# Mirror On

# 1936

ISBN: 9781674754901
© Liberty Eagle Publishing Ltd. 2019
All Rights Reserved

# INDEX

## JAN
| | | PAGE |
|---|---|---|
| 1st | London's Wild Welcome To New Year | 7 |
| 4th | Brothers, 'Lost' In The War, Meet Again | 8 |
| 7th | Lover's Grief In Death Mystery | 9 |
| 9th | Wonder Guns To Fight Air Raiders | 10 |
| 13th | More Divorces Than Ever | 11 |
| 16th | Soviet Army: 1,3000,000 Ready | 12 |
| 21st | The King Dies: His Hand Clasped By The Weeping Queen | 13 |
| 22nd | King Edward's First Speech To "My Subjects" | 14 |
| 30th | Queen Mary's Thanks | 15 |
| 31st | Doctor Fears Nazi Torture | 16 |

## FEB
| 7th | Secret Arms Supply For Palestine | 17 |
|---|---|---|
| 8th | King Edward's First Honours | 18 |
| 10th | Mr. De Valera's Son Killed Riding | 19 |
| 14th | Football Rough Play Must Stop - Says Inquest Jury | 20 |
| 17th | Sabotage In British Cruiser | 21 |
| 19th | Ten Feared Lost In British Ship | 22 |
| 20th | Duce Sends Secret Note To Hitler | 23 |
| 21st | Spy Gangs Stealing Our Secrets | 24 |
| 27th | Rebels Holding Out As Japan's Army Wavers | 25 |
| 29th | Hitler's "Let's Be Friends" Plea To World | 26 |

## MAR
| 2nd | 17 Officers Shot In Mass Suicide | 27 |
|---|---|---|
| 3rd | Oil Embargo - Or Peace - Within 48 Hours | 28 |
| 4th | Britain Awakes! Millions For Defence | 29 |
| 5th | New York General Strike Fear | 30 |
| 6th | They Welcomed The King With - "Good Old Teddy" | 31 |
| 9th | It Must Not Be War - Hitler's Peace Plan Should Succeed | 32 |
| 21st | Hitler Warns Powers Again "Our Demands Stand" | 33 |
| 23rd | 100 Measles Cases A Day In London | 34 |
| 24th | 2,000,000 Cheer The Ocean Queen To-Day | 35 |
| 28th | Serum Shortage Is Costing Lives | 36 |

# INDEX - 2

| APR | | Page |
|---|---|---|
| 2nd | Britain Takes Grave Step | 37 |
| 3rd | Dying Pilot Leaps With Parachute | 38 |
| 8th | Girl, Burned In Air Crash Calls Aid | 39 |
| 9th | £40,000,000 By-Pass For Nation | 40 |
| 13th | Overcoat Holiday To-Day | 41 |
| 17th | "Live" Shells On Doorstep | 42 |
| 22nd | What You Will Pay - Income Tax Up 3d. | 43 |
| 23rd | Rescuers' Pit "Tomb" Peril | 44 |
| 24th | Budget "Leakage" Storm | 45 |
| 30th | M.P.s Denounce The B.B.C. | 46 |

| MAY | | |
|---|---|---|
| 4th | Emperor A 'Prisoner' In French Hands | 47 |
| 7th | 'Crazy' Storms Flood Many Towns | 48 |
| 8th | Royal Oculist For Blind Boxer | 49 |
| 14th | Flaming Dancer Fires Night Club | 50 |
| 18th | Cloudburst, Fog And Lightning | 51 |
| 19th | Italians Arrest A Briton In Abyssinia | 52 |
| 23rd | Mr. Thomas On Why He Resigned | 53 |
| 27th | Sensational Backing Puts Boswell 8-1 | 54 |
| 28th | J.H. Thomas Speaks | 55 |
| 30th | The Queen Mary: Smashes 3 Records | 56 |

| JUN | | |
|---|---|---|
| 2nd | The Queen Mary Docks Safely | 57 |
| 6th | Vicar's White Slave Warning To Parents | 58 |
| 11th | Rescue Swim At 82 | 59 |
| 13th | "Send An Army To Palestine" | 60 |
| 19th | Quads To Be On Show - 6d. A Look | 61 |
| 22nd | 11-Ft. Flood's Havoc | 62 |
| 24th | Man Dives From Express To Escape Escort | 63 |
| 25th | R.A.F. 'Planes 'To Beat World' | 64 |
| 26th | Steel "Hand" To Capture Bandits | 65 |
| 30th | 'Now I Can Smoke When I Like' | 66 |

# INDEX - 3

| JUL | | Page |
|---|---|---|
| 3rd | "Escaped" Prisoner Found On Roof Of Gaol | 67 |
| 6th | Crash Kills Air Hero Of 22 | 68 |
| 7th | Britain Better Off Than For 6 Years | 69 |
| 11th | 300 Die As Great Drought Paralyses U.S. | 70 |
| 16th | British Babies Being Sold Abroad | 71 |
| 17th | Here Is The Man With Loaded Pistol | 72 |
| 27th | Mothers Weep As The King Greets Blind Heroes At Vimy | 73 |
| 28th | Ex-Wife Managed Husband's Money | 74 |
| 30th | The King To Go On Secret Cruise | 75 |
| 31st | Women As Pilots Of R.A.F. Bombers | 76 |

| AUG | | |
|---|---|---|
| 5th | English Wife Treated Like Oriental | 77 |
| 6th | Air Ministry Chief Dismissed By Premier | 78 |
| 8th | Rich Island Queen Marries Fisherman | 79 |
| 12th | Lovers In Childhood Wed At 75 | 80 |
| 13th | Games Star Gives Up Fame To Be 'Just A Wife' | 81 |
| 15th | R.A.F. Camp Raided - As Joke | 82 |
| 19th | Month Of War Cost Spain £125,000,000; 20,000 Men | 83 |
| 24th | Seized British Ship - Then Apologised | 84 |
| 25th | Hitler Doubles Army - Duce Increases Air Force | 85 |
| 31st | The Queen Mary Wins Riband For Britain | 86 |

| SEP | | |
|---|---|---|
| 1st | Briton Of 21 Shoots Down Enemy During An Air Duel | 87 |
| 2nd | 3½lb. "Cotton-Wool" Baby Becomes A Champion | 88 |
| 7th | Reds Prepare To Blow Up 1,200 Trapped In Fortress | 89 |
| 11th | Pound-Note Woman's Tour Of Mercy Secret Out | 90 |
| 12th | Famous Sports Cup Stolen Under Eyes Of Crowd | 91 |
| 15th | Husband's Death May End Norma Shearer's Film Career | 92 |
| 16th | Bride Sees Husband And Two Others Die In Air Wreck | 93 |
| 17th | Randolph Churchill Dashes To U.S. On Trail Of His Sister | 94 |
| 24th | 17 Die As Pilgrim Train Is Wrecked By Express | 95 |
| 30th | Highest-Ever Pilot Saved Life With Knife | 96 |

# INDEX - 4

## OCT
| | | Page |
|---|---|---|
| 2nd | Big British Arms Speed-Up: Extension Of Defence Plan | 97 |
| 3rd | Chain Cafes Want More For Cup Of Tea: Is It Justified? | 98 |
| 5th | 84 Arrests As Thousands Stampede In London Riots | 99 |
| 6th | Girl To Marry Man Of 78 She Will Never See | 100 |
| 16th | Jean On Perilous 1,100 Miles' Dash Over Tasman Sea | 101 |
| 17th | Blood Rite At Gipsy Wedding | 102 |
| 20th | Boy Sentenced Over An Egg Is Cleared On Appeal | 103 |
| 23rd | Pretty Girls Eject Men In Wild Fight At Meeting | 104 |
| 24th | Husband Dies On Day Wife's Body Is Exhumed | 105 |
| 26th | Boy Of 4 Inherits £500,000 From Aunt He Saw 6 Times | 106 |

## NOV
| | | |
|---|---|---|
| 3rd | Famous K.C. Dies As Diners Laugh At His Jokes | 107 |
| 4th | Banned Play That Portrays God To Go On Screen | 108 |
| 5th | Flat On Coronation Route Cost £472 For A Week | 109 |
| 9th | Praying Children Killed By Bomb: Madrid In Flames | 110 |
| 12th | At His Mother's Side The King Leads The Nation | 111 |
| 14th | Baldwin Betrays His Convictions For Votes | 112 |
| 19th | "Something Must Be Done" - The King | 113 |
| 26th | Stalin Challenges Fascism As 'Plotters' Are Shot | 114 |
| 28th | Doctor 'No Right In Homes Of Women' | 115 |
| 30th | Ex-Millionairess Fights To Clear Dead Man's Name | 116 |

## DEC
| | | |
|---|---|---|
| 1st | Fire Wrecks Crystal Palace: Royal Duke Watches | 117 |
| 3rd | The King Wants To Marry Mrs. Simpson | 118 |
| 5th | Tell Us The Facts Mr. Baldwin! | 119 |
| 9th | The King And Brothers Have Five Hour Conference… | 120 |
| 10th | The King Decides: Abdication Plans | 121 |
| 11th | King Edward Will Broadcast To-Night | 122 |
| 12th | Ex-King Sailed This Morning In Yacht | 123 |
| 17th | Eight More Die In Third Day Of Britain's Great Storm | 124 |
| 24th | The King Gives Back Jobs To All At Sandringham | 125 |
| 28th | Streets Red Hot In Blaze Under Heart Of Berlin | 126 |

THE DAILY MIRROR, Wednesday, January 1, 1936.

Broadcasting—Page 18

# Daily Mirror

THE DAILY PICTURE NEWSPAPER WITH THE LARGEST NET SALE

## A HAPPY NEW YEAR TO YOU

No. 10,011  Registered at the G.P.O. as a Newspaper.  WEDNESDAY, JANUARY 1, 1936  One Penny

Amusements: Page 16

# LONDON'S WILD WELCOME TO NEW YEAR

## 60,000 Join in Midnight West End Revels

WITH hopes higher than at any time since the War, millions of people all over Britain last night welcomed 1936.

Streets were gay. Restaurants were thronged with merry-makers. The business outlook was optimistic. But there was a note of regret in the farewell to 1935. The year had been a good friend. It had seen the Empire united in homage to its King. It had laid the foundations of Britain's recovery laid anew.

News from Treasury experts earlier last evening had shown how surely those foundations had been laid.

In spite of heavier expenditure a Budget surplus is likely in March. Revenue is up £22,611,755. Income-tax is ahead of estimate.

### Floodlit Walls

Everywhere in London there was rejoicing.

Within the floodlit walls of St. Paul's Cathedral last night a devout congregation of ticket-holders celebrated the advent of the New Year with dignified ceremonial.

Outside, where two giant Christmas trees, given by the King, stood out in a blaze of light, a vast crowd of Cockney revellers welcomed 1936 with a tumult of conflicting sound, madly waving streamers, balloons and ticklers.

For the first time in the history of this crowd pageant, staged within sight of the great cathedral, Londoners came into their own.

The traditional Scotsman, sometimes kilted, but always unmistakably on Hogmanay bent, was swamped by sheer weight of numbers.

Reinforced by visitors from overseas, the revellers swept up Ludgate Hill in a wave of wildly shouting humanity.

When the tones of Big Ben, faintly audible from the mouth of a giant loud speaker, betokened that 1935 was dying, the clamour increased a thousand-fold.

The strains of "Auld Lang Syne" were drowned in the overwhelming torrent of "You Can't Do That There 'Ere."

### Fire-Engine Dance

On a platform in front of the Queen Anne statue, which dominates the west entrance to St. Paul's, Dick Sheppard, canon-in-residence of the Cathedral, strove valiantly to lead the huge concourse in less secular tunes.

Although he was aided by loud speakers, he was powerless to reach all save those within a radius of a few yards.

Earlier his energetic, cassock-clad figure had moved about among the revellers. With characteristic good humour he had parried the sallies of the swaying crowds.

Despite the tremendous crush right from the foot of Ludgate-hill to the steps of the Cathedral, there were surprisingly few casualties.

On the way down Ludgate-hill a group of revellers fell through a shop window. Their

(Continued on back page)

### FIRST 1936 BABY

A BABY was born just as the clock struck the last stroke of midnight in Queen Charlotte's Hospital, W.

It was the first baby of the New Year. The baby is a boy, weighing 7 lb.

Gathered to greet the New Year—last night's crowd around the statue of Eros. See also page 12.

## GREETING 1936 IN PICCADILLY

## POLICE GUARD ON COTTAGE AFTER SECRET INQUEST

FROM OUR SPECIAL CORRESPONDENT

SHERBORNE (Dorset), Tuesday.

POLICE guarding a dead man's cottage which stands on the slopes of a lonely valley and is reached only by a cart track was a dramatic development here to-day when rumours concerning the man's death were followed by the arrival of Scotland Yard detectives to make investigations.

All visitors were turned away from the cottage. Relatives have been instructed to make no statements and the whole affair is being shrouded in the deepest secrecy.

The dead man was Frederick John Bryant, aged thirty-nine, a cowman, who lived with his wife and five children at the little hamlet of Coombe, two miles from this town. For the past two years Bryant had been employed by a farmer in the neighbourhood.

A fortnight before Christmas he was taken ill. On December 22 he was removed to the Yeatman Hospital, Sherborne, and died.

When the inquest was opened on Christmas Eve no members of the public or Press were present. Only evidence of identification was given by the widow, and the inquest was then adjourned until January 14.

Later certain organs, finger nails and hair were sent to London for examination. As a result of a preliminary report some days ago Chief Inspector Bell, of Scotland Yard, and another officer arrived at Sherborne to-day.

Early to-day Bryant's children were taken away by car. The widow left home early this morning and was interviewed by the police for some time.

### Stealing the Judge's Thunder

MR. Justice Greaves-Lord is wondering whether two men and a motor-car are still staggering under the weight of a couple of 150lb. bronze cannon.

The cannon used to stand on the lawn of Windygap, his home on the Seaford cliffs, in Sussex, pointing out to sea. Now they have vanished, and the police believe they were stolen.

"I am hoping," Mr. Justice Greaves-Lord said last night, "that the thieves, embarrassed by the weight of the cannon, will have left them in a ditch somewhere."

## HONOURS FOR WOMEN

### Christabel Pankhurst Receives D.B.E.

WOMEN receive high honours in the New Year list issued last night.

The Duchess of Abercorn and Miss Christabel Pankhurst, who became famous years ago as a pioneer fighter for the enfranchisement of women, become Dames of the British Empire.

Miss Myra Hess, the pianist, and Miss Olga Nethersole, of the People's League of Health, are also honoured.

Many other women are included in the list. There are two new viscounts—Lord Hanworth, lately Master of the Rolls, and Lord Trenchard, lately Commissioner of the Metropolitan Police—four barons—including Sir Ian Macpherson, who recently resigned as M.P. for Ross and Cromarty—four baronets and thirty-four knights.

An honour unusual for members of the forces is the award of the Order of Merit to Field-Marshal Sir Philip Chetwode, formerly Commander-in-Chief in India.

He has the distinction of being the only soldier O.M. in the realm. A posthumous award of the King's Police Medal for gallantry is made to Reginald Cyril Victor Mott, who was a constable in the British section of the Palestine police, and who was killed by brigands while calling on them to surrender last November.

His home is in Colenman-street, Chatham.

The new C.B.s include a V.C., Major-General Bernard Cyril Freyberg, late of the West Surreys and the Grenadier Guards.

A list of principal honours is on page 4.

Miss Christabel Pankhurst.

# Daily Mirror

**THE DAILY PICTURE NEWSPAPER WITH THE LARGEST NET SALE**

Broadcasting—Page 18

**THE SAINT IS COMING!**
See Monday's Great New Serial——by
**LESLIE CHARTERIS**

Amusements: Page 14

No. 10,014 Registered at the G.P.O. as a Newspaper. SATURDAY, JANUARY 4, 1936 One Penny

## BROTHERS, 'LOST' IN THE WAR, MEET AGAIN

### Hospital Reunion After 18 Years

SPECIAL "DAILY MIRROR" NEWS

EIGHTEEN years ago two brothers went "over the top" together into the Battle of Cambrai. Each had since believed the other killed.

**Yesterday they met in adjoining beds of a London hospital.**

Edward and Charles Walters are the brothers. They had not seen each other since November 22, 1917, at Bapaume.

Yesterday, Edward lay in a London County Council hospital, recovering from an abdominal operation, when a patient was brought in to occupy the next bed.

"The new patient has the same name as yours," the nurse said, and Edward looked, hesitated, stared and spoke.

A fervent handclasp reunited the brothers.

"I was reading a newspaper when the nurse told me that the newcomer had the same name as mine," Edward told me, and I gave it no thought

### Chance Plays a Part

"Even when I saw a family resemblance I hesitated at first to speak to him—then at last I felt I just had to. I was overjoyed."

Charles told of the remote chance which brought him to the hospital. "A fall of stonework on my foot while at work brought me here," he said. "It was the first work I have had for nearly three years, and I started just before Christmas.

"It may mean more unemployment now, but that doesn't matter, for it has brought me back my brother whom I thought had gone under' at Bapaume.

"When I returned from France I had no home so I roamed the country looking for work."

The brothers have been visited by their stepmother, with whom Edward, who is a fruit salesman, has been living in West Kensington since 1918. The men were privates in the West Yorkshire Regiment.

Standing on a tumbler half filled with wine, from which he leaps without spilling any of the liquid. The leader of the team of five Basque dancers who arrived in London yesterday from Soule, in the French Pyrenees, demonstrating the feat he will perform at the National Folk Dance Festival in the Albert Hall to-day.

## Prince of Wales to See All Blacks

NO international Rugby match of recent years has aroused so much interest as the great game to be staged at Twickenham to-day when England will try to emulate Wales's feat in beating the All Blacks.

The Prince of Wales and the Crown Prince of Egypt are expected to attend. All seats were sold some time ago. The kick-off is at 2.15.

The England team has reported fit, but there is still a doubt about T. H. C. Caughey, the All Blacks' star five-eighth, being able to play.
**England's Chances—Page 22.**

## PEER'S SON IN SLED PERIL

ST. MORITZ, Friday.

OVER-CAUTION, due to a narrow escape from disaster earlier in the race, has by a bare tenth of a second robbed the Hon. B. L. Bathurst, Viscount Bledisloe's son, of victory in the Carlton Cup, first big race on the Cresta Run this season.

In his second course Bathurst took Shuttlecock Corner alarmingly high and was within an ace of going over the top. As a result of this unnerving experience he was less daring on his third course.

The winner was Jim Lawrence, with an aggregate time of 142.8s., and individual courses of 47.7s., 47.9s, and 47.2s.

Bathurst's aggregate was 142.9s., made up of runs of 47.2s., 47.2s. and 48.5s.

The 47.2s. done by both Lawrence and Bathurst were the fastest runs of the race, which had been postponed, owing to bad conditions, from December 30.

The Hon. B. Bathurst

## ARTIST MODEL WEDS SECRETLY

### She Did Not Tell Her Mother

SPECIAL "DAILY MIRROR" NEWS

A HIGH-SPIRITED girl wished her elderly mother a Happy New Year, and then said good-bye. She did not say that she was going out to get married.

She is twenty-four-year-old Miss Madeline Lucy Burt, an artist's model, celebrated in art circles as Miss Holland of the lovely figure and exquisite mouth.

She married fifty-six-year-old Mr Henry Savage, the well-known writer. They are spending their honeymoon at Winchelsea Beach, Sussex.

They were married at Caxton Hall on January 1. The marriage was a complete secret, even to her close friends.

When the news was broken last night to her silver-haired mother at Chester-terrace, London, S.W., she said it came as a complete surprise to her.

### Very Modern

"She is an extremely independent girl of highly artistic temperament and with very modern ideas," said Mrs. Burt. "She was at a boarding school in Montreux, and ever since she has pursued a path of her own.

"About two years ago she suddenly announced that she was going to Spain. She was away there for several months.

"Formerly she was a mannequin, and soon became famous for her beautiful figure. She has sat for Mr. James Gunn, the artist, for the Byam Shaw Art School, and for other noted artists.

"She came to see me on New Year's Day, but told me nothing of her plans.

Mr. Henry Savage is a poet, has published numerous books, and has travelled in many countries. His former wife was Miss Mary Elizabeth Rayne. This marriage was dissolved.

### TO WED HIS TYPIST

SIR Edmund Spriggs, the physician-in-charge of Ruthin Castle Private Hospital, North Wales, is to marry Miss Janet Macintosh, who has been a typist at the hospital for fifteen years. Miss Macintosh is aged forty-one. They are to marry on January 14.

Mr. Henry Savage's bride, Miss Madeline Lucy Burt.

## FOUND A 'BOMB' ON HIS OWN DOORSTEP

FINDING a wicker basket on his front doorstep when he arrived home last night, Mr. Arthur Bailey, of Branksomeroad, Southend, examined it and found it was a crudely-made bomb.

The basket contained two tins. The smaller tin was packed with gunpowder, pieces of iron, nails, stones and broken glass.

This was contained in a larger tin packed with paper and rags saturated in paraffin.

There was a hole in the smaller tin with a piece of rag leading into it.

Mr. Bailey took the basket to the Southend police, who are making inquiries.

## Abyssinians Fire on R.A.F. 'Planes

Royal Air Force patrols over the Kenya border have twice been fired on by Abyssinians on the banks of the Dawa River. None of the planes was damaged, says Exchange.

Believing that the Abyssinians must have mistaken the 'planes for Italian aircraft, the authorities at Manderi got into touch with the commander of the Abyssinians asking him to indicate to his troops the distinction between British and Italian planes.

Since this communication was made the firing has ceased.

# Daily Mirror

**THE DAILY PICTURE NEWSPAPER WITH THE LARGEST NET SALE**

Broadcasting - Page 20

DOROTHY DIX - - - Page 7
EUSTACE - - - - - Page 13
QUIET CORNER - - Page 14
DOCTOR'S DIARY - Page 17
SERIAL - - - - - - Page 19
BELINDA - - - - - Page 22

No. 10,016 Registered at the G.P.O. as a Newspaper.
TUESDAY, JANUARY 7, 1936
One Penny

Amusements: Page 22

## LOVER'S GRIEF IN DEATH MYSTERY

### Tragedy of Clever Young Doctor

Dr. John C. White, found dead in a chair.

By A SPECIAL CORRESPONDENT

POLICE are investigating the death of twenty-six-year-old Dr. John C. White, found dead yesterday five days after his appointment as resident surgical officer at St. Bartholomew's Hospital, Rochester.

Dr. White was found dead in the hospital dispensary with two closed books on the desk in front of him.

It is believed that he had gone to the dispensary, the door of which was not locked, to make up some emergency drugs.

Last night I learned that Dr. White's fiancee, heartbroken, is now in the country.

She is Sister Peggy Stratton, a nursing sister at the Middlesex Hospital, Mortimer-street, W.

"Sister Stratton was semi-officially engaged to Dr White, but she did not wear a ring," a member of the nursing staff at Middlesex Hospital told me last night.

### "Great Friends"

"A telephone call was received by the matron this morning from the dead man's father, who is also a doctor on the staff of St. Bartholomew's Hospital, Rochester, asking her to break the news to Miss Stratton.

"She was terribly distressed and she was sent away with another sister.

"Sister Stratton joined the nursing staff here in 1927, and became a sister in 1933. She met Dr. White here while he was training, and they had been great friends for some years."

A porter at the Rochester Hospital found Dr. White's body.

It is not known how long the doctor had been in the dispensary, but as there was no light on it is believed he entered the room some time on Sunday afternoon.

### At Dance

On Saturday Dr. White was at the hospital staff dance and turned up for duty on Sunday morning.

The doctor was seen after eleven o'clock on Sunday morning.

Dr. White was the only son of Dr Clement White, an honorary physician to St. Bartholomew's Hospital, Rochester, who lives in Star Hill, Rochester.

He was regarded by many as having a brilliant medical future. He qualified a year ago and was on the staff of St. Mary's Hospital, Stratford, E.

## COW CAUSES PANIC

### Man Trapped in Shop —Crowd Stampede

WOMEN fled in panic when a cow, eluding its drover, spread havoc in busy Bristol streets yesterday. The animal—

Dashed into a tobacconist's shop and wrecked the counter;
Ran amok in a draper's shop; and
Scattered crowds of women bargain hunters before being cornered and killed.

Mr. W. C. Rowley, confectioner, was trapped in the room behind his shop while the cow took his place behind the counter.

"I had to stand watching it smash the fittings," said Mrs. Gould, whose husband owns the property.

"It trampled on milk and lemonade bottles and broke several 28-lb. bottles of sweets."

Driven out, the cow disappeared into the draper's.

After another rest it continued its course, driving hundreds of shoppers into side streets and doorways.

It covered two miles through the heart of the city before falling into a garage—for its last round-up.

## "BABY MASSACRE" FEAR SWEEPS CITY

NEW YORK, Monday.

EXCITED mothers crowded the streets of East Side, New York, to-day and chased their children into their homes.

The cause was Jessie Friedman, aged forty-five, who was recently released after twenty years in a mental asylum.

It was rumoured that Friedman had planned to drown every child she could.

She was later seen pushing a child towards the river and was arrested. She is suspected of drowning a baby who was kidnapped from a perambulator yesterday.—B.U.P.

### DUCHESS OF YORK

"The condition of the Duchess of York shows a steady improvement, and convalescence is approaching," it was stated last night.

---

### MOTHER AND DAUGHTER

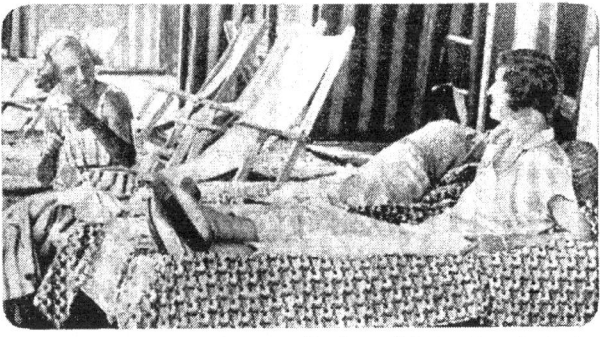

Miss Anne Cooper Hewitt, with her mother Mrs. George McCarter (whom she is suing for £100,000 damages), on the Excelsior beach at the Lido, Venice.

## £2,000,000 HEIRESS SUES MOTHER AFTER OPERATION

### Prevented from Having Children Claim

A TWENTY-ONE-YEAR-OLD heiress to 10,000,000 dollars (£2,000,000), who is alleged to have been the victim of an operation, on her mother's orders, as a result of which she cannot have children, yesterday filed a suit against her mother claiming £100,000 damages.

The girl is Anne Cooper Hewitt, whose father, Peter Cooper Hewitt, left a will containing the proviso that if Anne married and bore children they were to receive a share of his fortune.

If, however, she died childless the money would revert to the mother.

Mr. Russell P. Tyler, an attorney (says the B.U.P. from San Francisco), had announced that he would file the suit against the mother and two surgeons, who performed the operation.

### Surgeon's Admission

He alleges that the mother had the operation done in order to gain control of the £2,000,000 fortune.

Dr. Samuel G. Boyd, one of the two surgeons cited, has admitted that he performed the operation at the request of the girl's mother, but the other surgeon, Dr. Tillman, at first said he had no knowledge of the case.

Later Dr. Tillman, who said he was a childhood friend of the mother, Mrs McCarter, said he was present at the operation but took no part in it. He added:

"The girl is feeble-minded. Mrs. McCarter came to me and said that she wanted her daughter examined."

### "Within Her Rights"

"I had her under observation for six or eight months Mrs. Scully (a Californian State mental specialist) gave the girl tests and confirmed my observation regarding the girl's mentality.

"The actual operation was performed by Dr. Boyd. In such a case Mrs. McCarter was within her legal rights in deciding to have the operation performed."

Mr. Tyler denies that the girl is feeble-minded, claiming that she is normal but that her education has been retarded. He asserts that the girl thought that she was being operated upon for appendicitis.

Mrs. McCarter's marriage with Baron D'Erlanger was annulled in 1925. A year later she married George W. C. McCarter, of New York, who was a son of the former Attorney-General, Mr. Robert H McCarter.

---

King Gustavus of Sweden in the little motor-boat he often uses at Stockholm, that Venice of the North. It is his way of getting an airing.

## Drugs to Kill 14,000 Stolen

POISON capable of killing 14,000 people, stolen from Community Hall, Townsend-avenue, Liverpool, was being sought by the police last night.

A warning to all schools and an appeal to the public to help to recover it were issued.

Although the theft occurred last Thursday it was not until last night that it was discovered.

The Community Hall is used as headquarters for the local tenants' association and as a welfare clinic.

The intruders broke in by smashing a ground-floor window. They left by the main door with the packages of drugs.

The poison was in a cardboard carton measuring four inches by two inches and marked "poison."

In this carton was a triangular-shaped bottle containing 100 tablets red in colour, and the size of a threepenny piece.

These tablets are of a deadly poison, the maximum dose being one-sixteenth of a grain. Each tablet contained eight and three-quarter grains.

THE DAILY MIRROR, Thursday, January 9, 1936.

Broadcasting - Page 20

# Daily Mirror

THE DAILY PICTURE NEWSPAPER WITH THE LARGEST NET SALE

No 10,018  Registered at the G.P.O. as a Newspaper.  THURSDAY, JANUARY 9, 1936  One Penny

DOROTHY DIX - - - Page 7
EUSTACE - - - - - - Page 8
QUIET CORNER - - - Page 14
DOCTOR'S DIARY - - Page 17
SERIAL - - - - - - - Page 19
BELINDA - - - - - - Page 22

Amusements: Page 20

# WONDER GUNS TO FIGHT AIR RAIDERS

## And Only Britain Has Them

The Lord Mayor and Lady Mayoress, Sir Percy and Lady Vincent, receiving a guest at the Juvenile Fancy Dress Ball which was given at the Mansion House, E.C., last evening. Right: The footman stoops to conquer the little arrival's admission ticket.

**BRITAIN HAS THE BEST SECRET ANTI-AIRCRAFT GUN IN THE WORLD.**

THIS was the assurance given by experts to the *Daily Mirror* last night following the revelation before the Royal Commission on Arms (reported on page 5) that a new anti-aircraft gun "proved to be the best in the world" was being bought by foreign Powers while not one had been ordered by Britain.

General Sir Herbert Lawrence, chairman of Vickers, the famous armament and engineering firm, made the announcement before the Commission.

**Inquiries revealed that Britain's naval and armament authorities are not perturbed.**

An eminent naval authority said that the British Navy had been developing multiple-barrelled anti-aircraft guns for years.

These guns, called multiple "Pom-Poms," had recently been perfected.

It was the opinion of the Admiralty experts, he said, that no single-barrelled gun, however perfect, could compete with these multiple "Pom-Poms"—guns no other Power possessed.

On the battleships, like the Rodney, the gun has eight barrels and is equivalent to eight guns mounted in one. On the cruisers they must necessarily be lighter and have four barrels.

The nearest that any foreign Power has to a gun of this type is one with two barrels.

These "Pom-Poms" are stated to fire with amazing rapidity, setting up a barrage that it is almost impossible for aircraft to penetrate.

The theory of the gun is that it shall fire at enemy aircraft at the moment when it flattens out after diving from a great height before dropping its bombs or torpedoes.

# PRINCESS REBURIED BY LIGHT OF HURRICANE LAMPS

## Last Wish of the King's Sister Fulfilled

FROM OUR SPECIAL CORRESPONDENT

WINDSOR, Wednesday.

AS dusk was falling to-day the body of Princess Victoria, the King's sister, was removed from the royal tomb house beneath the Albert Memorial Chapel, where it has rested since the funeral in December, and was taken to the Royal Cemetery at Frogmore.

It was at the special wish of the late Princess that this reburial was undertaken.

By the light of torches carried by members of the Windsor Castle Fire Brigade, the coffin, unadorned by flag or flower, was carried by them to the waiting motor hearse.

The short journey to Frogmore was made slowly via the Grand Quadrangle and the Sovereigns Entrance, two private cars following the hearse.

As the cortege left the Castle sentries of the 1st Battalion Coldstream Guards presented arms.

At Frogmore the open grave was lit by hurricane lamps, and a tarpaulin shielded those taking part in the service from the wind and rain.

The Dean of Windsor, Dr. Albert Baillie, offered special prayers as the coffin was placed in the grave.

Later, when the earth has settled, a marble slab will record the fact that the Princess Victoria is buried there.

## THAMES IS RISING

FLOODS returned with the rain last night in many parts of southern England.

In some places the Thames is rising. The rate of flow at Teddington yesterday was 500 million gallons more than on Tuesday.

Better weather in France, however, has eased the flood situation says Reuter.

# 'TIPS' FORTUNE FOR THE BLIND

## Ship's Steward Who Left £20,000 to St. Dunstan's

ST. Dunstan's, the institution for war-blinded soldiers, sailors and airmen, benefits by more than £20,000 from the will of Mr. Richard Thomas Hughes, of Kirkdale, Liverpool, who died four years ago, aged seventy-four, leaving about £27,000.

Mr. Hughes left a life interest to a brother who recently died, and now, in accordance with the provisions of the will, £20,000 has come to St. Dunstan's.

Mr. Hughes was a ship's steward, and the bulk of his fortune was made by "tips" obtained throughout his long sea career.

When he retired he lived ashore in a small house in a working-class neighbourhood on about only £2 a week with the express idea of ultimately benefiting those blinded during the war.

## Guided 12,000 Feet by Radio to See Eclipse

AN air pilot, radio operator, photographer and passenger, climbing 12,000ft. despite atrocious weather, were among the few people who saw last night's total eclipse of the moon.

The pilot was Mr. Roland Falk, employed by a firm operating from Heston, Middlesex. Owing to low-flying clouds he had to "fly blind" most of the way, guided by wireless from the control tower at Heston.

Thousands of shots were fired by ignorant and superstitious Turks to "frighten away the Devil" during the eclipse, says Reuter from Istanbul.

Earth tremors occurred in Southern Austria and Northern Yugoslavia at the time of the phenomenon, states a B.U.P. message.

## RADIO PRIEST'S CHALLENGE

FATHER Coughlin, the United States "Radio Priest," with millions of followers, is the latest challenger of the Federal laws.

He says the Federal Reserve Act is unconstitutional and that he is going to court to challenge it and all its amendments.

His announcement follows the success of the challenge to President Roosevelt's agricultural New Deal, which bids fair to start a vogue for challenging laws.

Father Coughlin, who is founder of the National Union of Justice, has repeatedly broadcast attacks against the "privately-owned" Federal Reserve system, demanding the establishment of a Bank of the United States on the lines of the Bank of England.

He states, says Reuter, that his motive in filing his suit challenging the act is "to restore to Congress control over money."

ENGLISH GIRL TURNS HINDU.—Miss Mary Oldfield, who has embraced the Hindu religion at Lahore (India) and has been renamed Indumati. Her marriage is expected shortly to take place to Mr. Rupkrishan, an artist. She herself studied under Sir William Rothenstein at the Royal College of Art in London.

# Daily Mirror

**THE DAILY PICTURE NEWSPAPER WITH THE LARGEST NET SALE**

Broadcasting - Page 20

DOROTHY DIX . . . Page 7
EUSTACE . . . . . . . Page 13
QUIET CORNER . . . Page 15
DOCTOR'S DIARY . . Page 17
SERIAL . . . . . . . Page 19
BELINDA . . . . . . Page 22

No. 10,021 Registered at the G.P.O. as a Newspaper  MONDAY, JANUARY 13, 1936  One Penny

Amusements: Page 21

## SERVICE IN A CIRCUS RING

## MORE DIVORCES THAN EVER

### Law Attacked—and Mothers Blamed

BY A SPECIAL CORRESPONDENT

THERE ARE MORE DIVORCES IN BRITAIN TO-DAY THAN EVER BEFORE.

The Registrar-General's return, issued to-day, shows a total of 3,934 in a year.

Divorce Judges this morning begin hearing 1,300 applications for the dissolution of marriages as well as nullity and judicial separation suits—the biggest list ever for the time of year.

SERVICE IN THE CIRCUS.—The Bishop of Willesden conducting divine service in the circus ring at Olympia yesterday afternoon. Performers and members of the staff of Bertram Mills's circus attended, and the circus band played the hymns during the service.

Publication of these figures last night coincided with an attack on "Godless, worldly mothers" by Father Woodlock. He held them responsible for their "modern" children's failures in life—and marriage.

It also coincided with a sensational "open letter" from a young woman— "a wife without a husband." Her choice lies between adultery and loneliness and her challenge—quoted on page three—is a terrible indictment of the present divorce laws.

The cases of such wives-without-husbands was used by a well-known sociologist to whom I spoke last night as part of his argument for even more divorce.

"Not half enough even now," he said when I read to him the figures.

### Scotland's Way

"I would almost say give the King's Proctor a holiday!" he added with a laugh.

"Also I should like to see the law altered to make incurable insanity and physical or mental cruelty of a grave nature grounds for divorce."

Sir Arnold Wilson, M.P., also had a word to say for the deserted wife.

"They do these things better in Scotland," he said, "where wilful desertion by either party is a legal reason for an application to the Court for divorce by the other."

Father Woodlock's attack on mothers was

(Continued on back page)

## Wedding Hitch Dream That Came True

FROM OUR SPECIAL CORRESPONDENT
FRENSHAM, Sunday.

THREE nights before a wedding at Frensham Parish Church, Surrey, yesterday, the bride's brother Mr. George King, of Crooksbury Anstey-lane, Alton, Hants, dreamed there would be no parson to conduct the ceremony.

His dream came true.

The marriage of Miss Phyllis Mary King to Mr. Frederick John William Woolley, of Mead-lane, Farnham, was due to take place at 3 p.m.

### Guardian of Keys

Three bridesmaids, the groom, the best man, and about fifty guests assembled at the church. But the vicar of Frensham, the Rev. M. H. C. Collet, was missing.

Mr. Ernest Eustace, the best man, dashed to the vicarage, but the vicar was out.

So Mr. Eustace drove by car to the neighbouring parish of Duckenfield, about three miles away, to persuade the Rev. Stanhope-Ward, curate in charge, to conduct the service.

Mr. Ward had been resting as he is to undergo an operation this week, but he hastily dressed and returned in the car.

The ceremony was duly performed, but when the bride and bridegroom went to sign the register it was locked in the vestry safe.

The best man discovered that the vicar's gardener was the guardian of the keys.

It was 4.30 before the ceremony ended.

THE LOW-DOWN on that famous hare v. tortoise race! The tortoise must have had as charming a jockey as this lucky turtle at Miami, Florida.

## STOPPED WATCH CLUE TO CLIFF TRAGEDY OF UNKNOWN WOMAN

ON the wrist of the body of a woman found yesterday at the foot of Beachy Head was a watch which had stopped at 5.40—the only definite clue in a mystery which is engaging the attention of the Eastbourne police.

She is described as about sixty-five years old, 5ft. 1in. tall and of slim build.

She wore a thick brown blanket-cloth coat with light plaid pattern collar and strips of the same material on the elbows and edge of pockets, a two-piece plum-coloured square-pattern knitted suit, brown underslip and underclothes. There were two small coloured handkerchiefs in the pockets.

A man walking on the beach discovered the body, terribly injured. It was recovered last night by police using a boat.

It is believed death took place about three days ago.

## Sophistication—by a "Bachelor" Girl

"SOPHISTICATION—or at least a pretence of it—is the greatest safeguard of the modern girl, and you can't have sophistication with an utterly unworldly upbringing."

This was the opinion of a "bachelor girl" who has looked after herself since she was nineteen.

"Father Woodlock attacks mothers for their worldliness," she said, "but surely girls who are brought up in an ultra-sanctified home atmosphere are doomed to a nasty shock when they get out into the world; they are unarmed.

"Vanity, too, is a good thing in small doses—it gives a girl the protection of a sense of self-assurance and self-respect—it is more useful than sweet innocence, if the girl has common-sense as well."

# Daily Mirror

THE DAILY PICTURE NEWSPAPER WITH THE LARGEST NET SALE

Broadcasting - Page 20

EUSTACE — Page 8
QUIET CORNER — Page 15
DOCTOR'S DIARY — Page 17
SERIAL — Page 19
DOROTHY DIX — Page 22
BELINDA — Page 22

No. 10,024 Registered at the G.P.O as a Newspaper. THURSDAY, JANUARY 16, 1936 One Penny

Amusements: Page 16

## SOVIET ARMY: 1,300,000 READY

### Germany and Japan Warned

RUSSIA has an army of 1,300,000 men ready in case countries such as Germany and Japan desire to try conclusions with her.

She is building more submarines and warships, increasing the numbers of her trained soldiers and officers, and improving her tank corps and gas warfare department.

Her army has been increased by 360,000 men in one year. To build up morale, soldiers' and officers' pay will be increased 57 per cent.

All this was revealed by M. Tukashevsky, Assistant Commissar for War, yesterday, when he addressed the Central Executive Committee of the Soviet Union—the Union's Parliament—says B.U.P.

He made a passionate appeal for the passage of the military Budget, which reaches £550,000,000. Cheers greeted his speech.

### Finland's Airports

M. Tukashevsky, adorned in the new uniform of a Soviet Marshal—with decorations—made no secret of the countries that Russia fears, mentioning openly the alleged designs of Germany and Japan.

Poland was friendly to Germany, he went on, and Finland had more aerodromes than she could possibly use.

Turning towards Japan, he quoted an unnamed Japanese officer as telling his troops that they must accustom themselves to Siberian food.

His statement coincided with the report of another "border" incident. According to an official Soviet report a Mongolian detachment captured seven Japanese and Manchukuo soldiers near Lake Harmur.

Japan was causing anxiety in another sphere yesterday. Her withdrawal from the London Naval Conference brought authoritative indications that the U.S. Navy Department may soon ask Congress for money to increase capital ship strength, says Reuter.

Rome foresaw in Japan's move an open clash between Eastern and Western imperialism in the Pacific.

Germany talked of considering the Anglo-German Naval Pact jeopardised.

Geneva was gloomy. It is feared that a naval armaments race may develop.

LIT BY THE GLARE of the flames as they poured water on them from lofty water-towers. Men of the London Fire Brigade fighting a blaze last night at a four-story building near the junction of Eastcheap and Gracechurch-street, close to the spot where the Great Fire of London started. Six water towers were used.

## Hermit Said He Would Never Die

### BUT HE DID AFTER 20 YEARS IN WOOD

A MAN who said he would never die died yesterday.

He was the Cadmore hermit, a strange figure with waist-long hair and pilgrim's staff, who had lived in a little hut of boughs, deep in a Buckinghamshire beech wood, which had been his home for nearly twenty years.

Villagers regarded him with an almost superstitious awe. Few visited him by day and none by night, when he crouched by his camp fire writing endlessly on scraps of paper.

One of the villagers said last night:—

"His name was Jack Butler, and he was born at Cadmore End. He was brought up by his grandmother, and had a good education. For years he earned his living tying up bundles of firewood.

"He built his little house of boughs in the Levgrove Wood on Lord Parmoor's estate about twenty years ago. People used to come a long way to see him.

"He never talked to strangers and seldom to the few people who used to bring him food and provisions.

"Sometimes he would say that he was not as other men and that he would never die. He called himself a prophet, and one of his prophecies was that the time will come when men will eat grass.

"He was eighty-eight—a tall figure, bent with age."

Dr. G. Nunn, of Lane End, who was called when the hermit was found seriously ill, said:—

"Butler thought he was greater than other men and that he had a mission on earth."

Countess Poulett (Oriel Ross).

## Countess Danced On—Did Not Know of Fire at Her Home

WHILE Countess Poulett, whose stage name is Oriel Ross, was dancing her way through a Manchester pantomime last night, fire broke out at her husband's Somerset home.

Their home is Hinton House, at Hinton St. George, near Crewkerne. The fire is stated to have started in the maids' quarters and the servants' wing. One room was damaged. The main building, containing valuable pictures, was not touched. When the alarm was given the Hinton House Brigade, consisting of men employed on the estate, turned out and, with water from a pond in the grounds, they had the fire out before the arrival of the Crewkerne Brigade.

Earl Poulett told the Daily Mirror that the room damaged was a bedroom.

He himself had installed fire hydrants round the house, and had inaugurated regular fire practice among members of his staff.

### Cause Unknown

There was no one in residence at the mansion at the time and the cause of the fire is unknown.

Countess Poulett is appearing in "Jack and the Beanstalk" at the Palace Theatre, Manchester.

The Earl is twenty-six years of age and Miss Ross twenty-eight. They were married last June.

Two hundred firemen fight London blaze.—See back page.

## Another Operation on Hitler?

WILL Hitler, the German Dictator, have to undergo another operation for throat trouble? Statements were made yesterday indicating this possibility.

The Paris Soir said last night that Professor Portmann, a well-known surgeon of Bordeaux and a French senator, had been asked to perform a throat operation upon Hitler.

Professor Portmann, however, told the Central News correspondent that he had received no official proposal from Berlin.

In any case, should such an invitation come he did not know what decision he would take. He thought there were several capable surgeons in Germany in whom Hitler could have every confidence.

The "Paris Soir" also stated that there are various rumours about Hitler's throat, and that Professor Saurbruch, a well-known German surgeon, refused to take such a responsibility as an operation.

Professor Karl von Eicken, the laryngologist, who last year operated on Hitler's throat, denied yesterday (says Reuter from Berlin) rumours that Professor Portmann had been called to Berlin for consultation.

Hitler's operation last May was for polypus (a kind of tumour) on the right vocal chord.

## KIPLING IS SLIGHTLY BETTER

AFTER a very restful day Mr. Rudyard Kipling was maintaining early to-day the progress reported last night.

Just before the issue of the night bulletin Mrs. Kipling paid a short visit to the Middlesex Hospital.

That he is making a "gallant fight"—the words of one of the nurses is borne out by a little incident.

Looking up from his bed he recognised her. "Ah," he said, "so it is you. They would set you over me." Then he smiled wanly.

The first bulletin issued yesterday said that Mr. Kipling's condition was still critical, but he had slept quietly.

# Daily Mirror

**THE DAILY PICTURE NEWSPAPER WITH THE LARGEST NET SALE**

No. 10,028 — Registered at the G.P.O as a Newspaper. — TUESDAY, JANUARY 21, 1936 — One Penny

# THE KING DIES: HIS HAND CLASPED BY THE WEEPING QUEEN

## Nation of Grieving Homes

THE "Daily Mirror" announces with the deepest regret that his Majesty King George V died last night at Sandringham. He was aged seventy.

THE FOLLOWING OFFICIAL BULLETIN WAS ISSUED JUST AFTER MIDNIGHT:—

"DEATH CAME PEACEFULLY TO THE KING AT 11.55 P.M. IN THE PRESENCE OF HER MAJESTY THE QUEEN THE PRINCE OF WALES, THE DUKE OF YORK, THE PRINCESS ROYAL AND THE DUKE AND DUCHESS OF KENT. SIGNED: FREDERIC WILLANS, STANLEY HEWETT, DAWSON OF PENN."

**The Queen, with tears running down her cheeks, sat with the King's hand clasped in her own.**

**The King lay motionless in his bed. He made no sign of recognition to the other members of his family who were sharing the Queen's vigil.**

As his life slowly ebbed away he passed into a deep coma.

When she realised the end had come, the Queen turned to her son—the new King—and mother and son exchanged an affectionate embrace.

Edward Windsor, now Edward VIII of England, turned to his brothers and his sister with sad face, and the royal party moved slowly out of the death chamber.

Then the Queen, whose iron self-control had kept her calm throughout the long, anxious days, broke down

The sad news was flashed to all parts of the world. The nation, sitting at its fireside, heard it over the wireless.

With the chimes of Big Ben as a majestic requiem, the King's passing was announced by the B.B.C. at 12.15 this morning

**For the first time, wireless had told a sorrowing kingdom of the passing of a British Sovereign.**

Sir John Reith, director-general of the B.B.C., himself went to the microphone.

"It is with great sorrow," he said, "that we make the following announcement: His Majesty the King passed peacefully away at a few minutes before twelve."

Listeners in their homes, the crowds round Buckingham Palace and at Sandringham, knelt in silent prayer. Many wept. The King was at rest.

# Daily Mirror

**THE DAILY PICTURE NEWSPAPER WITH THE LARGEST NET SALE**

**NATION'S DAY OF MOURNING**

No. 10,029. Registered at the G.P.O. as a Newspaper. WEDNESDAY, JANUARY 22, 1936. One Penny

# KING EDWARD'S FIRST SPEECH TO "MY SUBJECTS"

## Pledge to Work for Their Happiness

In his first speech to his subjects, when he was proclaimed King at the Privy Council yesterday, Edward VIII announced his determination to follow in his father's footsteps.

HIS speech followed a solemn ceremonial at a meeting attended by more than 100 members of the Privy Council in St. James's Palace, while great crowds thronged the Mall outside.

The Lord Chancellor (Lord Hailsham) and the Archbishop of Canterbury led him by the hand from an adjoining room into the Council Chamber, as an official announced, "His Majesty the King."

It was then that his Majesty made his historic declaration. He said:—

"The irreparable loss which the British Commonwealth of Nations has sustained by the death of his Majesty, my beloved father, has devolved upon me the duty of sovereignty.

"I know how much you and all my subjects, with I hope I may say, the whole world, feel for me in my sorrow, and I am confident in the affectionate sympathy which will be extended to my dear mother in her overpowering grief.

"When my father stood here twenty-six years ago he declared that one of the objects of his life would be to uphold constitutional government.

"In this I am determined to follow in my father's footsteps and to work, as he did throughout his life, for the happiness and welfare of all classes of my subjects.

"I place my reliance upon the loyalty and affection of my peoples throughout the Empire, and upon the wisdom of their Parliaments to support me in this heavy task, and I pray that God will guide me to perform it."

The Lords of the Council then requested that his Majesty's declaration be made public and the King ordered this to be done.

Miss Margaret Bondfield, who was present as a Privy Councillor, is the first woman Councillor to assist at the proclamation of a British King.

### Public Proclamation

King Edward, who by flying to London from Sandringham to attend the Privy Council, became the first British Monarch to travel by air, will be publicly proclaimed King at ten o'clock this morning.

Outside St. James's Palace the Proclamation will be made by the Garter King-of-Arms, Sir Gerald Woods Wollaston. The heralds will then enter state carriages, and, with their escort, go to Charing Cross.

There the Proclamation will be read by Mr. Archibald Russell, Lancaster King-of-Arms, and afterwards it will be read at Temple Bar, Chancery-lane, by Mr. Algar Howard, Norroy King-of-Arms, and at the Royal Exchange by Mr. Arthur Cochrane, Clarenceux King-of-Arms.

(Continued on Back Page)

KING EDWARD VIII and the Duke of York, his brother and his heir, on their way from Sandringham to Bircham Newton aerodrome, whence they travelled by 'plane to Hendon.

## Last Thoughts for His People

IN the last hours of his life, King George's thoughts were with us—his people.

"How is the Empire," he asked his secretary in one of the brief periods of consciousness, and, on being told, "All is well, Sir, with the Empire," smiled and lapsed again into unconsciousness.

Mr. Baldwin told this moving incident to the Empire in a message he broadcast last night.

### PUBLIC TO GO INTO MOURNING TO-DAY

BY an order issued last night by the Duke of Norfolk, Earl Marshal of England, the general public are asked to go into mourning for King George to-day.

A black tie or an armlet, the "Daily Mirror" learns, is sufficient, and should certainly be worn until after the funeral next Tuesday.

Women may wear an armlet and dark clothes if they so wish.

It has not been decided when the mourning period will end. An announcement on this point may be made later.

His speech was heard in three continents—Europe, America and Africa.

King George, said Mr. Baldwin, inherited his position on the Throne, but he won his way to the hearts of his people.

"Great power, which corrupts weak natures, ennobled our King's character," said Mr. Baldwin.

"As the knowledge of the King's complete dedication to duty grew and spread, so the reign proceeded, so did the respect of his people turn into reverence and reverence into love.

"It is literally true that he won our hearts and during the Jubilee they made that manifest to him.

"We can best honour the noble memory of King George by gathering around and sustaining the young King who for so long we have delighted to know as Prince of Wales."

And of the Queen, Mr. Baldwin said:

"There are millions of hands which, if they could reach the Queen, would be stretched out to her and tears of sympathy would be shed with her."

Mr. Baldwin's message is given in full on page 2.

## LONELY GRIEF OF THE QUEEN

FROM OUR SPECIAL CORRESPONDENT
SANDRINGHAM, Tuesday.

ALONE with her grief, at times inconsolable, this has been a day of infinite sadness to the Queen.

Early to-day her son, the new King, went to her rooms in Sandringham House to say good-bye to her.

He was leaving with his brother, the Duke of York, to fly to London, there to be formally proclaimed King Edward VIII of England.

But history was forgotten at this visit. Those few moments of parting served to intensify the personal loss which each had sustained—the loss of a husband and of a father.

For a few moments they remained alone together, mother and son, stricken with the great burden of their grief—then the son left to fulfil the duties of King.

When the King had left, the Princess Royal, who has been her mother's constant companion through the recent days of anxiety, went to comfort Queen Mary.

The only visitors they received were the Duke and Duchess of Kent, who have remained at Sandringham to be near the Queen.

# Daily Mirror

**THE DAILY PICTURE NEWSPAPER WITH THE LARGEST NET SALE**

Broadcasting - Page 20

EUSTACE - - - - - - Page 6
QUIET CORNER - - Page 15
DOCTOR'S DIARY - - Page 17
SERIAL - - - - - - - Page 19
DOROTHY DIX - - - Page 22
BELINDA - - - - - Page 22

No. 10,036 — Registered at the G.P.O. as a Newspaper. — THURSDAY, JANUARY 30, 1936 — One Penny

Amusements: Page 20

# QUEEN MARY'S THANKS

## Her Deep Gratitude to Nation—"How I Shall Miss Him"

## "GIVE ME YOUR PRAYERS"

*The following message to the nation from Queen Mary was issued last night from Buckingham Palace and broadcast in the second news bulletin:—*

I MUST send to you, the people of this Nation and Empire, a message of my deepest gratitude for all the sympathy with which at this time of sorrow you have surrounded me.

It is, indeed, a gratitude so deep that I cannot find words to express it. But the simplest words are the best. I can only say—with all my heart, I thank you.

In my own great sorrow I have been upheld not only by the strength of your sympathy, but also by the knowledge that you have shared my grief.

For I have been deeply moved by the signs, so full and touching, that the passing of my dear husband has brought a real sense of personal sorrow to all his subjects.

### "I TRUST I MAY STILL SERVE"

In the midst of my grief I rejoice to think that after his reign of twenty-five years he lived to know that he had received the reward, in overflowing measure, of the loyalty and love of his people.

Although he will be no longer at my side—and no words can tell how I shall miss him—I trust that with God's help I may still be able to continue some part at least of the service which for forty-two years of happy married life we tried to give to this great land and Empire.

During the coming years, with all the changes which they must bring, you will, I know, let me have a place in your thoughts and prayers.

I commend to you my dear son as he enters upon his reign, in confident hope that you will give to him the same devotion and loyalty which you gave so abundantly to his father.

God bless you, dear people, for all the wonderful love and sympathy with which you have sustained me.    MARY.

### 'QUEEN MARY'—OFFICIAL TITLE

THE Court Circular from Buckingham Palace last night contained the following announcement:—

"Queen Mary wishes to express her sincere gratitude to all those who have so kindly sent tributes of flowers in memory of her late Majesty.

"They were so numerous that it has proved impossible for them to be acknowledged separately, but her Majesty hopes that everyone who has sent tributes of affection and sympathy will accept this acknowledgment as an assurance of her warmest thanks."

Since King George's death her Majesty has been referred to, in the absence of any official designation, as "The Queen," "The Queen Mother" and "Queen Mary." It is to be noted that the official designation now given in the Court Circular is "Queen Mary."

### OUR OTHER ARMY!

"MOST ludicrous," was the official reply given in London yesterday to a broadcast from Rome which alleged that:—
"During the battle against Ras Desta it was proved again that every Abyssinian battalion is under the command of European officers, most of whom are British."

### THREE LAZIEST BOYS

THREE boys accused at Wolverhampton Juvenile Court yesterday with theft were stated to be so lazy that—

One put fingers in his ears when the word "work" was mentioned.

Another left a good job because he got his hands dirty.

A third refused to work while his father had a job.

The boys' parents all expressed a wish to have their sons "put away for a time."

The magistrates ordered the boys to be sent to a remand home for a week.

### Germany Pledges "No Violation" of Rhineland

Paris, Wednesday.

FRENCH delegates who returned to Paris to-day from London have told the French Foreign Office that Germany has promised Britain that she will not violate the demilitarised zone of the Rhineland.

The British Government, it is stated, communicated Germany's pledge to M. Flandin, France, it is declared, now considers that Herr Hitler's promise completely closes the problem which the French had considered in the past to be the most acute difficulty of their present foreign policy.—B.U.P.

THE DAILY MIRROR, Friday, January 31, 1936

# Daily Mirror

THE DAILY PICTURE NEWSPAPER WITH THE LARGEST NET SALE

Broadcasting - Page 22

EUSTACE - - - - - Page 8
QUIET CORNER - - Page 17
DOCTOR'S DIARY - - Page 19
SERIAL - - - - - - Page 21
DOROTHY DIX - - - Page 24
BELINDA - - - - - Page 24

No. 10,037  Registered at the G.P.O. as a Newspaper.  FRIDAY, JANUARY 31, 1936  One Penny

Amusements : Pages 26 and 27

# DOCTOR FEARS NAZI TORTURE

## LEAVE-TAKING

There were several falls at Kempton Park yesterday, and here are T. Dart and Lester Boy falling severally after coming to grief at the open ditch in the Cranford Handicap.

## Sobbing Nurse Sees Baby in Cell
### After Murder Verdict

SOBBING hysterically in a police cell at Nottingham Guildhall—the same building in which she had been committed on a coroner's warrant for the alleged murder of Miss Ada Louisa Baguley—Nurse Waddingham last night thought only of the three-month-old baby whom she had left in her home at Devon Drive, Sherwood.

Her youngest child was brought to her, and for a few precious minutes she was left alone with it. Later the baby was taken away by the matron to a nearby house.

**Each day during the proceedings Nurse Waddingham has said good-bye in the morning to her five children.**

The inquest on Miss Baguley, fifty, who died in a nursing home carried on by Nurse Waddingham and Ronald Joseph Sullivan, closed yesterday with this finding: —

"The unanimous verdict of the jury is that Ada Baguley met her death by a fatal dose of morphine or heroin, or both. Our considered opinion is that there was a joint conspiracy. Our verdict is one of Wilful murder against Ronald Sullivan and Nurse Waddingham."

Nurse Waddingham collapsed.

The couple, it is understood, will appear at Nottingham City Police Court this morning.

**Coroner's summing-up.—Page 9.**

## Ex-Wife Fights to Save Him

### PLEA FROM LINER

BY A SPECIAL CORRESPONDENT

FEARING that her former husband, bound from New York to Hamburg on a deportation order from the U.S.A. to Germany, is being taken back to death or torture, a beautiful woman is to fight to save him.

"I would not let my worst enemy go back to Germany to face the fate which must be confronting him," she told me last night.

For her former husband is Dr. George Bresin, Man Without a Country, a fanatic fighting for freedom for all men, America's leading anti-Nazi propagandist, who fled from Germany in 1933.

Dr. George Bresin, deported from U.S. to Germany.

He is a passenger on board the U.S. liner President Roosevelt, which called at Plymouth yesterday. From the ship he issued a statement saying he had been "kidnapped," and making an impassioned plea for the British Government to intervene on his behalf, as he possessed "Nazi secrets affecting British interests."

Mrs. Lily Bresin, dark-haired and dark-eyed, was overcome with emotion as I spoke to her in her home in Glendale-avenue, Edgware.

She revealed to me that her marriage was dissolved four years ago.

"I knew something like this would happen," she said. "I always told him that no happiness would come to us if he meddled with politics. Why didn't he listen to me? That is the only reason we parted.

"I wanted my children to be brought up in England, where there is a wonderful feeling of security."

### War Ordeal

Then Mrs. Bresin told me of her life during the past twenty-five years.

"Dr. Bresin and I met in Berlin in 1911. He had a flourishing practice in a fashionable quarter of the city, and during the first few years of our married life we were supremely happy.

"Then came the war. My husband was of French birth, though he had spent most of his life in Germany. He was torn between a desire to fight for his native land or the country of his wife and child.

"After a great deal of investigation he was permitted to join the German Army as a medical officer. He served throughout the war on various fronts, and it was during that time that he became embittered.

"It was torture for him to see the sufferings of German men and youths. When he came home on leave he often raved about the

(Continued on back page)

## FRIEND OF QUEEN MARY DEAD

SUSAN Duchess of Somerset, a personal friend of Queen Mary and a well-known hostess of the Victorian and Edwardian periods, died last night at her house in Grosvenor-square, London, aged eighty-three.

Her husband, the fifteenth Duke of Somerset, who died in 1923, bore the orb at the coronations of both King Edward VII and King George V.

Always outspoken, the Duchess held unorthodox views.

She had an adventurous life in her younger days, accompanying her husband on a ranch in the West, where they lived primitively.

She wrote "Impressions of a Tenderfoot," a book describing her Wild West adventures.

## RONALD COLMAN HIT BY KNIFE IN FILM SCENE

HOLLYWOOD, Thursday.

RONALD Colman, British film star, was injured in an accident while making a scene of a film in Hollywood to-day.

He was struck in the chest by a knife thrown during the shooting of a scene of the film, "Under Two Flags." The knife was deflected slightly by a post and hit Colman.

The knife was thrown by a Yaqui Indian, Steve Clemente, a veteran knife thrower, who earns £50 for each knife he throws in films.

Clemente said that this was his first accident in twenty years, and claims that he was distracted for a fraction of a second by "someone looking at me."

He had previously warned bystanders against looking in his eyes.—B.U.P.

## 30,000 Torches in Hitler Parade

BERLIN, Thursday.

HERR Hitler, standing on a balcony of the Chancellor's palace to-night took the salute of 30,000 members of the original Storm Troops in celebration of the third anniversary of his accession to power.

With torches aflame the long columns of Brownshirts marched through the famous Brandenburg Gate, down Unter den Linden and the Wilhelmstrasse to the Chancellor's palace, where Herr Hitler stood to take the salute.—Reuter.

**Bombs to Keep Order—Page 7**

## LINDBERGH INQUIRY

TRENTON (New Jersey), Thursday.

INVESTIGATION into the kidnapping of the Lindbergh baby has been reopened by order of Governor Hoffman.—Reuter.

# Daily Mirror

THE DAILY PICTURE NEWSPAPER WITH THE LARGEST NET SALE

Broadcasting - Page 20

DOCTOR'S DIARY Page 6
EUSTACE ........ 7
QUIET CORNER --- 14
SERIAL .......... 19
BELINDA ........ 20
DOROTHY DIX --- 24

No. 10,043  Registered at the G.P.O. as a Newspaper.   FRIDAY, FEBRUARY 7, 1936   One Penny

Amusements : Pages 22 and 23

# SECRET ARMS SUPPLY FOR PALESTINE

## Dhows Used for Gun-Running

BY A SPECIAL CORRESPONDENT

Grave unrest in the Near East . . . secret arming in Palestine . . . Damascus and Beirut as storm centres . . . dhows used for gun-running.

THIS alarming situation was revealed last night in foreign messages and in a question asked in the House of Commons. Palestine is rapidly becoming an armed camp.

Major Milner, M.P., asked the Secretary for the Colonies in the House of Commons last night whether he was aware that:

Secret arming was going on at a rapid rate in Palestine, both by Jews and Arabs.

Arabs, Japanese and Greek agents were helping to import cheap arms into the country, mainly through the north and east.

He asked what action was being taken by the Government to stop it.

The existence of a limited traffic in arms in Palestine was admitted by Major Davies, Lord of the Treasury, replying for the Secretary for the Colonies.

### No Reply

He said that the Secretary was aware of what was going on, that all possible steps were being and would be taken by the authorities to check the traffic.

When another member asked what the object of the people was in arming no reply was given.

In Damascus, in the French mandated territory of Syria, there has been rioting arising out of the Nationalist agitation against the Government.

A B.U.P. message from Jerusalem last night states that merchants in Damascus who attempted to open their shops yesterday were subjected to a window-smashing campaign by Syrian Nationalists, and smoke bombs were thrown by the mob. Demonstrators smashed the windows of the offices of the President of the Syrian Republic and demanded his arrest.

Already during the riots nearly 300 Syrian youths have been sentenced to various terms of imprisonment.

The Government have had to take in hand the food supplies for their officials.

In Beirut, some fifty miles away from Damascus, states Reuter, there was a clash between soldiers and Nationalist demonstrators at Hama yesterday.

The troops were called out after the crowd had started stoning public buildings following a meeting at a mosque.

Up to yesterday there had been four deaths as a result of the riots in Damascus and two more in Aleppo.

### ALFONSO'S SON DYING

HAVANA, Thursday

THE Prince of the Asturias (ex-King Alfonso's son) is reported to be dying in Havana, where he has been living for some time with his Cuban wife. The Papal Nuncio, Monsignor Caruana, is stated to have given extreme unction at 7.30 p.m. (12.30 a.m. Friday G.M.T.).—B.U.P.

Boarding party from a British warship alongside an Arab dhow in the Eastern Mediterranean to search for arms. An officer is interrogating the master of the dhow while his boat's crew stand by.

## "God Told Me How to Act"

### RAIL HERO WHO AVERTED TRIPLE CRASH

"It is due to this, sir. God told me how to act. His spirit spoke to me through this book."

HOLDING aloft a small Testament, which he produced from his waistcoat pocket, a railway hero made this declaration in a tense scene at a Loughborough inquest yesterday.

The man is John Robert Frank Wilson, of Derby, the driver of a Derby train, aged thirty-seven. It was revealed that he had averted a triple crash.

He had just been complimented by the coroner and the barrister representing the L.M.S. railway at an inquest on a guard who was killed in a collision.

Returning a verdict of Accidental death, the jury announced that there was no criminal negligence by anyone.

Wilson was the pilot of a double-headed goods train travelling from Brent to Derby in the early hours of January 21.

Two miles from Loughborough his engine crashed into the rear of another goods train which had pulled out from a siding and on to the same line, killing the guard, Thomas Frank Busby, aged thirty-six, of Childs Hill, Cricklewood, N.W.

"I was shot into the corner of my cab," Wilson told the coroner. "I jumped down on to the line, ran along the bank flashing a small white light to warn an oncoming train."

Mr. Mathew Beale, a Birmingham barrister, expressing the railway company's gratitude to Wilson, disclosed that not only did Wilson avert a collision at one end of the wreckage, but ran back to the other end of the mix-up and held up a second train in the nick of time.

### JOCKEY WEDS

Arthur Wragg, the popular jockey, and his bride, Miss Phyllis Wood, were well pelted with confetti as they left Caxton Hall Register Office, Westminster, after their marriage yesterday. Among the guests was his brother, Sam Wragg.

### ROSE LEAVES CAIRO

CAIRO, Thursday.

Flight-Lieutenant Tommy Rose, who is attempting to break Mrs. Mollison's England-Capetown flight record, left here for Khartoum at 10.10 p.m. G.M.T.—Reuter.

## BOY DIED AS HE READ IN BATH

DESCRIBED by his friends as "a book worm," a fourteen-year-old boy was found drowned in his bath, a book in his hand, at his home in Wimbledon, S.W., last night.

He was Cyril Ernest Embleton, of Queens-road, Wimbledon.

For three-quarters of an hour he was left in his home while his parents were out.

During that time he went to the bathroom, where his bath had been left ready for him. It is believed that he had been reading in the bath and fainted.

His parents found him dead on their return.

## MARRIED 2 DAYS AFTER THEY MET

MET for the first time on Tuesday, married yesterday—that is the story of the romance of Mr. Harris Bate, seventy-year-old widower of Devonshire, and Mrs. Sarah Booted, sixty-six, of Stoke Newington, London.

Loud greetings of "mozeltov," the Hebrew equivalent of "Good luck," were exchanged when the ceremony was performed with full ritual at Plymouth Synagogue. The bridegroom crushed a wineglass under his foot.

"Daily Mirror" correspondents for the occasion exchanged photographs.

# Daily Mirror

THE DAILY PICTURE NEWSPAPER WITH THE LARGEST NET SALE

Broadcasting - Pages 20 & 21

EUSTACE . . . . Page 13
QUIET CORNER . . . 15
DOCTOR'S DIARY . . 17
SERIAL . . . . . . . 19
DOROTHY DIX . . . . 22
BELINDA . . . . . . 23

No. 10,044 Registered at the G.P.O. as a Newspaper. SATURDAY, FEBRUARY 8, 1936 One Penny

Amusements: Page 20

## KING EDWARD'S FIRST HONOURS

**COUNT OF COVADONGA AND HIS CUBAN WIFE**

The Count of Covadonga, formerly Prince of the Asturias, with his wife, the daughter of a wealthy Cuban. Before marriage she was Senorita Edelmira Sanpedro-Ocejo.

## Three Drops of Blood a Minute to Save a Prince's Life

THREE drops of blood a minute are keeping alive King Alfonso's eldest son, the ex-Prince of the Asturias. For two days he has lain desperately ill in Havana.

Doctors fear he may not last for many hours. Haemophilia (bleeding)—a disease which has already caused the death of one of his brothers—is taking its toll.

But a blood transfusion, at first considered impossible, owing to the Prince's weak state, was successful yesterday. The operation, consisting of giving three drops of blood a minute, lasted eight hours.

Some time after the operation, says B.U.P., the Prince was resting easily, greeting visitors and taking liquid refreshment.

It is understood that renewed hopes are now entertained of his recovery.

At the bedside is the Prince's wife, the beautiful daughter of a wealthy Cuban sugar planter.

It was for love of her that the Prince defied his father's wishes, renounced his rights to the Spanish throne and became the Duke of Covadonga.

## British Officers Cut Down by Mob

AN Indian police officer was killed and the Zanzibar Commissioner of Police and two other European officials were seriously wounded by a mob of Arabs in severe rioting at Zanzibar yesterday, says Reuter.

Arabs, armed with swords surrounded European officers, including the Produce Inspector and the Assistant District Commissioner.

The riots were a protest against the new law to prevent the adulteration of copra.

## Soldier Accused of Attack on Girl

THE story of an alleged assault by a soldier on a domestic servant at Wrecclesham, near Farnham, Surrey, was related at a special Court at Farnham yesterday.

Leslie Hayde, a private stationed at Bordon Camp, was charged with unlawfully assaulting the girl with intent to commit a serious offence.

Accused in custody was ordered until next Thursday, when Hayde will appear at Camberley.

Police-Sergeant W. H. West said that after the girl had made a statement at Farnham Police Station he saw Hayde at Brookhead Common, Bordon. When charged Hayde denied all knowledge of the offence.

At Bordon Hayde was put up for identification with twelve other soldiers. He was immediately picked out by the girl as the man who had assaulted her.

## Man Who Saw Crown Gems Fall

AS the first honours bestowed by King Edward VIII were being made known last night, the Scottish Nationalist Party decided to launch a petition to the King asking him " to refrain from using his wrong title."

The party, which met privately in Glasgow, object to the new King being known as King Edward VIII. They base their claim on the fact that before the Union of the Crowns there had never been a King Edward of Scotland, although there had been six in England, and that therefore the present King is King Edward VIII of Great Britain and Edward II of Scotland.

In last night's "Honours List" are seventeen naval and Army officers and two gunners who helped to draw the body of King George to Westminster Hall for the lying-in-state and on the last funeral procession.

### Frontier Heroes

The honours—the first of the new reign—take the form of appointments to the Royal Victorian Order.

Lieutenant Arthur Charles Huntington, of the Grenadier Guards, the officer in charge of the bearer party when the coffin was brought from King's Cross Station to Westminster Hall for the lying-in-state, becomes a member of the fourth class of the Order.

He picked up the cross of the Imperial Crown when it fell to the ground during the procession.

Other honours are conferred on officers and men who were engaged in the operations on the North-West Frontier last year, when British troops at length dislodged the tribesmen of the Fakir of Alingar (the Mad Fakir), following border raids.

### ROYAL VALET ILL

A further drama of the royal funeral was revealed last night, when it was announced that Mr. Richard Howlett, devoted servant of King George and superintendent of his Majesty's wardrobe, lies seriously ill at Ambassador's Court, St. James's Palace.

His illness, caused by a chill, is due to his devotion to his beloved master.

Although far from well, he insisted on walking all the way in the funeral procession.

He was warned that it was more than his strength would bear, but doggedly he plodded on to St. George's Chapel, Windsor. He overtaxed his powers of endurance. Afterwards he was taken ill.

Last night he was reported to be making progress towards recovery.

Mr. Richard Howlett.

## NAZI CHIEF'S ASSASSIN

David Frankfurter, self-confessed murderer of Dr. Wilhelm Gustloff, Nazi leader in Switzerland, waiting to be taken to prison from Davos Town Hall. Frankfurter, who is twenty-six and a Yugoslav Jewish medical student, called at Dr. Gustloff's flat, fired five shots as his victim entered, and then gave himself up.

### Biscuit-Tin Raiders

TWO men entered an antique shop in Tooting yesterday and asked the assistant if they could see some daggers.

As the assistant turned to find the daggers, the two men jammed a biscuit tin on his head and made off with three daggers.

### "RED MAX" RIDDLE

## SUSPECT'S WIFE IN COURT DRAMA

PARIS, Friday

LACROIX, the man arrested in Paris in connection with the shooting of Max Kassel, whose body was found near St. Albans on January 24, was confronted here to-day with a woman who claimed to be his wife.

The two faced each other before M. Rousel, the examining magistrate.

The examining magistrate stated later that Lacroix was obviously astounded at the sight of the woman.

Indeed, the prisoner is reported to have said before the interview, "I noticed my wife in the passage. I want to speak to her. I want to kiss her."

During his appearance before the magistrate, M. Rousel: You have every interest in staying in France, British justice is much more severe.

Lacroix: Only if I am guilty. I am innocent. I demand extradition.

Suzanne Bertron, the woman who was arrested with Lacroix, will not be examined by the magistrates until next Thursday.—Reuter.

# Daily Mirror

**THE DAILY PICTURE NEWSPAPER WITH THE LARGEST NET SALE**

Broadcasting - Page 20

EUSTACE . . . . Page 13
QUIET CORNER . . . . 15
DOCTOR'S DIARY . . 10
SERIAL . . . . . . . 19
DOROTHY DIX . . . . 22
BELINDA . . . . . . . 22

No. 10,045 Registered at the G.P.O as a Newspaper. MONDAY, FEBRUARY 10, 1936 One Penny

Amusements: Page 21

## A-HUNTING WE WILL GO!

THE famous Dionne quintuplets "go for a ride" on the chairs in their nursery at Callander, Ontario, Canada. Yvonne, laughing, on the left, enjoys her ride, while Marie, next to her, whips up her steed.

## HEIRESS WEDS MAN WITHOUT A COUNTRY

### Mother Denies Fortune Was Sacrificed

BY A SPECIAL CORRESPONDENT

A twenty four-year-old Cheshire heiress was married in London this week-end to Andre Michelson, a man without a country.

The bride is Pamela Moseley. Reports that she had given up a fortune by marrying were denied by her mother yesterday.

From her lovely old house at Prestbury, Cheshire, Mrs. Reginald Moseley made this statement to the *Daily Mirror*.

"It is absurd to suggest that Pamela, our only child, has been cut off by us.

"I was present at her wedding. My brother gave her away and most of our relatives were present.

"True, we did not really wish her to marry this man, but Pamela is old enough to decide for herself.

"She will still have her private income from us as if nothing had happened. We shall correspond and occasionally see each other.

"We are just a little worried about the fact that her husband as a White Russian has no nationality, but we have no intention whatsoever of breaking all links with our only daughter on that account."

## Germans Howl Down Nazi Cries of "Heil Hitler"

MUNICH, Sunday.

NAZIS were howled down by a crowd of 4,000 people outside St. Michael's Church here to-night, in an amazing demonstration after Cardinal Faulhaber, Archbishop of Munich, in a sermon had denounced Nazi "lies."

Ex-Crown Prince Rupprecht of Bavaria was among the 10,000 people in St. Michael's Church and he and the Archbishop received a great ovation.

In another church close by, to which the Cardinal's words were relayed, every inch of room was filled. Many hundreds of people were turned away from both churches.

Afterwards the crowds blocked the streets round the church and traffic was disorganised.

Nazis tried to stage a counter-demonstration on the doorsteps of the police headquarters opposite the Cardinal's church. Their cries of "Heil, Hitler!" were howled down.

The Archbishop's sermon was a powerful defence of the Pope and the Catholic Church and an attack on Nazi methods of prejudicing the young against Christianity and against the Catholic Church.

He did not mince matters when he referred to some of the Nazi allegations as "lies," and to a certain type of Nazi fanatic as "Brown-coated Communists."—Exchange.

## MR. DE VALERA'S SON KILLED RIDING

### Father at Bedside

Mr. de Valera.

FROM OUR OWN CORRESPONDENT

DUBLIN, Sunday.

MR. De Valera stood by the bedside of his dying son in a Dublin hospital to-day. The President of the Free State Executive Council had been urgently called there when his son Brian, aged twenty, had been injured in a riding accident in Phoenix Park, Dublin.

Standing with him were two other sons and a cousin, with whom he had been riding.

Mr. de Valera, controlling his own emotion, strove to comfort them in their distress.

The youth, suffering from concussion, died without being able to speak to his father.

### Struck a Tree

Brian de Valera, with his cousin, Dr. Flanagan, was taking a morning ride in the park, and, when galloping under a tree, his head struck an overhanging branch. He was thrown unconscious from his horse.

His cousin rushed to his aid, and calling others to help, had Brian taken to hospital.

An urgent summons was sent to President de Valera at his home at Black Rock, five miles away.

Despite all the surgeons and doctors could do, Brian died at 4 p.m.

The iron control of Mr. de Valera gave way when the doctors announced that all was over.

In the same hospital another son of the President is a medical student.

### Brother in London

Brian de Valera was a student in the engineering school of the National University. He is described as having been very brilliant.

President de Valera has four other sons and two daughters. Brian is the third son.

His eldest son, Vivian, is touring England as a member of the Irish students' debating team and spoke yesterday at University College, London. A message was sent to Vivian informing him of the tragedy, and he is returning home at once.

### £450,000 FIRE

DAMAGE estimated at £450,000 was done by a disastrous fire at Elstree, Britain's "Hollywood," yesterday.

See story on back page; pictures on pages 14 and 15.

### TOWN'S BLACK-OUT CHAOS

SLOUGH (Bucks) was in darkness for more than an hour last night when the electric light supply failed.

Many houses were in complete darkness and people were unable to obtain candles as it was Sunday.

At the police station and the nursing home work was carried on by the light of candles. Along the Bath road traffic lights failed and constables were sent out to control the traffic.

Mrs. Andre Michelson.

## WOMAN OF 75 SCARES RAIDERS

A SEVENTY-FIVE-YEAR-OLD woman scared raiders who broke into her house in Friern Barnet-lane, Friern Barnet, Middlesex, yesterday.

She was Mrs. K. McLeod, who was alone in the house at the time.

As she sat asleep in her chair, one of the intruders entered and awakened her. She called out, "Who is there?" and the man and a companion ran off.

The men had ransacked another bedroom before going to her room.

## Police Guard Chase Carol's Car

DETECTIVES guarding King Carol of Rumania while he is in France are not to be fooled twice.

When the King left his hotel on Saturday by a back door, the detectives did not discover that he had gone until a quarter of an hour later.

Then followed a wild race between the King's car and the black cars and motor-cycles of the Sureté Générale.

Stopping his car, King Carol had a short but fiery conference with the pursuing detectives. When the King entered the Château de Belleme he gave strict instructions that he was not to be disturbed. News seekers were met by gendarmes and fierce dogs.

19

# Daily Mirror

THE DAILY PICTURE NEWSPAPER WITH THE LARGEST NET SALE

Broadcasting - Page 22

EUSTACE . . . . Page 13
QUIET CORNER . . . . 15
DOCTOR'S DIARY . . 10
SERIAL . . . . . . . . 19
DOROTHY DIX . . . . 22
BELINDA . . . . . . . 22

No. 10,049 — Registered at the G.P.O as a Newspaper. — FRIDAY, FEBRUARY 14, 1936 — One Penny

Amusements: Pages 26 and 27

## MOB'S SAVAGE ATTACK ON A STATESMAN

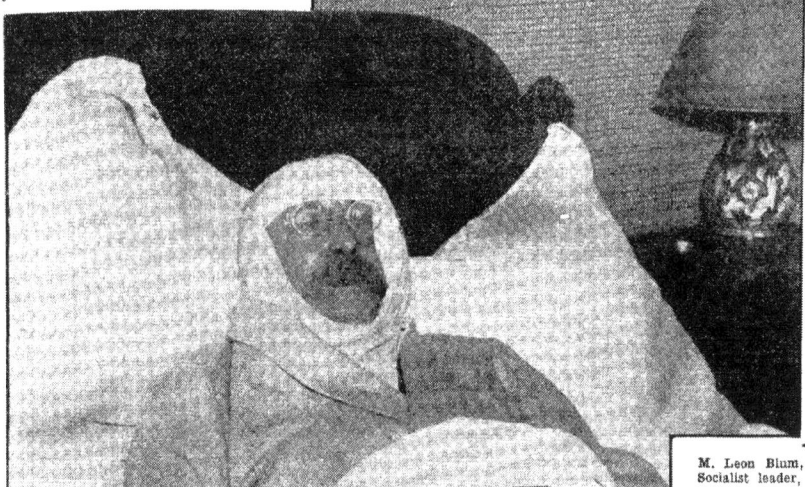

M. Leon Blum, the French Socialist leader, in bed with his head bandaged after receiving severe injuries when attacked in Paris yesterday by members of a royalist organisation. See page 3.

## FOOTBALL ROUGH PLAY MUST STOP

—Says Inquest Jury

### Demand After Player's Death

"The Management Committee of the Football Association should be asked to instruct all referees that they must exercise stricter control over players so as to eliminate such incidents."

THIS was the view of a Sunderland inquest jury last night after they had heard evidence of the Sunderland-Chelsea match at Roker Park on February 1.

They added it as a rider to their verdict at the resumed inquest on James Thorpe, the Sunderland goalkeeper, who collapsed shortly after the match.

The jury found that his death was due to diabetic coma, accelerated by the rough usage he had received.

### New Style Blamed

When Sir Frederick Wall, formerly secretary of the Football Association, was told of the findings he said:—

"I feel that an inquiry should be held in order to take action upon the recommendations.

"In my opinion, rough play has been developing in recent years. This has been the case more particularly during the past two or three seasons."

"One cause has been the introduction of the new system of re-arranging what one might call the field. I am thinking of the new formation which has been introduced, an attacking centre forward and an attacking half back, commonly called the stopper.

"That, in my opinion, has completely changed the style of play and had been conducive to unfair charging—a dangerous practice."

### Coroner on "The Game"

The coroner, in his summing-up, said:—

"You have heard described the game that was played that afternoon. One witness said the game was a disgrace to first-class football. From what I have heard, I quite agree with him. I think it was.

"I feel strongly that some of the men in this game have not been taught as I was taught.

"When we get First Division football teams playing we expect to get the cream of sportsmanship and the best of play.

"We find players in first-class football who resort to methods that are far from what is to be desired, and they do not really help their clubs or themselves or the game.

"If the referee had been where he should have been, watching the game, the continued ill-treatment to which the goalkeeper was subjected would not have been continued as long as it was—if the referee had done his duty.

### "Lost His Grip"

"But he seems, from all accounts, to have lost his grip of the game, and not been able to hold the players in check."

The coroner asked the jury not to pass a vote

(Continued on page 4)

## CONVICT MAY BE PRESIDENT

### Tom Mooney, in Gaol, Agrees to Stand

Tom Mooney, one of the principals in the celebrated Mooney-Billings case, who is imprisoned in California, has acceded to the plan of the Communist Party of the United States to run him against President Roosevelt in the forthcoming Presidential election.

MR. Jay Lovestone, secretary of the group, whose leaders were expelled from the official Communist Party six years ago, is sponsoring the plan.

"If it is the desire of all working-class political parties to so honour me, I would be happy to accept and would do everything in my power to fulfil the requirements such an obligation imposes," declares Mooney, answering a telegram the Communist leaders sent to his prison quarters in California.

### Twenty Years

Mr. Bertram Wolfe, agent for the Communists, admitted he did not know how Mooney could be got out of prison if he should be elected.

The suggestion is that Mooney should be a rallying figure for Communists Socialists and Radical Farmer groups.

He had spent twenty years in prison, states Reuter, after being convicted for the 1916 Preparedness Day bomb outrage in San Francisco.

Mooney claims an alibi and alleges he was "framed" by perjured evidence procured by the police.

## DEAD WIFE RIDDLE TO GO TO HOME OFFICE ANALYST

BY OUR SPECIAL CORRESPONDENT

INQUIRY into the riddle of the death of the young wife of a minister in an empty house which was formerly her home will be opened at a Middlesex inquest to-day.

The "Daily Mirror" learns that the hearing will be adjourned by Dr. J. S. Crone, the deputy-coroner for the county, for certain of the organs to be examined by Dr. Roche Lynch, the Home Office analyst.

On Tuesday evening last Mrs. Winifred Alice Hamilton, twenty-six, was found dead in a room of a house in Joel-street, Eastcote, Middlesex. The house is on a new estate and until recently was occupied by the dead woman and her husband, who is the Rev. Herbert Hamilton, recently appointed an associate minister of Union Church, Mill Hill.

Early this year the house was given up and the Rev. and Mrs. Hamilton resided elsewhere.

On February 1 Mrs. Hamilton disappeared and her husband could find no trace of her. On Tuesday last he had occasion to return to Joel-street, where there were still some of his wife's belongings.

### No Foul Play

He found her lying on the floor of the bedroom dead.

The body was taken to the mortuary and yesterday a post-mortem was carried out by Dr. Harold Broadbridge, of Harley-street.

No definite cause of death has been discovered, and it has been decided to remove certain organs, which will be examined by Dr. Roche Lynch.

Mrs. Hamilton had been married for five years, and is believed to have relatives at Stockport. Her husband is an official of a London mission.

The police are satisfied that there is no suspicion of foul play.

James Thorpe playing in the match in which he received the injuries that were followed by his death.

# Daily Mirror

**THE DAILY PICTURE NEWSPAPER WITH THE LARGEST NET SALE**

Broadcasting - Page 22

EUSTACE .... Page 13
QUIET CORNER ... 15
DOCTOR'S DIARY .. 17
5-DAY SERIAL ... 18
BELINDA ....... 22
DOROTHY DIX .... 24

No. 10,051   MONDAY, FEBRUARY 17, 1936   One Penny

Amusements: Page 23

# SABOTAGE IN BRITISH CRUISER

## Third Case in Three Months

### ADMIRALTY INQUIRY

Sensation was caused early this morning when the Admiralty announced that a case of sabotage had occurred in the British cruiser Cumberland, stationed at Chatham.

H.M.S. Cumberland, the cruiser concerned in the latest outbreak of sabotage, photographed arriving at Chatham to refit some months ago. The cruiser was completed in 1928. She was the first vessel in any navy to be equipped with quadruple torpedo tubes.

TO the bare announcement of the discovery of the outrage the Admiralty added the following information:

"The matter is under investigation and it would not be in the public interest to make any statement."

This is the third case of sabotage in a British warship in three months.

It is understood that Cumberland is being refitted at Chatham.

She is a cruiser of 9,750 tons, and was paid off into dockyard control at Chatham on March 12, 1935. According to the current Navy List her commander is Commander H. G. Hopper.

Completed in 1928, she was continuously on the China station from that year. Estimates for her overhaul amounted to £386,532.

She was the first vessel in any navy to be equipped with quadruple torpedo tubes.

One thousand men are at present working on the Cumberland.

### Previous Attempts

In December officers of M.I.5, the intelligence department of the fighting services, were investigating damage done to the battleship Royal Oak, and the big submarine Oberon.

The electrical equipment on the Royal Oak completely failed and refitting work had to be held up for three days while search was made for the fault.

It was then found that an electric cable to the control tower of the battleship had been short circuited. A filed sail-pin had been driven through the cable. Repairs cost over £300.

The trouble in the Oberon was also in the electrical equipment. It was discovered that a commutator had been tampered with.

Sabotage in December last on the new U.S.A. heavy cruiser Quincy when the turbine reducing gears were ruined cost £20,000 to repair.

## ITALY CLAIMS NEW VICTORY

### "20,000 Abyssinian Casualties"

ITALY'S claim to have achieved on the Northern front the greatest victory since the start of the Abyssinian war was announced in a special communique issued in Rome yesterday, says B.U.P.

In the Battle of Enderta, which began on February 11 and developed at the beginning of the week-end it is claimed that—

Twenty thousand Abyssinians were killed or wounded. Italian losses reported by Marshal Badoglio were 400 killed and 500 wounded.

### FAMOUS BEAUTY IN THE NEWS

Mrs. Sylvia Gough, beautiful ex-chorus girl and daughter-in-law of the late General Gough, who has been cited as a witness in the police court proceedings against Douglas Burton, of Hungerford-road, Holloway, N., a book reviewer, charged with the murder of Douglas Boase, author, at Canonbury. In pre-war days she was a toast of London society. Burton is thirty. See page 3.

## Stranded British Liner Refloats After Vigil by 3 Destroyers

WITH 338 passengers on board, the Winchester Castle, 20,000-ton luxury liner of the Union Castle Line, was refloated at 12.55 this morning, nearly three hours after running aground in dense fog on the treacherous rocky coast near Portland, Dorset.

Three destroyers, four Admiralty tugs and the Weymouth lifeboat had answered the liner's distress flares and S O S. With high tide, at midnight, strenuous and successful efforts were made to refloat the vessel, bound for Southampton from Durban. Captain J. H. Kirby had already wirelessed that his ship was in no immediate danger.

The Winchester Castle moved off under her own power and passed slowly out to sea with tugs standing by. She had apparently suffered no damage.

Visibility was poor when the liner went aground, but by midnight the fog had cleared and the sea was calm. The liner was stranded about a mile from the shore, 200 yards south of Blackmore Fort, a spot well known to holidaymakers.

Orders of the officers to the crew were distinctly heard by the crowd which gathered on the coast.

Coastguards clambered down the 300ft. cliff and maintained communication with the Winchester Castle by flashlamps.

The Winchester Castle is the second largest vessel of the Union Castle fleet, and is the sister ship of the Warwick Castle, which is slightly larger.

Among her passengers was Earl Howe.

Coastguards noticed the rocket signal of distress and telephoned the coxswain of Weymouth lifeboat, Mr. J. Vine, a Daily Mirror reporter was told.

The crew of eight were called to the station by rocket signal and put to sea.

Lloyd's telegram received from Niton Wireless Station stated: "S O S received from British motor vessel Winchester Castle at 10.3 p.m. G.M.T.: 'Ashore west side of Portland. Want immediate assistance.'"

Coastguards and life-saving crews were mobilised and assembled on Portland Bill

## MURDERED AND FLUNG IN CANAL

### All-Night Hunt for a Woman's Attacker

FROM OUR OWN CORRESPONDENT

Dudley, Sunday.

It was revealed by a midnight post-mortem examination that the twenty-five-year-old woman whose body was found in the canal at Tipton, Staffs, had been murdered and then thrown in the ice-covered water.

CLOSE secrecy was observed regarding the post-mortem that was conducted at Bilston, near here.

Four doctors were present, including Dr. Menton, a pathologist, of Stafford. Afterwards certain organs were taken by police car to Dr. Menton's laboratory.

The dead woman was Eliza Jane Worton, of Phoenix-street, Greets Green, West Bromwich.

### Identity Parade

Her head had been battered in and twenty yards from where her body was discovered by gipsies police found a crimson patch, believed to be blood, on the roadway.

Mr. M. Stafford, of Tipton, who lives close to the spot where the body was taken from the canal on Saturday morning, has given valuable information to the police.

He said that about 10 p.m. on Friday he saw a lorry standing on the canal bridge. Mrs. Worton is believed to have had a conversation with a lorry-driver about this time.

In the early hours of this morning Mr. and Mrs. Stafford visited Bilston police station for an identification parade.

They were then unable to make any identification.

### Search for Car

I understand that the police are also looking for the owner of a small black car with a Surrey registration number.

All the evidence gathered by the police so far points to a murder carried out on the spur of the moment.

Bilston police issued a statement today that they would be glad to interview any person who saw the woman alive on the evening of February 14.

Police-Superintendent Orford, who is in charge of the case, said: "Our inquiries are

(Continued on back page)

# Daily Mirror

**THE DAILY PICTURE NEWSPAPER WITH THE LARGEST NET SALE**

Broadcasting - Pages 22 & 23

EUSTACE . . . . . Page 9
QUIET CORNER . . . 17
DOCTOR'S DIARY . . 19
5-DAY SERIAL . . . . 21
DOROTHY DIX . . . . 24
BELINDA . . . . . . . 26

No. 10,053  Registered at the G.P.O as a Newspaper.  WEDNESDAY, FEBRUARY 19, 1936  One Penny

Amusements: Page 22

## POLICE CHARGE IN SPAIN

Armed police advancing on the crowd gathered in Barcelona to anticipate federal government in Catalonia as a result of the Spanish Left's election victory. Right: Barring the way to a demonstrator.

## RADIO SOS TO TRAGIC HUSBAND

### Wife and Child Killed in Road Accident

A RADIO call was broadcast last night for a man whose wife and one of his children had been killed in a motor accident and another child seriously injured.

The broadcast said:—

"Will Thomas Kay, a commercial traveller, of City-road, Old Trafford, Manchester, who is believed to be in the Hull district, return home, as his wife and children have met with a serious accident to-day."

Late last night the police had been unable to get into touch with Mr. Kay.

The accident took place near Stretford-road, Manchester.

It is understood that a motor-lorry skidded on the wet surface of the road, striking Mrs. Elsie Annie Kay, aged thirty-six, and her children, Gerald, aged nine, and Jean, aged five. A third child escaped injury.

The two injured children were taken to Manchester Royal Infirmary, where Gerald died later.

In the meantime doctors fought for the life of five-year-old Jean, and late last night they decided that unless an operation was performed her life could not possibly be saved.

They got in touch with Mrs. Kay's father, who broke down and wept as he gave them the necessary authority to perform the operation.

### MINERS ENTOMBED

NINE hours after a fatal accident in Kimblesworth Colliery, Co. Durham, miners at midnight had established communication with two workmates entombed as a result of an extensive fall of roof.

The dead man was Robert Atkinson, nineteen, a coal cutter, of Sacriston.

## Army's Midnight Revolt Stamped Out by Spanish Government

AN attempted coup by members of the Spanish Army met failure early this morning. The Government took swift action and is still in power. Two high army officials have been arrested. Meanwhile, prominent politicians, against many of whom the victorious Left parties have old scores, continued to flee the country.

Refugees, including a number of aristocrats, who fear vengeance, are pouring into Gibraltar. With them come British and other foreign visitors from Malaga.

Senor Juan March, political "boss" and patron of the Right party, has left hurriedly for France.

Senor Salazar Alonso, who, as Minister of the Interior in 1934, used a heavy hand to deal with a strike in Madrid, has gone to Portugal.

His successor, Don Eloy Gaquero, who put down the revolution in Asturias in the same year, and Don Angel Velarde, who was Governor-General of Asturias at the time, have chosen Gibraltar.

The Monarchist newspaper, "ABC," quoted by Reuter, comments on their departure:—"Those who flee from Spain at this hour are no more than cowards and traitors, who do not deserve to bear the name of Spaniard."

A "state of war" has been proclaimed in Saragossa, where one person was killed and six, including two women, were wounded when police clashed with demonstrators.

A thousand prisoners in Burgos Gaol rioted and set fire to their bedding. One warder was wounded (says the B.U.P.).

There was a brief mutiny among political prisoners at Oviedo, who fired their dormitory.

## Ten Feared Lost in British Ship

### WRECKAGE WASHED UP DURING GALE

WRECKAGE washed ashore yesterday during a gale on the desolate Shetland Islands is the only trace of the missing Newhaven (Edinburgh) steam trawler May Island, feared lost with all her crew of ten.

The May Island left last Friday for fishing grounds north of the Shetlands. Wreckage found yesterday included a lifebelt, a ship's lifeboat, a wireless set and fish boxes.

It is now feared she has been wrecked on a remote part of the coast.

Mr. Thomas Seales, of Newhaven, the owner, said he had been in touch late last night with the coastguards who first reported the wreckage, but had received no confirmation of the wreck.

Earlier in the day he had spoken to a sister ship of the May Island, which stated that the trawler was two hundred miles from the Shetlands.

The German steamer Condor (889 tons), from Bremen bound for Aalborg, in Jutland, is reported lost with all her crew of ten.

### Rescue Drama

Rescued in the nick of time from their sinking ship, the crew of the Greek steamer Stefanos Costomenis had the narrowest escape of the hundreds of seamen imperilled by storm last night.

The steamer sprang a leak in heavy seas to the south-east of Norfolk (Virginia), and sent out an SOS saying the deck was under water and the captain would abandon ship.

Her signals were answered by the City of Newport News, which, battling against heavy seas, safely took off the whole crew, says Reuter from Boston.

Wireless warnings were sent to shipping when a tug with no one on board broke adrift in heavy seas at the mouth of the Tees last night.

## Cooking Steak and Onions Over the Telephone!

FRENCH 'phone girls are broadcasting how useful they are. It appears that a hostess rang up the "S'il vous plait" information bureau and explained that she had thirteen guests, and what was she to do to stop bad luck? The bureau sent round two evening gowned 'phone girls!

That's nothing!

Listen to this:—

A girl in a London exchange recently answered a call and a man's voice said: "I say, miss, may I speak to you a minute?"

When she hesitated he said:—

"Well, miss, what I want to know is, can you tell me how to cook steak and onions?"

It turned out that his wife was away and he was alone in the house. He had the steak and the onions, but he did not know how to handle them.

Obviously, it was a genuine case of domestic difficulty. The Hello girl came to the rescue of the subscriber, who enjoyed his steak and onions immensely, was extremely grateful to her.

Can the Paris "S'il vous plait" service beat that for usefulness?

Or this?

The alarmed voice of a nursemaid came through to another operator. "My mistress is out," said the voice, "and the baby seems to have had a fit. Whatever shall I do?"

The operator advised her to put the baby in a warm bath and ring up for a doctor to go round at once.

"I saved the child."

# Daily Mirror

**THE DAILY PICTURE NEWSPAPER WITH THE LARGEST NET SALE**

Broadcasting - Page 22

EUSTACE . . . . . Page 8
QUIET CORNER . . . 16
DOCTOR'S DIARY . . 19
5-DAY SERIAL . . . . 21
DOROTHY DIX . . . . 26
BELINDA . . . . . . . 26

No. 10,054  THURSDAY, FEBRUARY 20, 1936  One Penny

Amusements: Page 18

## Duce Sends Secret Note to Hitler

### ALLIANCE FEAR IN EUROPE

BY OUR DIPLOMATIC CORRESPONDENT

NEWS of secret talks in Rome added last night to the growing fear of an Italo-German front in Europe—of an alliance between the world's two greatest dictators.

Experts believe that Herr Ulrich von Hassel, German Ambassador to Italy, who left for Berlin on Tuesday after seeing Signor Suvich, Italian Under-Secretary for Foreign Affairs, bears Mussolini's answer to Hitler's questions on the future of the Locarno Pact.

Cordiality between Mussolini and Hitler has grown rapidly in recent weeks.

Both are faced with the problem of expansion and are keenly interested in Africa—Italy in Abyssinia and Germany in her lost colonies.

Both are completely distrustful of France and fear the effect of the proposed Franco-Soviet Treaty.

Germany claims that this Treaty, due for early ratification, is part of an "encirclement" plan. She brands Russia once more as the disturbing influence in Europe

### Tokio Assurance

And yesterday Britain too was showing anxiety over Russia.

She was anxious lest the recent frontier "incidents" should lead to serious trouble between Russia and Japan. Sir Robert Clive, the British Ambassador in Tokio, had an hour-long interview with Mr. Shigemitsu, Vice-Minister for Foreign Affairs.

Mr. Shigemitsu is reported to have declared that a settlement was Japan's aim.

### Socialist Flare-Up

Meanwhile, Britain's supplementary Service estimates, amounting to over £7,000,000, necessitated by the Italo-Abyssinian war, has caused a flare-up in the Parliamentary Labour Party.

At the party's meeting yesterday more than one M.P. threatened to vote against the party's policy of opposing the estimates.

The Socialists are worried about the concentration of the Fleet in the Mediterranean.

After considerable wrangling, I am told, it was agreed that the estimates must be opposed because our action tended to become unilateral and not part of the League's policy.

## WHAT ROCKS DID TO LINER

TWO views of the damage done to the Union Castle liner Winchester Castle when, inward bound, she went ashore near Portland Bill on Sunday night. Left: Men cleaning torn and twisted plates of the bow in Trafalgar dry dock at Southampton yesterday. Below: Looking up at the holed bow when the dock had been emptied

## OSTRICH FEATHER MODE LEAD BY THE KING

By A SPECIAL CORRESPONDENT

THE King wants to see ostrich feathers come back into fashion. When he saw a display on the South African stand at the British Industries Fair yesterday he said: "I'd like to see them come back, but I don't know if I can move the fashions." Mr. Norman Hartnell, who designed the Duchess of Gloucester's trousseau, said: "Designers will be grateful to the King for this lead—we shall do all we can to bring them back.

"I know the King's words will have an immediate effect—often he has greatly influenced fashions in the past.

"The feathers began to be used a little more at the Jubilee. They are now dyed in the most beautiful colours. Nothing makes so alluring a frame for a woman's face.

"Many of the ostrich feathers used to-day are about six inches long. Lovely capes can be made from them, and they are unequalled for trimming evening dresses of chiffon and other similar materials.

"Probably the King saw them on toques or small hats—they make a most effective decoration in this way."

Another well-known designer told me that ostrich feathers were being much used in the latest creations coming from Paris.

An official at the office of the High Commissioner for South Africa said that there were good stocks of feathers in London.

An ostrich feather broker said that any increased demand for the feathers would create a great deal of employment in England.

The King's tour of the Fair—page 5.

## FELL IN LOVE WITH A PAINTING?

A MAN who went to an exhibition of paintings at Hove Art Gallery fell so deeply in love with a miniature of a girl that—he stole it!

This is the theory advanced yesterday to account for the mysterious disappearance of a "head and shoulders" of a girl with sparkling eyes and raven hair.

The portrait was valued at £20.

Many more valuable exhibits, contributed by the Eclectic Art Society, hung on the walls—but were untouched.

It is thought that this particular portrait cast a spell over a male visitor, who was unable to resist the temptation to take it down and slip it under his coat.

Police describe the miniature as being three inches by four. It is enclosed in a plain silver-gilt frame.

## NO HOPE FOR TEN IN TRAWLER WRECK

TWENTY men are feared dead in two British trawlers which vanished into a waste of wild waters while a gale lashed desolate northern coasts.

Owners of the Grimsby trawler Merrivale, wrecked in the Orkneys early yesterday, have abandoned hope for her crew of ten. It is thought she ran ashore in dense fog.

Siren calls were heard by the lighthouse-keeper at Pentland Skerries, and after the fog cleared he saw distress flares.

The lighthouse keeper, Mr. Black, told the Daily Mirror:—

"I tried to get into touch with headquarters by wireless telephone, but was unsuccessful. When dawn came I saw the mast of a ship. Slowly it disappeared into the waves."

There was no news yesterday to indicate that any had been saved from the Newhaven (Edinburgh) trawler May Island, believed wrecked with a crew of ten in the Shetlands.

## Girl's Body on Beach Mystery

The possibility that a woman was aboard the steamer Kentbrook, which foundered with all hands in West Bay, Dorset, last January, was raised at a Weymouth inquest yesterday on the partly-clothed body of a girl washed up at Chesil Beach.

The inquest was adjourned for a week.

## Chelsea F.C. Chief Dead

Mr. C. J. Pratt

CHAIRMAN and oldest member of Chelsea Football Club, Mr. Charles J. Pratt, died suddenly at his home last night, a few hours after discussing with his son his club's Cup-tie match. He was aged seventy.

He had attended matches regularly until last week, but he was unable to be at yesterday's game owing to illness.

His son, Mr. C. J. Pratt, junior, also a director of the club, described the match in detail to his father shortly before he collapsed and died.

This is the fourth official of the club to die since October, the others being Mr. J. T. Mears, the vice-chairman; Mr. A. J. Palmer, the secretary, and Mr. Claude Kirby, former chairman.

Mr. Pratt was an official of the Amateur Athletic Association for twenty years.

## In Court After Escaping Birch

Mr. Justice Goddard, at Notts Assizes yesterday had before him a fifteen-year-old Leicester boy who had been ordered twelve strokes of the birch at Leicester, the punishment later being remitted following an application to the Home Office by one of the local M.P.s.

The Judge said to him: "I can only say this, if you had undergone that sentence it is much less likely that you would be standing where you are now."

The boy was sent to an approved school for three years.

THE DAILY MIRROR, Friday, February 21, 1936.

# Daily Mirror

**THE DAILY PICTURE NEWSPAPER WITH THE LARGEST NET SALE**

Broadcasting - Page 22

EUSTACE . . . . . Page 8
QUIET CORNER . . . 16
DOCTOR'S DIARY . . 19
5-DAY SERIAL . . . . 21
DOROTHY DIX . . . . 26
BELINDA . . . . . . 26

No. 10,055 Registered at the G.P.O. as a Newspaper.  FRIDAY, FEBRUARY 21, 1936  One Penny

Amusements: Pages 26 and 27

# SPY GANGS STEALING OUR SECRETS

Lieut.-Commander A. A. Hogg with his fiancée, Miss Daphne Mulholland.

## Master-Mind Is Behind Leakages

By OUR PARLIAMENTARY CORRESPONDENT

International espionage on a large scale directed by a master-mind is suspected to be at the bottom of the sensational leakage of confidential Government information.

BRITAIN'S silent army—the Secret Service—is now investigating the leakage.

Only a month or two ago there was a leakage in Paris which led to the Hoare-Laval peace pact dilemma.

Mr. Baldwin's cryptic remark on that occasion: "My lips are not yet unsealed," indicates clearly that secret diplomacy is working overtime.

Someone is obtaining information from the capitals of Europe and thus sowing seeds of discord.

There have been other leakages, and obviously a number of highly confidential documents dealing with Italy and Abyssinia are in circulation.

All Whitehall is now asking how the Rome newspaper, *Giornale d'Italia*, obtained possession of a report on Abyssinia by a Government Committee presided over by Sir John Maffey, Permanent Under-Secretary of State for the Colonies.

### More Bitterness

The report, made to the Foreign Office last June, was marked "Secret" and circulated among certain Government departments concerned. It was definitely not communicated to Italy.

Although its conclusions are by no means unfavourable to Italy, and do not tally with

(*Continued on back page*)

## Glass Splinter Killed Naval Officer in His Cabin

FROM OUR OWN CORRESPONDENT

SHEERNESS, Thursday.

A TINY splinter of glass from a broken tumbler caused the death of Engineer-Lieutenant-Commander A. A. Hogg, whose body was found lying in a crumpled heap in his cabin on board the battleship Ramillies in Sheerness Harbour to-day.

This was indicated by a post-mortem completed late to-night by Dr. Madwar, of Sheerness.

Blood from throat wounds and splinters of glass on the floor were found by Commander Hogg's servant, who discovered the tragedy.

Tall, athletic and popular, Commander Hogg was to have married Miss Daphne Mulholland, daughter of the late Captain the Hon. A. E. S. Mulholland and the Countess of Cavan, this spring.

At the London home of the Earl and Countess of Cavan it was stated to-night that Miss Daphne Mulholland was staying with them at a friend's house in the country, and that news of Commander Hogg's death had been broken to her.

Later, with the dead officer's parents, Miss Mulholland and her mother arrived to stay the night as guests of the dockyard superintendent.

### Throat Injuries

Immediately the tragedy became known, Ramillies sent a signal to the police station ashore, and police officers, after removing the body to Sheerness mortuary, spent several hours examining the dead officer's cabin.

Commander Hogg's throat injuries were caused by the tumbler breaking as he fell after drinking from it.

Mr. E. C. Harris, coroner for East Kent, will hold an inquest, the time of which is not yet fixed.

Ramillies, 29,000 tons, belongs to the Home Fleet, but served with the Mediterranean Fleet last autumn, returning to Sheerness, her home base, on January 19.

## VICAR BANS FILM OF ROYAL FUNERAL

ABOUT 100 children who attend Tintwistle (Cheshire) Parish Church school were denied the opportunity of seeing a film of the funeral of King George yesterday because the vicar, the Rev. John Penrose, believes that "Christians should never go to the pictures."

The proprietor of the local cinema had invited all the schoolchildren in Tintwistle and Hadfield to attend, but owing to some misunderstanding the scholars of the Independent school there missed the performance, too.

Mr. Penrose last night strongly denied that he was unpatriotic.

"I am proud of my King and country," he said, "and am not slow to demonstrate this when it does not conflict with my religious convictions.

"I refused to allow the children to go because I am opposed to theatres and cinemas.

"In view of the fact that so many films are of a questionable character, I feel that the wisest and most Scriptural policy for a Christian to adopt is to keep away from the cinema.

"I listened to the broadcast of the funeral, but I refused to allow the children of my school to see the film because I believe it was in their own welfare that they should not see it."

## NIECE OF MILLIONAIRE MARRIES A COWBOY

Anne Gould

MISS Anne Gould, romantic grand-niece of the famous U.S. millionaire Frank Jay Gould, has been married again—to a cowboy who wore his cowboy clothes at their secret wedding.

He is Herman Asbury, and he lives at Cody, Wyoming.

The marriage, which was revealed yesterday, took place on Saturday, two days after Miss Gould's previous marriage had been dissolved, says Reuter.

The couple first met when Anne visited the Sunlight Ranch in 1933, says Mrs. Lillian Livingstone, Mr. Elsbury's sister, who added that the happy pair were going to New York.

In December, 1934, Miss Gould eloped with Mr. Frank Spencer Meador, a Texas actor. They separated after three months of a "love in a cottage" romance.

Miss Gould's great-uncle, Frank J. Gould, started as a farm boy and became one of the biggest financiers in America.

His millionaire son, Frank J. Gould, built the £1,000,000 casino at Nice, the Palais de la Mediterranée, which was later destroyed by fire.

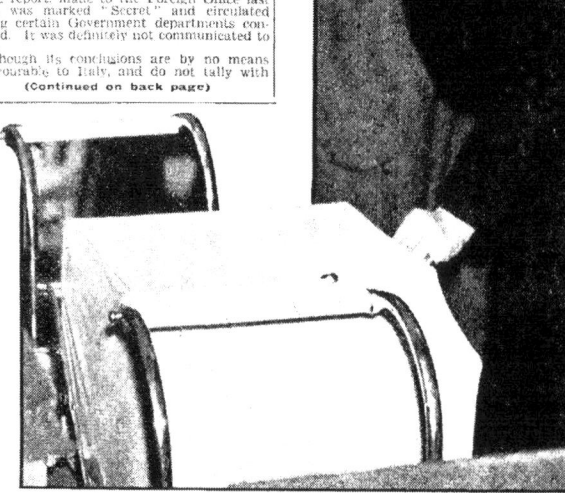

**A FATHER'S INTEREST**

The Duke of Kent during a visit yesterday to the Olympia section of the British Industries Fair taking a special interest, as the father of the baby Prince Edward, in the latest in perambulators. The visit lasted more than an hour.

THE DAILY MIRROR, Thursday, February 27, 1936.

Broadcasting - Page 20

# Daily Mirror

THE DAILY PICTURE NEWSPAPER WITH THE LARGEST NET SALE

EUSTACE .... Page 8
QUIET CORNER ... 15
DOCTOR'S DIARY .. 17
5-DAY SERIAL .... 19
BELINDA ....... 22
DOROTHY DIX .... 22

No. 10,060  Registered at the G.P.O as a Newspaper.  THURSDAY, FEBRUARY 27, 1936  One Penny

Amusements: Page 16

# REBELS HOLDING OUT AS JAPAN'S ARMY WAVERS

## Buildings Besieged This Morning

Admiral Saito.

General Watanabe.

Rebel troops who yesterday seized power in Tokio were this morning still in possession of many of the main Government buildings in the city, and little attempt had apparently been made to dislodge them.

MANY OF THE REBELS BELONG TO THE "WANT WAR" PARTY—MEN WHO ARE DETERMINED TO EXTEND, BY FORCE IF NECESSARY, THEIR POSSESSIONS ON THE MAINLAND. THEY ALSO DESIRE WAR WITH RUSSIA.

It is believed that actually there is much official sympathy for the rebels, and though martial law has been declared by Imperial edict, the "loyal" troops have been ordered to avoid a clash.

Fears were expressed in many of the world's capitals yesterday that a great military dictatorship was being established in the Far East, and as the news came in during the day and night this fear was strengthened by the apparent apathy of the Japanese Government.

Among the buildings still in the possession of the rebels are the police headquarters and Government offices.

This grave situation followed yesterday's early morning attempt of 3,000 Army mutineers, led by junior officers, to seize the reins of government in Tokio.

These men, belonging to the Third Regiment, were on their way to entrain for service in Manchukuo.

They seized a number of public buildings, while separate detachments rushed the residence of Admiral Okada, the Prime Minister, who was shot dead in his bed.

The same fate overtook Viscount Saito, his predecessor, and General Watanabe, Director-General of Military Training.

Murderous attacks were also made on the Minister of Finance, Mr. Takahashi, who, according to some reports was killed, but according to others, was only injured.

### Ammunition Issued

Units of the Imperial Guard and Marines who were stationed in the capital were called out to restore order.

Mr. Goto, the Home Minister, took over the Premiership temporarily, but last night resigned.

The rebels were led by a Captain Nonaka and their coup was facilitated by the fact that ball ammunition had been issued to them as they were under orders for Manchukuo.

The disturbances are attributed to the extreme militarists who are impatient of the Liberal policy of the Government.

For instance, Admiral Okada was believed to be opposed to the more violent exponents of Imperialism in China; Viscount Saito, veteran sailor and politician, favoured a moderate policy in foreign affairs, and Mr. Takahashi firmly opposed increased military

(Continued on back page)

## TEACH THEM FRENCH —AT AGE OF THREE!

A SUGGESTION that foreign languages might be taught in nursery schools to children between the ages of three and five was made to the L.C.C. Education Committee yesterday.

The Committee was discussing a proposal to make grants to teachers of foreign languages to enable them to go abroad to study the languages they teach.

Major Robert Spencer said that in the early stages of life the power of mimicry was more highly developed than in the later stages.

### The Sensitive Ear

"Under certain conditions," he went on, "children are more capable of taking in what they hear around them. The ear of the younger child is much more sensitive to sound, and when that sound later has to be repeated they can reproduce it more effectively than they would do had they not heard it before.

"Is it possible to contemplate, in the not too distant future, French or other foreign languages being taught in the nursery schools and classes?"

The Committee agreed to make grants of £20 or £25 to certain teachers to assist them to attend foreign holiday courses, the total annual sum being £1,100.

WEARING MOURNING for her grandfather. Princess Elizabeth, elder daughter of the Duke and Duchess of York, accompanied by a friend, exercising her dog in Hyde Park.

## Died with £4,000 Hidden in House

LAWYERS were yesterday searching for the heirs of a seventy-eight-year-old recluse who died at Brighton and left more than £4,000 in cash and securities in his desolate house.

He was Julian White, retired grocer. He was found dead in an old armchair at his home in Victoria-place on January 20.

He had been living alone since the death of his wife in November.

The discovery was made by a relative of the dead wife who went to visit the old man. The relative called in the police, and a post-mortem examination revealed that White died from natural causes.

A search of the house revealed that he had left a small fortune.

The securities included the title deeds of four houses and valuable share certificates. The searchers also found about £30 in cash hidden in a pile of coal and three sovereigns wrapped in paper.

Filling the rooms in confusion were antique furniture, pictures and articles of little or no value which the old man had apparently kept for sentimental reasons.

Since the death of his wife, with whom he had lived in the house for forty years, White had become solitary and was rarely seen by neighbours. It is believed that he had relatives in other parts of the country.

### MEMORIAL TO KING GEORGE

THE Duke of York attended a meeting with the Prime Minister and party leaders at the House of Commons yesterday to discuss the subject of a memorial to King George.

# Daily Mirror

**THE DAILY PICTURE NEWSPAPER WITH THE LARGEST NET SALE**

Broadcasting - Page 20

EUSTACE ..... Page 8
QUIET CORNER ... 16
DOCTOR'S DIARY .. 19
5-DAY SERIAL .... 21
DOROTHY DIX .... 26
BELINDA ....... 26

No. 10,062  Registered at the G.P.O. as a Newspaper.  SATURDAY, FEBRUARY 29, 1936  One Penny

Amusements: Page 22

# HITLER'S "LET'S BE FRIENDS" PLEA TO WORLD

## An Exclusive Interview with "Daily Mirror"

### "I APPEAL TO REASON"

Passionately...fervently...in the plain words of a Man of the People, Adolf Hitler, Leader and Master of Germany, in an exclusive interview with the "Daily Mirror" yesterday, pleaded with the world:—

#### "LET'S BE FRIENDS"

"I appeal to reason in international affairs," he said. "I want to show that the idea of eternal enmity is wrong. We are not hereditary enemies."

The "Daily Mirror" challenged his views with those in his book, "My Struggle." "My justification," said the Leader, "I shall write in the great book of history."

## Man of Destiny Speaks

*By BERTRAND DE JOUVENEL*

IN the room where the destiny of Germany is planned her Man of Destiny sat to receive me.

Simply dressed, sitting at his desk, he unburdened to me his heart ... his hopes ... his fears.

He eyed me keenly for a moment.

Then ... slowly, this man who sees into the mind said:

"Yes, I know what you are thinking. You say to yourself, 'Hitler makes precise declarations to us, but is it in good faith? Is he sincere?'

"Instead of giving yourselves up to psychological guesses, would you not do better to reason, to make use of logic?

"This logic, in which the French profess implicit belief—does it not lead you to think that it would be obviously to the advantage of France and Germany to maintain friendly relations?

"Would it not be ruinous for them to meet in conflict on new fields of battle?

"Is it not logical that I should wish for what is the most advantageous for my country?

"AND THE BEST THING FOR MY COUNTRY IS PEACE.

"People imagine me as someone quite different from what I am.

"They know quite well that I started at the bottom, and have become the master of Germany, which is rather an astonishing achievement, and there must be some extraordinary reason for it.

### "Mysticisms, Chance, or—?"

"Some say that it is due to violence that I have become chief of the German nation. As you know, there was only a handful of us to start with. We would have had our work cut out to capture by violence a nation of 65 million.

"Others say that my success is due to the mysticisms that I have created. Still others declare that it is due to chance.

"I must tell you what has brought me to where I am."

Hitler's face took on a change. His eyes took on their fighting light; his fists clenched.

"Political problems appeared complicated. The German people did not understand them.

"They preferred, in such conditions, to leave to professional politicians the task of freeing them from these complications.

"I simplified these problems. I reduced them to simple terms.

"The Germans understood—and they followed me.

"And so the class-war—that notorious war of the classes—was shown to be an absurdity.

"I demonstrated its absurdity and the people understood me!

"NOW I AM MAKING AN APPEAL TO REASON IN INTERNATIONAL AFFAIRS.

"I WANT TO SHOW MY PEOPLE THAT THE IDEA OF EVERLASTING ENMITY IS ABSURD; AND THAT WE ARE IN NO WAY HEREDITARY ENEMIES. THE GERMAN PEOPLE UNDERSTAND THAT, TOO.

"The German people have followed me in a reconciliation that has been infinitely more difficult—the reconciliation of Germany and Poland.

"By some the agreement between Germany

*(Continued on back page)*

## Rest of the News

Countess Haugwitz-Reventlow, formerly Miss Barbara Hutton, the Woolworth heiress, who gave birth to a son on Monday, was last night stated to be gravely ill after an operation. See back page.

Poor Family's Missing Home .... Page 2
Memorial to King George .......... " 2
Good News ........................ " 2
Children At Loose Herd ........... " 3
Football Clubs Deal of "Hush Hush" " 3
Things to Come ................... " 4
Painted King George Lying in State " 5
Postman Leaves £25,000 ........... " 5
Building New Press on a Moor ..... " 5
Life or Death in a "Twist" ....... " 6
Four Heroines of Commons ......... " 13
Sir Austen and Rearmament ........ " 24

THE DAILY MIRROR, Monday, March 2, 1936.

Broadcasting - Page 20

# Daily Mirror

THE DAILY PICTURE • NEWSPAPER WITH THE LARGEST NET SALE

EUSTACE . . . . . Page 8
QUIET CORNER . . . 16
DOCTOR'S DIARY . . 19
5-DAY SERIAL . . . . 21
DOROTHY DIX . . . . 26
BELINDA . . . . . . . 26

No. 10,063  Registered at the G.P.O as a Newspaper.   MONDAY, MARCH 2, 1936   One Penny

Amusements : Page 21

# 17 OFFICERS SHOT IN MASS SUICIDE

## Tokio Rebels Obey Last Order to 'Fire'

Titayna, the French journalist.

THE nineteen officers who led the Japanese regiment which last week assassinated three statesmen are dead. Tokio does not know; it believes them still to be confined in disgrace.

But the *Daily Mirror* is able to tell exclusively in Britain the tragic story of their end.

. . . of eighteen men who asked to be left alone in the room of the Premier . . . of their last obeisance to the spirits of their ancestors . . . of seventeen revolvers pointing to seventeen heads . . . the word "Fire" from the senior . . . and seventeen bodies that sank to the carpet together.

And, lastly, of two seniors of that proud caste, the Samurai, who committed hara-kiri—"honourable death" by the sword.

### TWO FAMOUS CORRESPONDENTS

The story is told in a telephoned message from Madame Titayna, the *Paris Soir* and *Daily Mirror* special correspondent in Tokio. It was Madame Titayna who secured for the *Daily Mirror* the exclusive interview with Venizelos during the Greek revolt.

Only on Saturday another *Daily Mirror* special correspondent, Bertrand de Jouvenel, obtained an exclusive interview with Herr Hitler, which during the week-end attracted world-wide attention.

## HIS LIFE FOR PREMIER

By MADAME TITAYNA, Special Correspondent of the "Paris Soir" and the "Daily Mirror"

IN the first telephone message to be allowed from Japan since the assassination orgy, I am able to give complete details of how Colonel Matsui gave his life for his brother-in-law, Admiral Okada, the Prime Minister.

I can tell, also, the moving and tragic story of how the officers who led the revolt committed suicide after they had communed with the spirits of their ancestors than which no more solemn or sacred ceremony exists in the land of the Mikado.

When the rebels, led by their officers, besieged Admiral Okada's house, the Prime Minister was working with Colonel Matsui, his secretary and counsellor.

Both men, who lived alone without servants since the death of Mme. Okada (Colonel Matsui's sister) were in their office.

### The Samurai Sacrifice

Colonel Matsui, remaining perfectly calm, told his brother-in-law to hide in a room in the cellar while he talked to the rebels.

As the rebels forced their way into the room with revolvers drawn, Colonel Matsui, taking advantage of his strong resemblance to his brother-in-law, said: "I am Admiral Okada. What do you want?"

There was a brief discussion. What was said will probably never be known. Feeling that no argument could convince the rebels,

(Continued on back page)

---

### POOLS? S-SH!

Mr. C. E. Sutcliffe, vice-chairman of the Football League, arriving in London for last night's meeting.

**HUSH-HUSH FOOTBALL**

## MORE SECRECY NEXT SATURDAY

Football fixtures for next Saturday will be "hush-hush." Clubs will not know their opponents until Friday.

THIS decision on the "secrecy" policy in the "pools" war was taken by the League Management Committee early to-day after a four-hour sitting in a London hotel.

Mr. Fred Howarth, secretary of the Committee, told the *Daily Mirror*: "We will meet the clubs in Manchester next Monday, when the whole situation will be discussed."

The "Daily Mirror" understands that radical changes in the policy of the Committee will be advocated at this meeting.

The "rebel" football clubs hold their meeting of protest against the secret fixtures scheme in Leeds to-day.

Thirty-one of the forty-four clubs of the First and Second Divisions will be represented at this meeting. Hull City, Grimsby Town, Portsmouth and Preston North End are the latest to accept invitations.

Only three clubs—Bury, Fulham and Nottingham Forest—have definitely refused to attend.

The meeting will be private, but an official statement will be issued afterwards.

---

## HEIRESS'S MOTHER ON DANGER LIST

JERSEY CITY, NEW JERSEY, Sunday.

MRS. Hewitt, the mother in the U.S. "heiress" claim, who was charged with attempted suicide on Friday following her admission to a hospital here suffering from an over-dose of narcotic, has been placed on the "danger list."

Her condition has suddenly worsened, and visitors are barred.

Mrs. Hewitt's daughter is bringing an action against her mother and two doctors alleging that an operation was performed on her to prevent her having any children.—Reuter.

### The King's Broadcast

The King's radio message . . . Page 3
Pictures . . . . . . . . . . Pages 14 and 15

---

## No Ups and Downs Here To-day!

No lifts? Oo-er!

AMERICA has had its ups and downs. It looks as if, from to-day, New York for a time would have neither downs nor ups.

A strike which, it is claimed, will affect 100,000 liftmen, porters and other employees in the service of 8,000 office buildings, flats, shops and hotels has been called for to-day.

If that happens thousands of workers instead of being up and doing will be down and out. If they tried to climb to their offices they would get there just in time to climb down again and go home.

The highest building in New York, the Empire State building, has eighty-six stories, approximately 1,600 steps. The Monument in the City of London has just over 300.

As a forerunner of the general walk-out and walk-up a sectional strike began yesterday. Flats and hotels situated in the extensive residential West Side district were left unattended.

Top flat dwellers were faced with a climb of about 500 stairs if they wished to leave their homes. The union, which is demanding better working conditions, is backing the strike with a fund said to amount to nearly £100,000.

Arrangements have been made for emergency strike duty in many of the big shops and business buildings.—Reuter and Exchange.

# Daily Mirror

**THE DAILY PICTURE NEWSPAPER WITH THE LARGEST NET SALE**

Broadcasting - Pages 20 & 21

| | |
|---|---|
| EUSTACE | Page 8 |
| QUIET CORNER | 14 |
| DOCTOR'S DIARY | 17 |
| NEW SERIAL | 19 |
| BELINDA | 22 |
| DOROTHY DIX | 24 |

No. 10,064 Registered at the G.P.O. as a Newspaper. TUESDAY, MARCH 3, 1936 One Penny

Amusements: Page 20

## OIL EMBARGO—OR PEACE —WITHIN 48 HOURS

Mr. Eden, who outlined Britain's policy yesterday at Geneva.

### Britain Will Give Lead

Unless Italy and Abyssinia accept mediation by the League of Nations within the next forty-eight hours, Britain is expected to take the initiative in securing an oil embargo against Italy.

THAT IS THE SITUATION AS A RESULT OF THE SPEECH BY MR. ANTHONY EDEN, THE FOREIGN SECRETARY, BEFORE THE LEAGUE COMMITTEE OF EIGHTEEN AT GENEVA YESTERDAY.

It is well known that Mussolini's attitude is: "Oil sanctions mean war." Last night it was reported from Rome that Mussolini has recently told the French Ambassador, M. Chambrun, that any extension of sanctions would hasten a catastrophe in Europe at a moment when there was hope of ending the conflict.

On the basis of this information M. Chambrun is credited with having advised M. Flandin, the French Foreign Minister against pushing an oil embargo at Geneva for the time being.

This is supported by the news from Geneva yesterday that M. Flandin proposed that the Committee of Thirteen, which is the League Council without Italy, should be convoked at once to make fresh peace proposals.

Mr. Anthony Eden supported M. Flandin. He also said (according to the B.U.P.):—

"His Majesty's Government favour the imposition of an oil embargo by members of the League, and are prepared to join in any application of such sanction if the other principal supplying and transporting States, who are members of the League of Nations, are prepared to do likewise."

This is taken to imply that the British Government is prepared to take action independently of the United States.

To-day the Sanctions Committee of Eighteen will meet and will probably send telegrams to Italy and Abyssinia urging them to accept mediation by the League of Nations.

League delegates expect the peace overtures to fail, and they believe that the oil embargo will be voted before the end of the week.

Italy, meanwhile, is growing more confident of a quick victory. The Government expects the Emperor of Abyssinia to abdicate within a fortnight in favour of his son, who would sue for peace.

Sir Roger Keyes's Malta revelations—Back Page.

### Our Arms Plan

LATE last night the Cabinet finally approved of the White Paper on National Defence.

The document of 7,000 words was taken to the Stationery Office for immediate printing.

It will be available at the House of Commons this morning, when M.P.s will know the outline of the Government's rearmament scheme.

### WOMEN'S QUEUE PICNIC BEFORE MURDER TRIAL

Picnic breakfast by women waiting for the Assize Court to open at Manchester yesterday for the first day of Dr. Ruxton's trial. One woman took up her position at 10.30 on Sunday night. The police put women in one queue, men in another. Report on page 4.

### HE WAS A BARONET FOR ONLY EIGHT DAYS

#### 3 People Hold Title in 9 Months

BY A SPECIAL CORRESPONDENT

AFTER only eight days the 300-year-old baronetcy of Vincent has changed holders again. The previous baronet held the title for eight months.

Sir Frederick Vincent died in London last night, aged eighty-four. He succeeded his great-nephew, Sir Anthony Francis Vincent, who had no male heir, eight days before.

Sir Anthony's father, Sir Francis Vincent, of Ormesby, Yorks, died last August in Brussels. The title now goes to seventy-nine-year-old Viscount D'Abernon, Sir Frederick's younger brother, who becomes the sixteenth baronet.

The first baronet was M.P. for Surrey in the reign of Charles I, and his father was knighted by Queen Elizabeth, having received the Queen at his mansion.

### LIFT STRIKER CRIES "USE A PARACHUTE"

Marooned on the twenty-sixth floor of an apartment house, a frantic woman shouted, "How can I get down?"

From a strike picket flashed the answer: "Use a parachute, lady!"

THIS was one incident of the great liftmen's strike which threatens to bring New York business to a standstill.

With thousands marooned on top floors of skyscrapers, and 19,000 police standing by to check brawls, Mayor Laguardia, of New York, yesterday declared a "state of emergency."

In his proclamation, states Reuter, the Mayor ordered all city departments to maintain health and safety.

### English Girl of 15 to Broadcast in Moscow

FIFTEEN-YEAR-OLD Audrey Mosson, Railway Queen of Great Britain, leaves London to-day to address the International Women's Conference in Moscow on March 8 and to broadcast from the Moscow Station.

She will be the first British Industry "Queen" to visit Russia since the revolution.

Miss Mosson, who is the daughter of a Blackpool railway guard, will be accompanied by her mother. She will be accorded an official welcome at the Russian frontier.

Miss Mosson, Britain's Railway Queen.

### SECRET NEW ARMS FACTORY DECISION

A SECRET new arms factory is to be established in South Wales.

Disclosing the decision in the House of Commons yesterday, Mr. Ramsay MacDonald said the Government had been pressing employers to found industries in the special areas.

"Now the Government itself proposes to adopt the recommendation which it is pressing upon private employers and to place important orders and plant new industries within those areas in the course of the development and execution of its rearmament schemes," he declared.

Official announcement of the exact location of the new factory is eagerly awaited.

M.P.s jeer Mr. R. MacDonald—Page 3.

THE DAILY MIRROR, Wednesday, March 4, 1936

Broadcasting - Page 22

# Daily Mirror

THE DAILY PICTURE NEWSPAPER WITH THE LARGEST NET SALE

EUSTACE .... Page 10
QUIET CORNER .... 16
DOCTOR'S DIARY .. 19
NEW SERIAL ..... 21
DOROTHY DIX .... 25
BELINDA ....... 26

No. 10,065  Registered at the G.P.O as a Newspaper.  WEDNESDAY, MARCH 4, 1936  One Penny

Amusements: Page 22

# BRITAIN AWAKES!

MILLIONS FOR DEFENCE

## More Men, Warships, Guns and 'Planes—Secret Alliance Fear

By OUR DIPLOMATIC CORRESPONDENT

BRITAIN'S re-armament scheme, announced yesterday, while the greatest which this country has put into being in peace time, will not be judged as excessive in view of the menacing international situation.

Gravest among the portents of coming trouble is the belief that Germany and Japan may have concluded a secret alliance. Both of these great powers are outside the League of Nations; both are seeking expansion.

It is significant that, in the British plan, most of the new arms factories will be on the west coast, as far away from the Continent as possible.

Germany is rearming, particularly in the air, at a prodigious rate, and it is generally regarded as probable that she will seize on the mutual assistance pact between France and Soviet Russia to free herself from her obligations under the Locarno Pact which guarantees the eastern frontiers of France.

In the White Paper giving the Government proposals (the text of which begins on page 5), the word "deterrent" appears many times.

That word emphasises the fact that our re-armament programme is not directed against any particular Power. It is a reminder to other nations to keep their hands off Britain.

A tremendous Air Force—larger than that provided for in the re-armament plans put forward yesterday by the British Government—a much stronger Navy and a highly mechanised Army are regarded as essential to the security of this country and of the Empire, and to enable Britain to fulfil her mission as a powerful factor in maintaining the peace of the world.

### Socialists Hostile

I learn that the Socialist Party dislike the proposals issued yesterday, and that they are determined to oppose the scheme unless the Government can convince them that re-armament is an essential part of the League's policy of collective security.

The scheme may, perhaps, be regarded as a definite hint to all members of the League of Nations to make a substantial contribution of their own.

The cost of our contribution will be staggering.

The main estimates of the three fighting services for the new financial year 1936-37 will be

Continued on back page

### How They Will Grow

THE NAVY:

TWO NEW BATTLESHIPS TO BE LAID DOWN. TWENTY NEW CRUISERS TO BE ADDED TO THE PRESENT FIFTY.

Steady replacement programme for destroyers and submarines. Modernisation of existing battleships.

NAVY PERSONNEL TO BE GRADUALLY INCREASED BY 6,000 MEN IN A YEAR'S TIME.

New aircraft-carrier and expansion of air arm.

ARMY:

Four new battalions of infantry. Army formations to be reorganised and to be EQUIPPED WITH THE MOST MODERN ARMAMENT AND MATERIAL, WITH ADEQUATE RESERVES OF AMMUNITION AND STORES.

Field artillery to be thoroughly modernised Territorial Army to support Regular Army abroad if required. Efficiency of the force to be increased.

THE AIR FORCE:

FIRST LINE MACHINES TO BE INCREASED TO 1,750, EXCLUSIVE OF THE FLEET AIR ARM.

Four new auxiliary squadrons to be formed for co-operation with the Territorial Army.

**£1,000-A-YEAR CLAIM**
Mrs. Margaret Irwin, of Holmbury St. Mary, Surrey, who, at Surrey Assizes yesterday, sued Mr. William Herbert Dunnett, of Leatherhead, alleging that he had made an agreement to pay her £1,000 a year free of tax. See story on page 4.

### Number Thirteen Won £350

THE result of the architectural competition for Harrow's new £85,000 civic centre at Knayston Court was made known last night when 131 designs were submitted. The winning design was No. 13, and was that of Mr. Verner O. Rees, of Bedford-place, London, W.C., who received the award of £350 offered by the Council.

## FOOD STRIKE BY OXFORD STUDENTS

OXFORD University started a new fashion in strikes last night. About 150 undergraduates of Pembroke refused to enter the hall for dinner, as a protest at what they alleged were "un-appetising meals" served.

The strike was complete. Not a single man dined. The men's move surprised the Dons of the college when they went to the head table.

An undergraduate stated that the extraordinary thing was that while they had been complaining "from time immemorial" at the poor quality of the food, the high table at Pembroke was looked upon as one of the best in the University.

A three years man said:
"Our strike is not only against the poor quality of the food, but against many of the rules obtaining in the college. At other colleges men can sign off hall as late as soon as 2 p.m., but at Pembroke we have to sign off by 10 a.m."

### The Cost

"We have asked that the meals shall be ready by ten, but have been told that is impossible. It has been a common thing for years for men to enter the dining hall and on seeing the menu at once leave and go into the city for dinner.

"It is not a question of the quantity of the food, but the quality. We pay 2s. for dinner plus one penny for a roll. We say we should get something more appetising than we have been getting for some time."

Another undergraduate told the Daily Mirror last night: "We shall go into Hall to-morrow as usual, but if the food is not improved we shall simply strike again and carry on until it is."

# Daily Mirror

**THE DAILY PICTURE NEWSPAPER WITH THE LARGEST NET SALE**

Broadcasting - Pages 22 & 23

EUSTACE .... Page 10
QUIET CORNER .... 16
DOCTOR'S DIARY .. 19
NEW SERIAL ..... 21
DOROTHY DIX .... 25
BELINDA ....... 26

No. 10,066 Registered at the GPO as a Newspaper

THURSDAY, MARCH 5, 1936

One Penny

Amusements: Page 18

### DID YOU HEAR HIM?

Patsy, a mongrel having a part in the play, "Storm in a Teacup," at the Haymarket Theatre, with Miss Ivy Des Voeux, another member of the cast. Last night an excerpt from the play was broadcast: Patsy attended at Broadcasting House, and was given a drink (of water) while waiting in a corridor for his cue. A gramophone record was ready in case he got stage fright, but as soon as the studio door opened and he saw Sara Allgood Patsy barked—his wireless debut was accomplished.

## THEY LEFT THEIR BABY ASLEEP ON THE CINEMA SEAT

A YOUNG married couple roused a Hampshire cinema manager from his bed in the middle of the night. They said they had left a very valuable article in his cinema.

Impressed by their anxiety, he let them in, and the couple began a frantic search of the empty building.

Eventually they found their "valuable article." It was their baby!

### Empty Cot Reminder

The child, who was fast asleep, had been left there by the couple when they hurried from the cinema. It was not until they reached home and saw the empty cot that they realised their loss.

This story was told by Lady Beedoe-Rees at a Romsey, Hampshire, N.S.P.C.C. meeting yesterday.

She said the couple had been warned about leaving their child alone at home at night and that was the result.

## Sabotage in Two More Warships

TWO more cases of sabotage, it was revealed in the Commons yesterday, are believed to have occurred in British warships.

Lord Stanley, Parliamentary Secretary to the Admiralty, stated that there had been damage or attempted damage in six ships undergoing refitting in royal dockyards.

In four cases, he said, sabotage was suspected. Official announcements concerning previous cases of sabotage had referred to four cases only.

In each instance it has been stated that the public interest would not be served by any further information.

Scotland Yard officers are understood to have been called in to investigate, but the utmost secrecy has been observed in connection with these proceedings.

# NEW YORK GENERAL STRIKE FEAR

## Armed Lawyer Leads "War" on Chaos

Compelled to climb thousands of steps to work and deprived of services in their homes, shivering New Yorkers were last night fighting back against the liftmen strikers who threaten to paralyse the city by calling a general strike.

FOLLOWING a night of terrorism in which 5,000 liftmen paraded Park-avenue—home of New York's elite—smashing windows and attacking strikebreakers, a "Tenants' Defence League" is being organised.

Lawyer Frederick C. Bellinger, decorated for bravery in the Battle of the Marne, is heading this movement.

Armed with a shotgun, he is running the lift of his apartment house. His league aims at protecting employees still at work and at improving existing conditions in buildings.

So bad are these conditions that one woman living in Park-avenue, determined to warm her apartment, and unable to obtain any fuel at the top of the building, used household furniture for fuel.

### Women Collapse

Nine women employees of a firm in the centre of the city collapsed after climbing twenty stories.

Soon afterwards an enterprising pedlar appeared with a placard reading: "Buy your corn plasters and foot powders here."

The liftmen's strike took a more serious turn last night, when the possibility of a general strike developed.

The stoppage is also threatening to spread to other towns. "Ready to pull out every building service employee in the U.S.," wired Chicago Building Service Employees' Union to New York colleagues last night.

### Fiery Leader

But it is the paralysis of all New York's services that is most feared.

James J. Bambrick, fiery leader of the Service Workers' Union, met other union leaders last night. Bambrick was ready to discuss a general strike.

He had shown his determination in a speech to his followers:—

"We are ready," he said, "to tear down the entire town and fight it out on the streets. If necessary, we can count on the support of the 950,000 members of trades unions in New York, who, with their families, total 3,500,000."

*Messages from B.U.P. and Reuter*

## BIGGEST 'ZEPP' TAKES THE AIR

### "PERFECT"

The world's largest airship, the Hindenburg, in flight at Friedrichshafen during her first trial yesterday afternoon. So successful was the flight that no further test will be made before demonstration to Germany's Air Ministry.

## Secret Defence Plan to Make the Free State England's Friend

**BY OUR DIPLOMATIC CORRESPONDENT**

SECRET negotiations are, I am told, now in progress between Great Britain and the Irish Free State. When a settlement is reached, Ireland will be Britain's western bulwark against aggression.

Peace seems very near for two reasons:

First, I am informed, a British munition factory drawing its power from the Shannon will shortly be erected on the west coast of Ireland;

Secondly, a great transatlantic seaplane base operated by the Imperial Airways and the Pan-American Corporation will soon be installed near Limerick.

When Ireland and Great Britain have "buried the hatchet," other seaplane bases and munition works will spring up.

I understand that Mr. Malcolm MacDonald, the Dominions Secretary, has one task to perform—the settlement of the Irish dispute.

The only obstacle to the settlement is Mr. de Valera, but even he may make terms if these will benefit his dwindling trade.

It is suggested that Southern Ireland may be retained in the Empire and receive the same status as that of the Union of South Africa.

Ulster, however, may rest assured that she will take a prominent place in the defence scheme.

## Petersen to Fight McAvoy in London

JACK Petersen is to defend his British and Empire heavy-weight titles against Jock McAvoy, British middle-weight champion, at the Empress Stadium, Earl's Court, London, at the end of next month.

Mr. Stanley Lonsstaff, match-maker at Earl's Court, told the "Daily Mirror" that the purse would be about £9,000—a record for an indoor fight in this country.

Petersen, as champion, will receive slightly the larger share.

McAvoy fights in America to-morrow week and leaves immediately afterwards for England.

*P. J. B. Wilson on the Big Fight—page 30.*

# Daily Mirror

**THE DAILY PICTURE NEWSPAPER WITH THE LARGEST NET SALE**

Broadcasting · Pages 22 & 23

EUSTACE .... Page 10
QUIET CORNER ... 16
DOCTOR'S DIARY ... 19
NEW SERIAL ... 21
DOROTHY DIX ... 25
BELINDA ... 26

No. 10,067   Registered at the G.P.O. as a Newspaper.   FRIDAY, MARCH 6, 1936   One Penny

Amusements: Pages 26 and 27

## THEY WELCOMED THE KING WITH— "GOOD OLD TEDDY"

Workmen surging round the King as he made his way to his car after tour of the Queen Mary. More pictures on page 17.

## Vatican Urges Peace, Warns World of Peril

A DRAMATIC appeal for "immediate peace" between Italy and Abyssinia was made yesterday in the Vatican official newspaper, the "Osservatore Romano." Growing fears of the spread of the conflict and for the peace of the whole world found expression in this paragraph:—

"The necessity for peace is urgent, not only for those who are fighting, but also for those who die and FOR THE ENTIRE WORLD."

In its reference to the Italo-Abyssinian war the paper urges European statesmen to obtain a "fair and lasting solution because the announced losses in human life in the recent battles in East Africa are terrifying," says B.U.P.

It observes that the best kind of peace is not that which is obtained on the battlefields, as was shown in the World War.

Political circles in Rome attach great significance to this plea.

Meanwhile an official spokesman of the Italian Foreign Office stated that Signor Mussolini has made no decision on the League's recent appeal for peace. He will wait until the Cabinet meeting on Saturday.

### Abyssinia Accepts

But Abyssinia has accepted the League suggestion.

The Emperor's answer is reported to stipulate that the negotiations must be in the spirit and the framework of the League. This is regarded in Geneva as a reiteration of the Emperor's previous view that Abyssinia will not accept a peace that involves the gift of territory to Italy without compensation.

League hopes that the Peace Plea might prove successful increased last night with the news of the Emperor's decision, which reached the Abyssinian Legation in Paris.

### 102 AND TOO ILL TO KNOW

MISS E. M. Crawford, of Queen Alexandra's-court, Wimbledon, was 102 yesterday.

But she was too ill to know it was her birthday.

She has only just taken to her bed, and until Christmas attended to all her normal duties and correspondence herself.

It is expected that she will be sufficiently recovered to celebrate her birthday to-day.

### TOMMY ROSE FLIES ON

Flight-Lieutenant Tommy Rose left Kisumu (Kenya) yesterday for the Sudan on his Cape-England record flight attempt, states Reuter.

He has now covered 3,354 of the 7,863 miles to London in less than two and a half days.

---

### THREE MOTHERS

THE FIRST MOTHER "just did what she could" to aid a helpless man of eighty—but a coroner yesterday said that her action exemplified "the extraordinary kindness poor people have for the poor." (Story on the back page.)

THE SECOND MOTHER read yesterday of the death of a daughter separated from her for fifteen years. But those years did not lessen her sorrow. (Page four.)

THE THIRD MOTHER is missing. Her return can save the life of her brokenhearted, thirteen-year-old daughter. (Page five.)

---

**THE KING SPOKE TO HIM**

Charlie Storrie, aged five and a half, who, when the King visited his aunt's house in Glasgow yesterday, asked, "Is that the new King, Auntie?" Patting his head, the King replied, "I am the new King, sonny."

## Royal Voyage on Giant Liner at Trials

### SEVEN-MILE TOUR OF THE QUEEN MARY

Before Britain's giant liner, the Queen Mary, goes into active service, the King may make a short cruise in her, probably during a trial trip.

THIS statement was made after the King had toured the liner in the Clyde yesterday. The King expressed his intention of visiting the ship again before she goes into commission.

Shouts of "Good Old Teddy"—a welcome that so often rang in the ears of his grandfather—greeted the King at the close of his tour of the liner.

As he came ashore hundreds of workmen surged round him, cheering wildly and demanding, "Speech, speech." One of them rushed forward and opened the door of his car.

His visit to Britain's new wonder ship was marked by an absolute absence of formality and ceremonial. Lines of cheering men, women and children were massed ten and twelve deep outside John Brown's shipyard to welcome him.

He used the workmen's gangway to board the ship and immediately set out on his seven-mile tour. At the end a number of workmen were presented to him.

After leaving Clydebank the King's first call in Glasgow was at Knightswood, a large housing area, where he visited two houses, those of

(Continued on back page)

THE DAILY MIRROR, Monday, March 9, 1936.

# Daily Mirror

THE DAILY PICTURE • NEWSPAPER WITH THE LARGEST NET SALE

Broadcasting—Page 22

EUSTACE . . . . Page 10
QUIET CORNER . . . . 16
DOCTOR'S DIARY . . 19
NEW SERIAL . . . . . 21
DOROTHY DIX . . . . 25
BELINDA . . . . . . . . 26

No. 10,069   Registered at the G.P.O. as a Newspaper.   MONDAY, MARCH 9, 1936   One Penny

Amusements: Page 23

# IT MUST NOT BE WAR
## Hitler's Peace Plan Should Succeed

## BUT FRENCH PREMIER HAS REFUSED TO NEGOTIATE

### Germany Called to League Council

*BY OUR DIPLOMATIC CORRESPONDENT*

Germany has flung a challenge to Europe that can lead to another great war—or a strong and lasting peace.
**IT MUST NOT LEAD TO WAR.**

THE FRENCH STATESMEN ARE, NOT UNNATURALLY, ALARMED AND ANGRY AT HITLER'S MARCH INTO THE DEMILITARISED AREAS OF THE RHINE—AN ACTION WHICH FLOUTS THE VERSAILLES PEACE TREATY AND TEARS UP THE LOCARNO PACT.

Last night the French Premier, M. Sarraut, refused even to examine Hitler's eight-point plan for peace, which the German Dictator put forward even as his troops marched.

I am told that Mr. Eden will strongly support France's contention on legal terms that the Treaties have been grossly violated by Germany.

But M. Sarraut is dependent on parties who hate war and favour negotiations with Berlin.

World attention will be centred on the British House of Commons this afternoon, when Mr. Eden makes his statement on the new situation which has so dramatically arisen.

It is anticipated, however, that when the French Government have reviewed Germany's proposals they will be prepared to give them careful consideration, and any dire results from the very delicate situation which exists will be avoided.

**HITLER'S ACT NO THREAT TO PEACE**

Although German bayonets are again within sight of her frontier fortresses, France is calm.

Another reassuring fact is that Germany has been invited to the meeting of the League Council next Friday, when her breach of the Locarno Pact and the Versailles Treaty in occupying the Rhineland with troops will be considered.

Serious as is this violation of the Locarno Pact (which Germany signed voluntarily) and the Peace Treaty, it is in itself no threat to the peace of Europe. The offer Hitler made of twenty-five-year peace pacts with his neighbours is one that should receive very thorough examination.

The "Let's Be Friends" appeal to France which Hitler made in the
*(Continued on back page)*

GERMAN MACHINE-GUNNERS establishing positions yesterday at a Mainz bridge, on the Rhine, after they had entered the demilitarised zone.

### What Hitler Demands

A dispatch from John Haydon, our special correspondent in Berlin, appears on page 12.

A little German girl waiting with a bouquet to present to the troops when they arrived in Cologne.

## ITALY HOLDS UP THE WAR

ACCORDING to reports from Asmara received early to-day, the Italian High Command has ordered suspension of all offensives against Abyssinia, including bombing raids (says Reuter).

The order, it is expected, will remain in force until the outcome of the Geneva negotiations is known.

It is significant that Marshal Badoglio, the Italian Commander-in-Chief, has returned to Asmara.

This dramatic move follows Italy's acceptance, without preliminary conditions, this week-end of a further effort by the League to make peace.

Mussolini recognises that Germany's action has put the Abyssinian war "in the background."

### STEAMER SUNK

THE Barrow steamer Sea Fisher (552 tons) is reported to have sunk in the North Sea last night, two and a half miles south-east of the Shipwash light vessel and sixteen miles off Harwich, following a collision with the Newcastle steamer Sutherland.

All the Sea Fisher's crew were saved and are believed to have been taken on board the Sutherland.

The collision occurred in a dense fog

# Daily Mirror

**THE DAILY PICTURE NEWSPAPER WITH THE LARGEST NET SALE**

Broadcasting - Pages 20 and 21

EUSTACE .... Page 13
QUIET CORNER ... 17
SHORT STORY ... 19
DOROTHY DIX .... 22
BELINDA ....... 22
DOCTOR'S DIARY .. 24

No. 10,080  Registered at the G.P.O. as a Newspaper.  SATURDAY, MARCH 21, 1936  One Penny

Amusements: Page 20

# HITLER WARNS POWERS AGAIN
# "OUR DEMANDS STAND"

### WRECKED BY THE FLOODS

## Only Rhine Token Force from Britain

By OUR DIPLOMATIC CORRESPONDENT

HITLER: We will not withdraw an inch from our equality demand. ... If the statesmen could only see beyond a few weeks or months, they would be afraid of the consequences of their action.

MR. EDEN: It is, unfortunately, necessary, however reluctant we may be to do so, to envisage the failure of the proposed negotiations.

M. FLANDIN: If Germany refuses the proposals, our Governments have already resolved to draft and apply in common the measures recognised to be necessary.

THESE declarations followed the announcement yesterday of the terms of the Locarno Powers (Britain, France, Italy and Belgium) to Hitler on his treaty-breaking march of troops into the Rhineland.

I am told that in the event of Germany rejecting the plan, Britain will send only a token force—probably one battalion—into the Rhineland.

Before then, long diplomatic discussions will have taken place and in League circles last night it was believed that some compromise would be effected before next

### POWERS' TERMS TO GERMANY

THE proposals of Britain, France, Italy and Belgium are:—
An international force, including British and Italian troops, in a neutral zone twelve miles deep from the frontier in the Rhineland during negotiations.
Dispute over Franco-Soviet Pact to be submitted to The Hague International Court.
A world conference on disarmament and economic relations, if Germany accepts the terms.
Immediate assistance to Belgium or France in respect of any measures jointly decided on.

May when the World Economic Conference (which is part of the Locarno Powers' plan) is provisionally fixed.

Hitler made his declaration last night amid roars of applause at Hamburg.

"The whole German nation stands behind me," he is quoted by the Exchange to have said.

"I pity the statesmen who think they can initiate a new order in Europe by a new defamation of Germany.

"It is a mistake to believe that Germany is under a dictatorship and that one can do with the German people as one will.

"Permanent order in Europe is only possible among nations of equal rights. Any other idea is crazy and foolish."

A high official at the German Foreign Office remarked last night that at first sight not one of the proposals was acceptable to Germany.

It is emphasised that Germany can never tolerate foreign forces, even if only described as police, in her territory.

Herr von Ribbentrop, Hitler's Ambassador-at-Large, has not yet made arrangements to leave London. He is in constant communication with Berlin.

He was received by the King yesterday, and was with his Majesty for about half an hour.

M. Flandin, the French Foreign Secretary, who was reported to have said in the French Chamber yesterday that he understood the Abyssinian war was to cease and sanctions be lifted, later denied the accuracy of the report.

It is expected that the Locarno Powers will meet in London again on Monday.

Mr. Eden's speech in Commons—page 4.

Peering into a partly-submerged coach on the Erie Railroad near Hamburg, New Jersey, to ascertain if anyone was inside. A picture that poignantly conveys the terrible conditions prevailing in the wide area swept by floods that have caused the deaths of 175 people in the eastern United States. Left: Alice Beady, wrapped in blankets and lying in a boat which rescued her at Singac, New Jersey, first from her house and then from flood waters into which she fell while being rowed to safety. Other pictures on page 15.

## Hauptmann Confesses: "I Met Jafsie Before Kidnapping"

FROM OUR OWN CORRESPONDENT

NEW YORK, Friday.

HAUPTMANN is talking at last. To-night he almost definitely saved himself from execution by confessing to his counsel that "he must have met Jafsie Condon" before and after the kidnapping of the Lindbergh baby.

News was rushed at once to Governor Hoffman, whose word can save Hauptmann.

Hauptmann while in Trenton Prison, New Jersey, has steadfastly refused to admit ever having seen Jafsie, the intermediary in the case. Now he tells how, before and after the baby's disappearance, he used to canoe from Dickson's boathouse near Condon's office.

"Perhaps I never spoke to Jafsie," said Hauptmann. "I may not even have known him by name, but I have seen him many times since March, 1932. I remember his face."

The contention is that Jafsie also knew Hauptmann by sight.

Governor Hoffman is expected to insist on Condon's talking.

### EXPRESS WEDDING

Jack Oakie, star of "Sailor Be Good" and "Sitting Pretty," announced yesterday that he intends to marry Miss Vanita Vardon, the dancer, in an express train in Yuma, Arizona, on their way to New York, says Reuter.

### CUNNINGHAME GRAHAM DEAD

ROUGH-RIDER, author, traveller and Scottish-national, Robert Bontine Cunninghame Graham died in Buenos Aires last night (reports Reuter).

He was aged eighty-four.

His career was glamorous, and with his romantic features, flowing mane of white hair and pointed beard, he was built for the part.

He showed superb horsemanship even during his later years, and he looked every inch a cavalier whenever he was seen riding in Rotten Row.

He had gone to Argentina for the naming of a town—Don Roberto—in his honour.

THE DAILY MIRROR, Monday, March 23, 1936.

Broadcasting - Pages 26 & 27

# Daily Mirror

**THE DAILY PICTURE NEWSPAPER WITH THE LARGEST NET SALE**

No. 10,081 Registered at the G.P.O as a Newspaper. MONDAY, MARCH 23, 1936 One Penny

**FASHION WEEK!**
FILM STAR FROCK P. 30
FASHION TEST ---- 19
FREE PATTERN --- 31
NEW SERIAL --- 22

Amusements: Pages 20 and 28

## 100 MEASLES CASES A DAY IN LONDON

### Radio for Nurses

WITH its hospitals now admitting 100 measles victims daily, London County Council has had to throw open two hospitals held in reserve for serious epidemics.

This week-end an appeal for voluntary nurses to cope with the 1,500 victims already in hospital was broadcast.

In addition, between 7,000 and 8,000 people are being treated in their homes. In the past three months 132 deaths from measles have been reported in London.

The "emergency" hospitals which have been opened are the Joyce Green and Orchard Hospitals, Dartford, Kent.

An official of the L.C.C. told me yesterday that though there had been a good response to the appeal for nurses, still more helpers were needed, particularly domestic servants such as cooks and ward maids.

**Serum Appeal**

Other parts of the country are suffering from the epidemic.

Because one in every six boys at Sedburgh School, Yorkshire, is a victim, the school has broken up for the Easter holidays two weeks earlier than usual.

Many undergraduates at Cambridge and Eton schoolboys are victims.

Nottingham and Leicester report slight outbreaks.

In the Irish Free State Dr. Dwyer, resident medical superintendent of Dublin, appealed in a broadcast message for serum to fight a serious outbreak of the disease.

"Unless we have serum to combat the serious outbreak of measles, we cannot save the lives of the children," said Dr. Dwyer.

**TOUCH OF DEATH**

AFTER touching his dead mother's forehead a sixty-two-year-old man collapsed and died as her funeral cortege left the house. He was Isaiah Bourne, of Filbert-street, Leicester.

Mourners attending the mother's funeral, including Bourne's two sons and one daughter, were unaware of his death until later.

**OFF FOR A SPRING DIP**

Two fair bathers, lured to the sea by the glorious spring weather yesterday, stroll along the front at Eastbourne in swimming costumes on their way to the water. Other week-end holiday pictures are on page 18.

## Detectives at Altar Watch Banned Vicar "Invade" Church

DETECTIVES standing beside the altar looked on while the banned Leicester vicar, Dr. Samuel Shannon, entered St. Luke's Church last night and began a service. The service already in progress was interrupted in the middle of the sermon preached by the Rev. H. J. Drummond, and abandoned after a remarkable scene.

Dr. Shannon, who was recently released from gaol after serving nearly nine months for contempt of Court in connection with bankruptcy proceedings, defied the Bishop of Leicester's ban by taking three services yesterday.

Mr. Drummond has been appointed to the temporary charge of the parish.

Dense crowds lined the approaches to St. Luke's when Dr. Shannon arrived to take his service at 6.30. Mr. Drummond was already officiating inside.

Dr. Shannon donned surplice and hood and exhorted the crowd to follow him in singing the hymn "Fight the Good Fight." Then the doors were flung open and Dr. Shannon, followed by 300 people, marched into the church.

Mr. Drummond, who was delivering his sermon, paused as the procession slowly went up the centre aisle.

Two detectives went to the side of the altar near the pulpit, where Mr. Drummond stood motionless.

His eyes filled with tears as he looked appealingly at Dr. Shannon.

After five minutes' suspense Mr. Drummond signalled to the choir boys, who entered the vestry. They marched out by the back door while Dr. Shannon proceeded with the service, Mr. Drummond having left the pulpit.

### Spring Brings Out Beach Girls

YESTERDAY was No-Overcoat Sunday. The first spring days drew thousands out of the towns to enjoy sun and fresh air in the country and seaside.

And, so the prophets say, there is more mild weather to come during the next day or two.

No part of Britain was left out when spring bestowed its first favours of the year. As far north as the Moray Firth coast there was a freak "heat wave."

There the thermometer registered 65 degrees in the shade—the highest March figure on record in the district.

Once again the main outlets from London were crowded with traffic.

Summer frocks were plentiful, and there was not an overcoat on the seven-mile stretch of sands at Southend.

A woman who ventured into the sea at Margate was cheered by the crowd of fishers and small boys on the pier. At Bournemouth, where many bathers went into the sea, girls outnumbered men by five to one.

### TWO PLANES...
## MEN CRASH 800 FEET—LIVE

### Girl Falls Few Feet and Is Killed

An aeroplane fell a few feet yesterday and a girl passenger was killed. Another aeroplane fell 800ft., both occupants escaping with slight injuries.

THE dead girl was Miss Mary Clark, aged about twenty-two, of Cardigan-road, Leeds.

She went up with a friend, Mr. Reginald Ernest Morris, of Yeadon, a member of the Yorkshire Aero Club, from the Leeds-Bradford Municipal Aerodrome at Yeadon.

Mr. Morris was about to land when the machine struck some telegraph wires on the boundary of the aerodrome and crashed in the car park in full view of a large crowd. The pilot escaped with slight injuries.

The two men who fell 800ft. and escaped were Mr. F. B. Alexander, of Chester-road, Stretford, Manchester, the pilot, and Mr. J. Cunningham, of Eccles New-road, Salford.

**Went Into a Spin**

They were flying on the outskirts of Lichfield, Staffs, when the machine went into a spin and fell into a field.

Rescuers, when they reached the wrecked 'plane, were surprised to find the men not only alive, but conscious, although the pilot collapsed soon afterwards.

Mr. Alexander was taken to Lichfield Hospital suffering from concussion; Mr. Cunningham had a slight cut over the left eye.

### FOUND DYING IN POLICE CELL

FOUND with throat wounds in a cell at Caledonian-road Police Station on Saturday, Albert Ward, forty, of Freegrove-road, Islington, N., died yesterday in the Royal Free Hospital.

Ward was detained in connection with alleged cheque offences. His wife, who was arrested with him, will appear at the North London Police Court to-day, charged with being concerned in the alleged offences.

### MORE OF THESE ALLIANCES?

Assembled in Rome for the three-Power conference on Danubian problems. A to B: General Goemboes (Hungarian Premier), M. de Kanya (Hungary), Baron Waldenegg (Austria), Signor Mussolini (Italy) and Chancellor Schuschnigg (Austria).

# Daily Mirror

**THE DAILY PICTURE NEWSPAPER WITH THE LARGEST NET SALE**

Broadcasting - Pages 22 & 23

**FASHION WEEK!**
FILM STAR FROCK P. 25
FASHION TEST . . . . 19
FREE PATTERN . . . 27
NEW SERIAL . . . 21

No. 10,082 Registered at the G.P.O as a Newspaper. TUESDAY, MARCH 24, 1936 One Penny

Amusements: Page 22

# 2,000,000 CHEER THE OCEAN QUEEN TO-DAY

## France Starts Liner Tonnage "Race"

Along the River Clyde, between fourteen miles of cheering throngs, the Queen Mary goes down to the sea to-day.

TWO million people will greet her as she passes.

Millions more in their homes will hear a B.B.C. broadcast, beginning at 10 a.m., and share in this proud day in British shipbuilding history.

For this is the liner that IS Britain's pride; the liner that WAS to have been the heaviest, the longest, the greatest liner in the world.

But France has stolen those titles (officially).

When her crack ship, the Normandie, was completed in 1934 her tonnage was given as 79,280.

The Queen Mary's tonnage was fixed yesterday at 80,773.

Last night it was announced that as a result of recent alterations the Normandie's tonnage is now 82,799.

A proud Clydeside was saying last night that it was a "stunt" tonnage.

### Vanguard Arrives

The vanguard of to-day's multitude arrived during the night.

Favourable weather is promised for the voyage. This morning's forecast is light to moderate south-easterly or southerly winds and visibility good to moderate.

The Queen Mary will leave the ship yard escorted by seven tugs.

On board will be two men who will have charge of the world's greatest feat of navigation. They are Captain Duncan Cameron, the Clyde's most experienced pilot, who holds a certificate for all the waters of the British Isles, and Captain J. L. Murchie, who will assist him.

The Queen Mary's special radio call sign was heard for the first time on the air yesterday. G.B.T.T. (dash, dash, dot; dash, dot, dot, dot; dash) came through to Post Office engineers in Carter-lane, London.

Shortly before - p.m. the voice of a radio engineer on the Queen Mary came through.

"Queen Mary calling. Hullo, London. Can you hear me now?"

The Triumph of Davie Kirkwood.—Back page

### TO-DAY'S TIME-TABLE

HERE is the time-table of the Queen Mary's fourteen-mile journey down the Clyde:—
10.0.—Broadcast begins
10.30.—All clear signal.
11.0.—The Queen Mary will be slowly manœuvred into mid-stream by the seven tugs.
11.45-12.9.—Beardmore Bend. The first difficult bend will be negotiated.
12.30.—The liner passes Erskine Ferry.
1.15.—At Bowling Bend, the worst bend on the river. Speeds will be "dead slow" and all the seven tugs will be hard at work slowly easing the liner round the bend.
2.0.—Port Glasgow. The worst is past.
2.30.—At Greenock. Where she anchors for the night.
Weather Forecast.—Light and moderate south winds; clear; water calm.

### BATH CHAIR FOR A DOG

Mrs. White, Margate resident, giving her fourteen-year-old dog Punch an outing in a specially constructed bathchair, the main element of which is a Sussex trug (or basket). Punch can no longer go for walks, but he needs fresh air.

### FLEETNESS OF FOOT SAVED HER LIFE

Princess Juliana of the Netherlands yesterday narrowly escaped being knocked down by a motor-lorry as she was returning to the palace from a cinema. She had stepped off the pavement when the lorry cut the corner. Princess Juliana jumped back to the pavement just in time.

## SISTERS DIVORCED —FATHER AND SON CO-RESPONDENTS

In successive divorce cases at Birmingham Assizes yesterday the respondents were two sisters, and the co-respondents were son and father respectively.

### Decree for Director

IN the first case, James Thornton Norman Wilson, a grain and flour importer's manager, of Allerton-road, Wallasey (Cheshire), was granted a decree nisi.

He accused his wife (née Edith Eleanor Rossell Smith) of misconduct with John Graham Bond, at Wannerton Park, Blakedown (Worcestershire).

In the next case, Mr. Harold Goodwin, a company director, who gave his address as the Impney Hotel, Droitwich, was granted a decree against his wife (formerly Frances Mary Rossell Smith).

She was accused of misconduct with Frank Nelson Bond, father of John Graham Bond, at the farm, Wannerton, and at a flat in Calthorpe-road, Birmingham.

## MARRIED? READ THIS!
# Ordered Coffin —Then Fell in Love at 70!

Alfred William Spry, blacksmith, was
**Melancholy,
Doleful,
Fed-up.**

BLACKSMITH Spry was meeting death half way—till love came along!

"He's ordered his coffin," said his cronies at Crownhill, Alfred's Devonshire home town. True—he had.

"He's prepared the grave. Yes—and that was not all.

On his sixty-ninth birthday he entertained six pretty girls to a party. They were "daintily attired" in—funeral garb, black and white silk. They were to be the bearers at his coming funeral. Mr. Spry made that clear in his will.

"I want to see how they will look," he told neighbours. "I believe in making proper preparations."

### Pretty Pall Bearers

The vault was ready too. The smith was a mighty doleful man; he spent his leisure in spreading yew trees.

At his seventieth birthday they were there again, the pretty pall-bearers. At his seventy-first, too.

But YESTERDAY— Alfred William Spry was seventy-two. Yes, I was there, writes a "Daily Mirror" reporter. But the cortege was missing.

"Funeral procession? Pall-bearers?" Mr. Spry was surprised.

"Oh—that! I've given up the idea now. You see, she wouldn't like it."

### Seaside Romance

SHE—
Kate Toll, spinster. He had met her at Exmouth last summer. They got on well, very well. Seventy-one fell in love with fifty—at first sight. And fifty wanted to live.

"Who wants to think of dying—now?" said Mr. Spry himself. "That was in the bad old days."

"Now I'm rejuvenated. I'm getting younger every morning. I was never fitter in my life. I'm just like a small boy again, since I married Kate.

"I want to live.

"AND I'M GOING TO LIVE!"

Kate Toll smiled.

## M.P.'s WIFE FLUNG OUT OF CAR

LADY Fildes, wife of Sir Henry Fildes, National Liberal M.P. for Dumfries, was gravely injured in a motoring accident near her home last night.

Soon after she left her home, Euton their Kerridge, near Macclesfield, her car went through a hedge on a steep hill and fell down an embankment.

The car overturned, a door was wrenched off, and Lady Fildes was flung out.

# Daily Mirror

**THE DAILY PICTURE NEWSPAPER WITH THE LARGEST NET SALE**

Broadcasting - Page 20

**FASHION WEEK!**
FILM STAR FROCK - 22
FREE PATTERN · · · 23
NEW SERIAL · · · 19

No. 10,086   Registered at the G.P.O. as a Newspaper.   SATURDAY, MARCH 28, 1936   One Penny

Amusements: Page 4

## HIGH OVER BECHER'S

What a jump it needs. Taking Becher's Brook, most famous obstacle on the Aintree course, in yesterday's Grand National, which was won by Reynoldstown. Golden Miller fell at the first fence. Stories on pages 2 and 25. Other pictures on pages 14, 17 and 28.

## SERUM SHORTAGE IS COSTING LIVES

### Treatment That Would Save Measles Victims

SHORTAGE OF A SERUM IS COSTING THE LIVES OF HUNDREDS OF CHILD VICTIMS OF MEASLES EPIDEMICS IN BRITAIN.

DOCTORS declare that this simple method of treatment would almost eliminate loss of life. But the serum is difficult to obtain.

Experts told the "Daily Mirror" last night that there was a definite shortage.

It is alleged that the failure of public health authorities to provide a sufficient supply of serum is hampering doctors in their fight against measles epidemics.

Attention has been drawn to this serious situation by recent outbreaks.

Two great cities—Bristol and Dublin—have in the last month had to send out S O S's for serum.

**Supplies for Hospitals**

A medical officer of health told the *Daily Mirror* last night: "There is a definite shortage of serum. Hospitals and institutions are taking nearly all available supplies.

"At the present time a private doctor can hardly obtain any. His only chance is to obtain a supply from the blood of a patient who has been previously affected with measles.

"The serum has been used for ten years. Generally, however, there has been a decided lack of push in seeing that there is always a sufficient supply to deal with epidemics.

"An abundant supply would certainly lower the death roll of an epidemic."

**3,000 Patients**

London, too, has had a grave epidemic. Three thousand patients are now in L.C.C. hospitals. But in London there is no shortage.

Dr. Somerville Hastings, chairman of the Hospitals and Medical Services Sub-Committee of the L.C.C., said: "It is true that there is a shortage. I think this shortage affects areas all over the country.

"So far as the L.C.C. is concerned our stock is sufficient.

"Some time ago we offered healthy people money for samples of blood to be made into serum."

A physician at the London Hospital explained that a child who receives an injection of the serum feels ill for at most forty-eight hours, but he is entirely protected from any complications of the disease.

## FEVER CASE IN THE QUEEN MARY

FROM OUR SPECIAL CORRESPONDENT
SOUTHAMPTON, Friday.

A RADIO operator was taken off the Queen Mary to-night suffering from scarlet fever.

His name is George Withy.

Shortly after the ship had docked here a doctor was summoned.

At half-past six this evening an ambulance drove to the King George V graving dock, and waited at the bottom of the gangway.

Withy was carried down in a stretcher and placed in the ambulance.

To-morrow, as a result of this outbreak, three rooms on the Queen Mary, including Withy's cabin, are to be fumigated.

The Southern Railway announces that restaurant-car excursions will be run to Southampton from London (Waterloo) on Sunday, Monday, Tuesday and Wednesday.

Members of the public who wish to view the giant liner will be admitted to the graving dock at a charge of one shilling.

Scenes at Southampton—Page 3.

## WANTED—A GINGER-HEADED SAILOR

IN her search for a husband, a woman has set the Mayor of Southampton, Alderman T. H. Sanders, a problem. She wrote to him:—

"Dear Sir,—Will you please help me? I have, since a small child, wanted to marry a ginger-haired sailor but so far have never met one.

"I am nearly thirty-six years of age. I am not good-looking and not ugly, neither slim nor stout; brown hair, blue-grey eyes, nice hands. I don't paint my nails or dance. I am very fond of good music.

"I should be very grateful if you could put me in touch with a cheery sailor."

### Mystery Baby

Police were trying last night to trace the parents of a sturdy, well-clothed eight-weeks-old baby girl found in an M.P.'s car in a garage at Hugh-mew' Hugh-street, Chelsea, on Thursday.

## For the Loss of Her Son—£15

How much is your son worth to you? A million pounds? A round thousand? Or—

Fifteen!

THAT, according to the law, is what Mrs. Sarah Foreman's son, lost in a pit accident at Garesfield Colliery, Co. Durham, was worth to her.

"You can keep it!" she shouted to Judge Thesiger yesterday. He had told her he could only make an order for the amount already paid into court by the company.

"You can keep it! How is it that miners are insured for several hundreds of pounds when they go into the mine, and I can only get £15 for my son?" asked Mrs. Foreman. She is a widow.

Her son, when he died, was fifteen years old.

She got £15 for him. One pound a year...

"I am sorry," said the Judge "exceedingly sorry. It is a tragic case, but I am bound to administer the law as it is."

The boy was earning 11s. a week when the accident happened.

It is to avoid such cases as these that a movement is now being organised to amend the compensation laws.

"There are 30,800 boys under sixteen employed in British mines," Mr. William Golightly, sixty-two-year-old president of the Northumberland Miners' Association and leader of the movement, said yesterday.

"Coalowners pay £15 for the burial."

Mr. R. Taylor, M.P. for Morpeth, intends to raise the matter in the House of Commons.

### HER BROKEN ROMANCE

MISS Virginia Clive, daughter of the late Lieut.-Colonel Percy Archer Clive, M.P., of Whitfield, Herefordshire. Her marriage to Mr. Stephen Wynyard Kaye, second son of the late H. W. Kaye and Mrs. Kaye, will not now take place.

# Daily Mirror

THE DAILY PICTURE NEWSPAPER WITH THE LARGEST NET SALE

No. 10,090 — Registered at the G.P.O. as a Newspaper — THURSDAY, APRIL 2, 1936 — One Penny

Broadcasting - Pages 22 & 23
QUIET CORNER Page 14
EUSTACE...... 15
SERIAL...... 21
DOCTOR'S DIARY.. 25
DOROTHY DIX.... 25
BELINDA...... 26
Amusements: Page 18

# BRITAIN TAKES GRAVE STEP

## Cabinet Send Guarantees to France and Belgium

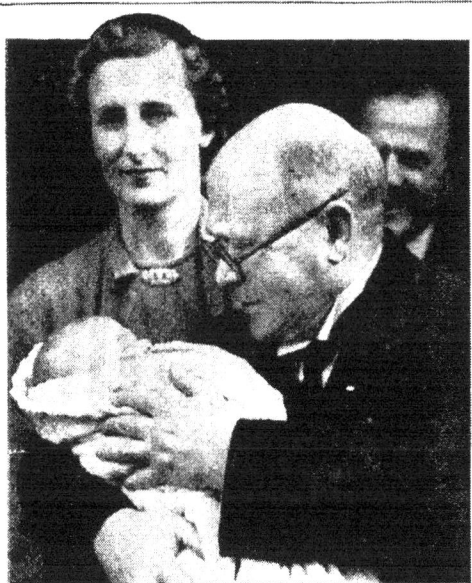

**HE IS A VERY PROUD GRANDPA**

Sir Edward Mountain, the insurance magnate, holding with legitimate pride his bonny grandson — son of Mr. and Mrs. Brian Mountain — after the child's christening yesterday at All Souls', Langham-place, W.

## "This Is Not Your Mother"— Wrong Body in a Coffin

FROM OUR OWN CORRESPONDENT
WELLINGBOROUGH (Northants), Wednesday.

"This is not your mother. It's a ginger-haired woman!"

THESE words, spoken by an astonished neighbour, shocked a daughter in a house in Little Park-street here as she was helping in the preparations for the burial of Mrs. Harriet Earl.

When the coffin was opened it was found to contain—the wrong body!

It had been brought from Northants General Hospital.

Miss Polly Fisher, daughter of Mrs. Earl by her first marriage, was in another room when the neighbour made her discovery.

"It was a terrible shock for us," Miss Fisher told me to-night. "We could hardly believe a mistake had been made.

"The coffin was quickly taken back to Northampton and the mistake was rectified."

It is not known how the confusion originally arose.

Mrs. Earl, the dead woman, was formerly Mrs. Fisher, wife of an officer of the Metropolitan Police Force.

She had been ill at the Northants General Hospital for some time.

"They were very kind to her there during her illness," said Miss Fisher to-night. "I would like to thank them."

### Two Men Hurt in Explosion

TWO men were seriously injured by an explosion as they were working on a mechanical sprayer in a shed at the back of premises in Berkeley-avenue, Bexley Heath, Kent, last night.

They are: Robert Boutell, twenty-one, of Franklin-crescent, Mitcham, and William Searle, twenty-one, of Glenister-street, North Woolwich.

### "AL" G.B.S.

AL Jolson, of "Sonny Boy" fame, is travelling to Hollywood from New York to confer with Warner Brothers about playing the part of George Bernard Shaw in a film based on the author's life.

### HUNT FOR A WOMAN

MR. Evans, a river bailiff, peering through a glass-bottomed box at the bed of the River Llede near Betws-y-Coed yesterday for traces of Miss Eileen Mary Salmond, thirty-two-year-old sportswoman who has been missing since Sunday. A coracle with a powerful electric light is also being used. The police wish to interview the owner of a car seen on Sunday at the spot where Miss Salmond's cap was found.

### GOVERNMENT DEFEATED!

IT really was All Fools' Day in the House of Commons yesterday.

First the Government was defeated; then it wasn't.

Even Mr. Baldwin was puzzled.

And it was all due to a woman—Miss Ellen Wilkinson.

The motion before the House was that the Speaker should leave the chair (a formality) so that the House could go into Committee of Supply on the civil and revenue estimates.

Miss Wilkinson moved an amendment that women Civil Servants should receive the same rates of pay as the men.

And the House agreed, defeating the Government by eight votes—156 to 148.

The Speaker then put Miss Wilkinson's amendment as a substantive motion and the House again went to a division.

Then, having shown its sympathy with the general principle of equal pay, the House rejected the substantive motion by deciding by 119 to 134 that the Speaker should not leave the chair.

Finally, the Prime Minister agreed to Mr. Attlee's motion for the adjournment.

Debate is on page 5.

## HITLER'S CONCESSIONS

FROM OUR DIPLOMATIC CORRESPONDENT

The Cabinet decided last night to send at once to France and Belgium letters guaranteeing the security of those countries in the event of a breakdown of conciliation with Germany.

They decided also that General Staff talks between Britain, France and Belgium should begin after an agreed agenda had been decided on, and should be held in London.

THESE grave decisions were taken after the Cabinet had studied the terms of Germany's reply, which made considerable concessions, to the other Locarno Powers (Britain, France, Italy and Belgium) on the Rhineland crisis.

Germany's counter proposals are officially regarded in London as definitely conciliatory. They afford ample matter for immediate negotiations tiding over an interim period.

Great Britain, backed by the League of Nations, will spare no efforts to bring about a round table conference.

An Exchange message from Paris last night said a superficial examination of the German reply in authoritative circles there had elicited the comment that the proposals were of rather a fantastic nature.

The General Staff conversations which the Cabinet decided upon last night, will possibly begin next week.

On the subject of these conversations, Hitler's reply says:—

"As is obvious from her offer, Germany has no intention ever of attacking France or Belgium, and, taking into consideration France's colossal armaments and the enormous fortresses on her eastern frontier, it is well known that such an attack would be senseless from the purely military point of view alone.

"For these reasons also the desire of the French Government for immediate General Staff discussions is incomprehensible to the German Government.

"The latter would regard it only as seriously prejudicial if such arrangements between General Staffs are arrived at before the conclusion of the new security pacts.

"They are of the opinion that such arrangements would in any case only take place as a result of the political obligations of the five Locarno Powers to render assistance, and then only on strictly reciprocal grounds."

An emphatic declaration that the German people are determined to preserve in all circumstances their freedom, independence and equality of status heads Germany's reply. But it adds:

"The German people most sincerely desire to co-operate with all their might in the great work of a general reconciliation and understanding between European nations."

For a period during which new non-aggression pacts guaranteeing European peace may be concluded, Germany proposes:

A limit of four months, during which she will make no reinforcements of troops in the

(Continued on back page)

Herr Hitler.

# Daily Mirror

THE DAILY PICTURE NEWSPAPER WITH THE LARGEST NET SALE

Broadcasting - Page 28

DOCTOR'S DIARY - P. 10
EUSTACE - - - - - - - 15
QUIET CORNER - - - - 16
SERIAL - - - - - - - - 25
DOROTHY DIX - - - - 31
BELINDA - - - - - - - - 34

No. 10,091 Registered at the G.P.O. as a Newspaper. FRIDAY, APRIL 3, 1936 One Penny

Amusements: Pages 32 and 33

## WHAT WILL THE UNION SAY?

Here are pupils of a nursery school—at North Shields—being builders, though only in play, of the school extension. And —

## THE 13th Crash

## DYING PILOT LEAPS WITH PARACHUTE

### Mid-Air Collision

DYING AS HE FLOATED GENTLY TO EARTH ON HIS PARACHUTE AFTER HIS 'PLANE HAD CRASHED IN MID-AIR, AN R.A.F. OFFICER WAS PICKED UP DEAD YESTERDAY.

The pilot of the second R.A.F. 'plane in the collision was trapped in his machine and killed.

It was the thirteenth R.A.F. accident this year. In previous crashes there have been twenty-four deaths.

The names of yesterday's victims, sole occupants of the machines, are:—

Acting Pilot-Officer Geoffrey Clive King George, aged twenty-one, who was educated at Eton, and

Leading Aircraftman Percy James Pugh, of No. 3 Flying Training School, who came from Wales.

The crash occurred at Colsterworth, about seven miles south of Grantham (Lincs).

### "Great Explosion"

An eye-witness said: "As the machines were flying overhead there was a great explosion as they appeared to collide.

"Both came tumbling down like a shower of fragments and one burst into flames.

"One of the pilots jumped out and I saw his parachute open perfectly. He landed on top of a tree 200 yards off. He was dead when help arrived. I found the second victim in the other machine."

Acting Pilot-Officer George was the only son of Mr. and Mrs. Clive King George, of Medina Villas, Hove, Sussex.

Mr. King George, who formerly lived at Guildford and was in the Grenadier Guards during the war, told the Daily Mirror that his son joined the R.A.F. six months ago.

"My son was a keen adventurous boy," Mr. George said.

"For two years he had been determined to join the Royal Air Force.

"About six months ago he passed the entrance examinations. I heard he was doing very well up there. I know he was always keen on flying."

## POLICEMAN ON DUTY WITH BROKEN SPINE

### 'Pain in Back' After Stopping Runaway

A YOUNG police-constable who had just stopped a runaway horse in Whitechapel, E., yesterday, complained afterwards of a pain in the back, so went off duty. He walked to hospital—and was found to have fractured his spine.

He is P.-C. Perigo, who is stationed at Bethnal Green Police Station, E.

He was on duty when a horse in a four-wheeled cart in Derward-street, Stepney, suddenly took fright at the back-firing of a car.

### Dragged 100 Yards

The terrified animal galloped into Vallance-road and traffic in the district was endangered.

P.-C. Perigo, seeing the danger, flung himself at the horse's head and, hanging grimly on to a rein and shaft, was dragged about a hundred yards into Whitechapel-road before he was able to bring the frightened horse to a standstill.

It was when all the excitement was over that he felt the pain in the back.

He walked to the London hospital and asked to see a doctor.

It was not until an X-ray examination was made that the surgeons made the amazing discovery that he had seriously injured the base of his spine. It is believed that he sustained his injury when he was thrown from his feet as the horse dashed into Whitechapel-road.

Police-Constable Perigo, who is only twenty-seven, is married and has a child aged three.

"I am not surprised that he did this," his wife told the Daily Mirror. "He does not know what danger is."

P.-C Perigo

## RESTAURANTHEATRE IS OPENED

BRITAIN'S first theatre-restaurant, the London Casino, opened last night.

Seven hundred and fifty people were there The Prince Edward Theatre in Old Compton-street has been transformed. Where the stalls and circle used to be there are tiers of little dining tables.

Last night every table was occupied, though the charge was £2 10s. a head (later it will be much the same as West End stalls prices).

First, dinner was served in the restaurant manner. In between courses diners danced on the stage.

Then came the show, an elaborate spectacular revue or super-cabaret produced by Clifford C. Fischer.

London Casino is not a gambling place, but it is a safe bet for a good show and a jolly evening. —B. B.

## FASTED 19 MONTHS

How a convict fasted nineteen months without ill-effect is revealed by Major H. Basil Rosair, superintendent of the Central Prison, at Bareilly, in the United Provinces, India, in this week's "Lancet."

The man, Munshi Khan, began his hunger-strike on May 18, 1934.

Major Rosair stated that it was the longest case of hunger-striking of which he was aware.

### THEY ARE GOOD AT IT TOO

—here, aged from six to twelve years, are acrobats and tap-dancers, the "Eight Wonder Kids" of Clitheroe, Lancs, trained by Mrs. Sherliker. And on page 5 you will find a children's corner—for parents only.

### HE DIDN'T KNOW, BUT

## Marriage Was Ended—Wife Wed Again

WITHOUT knowing it yesterday Wing-Commander Douglas Iron, in charge of the R.A.F. station at Eastleigh, Southampton, had his marriage dissolved. Then his wife remarried — still without his knowing it.

"That's the first I've heard of it," he said when the Daily Mirror spoke to him on the telephone early to-day.

The dissolution was granted at Reno on grounds alleging cruelty.

"My wife went to America about nine months ago to stay with her mother," Wing-Commander Iron said.

"That was the last I saw of her. Until you told me I had received no notification from America that I had been divorced."

Wing-Commander Iron has had a distinguished career. He was a pilot during the war and received the O.B.E.

His last appointment before taking up duty at Eastleigh was in charge of the R.A.F. units in H.M.S. Furious from 1931 until 1935.

Mrs. Phyllis Violet Iron was married a few hours after the case in the Reno courtroom to Dr. Rodney Wyman.

Dr. Wyman divorced his first wife, Hazel Wyman, in 1933, immediately marrying Ann Perone, a young American nurse. He divorced her last January.

### The King—Merchant Navy Chief Still

The King is to keep the title of Master of the Merchant Navy and Fishing Fleets.

Mr. Runciman made this announcement at the Chamber of Shipping banquet in London last night.

THE DAILY MIRROR, Wednesday, April 8, 1936.

Broadcasting - Pages 22 & 23

# Daily Mirror
THE DAILY PICTURE NEWSPAPER WITH THE LARGEST NET SALE

QUIET CORNER Page 14
EUSTACE . . . . . . . . 15
SERIAL . . . . . . . . . 21
DOCTOR'S DIARY . . 25
DOROTHY DIX . . . . 25
BELINDA . . . . . . . . 26

No. 10,095 Registered at the G.P.O. as a Newspaper. WEDNESDAY, APRIL 8, 1936 One Penny Amusements: Page 18

## GIRL, BURNED IN AIR CRASH, CALLS AID

### Staggers in Snow to Say '11 Dead'

WITH clothes burned and hands black with burns, a twenty-two-year-old "flying hostess" staggered half a mile through a snowstorm yesterday to a farmhouse from which she telephoned first news of a U.S. air liner disaster in which eleven people had been killed.

"Horrible accident," she gasped out. "Ship crashed. Started to burn. Both pilots and nine passengers killed.
"I dragged two from the 'plane before it got so hot that I had to quit. I tried to get several others but could see they were dead. I left the two lying on the grass."

Then the girl, Nellie Granger, borrowed some clothes and rushed back to the wreck

### Hit Mountain

The air liner belonging to the Transcontinental Western Air—known as the Lindbergh Line, because Colonel Lindbergh is its technical adviser—crashed into a mountain near Union Town, Pennsylvania.
The woman saved by Nellie Granger is Mrs. Ellenstein, the Mayor of Newark's wife.
Mrs. Ellenstein, states Central News, was so badly burned that doctors despair of her life. Her husband is flying to her side.
There were no British passengers on board Officials attribute the crash, adds British United Press, to the failure of the radio beam to "function accurately."

## GAS PROTECTION FOR FOOD AND WATER

ACTION to prevent food and water from becoming contaminated by poison gas has been considered by the Government, and protective measures will be embodied in instructions to be issued to the public.
In the House of Commons yesterday Mr. Geoffrey Lloyd, Under-Secretary to the Home Office said he proposed to make a considered statement in regard to the effectiveness of gas protectors
He said that advice would also be given for the protection of infants and young children. Alternative methods were being investigated.
As regards tube railways, the problem of whether gas could reach them depended on the protective measures for the supply of air to the railway.

### HOLD-UP IN SHOP

After he had been threatened at the point of a revolver a Gravesend shopkeeper gave chase to intruders last night
Mr. E. Moss, a wardrobe dealer, of Milton-road, Gravesend, returned from a cinema to find two men on his premises. They rushed by him, but Mr. Moss gave chase with a policeman on the running board of a car.
Later a man was detained
Mr. Moss was married on Sunday and there were valuable presents in the house

## Shattered Romance Vow
### Keeps Woman Indoors 40 Years

A BEAUTIFUL woman who for more than forty years had kept a vow to stay indoors—because of a shattered romance—died yesterday at the age of seventy-two. The woman was Miss Clara Jenkins, of Caerleon (Mon).
More than forty years ago she fell in love. Her parents interfered. Miss Jenkins made a vow always to stay indoors. She kept it until death.
She never saw motor-cars, aeroplanes or even tramcars.
Despite her vow, she was known to the children of two generations, for she kept a sweet-shop.
Towards the end she went into deeper seclusion, refusing to see anyone at all.
And at her funeral, by request, there will be no flowers.

### NIECE FOR DUCHESS OF KENT

PRINCESS Olga wife of Prince Paul, Regent of Yugoslavia, to whom a daughter was born early yesterday. The Duke and Duchess of Kent, her brother in-law and sister are staying with her at Belgrade.

## SHE LEAPS 1,500 FEET LIKE GETTING OFF BUS

BY A SPECIAL CORRESPONDENT

I TALKED yesterday with a girl who has never learned the meaning of the word "nerves."

Slim, smiling Miss "Joe" Nadin, who is twenty-one on Sunday, appears to think no more of parachute jumping than the average man does of stepping from a stationary bus.

Yesterday she made two further jumps at Broxbourne Aerodrome, Herts, to complete her ten jumps to gain the Air Ministry parachutist certificate.

I inquired how far one had to jump to suit the Air Ministry.

"Oh, between a thousand and fifteen hundred feet," said the self-possessed figure in white flying suit airily. "Not pull-offs, of course. I jump and when clear pull the rip cord."

"Doesn't it require rather a lot of nerve?"
"Oh, no," said Joe. "It is all a matter of doing what you want to do. I don't think there is much in it really, because I always wanted to do it and I like doing it. The bad part is the landing. One is liable to have all the corners knocked off."

Miss Nadin being unharnessed after coming to earth and (above) her parachute makes a perfect picture as it floats gracefully through the air.

## 350 TROLLY-BUS MEN STRIKE IN LONDON TO-DAY

ABOUT 350 trolly-bus workers, belonging to the Fulwell (Twickenham) branch of the Transport and General Workers' Union, decided early to-day to come out on strike as a protest against the new schedule.

The trolly buses they operate are in Hammersmith, Chiswick, Brentford, Twickenham, Hampton, Teddington, Kingston, Surbiton and Wimbledon.

Late last night it was also learned that an Easter bus strike, to begin on Good Friday, was threatened by the Nunhead (Camberwell) garage, which operates 100 buses on seven routes

A mass meeting is to be held at midnight to-night at the Unity Club, Albert-road, Peckham, when a decision will be taken.
Eleven other garages are sending delegates. They may come out in sympathy.
Mr. A. Collinson, secretary of the Nunhead branch of the Transport and General Workers' Union, who has been negotiating for a settlement of the men's grievances, said last night:
"The men feel that they have not been amply compensated for the speeding-up of the services

## Easter Will Be Mild and Sunny

Sunshine—mild weather—little or no rain.

THAT is likely to be the Easter weather. England is usually lucky at the year's first holiday. The "Daily Mirror" weather expert says that the chances are that Easter, 1936, will not let us down.
"The cold spell which set in late last week appears to be ending, and the warmer winds from the Atlantic will soon spread across the country," he says.

# Daily Mirror

THE DAILY PICTURE NEWSPAPER WITH THE LARGEST NET SALE

EUSTACE......P. 9
DOCTOR'S DIARY -- 10
QUIET CORNER---- 14
SERIAL--------- 21
DOROTHY DIX .... 26
BELINDA -------- 26

No. 10,096 — THURSDAY, APRIL 9, 1936 — One Penny

Broadcasting - Pages 22 & 23
Amusements: Pages 24 and 25

## EASTER EGG AS CRADLE

## £40,000,000 BY-PASS FOR NATION

## HOMES IN FOUR COUNTRIES

### As Memorial to King George

The world's greatest "by-pass" road—to cost £40,000,000 and to connect London and Glasgow without passing through a single town—is being discussed as a memorial to King George.

**M.P.s FOR THE DISTRESSED AREAS ARE TO CONSIDER THE SCHEME AS A MEANS OF BRINGING EMPLOYMENT TO THOUSANDS OF WORKLESS.**

All Britain would benefit by such a road. It would be more than 400 miles long. Birmingham, Manchester, Preston, Lancaster and Carlisle would particularly be well served by it.

The idea of this practical memorial comes from Mr. E. L. Leeming, surveyor to the Urmston Council, who is to discuss it with M.P.s next week.

If the suggestion is adopted the road would be protected from ribbon development, and would cross lesser roads over bridges.

"I am convinced that the road is a sound proposition," Mr. Leeming told the *Daily Mirror*.

"The present low rates of interest make it a favourable time to start.

"The road is planned to serve in a direct sense about 80 per cent. of the population.

"Indirectly it will serve the whole nation, with its improved access."

Mr. Leeming believes that the road could be constructed in five years, and estimates the cost at £40,000,000, a large proportion of which would be expended on wages.

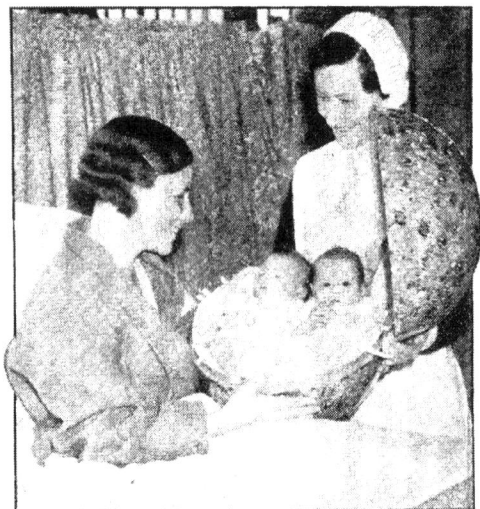

Peter and Paul, the twin boys born to Mrs. Lamb at University College Hospital, London, giving their mother a surprise when the monster Easter egg cradle presented to Mrs. Lamb by the nurses was opened.

### Country Wife's First Look at London

## Lifts—They Put Me in Cage: Buses—Them Tractors

FROM OUR OWN CORRESPONDENT
HEMPSTEAD (Essex), Wednesday.

"THEM tractors do go gurt fast.... I never seen so many in all my born days...."

This was now a forty-five-year-old Essex woman described her first visit to London which took place to-day when she had to give evidence in a divorce case.

She is Mrs. Julia Foster, of Riverside Cottages, Hempstead, and the Judge complimented her on the way she had given her evidence.

Late to-night she returned from what she said was the most exciting day of her life to the tiny cottage where she has spent the last twenty-one years.

"The queerest thing I see was those fellows in wigs," she told me, "but I didn't feel a bit scared. When they asked me questions I plucked up and answered quite boldlike.

"Then my friends took me round London on them tractor things...."

"Mother means buses," interrupted her pretty, seventeen-year-old daughter Nellie.

"Yes, buses." Mrs. Foster went on. "Then they took me to some wonderful shops full of pretty dresses and fur coats.

"They put me in a cage and shut the bars —and suddenly up we went into the air like. I had hardly knew what would happen next. We had some fish and chips in a great place full of people.... What most took my fancy was the world turning round, all done in coloured lights, right on top of a high building.

"This was my first long train journey. I en—
(Continued on page)

Mrs. Foster

## HOUSE OFFERED FOR A STAMP

BY A SPECIAL CORRESPONDENT
House for sale—or would exchange for a postage stamp.

THAT, in effect, is the offer made by a wealthy stamp-collector who wishes to dispose of his seven-roomed house at Copse Hill, Wimbledon, Surrey, in the Wimbledon Common and Richmond Park area.

Mr. Robson Lowe, an expert philatelist, who at present lives in the house, is negotiating the "swap" for a client.

"We thought we might get some interesting offers if the house were offered in exchange for a valuable stamp collection—or even a single stamp, provided it was worth the £1,650 which is the reserve price put on the house," Mr. Robson Lowe told me last night.

"The same client had a £2,000 car some time ago, and wanted to sell it after two months, but was offered only £750 for it. I advertised that the car could be exchanged for a stamp collection, and it was 'swapped' for a £1,000 collection, which was actually worth about £1,300 to my client. We could have done the deal twenty times over.

"So I am trying again—with a house this time. My client, who is a keen collector, has left the negotiations entirely to my judgment."

## NO PEACE FILM BAN

The censor has raised his ban on the film, "The Peace of Britain." It will be shown publicly at the London Pavilion to-day.

The Duchess of Leeds, who is always perfectly dressed and is at home in no fewer than four countries. She is the daughter of the late Iskender de Malkharzouny, of Serbia, and in addition to the ducal seat, Hornby Castle, Bedale, Yorks, has one residence in Italy and another in Paris. She was married in 1933.

## EMPEROR DISGUISED TO ESCAPE CAPTURE

EMPEROR Haile Selassie, who is fleeing before the advancing Italian troops, has disguised himself to escape capture (says British United Press).

According to one inhabitant of the village of Aloman, the Emperor had shaved off his beard when he passed through the village towards Dessie after the Ashangi battle. It was stated that he feared capture by Azebo-Galla tribesmen, who have been setting various traps to catch him.

More than 100,000 Italian soldiers and labourers are in working parties constructing motor roads and improving the existing tracks at the rear of the front lines in the north, to make a speedier advance possible.

Italian patrols of Askaris have occupied the village of Gobbo and are continuing their advance towards Dessie without meeting resistance, it is reported.

Britain's proposed inner by-pass

# Daily Mirror

**THE DAILY PICTURE NEWSPAPER WITH THE LARGEST NET SALE**

Broadcasting - Page 20

EUSTACE . . . . . . . P. 9
DOCTOR'S DIARY . . 10
QUIET CORNER . . . . 14
SERIAL . . . . . . . . 21
DOROTHY DIX . . . . 26
BELINDA . . . . . . . 26

No. 10,098 Registered at the G.P.O as a Newspaper. MONDAY, APRIL 13, 1936 One Penny

Amusements: Page 21

# OVERCOAT HOLIDAY TO-DAY

## First Easter Snowfall for Nineteen Years

### BRITAIN BRAVED IT

**FORECAST FOR TO-DAY:** Squally north wind, wintry showers, brighter intervals, cold.

BUTTON up your overcoat. You'll need it at the seaside, in the country or in city streets to-day.

For yesterday's bitter weather—when snow greeted Easter Sunday for the first time for nineteen years—will continue.

The lowlands of Thames-side were under a light covering of white. Elsewhere the snow melted.

The weather experts last week prophesied a fine and warm Easter. But Buchan, the weather expert who has been dead for 107 years, put this week-end as one of his cold spells. And Buchan was right!

Not even a fixed Easter would have saved us blue noses and dripping umbrellas. For the "fixed Easter" advocates would make Easter the Sunday after April's second Saturday—which was yesterday.

But Britain braved the cold.

Seventy-six-year-old W. P. Haskett-Smith, of London, celebrated the fiftieth anniversary of his climb of Napes Needle of Great Gable—which laid the foundation of British rock climbing—by climbing the Needle once more.

At Rhyl girls went down to the sea in fur coats. Off came the coats. Into the sea went the girls. They got wet—then made a dash for the fur coats again.

Southend had a hero—the solitary man who ventured into the sea.

At Yarmouth a girl was seen wandering about with a bottle of sun-burn oil in her hand. She was the OPTIMIST.

At Bournemouth a man appeared on the shore with a waterproof sheet which he made into a tent. He was the PESSIMIST.

### Dog Delays Royal Car

Hundreds of visitors cheered the King and other members of the Royal Family when they arrived at Windsor Castle to attend divine service in the private chapel yesterday morning.

The King motored from Fort Belvedere. Queen Mary followed with the Duke and Duchess of York.

When the second car was near Frogmore a small dog broke away from its mistress and ran in front of the car. The chauffeur pulled the car to a standstill with inches to spare. The frightened animal crouched down in the roadway and its owner ran and picked it up, much to the amusement of the Queen and the Duke and Duchess.

The owner then thanked the chauffeur and bowed to the Queen, who returned the bow.

Princess Elizabeth and Princess Margaret Rose were in a third car and they acknowledged the cheers by waving their hands.

On the roads there were few accidents reported due to the fact that the holiday rush

*(Continued on back page)*

### TO SUIT THE DAY

Hat seen in Hyde Park yesterday during one of the short spells of sunshine. The wearer was wisely prepared for the cold.

Eustace got there first! These folk, sheltering from yesterday's snow in a sentry-box outside Buckingham Palace, are evidently following the example set by Useless Eustace in the cartoon on the right, published in the "Daily Mirror" a fortnight ago. They are, however, luckier than Eustace, for no sentry has arrived to dislodge them.

"No! I'm hanged if I'll come out! I got here first!"

## Midnight Search for London's Flying Doctor—Lost in Blizzard

SEARCH was being made early to-day for London's flying doctor, Mr. W. Richardson, who in his sail-plane had been missing for twelve hours over desolate, blizzard-swept Derbyshire mountains.

Arrangements were made for two aeroplanes to take off at dawn to-day, and the Manchester Ramblers' Federation was asked to co-operate in the search.

Dr. Richardson, a member of the London Gliding Club, was flying in the open meeting of the Derbyshire and Lancashire Gliding Club, and was launched into the air from Mam Tor at 1.17 p.m. He circled about for two hours. Then a snowstorm swept the valley and visibility was reduced to a few yards.

Two other sail-planes which were in the air at the time made for Camp Hill Farm, Great Hucklow, the club's headquarters, and landed safely four miles from where they were launched.

When the storm cleared, Dr. Richardson was not to be seen. Darkness descended and there was still no sign of him. Anxious inquiries were made by telephone to police stations for miles around.

### MRS. BARTHOLOMEW FOUND

MRS. Bartholomew, the mother of the £15,000-a-year boy film star, who has been missing since she landed in New York from England on Wednesday, has been found.

The Bureau of Missing Persons stated last night that she would arrive at the Biltmore Hotel, Los Angeles, within a few hours.

Her husband had feared she had been kidnapped.

### Place in the Sun

IF you want a glimpse of the sun—bask in it with Rummy on page 9.

If you stay indoors and you would like to try hypnotism to amuse your friends—turn to page 4.

If you want to make the most of the holiday—turn to page 10.

## Naked Woman at St. Paul's Altar Steps

### 1,000 WATCH SCENE

BEFORE a thousand people in St. Paul's Cathedral last night a beautiful woman stood naked at the altar steps.

The woman had walked towards the altar from one of the pews just as the choir was leaving the vestry.

From her shoulders hung a long cloak. As she neared the altar officials noticed her and moved forward to intervene.

Then suddenly the cloak dropped from the woman's shoulders. For a minute she stood motionless, her back to the congregation.

An official stepped forward. The cloak was placed around the woman's shoulders and she was led to a vestry.

A member of the congregation told the "Daily Mirror": "The woman was very pretty and about twenty-five years of age.

"When she was taken away by police officers she appeared quite normal and composed.

"She remained quiet and offered no explanation."

The woman was later taken to an institution.

### MOLLISON BURNED

Mr. J. A. Mollison, the airman, was injured by burns through a fire in the bedroom of his hotel in Singapore during the night, says a British United Press message. The bedding and mosquito net were set alight.

# Daily Mirror

**THE DAILY PICTURE NEWSPAPER WITH THE LARGEST NET SALE**

Broadcasting - Page 24

EUSTACE . . . . . . . P. 9
DOCTOR'S DIARY . . 10
QUIET CORNER . . . . 14
SERIAL . . . . . . . . . 21
DOROTHY DIX . . . . 26
BELINDA . . . . . . . . 26

No. 10,102  Registered at the GPO as a Newspaper.  FRIDAY, APRIL 17, 1936  One Penny

Amusements: Pages 28 and 29

# "LIVE" SHELLS ON DOORSTEP

## Girl Put Them in Bedroom

### 'SABOTAGE' SCARE

FROM OUR OWN CORRESPONDENT

PLYMOUTH, Thursday.

WITH two "live" 14lb. shells which she had found in a parcel on the doorstep, a fourteen-year-old girl to-day struggled up a flight of stairs and placed them at her grandmother's bedside thinking they were a present.

**Her discovery brought Secret Service men hurrying to Plymouth to-night.**

A grave view is taken of the find. The shells must have been stolen from a Government base. They were stamped and marked as Government material.

**The incident is believed to be connected with the recent attempts at sabotage.**

The most serious aspect of the case is that such bulky material can have been stolen from a munition dump without the thief being discovered.

An inquiry will be held.

### Tied with String

The two shells were found standing upright wrapped in a sheet of newspaper and tied loosely with string.

The finder was Aileen Edwards, of the Old Vicarage, Higher Budeaux, Plymouth.

Miss Edwards was leaving her home this morning at seven o'clock when she saw the parcel on the doorstep. There was no address on it, and she asked her mother, Mrs. Georgina Edwards, if she was expecting a parcel. Mrs. Edwards said "No," and suggested it was a delayed Easter gift for Aileen's grandmother, Mrs. Mary Sparks, who also lives in the house.

Aileen picked up the parcel and managed to carry it into her grandmother's bedroom, where she placed it at the bedside.

Mrs. Sparks awakened and excitedly opened the parcel, thinking it was an Easter gift.

Then she uttered a cry of alarm, and in her astonishment she jumped out of bed a moment later and dressed only in her night clothes, ran on to the lawn with the shells.

### "I Almost Fainted"

She placed the shells on the lawn and ran into the house to get the remainder of the family outside.

They stood at a considerable distance from the house, scantily clad, while a friend telephoned the police, who quickly arrived and took the shells away.

Mr. Edwards told me: "It was a terrible fright for us all. We believe that the person who placed the shells on the doorstep was trying to reach the cemetery which adjoins our garden. He must have been disturbed and placed the shells on the doorstep before running away."

Mrs. Sparks told me how she eagerly opened her supposed Easter gift to discover the two cold, steel shells.

"I almost fainted with fright," she said. "I jumped out of bed quicker than ever in my life."

It is thought that the person who left the shells did so with no malicious intent against anyone in the house.

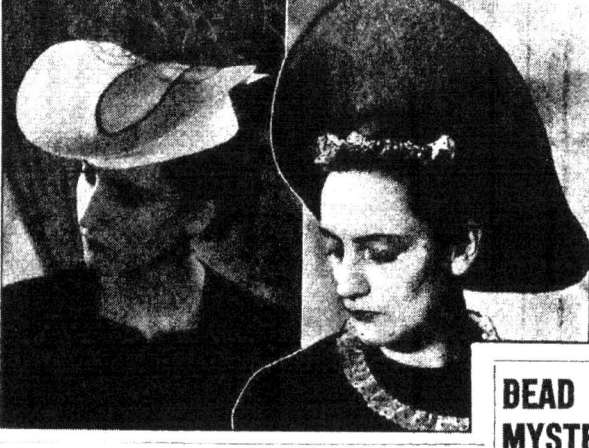

### WORN ABOVE THE HAIR

Variations with two colours. Left: White straw decorated above with green tulle, and right: Green straw decorated below with white lace.

### BEAD WOMAN MYSTERY: MURDER SUSPECTED

THE body of Mrs. Jeanette Cotton, aged about forty, was found last night on the floor of a room in Lexington-street, London, W.

A silk handkerchief was tied tightly round the lower part of her face.

Scotland Yard officers who were called to the house shortly after the body was discovered at 8.45 p.m., suspect that the woman was murdered.

### CINEMA CROWDS HUNT MISSING BOY

PEOPLE leaving a cinema joined with police, firemen and Boy Scouts in a search at Buntingford (Herts) last night for seven-year-old John Shuttleworth.

After a dam in the River Rib had been opened the child's body was recovered.

### SLIMMING RECORD

Fastest slimming treatment in history ended yesterday at Harper Hospital, Detroit, with a reduction in the weight of a 22st. 7lb. woman to 8st. 8lb. in ten days, says the *Daily Mirror* New York correspondent.

The woman is Mrs. John Crawford, aged fifty-eight, formerly of Ayr, Scotland.

Miss Palmer as a bride

### 'Feed the Goldfish' —But Clerk Didn't

OLDHAM'S workhouse master expects his clerks to do their duty. Up to a day or two ago he had his expectation fulfilled. Then the workhouse goldfish, bobbing up and down with wide-open mouths in the ornamental pond near the master's office wanted feeding.

"Feed the goldfish," came the master's order to William Melia, a twenty-one-year-old clerk in the master's office.

That order fell on deaf ears, and because Mr. Melia refused to feed those goldfish the master has suspended him for a week, with loss of pay.

Yesterday a sub-committee of the Public Assistance Committee sat in solemn conclave to consider Mr. Melia's claim that feeding goldfish does not come within his duties as a clerk. They turned it down.

← *This Wedding Was Her Own*

## BRIDESMAID AND BRIDE IN 3 HOURS

WITHIN three hours of acting as bridesmaid at her brother's wedding, a Bournemouth girl was married to a footballer belonging to the local Queen's Park Club, of which her brother is captain.

She was Miss Ada Doroth. Palmer whose parents live at Grantham-road, Bournemouth. During the morning she was a bridesmaid at the marriage of her brother, Mr. Alfred William Palmer, to Miss Constance Olive Turner. In the afternoon she was wedded to Mr George Hopkins.

Some of the bridesmaids attended both ceremonies, with different dresses for each.

Two receptions were held at the home of Mr. and Mrs. Palmer, senr., and the same guests, numbering 150, were present at both.

Both wedding ceremonies took place at St. Clement's Church, and Miss Turner and Mr. Hopkins had both been living in Wheaton-road.

### THIS CAT CAME BACK

THIS is the cat that walked by itself — 100 miles from Eastbourne to Bournemouth. It belonged to Mr. and Mrs. N. A. Whittingham, who lived at South Bournemouth. Recently, they removed to Eastbourne, taking the cat with them. Pussy, however, preferred Bournemouth, and within ten days was back again. The old home was locked, but Mr. and Mrs. Whittingham's next-door neighbours have taken charge of puss.

# Daily Mirror

THE DAILY PICTURE NEWSPAPER WITH THE LARGEST NET SALE

Broadcasting - Pages 24 & 25

EUSTACE ....... P. 9
DOCTOR'S DIARY .. 21
SERIAL ........ 23
QUIET CORNER ... 25
BELINDA ....... 26
DOROTHY DIX .... 28

No. 10,106  Registered at the G.P.O as a Newspaper.  WEDNESDAY, APRIL 22, 1936  One Penny

Amusements : Page 24

# WHAT YOU WILL PAY

## Income Tax Up 3d.—with Some Benefits

### TEA DUTY BLOW TO EVERY HOME

HARDSHIP FOR MILLIONS
2d. A LB. ON TEA DUTY

**THE MARRIED MAN WITH CHILDREN AND AN INCOME OF UP TO £800 A YEAR COMES BEST OUT OF THE "SACRIFICE FOR SAFETY" BUDGET WHICH THE CHANCELLOR OF THE EXCHEQUER (MR. NEVILLE CHAMBERLAIN) PRESENTED YESTERDAY.**

BACHELORS and higher salaried men will have to bear the brunt of the sacrifices which are vital to enable Britain to restore her defences.

**What YOU will have to pay is shown in detail on Page 3.**

Probably the greatest blow of all is the increase of 2d. a lb. on tea duty, which affects every household in the country. It will be unpopular among all parties. The price of tea will go up in the shops to-day.

To what extent rearmament has been responsible for these new demands is shown by the fact that during next year the taxpayer will have to find £50,000,000 more than last year for defence. That is the price of safety.

Part of this will be raised by:—

3d. on income tax.
2d. a lb. on tea duty.
£1 a barrel surtax on non-Empire imported beer.
£5,000,000 raid on Road Fund.

The plum has been reserved for the family man. He will receive an additional £10 income tax allowance as a married man and an extra

### Budget at a Glance

ESTIMATED REVENUE ... £798,381,000
ESTIMATED EXPENDITURE £797,897,000
PROSPECTIVE SURPLUS     £484,000

£10 for each child. This concession will benefit 1,100,000 of the 1,400,000 income tax payers.

In many cases this concession will outweigh the extra 3d. in the pound.

Until a household's income rises to about £800 a year it will continue to benefit under the proposals.

In spite of the need for new taxation, Mr Chamberlain believes that 1936 will see an increase in national prosperity.

The estimated expenditure of more than £798,000,000 is the highest for many years.

Both in his Budget statement and in a broadcast speech last night, Mr. Chamberlain

(Continued on back page)

### THE KING IN THE RAIN

Walking through yesterday's chilly downpour like any ordinary Londoner ... umbrella in hand and overcoat collar upturned. The King on his way from Buckingham Palace to preside over a meeting of the Council of the Duchy of Cornwall at the offices in Buckingham Gate. This is the second time that King Edward has left the Palace on foot.

Sir F. Hopkinson

## 'Don't Marry Young,' Says Knight—to Wed at 73

"NEVER since I had my first bicycle sixty years ago have I been so excited," said Sir Frederick T. Hopkinson, of Wimbledon Common, London S.W.—the man who built the Sennar Dam—discussing with the *Daily Mirror* last night his intention to marry again at the age of seventy-three.

His bride is to be Mrs. Lionel Booth, widow, of Wimborne, Dorset, and the wedding will take place in June.

Date and details are to be kept a close secret. Only members of the two families will be allowed to attend.

The honeymoon will be spent on the Continent, where Sir Frederick goes every winter.

### "Too Old at 40" Myth

"It is all nonsense to talk about men being too old at forty," he declared. "I was in my prime long after I passed that age. In my opinion marriages fail because the parties are too young.

"Marriage is the biggest responsibility in the world, and the older one is the nearer one has come to a perfect understanding of life.

"People say it is impossible for old folk to be thrilled. Not a bit of it!"

### HERE'S LUCK

*Do you find the Budget depressing this morning? Then read this*

A MAN, who for long has been out of work, walked from London to Epsom yesterday hoping for a job at the races.

There were no jobs. He was about to leave the course when a man asked him to help in unloading a lorry. He received two shillings; spent one shilling on food.

He went up to a bookmaker and put his last shilling on a twenty to one chance, Marcus Antonius—and it won.

So the out-of-work had a bet on each race, doubling his stakes on certain races. He went "through the card." When the last race was over he had won £400.

He left the course by taxi-cab, bought some clothes, and caught the night train back to Newcastle, his home.

THE DAILY MIRROR, Thursday, April 23, 1936.

# Daily Mirror

**THE DAILY PICTURE NEWSPAPER WITH THE LARGEST NET SALE**

Broadcasting - Pages 22 & 23

EUSTACE . . . . . . P. 9
DOCTOR'S DIARY . . 15
QUIET CORNER . . . 16
SERIAL . . . . . . . 21
BELINDA . . . . . . 26
DOROTHY DIX . . . . 26

No. 10,107 Registered at the G.P.O as a Newspaper. THURSDAY, APRIL 23, 1936 One Penny

Amusements : Page 22

# RESCUERS' PIT "TOMB" PERIL

## Unable to Drag Men to Safety

### 10-DAY ORDEAL

**FROM OUR SPECIAL CORRESPONDENT**

MOOSE RIVER (Nova Scotia), Wednesday.

**TWO MEN, ENTOMBED FOR TEN DAYS IN A GOLD MINE HERE, ARE STILL ALIVE. RESCUERS HAVE REACHED THEM. BUT THE RESCUERS THEMSELVES ARE IN DANGER. THE ROOF OF THE MINE MAY COLLAPSE AT ANY MOMENT.**

AN excited miner dashing from the pithead shouting: "We've got through," gave the news to the world that Dr. Robertson and Mr. Scadding, had been reached.

The crowd of thousands, held back by Canadian Mounted Police, cheered wildly. They were asked to be silent, as the noise might seriously affect the victims.

Among them were three women beseeching officials to allow them to go down the mine. They were the wives of Robertson, Scadding and the widow of Magill. Magill was one of the three originally entombed and died on Monday.

Smiling through her tears Mrs. Magill tried to congratulate the other women, as they wept for joy.

### Asked for Drugs

Dr. Davies, Nova Scotia's Minister of Mines, struggled down to the men. In his hand he carried a hypodermic syringe with which to deaden their agony.

When the last barrier to the underground tomb was being broken down, Robertson had made the pathetic request that a syringe should be in readiness, for both longed more than anything for an end to their pain.

But the hole into the cavern was so small that it was impossible to drag the men through without injury.

Miners seeing the cavern where the two men lay gasping were deeply moved.

"It is a miracle that the two could have survived this little hell," said one.

Stretchers were carried down to bring the men to the surface.

In Ottawa the news that the men had been reached was announced by the Prime Minister of Canada, Mr. Mackenzie King.

## Big Fight on the Radio To-night—Perhaps!

**By A SPECIAL CORRESPONDENT**

LISTENERS may—or may not—hear a broadcast commentary of the Petersen-McAvoy fight for the British and Empire heavy-weight championship to-night.

The decision is in the lap of the gods and the hands of the promoters and B.B.C.

The promoters will not start the bout later than 9.40.

The B.B.C. will not start the broadcast earlier than ten o'clock.

In any event listeners will not hear the start of the fight, which is at the Empress Stadium, London.

Here is a commentary on the "fight" between the promoters and the B.B.C.:—

"The match will start not later than 9.40, or as early before that as can be arranged," an official of the promoters told me last night. "We conferred with the B.B.C. this afternoon. The B.B.C. would not alter the time, and we would not let the fight start later than 9.40.

"If the B.B.C. wants to come and pick up' the fight it can—though the knock-out may be twenty minutes before the broadcast gins.

"It seems to me the B.B.C. has reduced the thing to a farce."

This is the decision of the B.B.C.: "We are adhering to the published times for the boxing broadcast—10 till 11 p.m. If Mr. McAvoy and Mr. Petersen are still on their feet when we begin then the public will hear them.

Other news of the fight on page 30

Thus far and no farther. . . . Clearing snow from a car in deep drift since Tuesday in Wales. . . . Above: Looking along main Treherbert-Swansea route, only link between Rhondda and Swansea valleys.

## PILOT'S SKILL SAVES CHILDREN AS HE CRASHES IN BOMBER

**By A SPECIAL CORRESPONDENT**

FORCED down in a blinding snowstorm, an R.A.F. bomber yesterday—

Crashed into a hedge, knocked down a small tree, narrowly missed some builders' sheds, shattered both wings and damaged the propeller.

The pilot, Flying Officer M. P. Forte, was unhurt. He had to make the forced landing less than two hundred yards from a new housing estate at Fryent-way, Kingsbury, Middlesex.

A London Transport conductor told me that Flying Officer Forte's skill prevented a terrible accident to a group of children.

"The children were in a sunken roadway on the other side of the field from Fryent-way when the 'plane swooped down only a few feet from their heads.

"Women at the windows of nearby houses screamed. Some of the kiddies looked up, then cowered down to the ground.

"I thought I was about to see a terrible accident. I could not see the pilot, but he seemed to lift the plane clear over their heads to where it flopped in the field. It was a magnificent piece of work."

This was one of the incidents in a day of shivers.

At one time the temperature in London fell to 38—nearly 20 deg. lower than the normal for this time of the year.

Bus queues were broken up, and shivering crowds flocked to Underground stations.

### HITLER'S WREATH

A WREATH of arum lilies from Herr Hitler adorned the coffin at the cremation yesterday of one of the five English schoolboys who lost their lives in the Black Forest last week-end.

How the bodies were met in London is described on page 10.

Dr. Robertson and (right) Mr. Scadding

THE DAILY MIRROR, Friday, April 24, 1936.

# Daily Mirror
### THE DAILY PICTURE NEWSPAPER WITH THE LARGEST NET SALE

Broadcasting - Pages 22 & 23

DOCTOR'S DIARY - P. 8
EUSTACE - - - - - - 9
QUIET CORNER - - - 17
SERIAL - - - - - - - 21
BELINDA - - - - - - 26
DOROTHY DIX - - - - 26

No. 10,108  Registered at the G.P.O as a Newspaper.  FRIDAY, APRIL 24, 1936.  One Penny

Amusements: Pages 24 and 25

# BUDGET "LEAKAGE" STORM

## Chancellor Is "Deaf" to M.P.s' Demands

### INQUIRY CALL

FROM OUR PARLIAMENTARY CORRESPONDENT

Clamour for an inquiry into an alleged leakage of a Budget secret which resulted in a huge gambling on the nation's fortunes grew last night.

IN the House of Commons M.P.s repeatedly raised the question. The Chancellor of the Exchequer (Mr. Neville Chamberlain) was asked for assurances that such a leakage would not be allowed to occur again.

Then the Chancellor spoke in last night's Budget debate—and never mentioned the leakage. M.P.s were indignant. They are demanding that this matter must not be hushed up. Inquiry must be as rigorous as when a British secret document was published in Italy.

In the Civil Service and at Government printing offices inquiries have been made. No leakage has occurred there. Before Easter every Cabinet Minister had the outlines of the Budget communicated to him. But they were bound to secrecy. Their "lips were sealed."

In an effort to solve the mystery, Lloyd's are to ask underwriters who dealt in last-minute insurances against risks of increases in income-tax or tea duty to disclose details.

### 40 per Cent. Jump

During the Commons debate, Sir Assheton Pownall (Cons., Lewisham, E.) explained the evidence pointing to a leakage.

Last week normal rate of insurance against higher income-tax was 5 to 10 guineas per cent. On Monday it was 15 guineas. On Tuesday the rush was so great that it rose to 45 per cent.

No one would have paid that rate without certain knowledge of the Chancellor's secret.

Mr. Arthur Greenwood (Soc., Wakefield) said: "I am not asking the Chancellor to apply methods of the third degree, but I do ask him to do his best, to find out how it is these leakages occur."

Mr. E. W. Collin, eighty-year-old father-in-law of Sir John Abercrombie, leaving St. James's, Spanish-place, with his bride, Mrs. Jane Gray.

Sir Frederick Hopkinson and his bride, Mrs. Lionel Booth, after their wedding at St. James's, Piccadilly.

## "SECRET" WEDDING OF SCIENTIST

BY A SPECIAL CORRESPONDENT

SIR Frederick Hopkinson, the seventy-three-year-old scientist, was married 'secretly" at St. James's Church, Piccadilly, London, yesterday, to Mrs. Lionel Booth, a widow, of Wimborne, Dorset.

The date and place of the wedding had been kept from everyone but the closest friends.

When he was engaged he told everyone that the wedding would probably take place in June, and there were fewer than twenty-five people "in the know."

Mr. Edward Woodfield Collin, the eighty-year-old father-in-law of Sir John Abercrombie, was married yesterday at St. James's Church, Spanish-place, London, W., to Mrs. Jane Gray, a widow of fifty-seven, a well-known Catholic social worker.

### S O S After Seven Months

An S O S message to a man who disappeared seven months ago was broadcast last night. Last September Mr. John William Hampson, fifty-three, licensee of the Tempest Arms, Bolton, left home.

His wife is lying dangerously ill at Townley's Hospital, Farnworth, and Hampson is asked to go to see her.

## OPERATION ON WIDOW WHO AWAITS TRIAL FOR MURDER

MRS. Charlotte Bryant, the twenty-nine-year-old Sherborne widow, who is awaiting trial on a charge of murdering her husband by poisoning, has undergone an operation in a London hospital.

She has been suffering from ear trouble for some time.

After her committal to the assizes she was taken to Holloway Prison, where an operation was considered necessary.

Mrs. Bryant's identity was kept secret from other patients.

Her three children are still in Sturminster Institution. Her schoolboy son, George, who has been worrying about the absence of his mother, is to go to Weymouth shortly for an eye operation.

### They Want To Be Eve

THE Carnival Committee of Bramley, near Leeds, have been swamped with applications from girls anxious to appear as Eve at the annual carnival which is to be staged next month.

---

CONSTABLE by name and constable by profession is this twenty-six-year-old Scottish girl selected from sixty applicants to be Leicester's second policewoman.
She is Miss Anne Constable, M.A. of Edinburgh.

## PETERSEN WINS— AND THE B.B.C. DID SAY SO

Jack Petersen kept his British and Empire heavyweight boxing titles by defeating Jock McAvoy, of Rochdale, on points over fifteen rounds at the Earl's Court Stadium last night.

BY A SPECIAL CORRESPONDENT

THE B.B.C. broadcast the Petersen-McAvoy fight after all.

But the commentary on the first round and part of the second was almost missed by listeners because of the dreary strains of orchestral music, which did not cease until ten o'clock.

Though spectators appeared to find the fight dull, the piquant comments of Bob Bowman, the Canadian ice hockey commentator, enlivened matters for listeners.

### His Accent

The running commentary was given by Mr. Lionel Seccombe, with Bob Bowman giving, in his broad Canadian accent, a short summary of each round after the interval.

During the tenth round, when there was a great deal of booing among the spectators at the Empress Stadium, Bowman said:

"I cannot see what they are grumbling at. It is a case of a big man against a little man, and the little man is cleverly avoiding the blows."

Later, when McAvoy was breathing heavily, Bowman said: "That strange, sniffing noise you hear comes from McAvoy."

### "No Blood"

Nearing the end of the contest Bowman said: "The end of the thirteenth round, and not a drop of blood from either of them."

This is the first time the B.B.C. have employed a commentator to give a summary of a fight between rounds.

Full report of the fight on page 30

THE DAILY MIRROR, Thursday, April 30, 1936.

# Daily Mirror

**THE DAILY PICTURE NEWSPAPER WITH THE LARGEST NET SALE**

Broadcasting · Page 22

EUSTACE · · · · · · · P. 9
DOCTOR'S DIARY · · 10
QUIET CORNER · · · · 14
SERIAL · · · · · · · · 21
DOROTHY DIX · · · · 26
BELINDA · · · · · · · · 26

No. 10,113 Registered at the G.P.O. as a Newspaper

THURSDAY, APRIL 30, 1936

One Penny

Amusements : Page 22

## M.P.s DENOUNCE THE B.B.C.

### "Dictatorship Over Private Lives"

### ACTION DEMAND

BY OUR PARLIAMENTARY CORRESPONDENT

SLASHING attacks by M.P.s on the B.B.C. last night raised the Commons to a pitch of excitement. "Unlimited dictatorial autocracy" by the Director-General (Sir John Reith) and that the B.B.C. had been "one of the most anti-religious influences in recent years" were among the charges made.

Major Tryon, Postmaster-General, replying to the debate, said the Government were going into the staff conditions on the B.B.C. very fully.

The Government would announce their proposals concerning the B.B.C. in a later debate. Sir Stafford Cripps who attacked Sir John Reith, said:

There had been a completely arbitrary selection of persons, whether at the top or bottom of the list of staff.

Sometimes most unsuitable people had been chosen. In some cases quite heavy sums in compensation had been paid to individuals who had been forced to resign because of their incompetence, so that no trouble or publicity might result.

#### "Black Marks"

There was a complete absence of security. At any moment an agreement might be terminated without reason stated.

This play of dictatorship within the B.B.C. allowed the very maximum of interference with the private lives of the staff.

The dictatorship was carried into the sports field and there was supervision over the private lives of the staff.

Any person who was the so-called guilty party in divorce proceedings was at once dismissed even if there had been no publicity in connection with the divorce.

Anything unorthodox was not tolerated and even if it did not lead to compulsory resignation it formed the subject of a black mark against the employee.

If necessary the Postmaster-General should organise some method of ascertaining the wishes of the staff of the B.B.C. and if the dictatorial character of the Director-General

(Continued on back page)

MR. Leslie John Alexander, of Leyton, found hanged after learning that his six-year-old daughter Pat (seen with him), had only a short time to live.
Pat is in hospital and doctors are to operate again in the hope of saving her life. There is now one chance in a hundred that she will live. See page 8.

### Patient's Gift to Princess

A LITTLE girl patient at Queen's Hospital for Children, Hackney-road, London, yesterday gave the Duke of York a large purple and yellow pansy in a pot decorated with a coloured cloth and blue silk ribbon.
Asked whom it was for she said firmly: "Princess Elizabeth."
"It is lovely, isn't it?" remarked the Duke as he handed the pot to his equerry.
The Duke, who presided at the annual meeting of the Court of Governors of the hospital, spent several minutes studying an oxygen chamber in which a baby suffering from bronchial pneumonia had been lying for ten days.
He remarked jokingly: "I should not like to be put in there. Suppose someone turned off the gas?"

### MILLIONAIRE'S WIFE HIDDEN IN LINER

MRS. Hazel Draper, wife of a Boston (Mass.) millionaire textile manufacturer, for whom the Cunard-White Star liner Georgic was searched without avail at New York, was found yesterday when the vessel was in the Channel.

A member of the crew said that she was in the tank room on the promenade deck.
Mrs. Draper was believed to have sailed from New York in the Georgic, though her name did not appear on the passenger list, and she was not found among the passengers. It is understood that Captain Townley had received a wireless message to search the ship.
There was a check-up of passengers soon after the liner left New York and before the vessel reached Southampton, and the captain replied that no one answering the description was on board.

#### Note at Hotel

This led to fears that Mrs. Draper, who left a note at her New York hotel saying that she intended sailing in the Georgic, might have been lost overboard.
A cable was sent to her husband last night reporting her safe arrival. It is believed that she accompanied friends to London.
Money is to be forwarded for Mrs. Draper's return to America. Meanwhile she is to be looked after by the American Consul in London.

### WIFE WANTED UNAMBITIOUS BUS CONDUCTOR TO "IMPROVE"

BY A SPECIAL CORRESPONDENT

DURING intervals of punching tickets, a tall, handsome London bus conductor told me yesterday why his marriage has been unsuccessful.

He was Mr. George Frederick Price, of Manor-road, Mitcham, Surrey. Earlier Wimbledon magistrates decided that he must pay his wife £1 a week on a maintenance order.

"I suppose it's just another of those cases of incompatibility of temperament," he said. "We have been married since 1924, and three years ago we decided that it was best to part. I must abide by the magistrates' decision.

"In court I said that my wife had a great opinion of herself. I still maintain that, but I do not want to enter into details which are painful to both of us."

Asked about a letter which his wife stated she had sent him from South Africa, suggesting how he might improve his position, Mr. Price said: "I don't remember receiving that letter; at any rate I did not read it."

His wife, Mrs. Ida Lilian Price, a smartly-dressed woman in evidence at the Court, said:—

"I am not ashamed of my husband's occupation. What I blame him for is that he refuses to accept opportunities to improve his position."

Mrs. Price said to me last night:—
"I am terribly fond of my husband.
"Actually, he comes from a noble English family—titled—and his present position is due entirely to the war, which changed everything.
"We have been married thirteen years. It was his terrible life as a bus conductor which ruined our marriage.
"I still want my husband. I am fond of him and would sacrifice anything—even at this stage—for a reunion."

### NAVY JUMPS TO IT!

Fast workers on Whale Island, Portsmouth. The Navy can show the Army something when it comes to gun drill. Competition was keen in this field gun contest and display, preliminary to Royal Tournament.

THE DAILY MIRROR, Monday, May 4, 1936.

Broadcasting - Page 24

# Daily Mirror

THE DAILY PICTURE NEWSPAPER WITH THE LARGEST NET SALE

EUSTACE - - - - - - P. 9
QUIET CORNER - - - 16
DOCTOR'S DIARY - - 19
NEW 5-DAY SERIAL 22
DOROTHY DIX - - - - 26
BELINDA - - - - - - 26

No. 10,116  Registered at the G.P.O. as a Newspaper.   MONDAY, MAY 4, 1936   One Penny

Amusements : Page 25

# EMPEROR A 'PRISONER' IN FRENCH HANDS

## Under Guard for Own Safety— London Doctor Shot in Addis Looting

Haile Selassie, Emperor of Abyssinia, Conquering Lion of the Tribe of Judah, the Elect of God, King of the Kings of Ethiopia, is a "prisoner" in the hands of the French Governor in Djibouti (French Somaliland).

HE reached there yesterday, fleeing from his country. He wanted to leave at once for Geneva to whip up support for his cause. But the French Government decided that it would be better if he remained in Djibouti.

It is felt that if he went to Geneva he would present his case so dramatically and movingly that the smaller nations—probably fearing for their own future—would support him, and that this would lead to grave international complications.

Ostensibly, therefore, he is a "guest under guard." But he cannot bid his hosts good-bye.

The British Government is prepared to offer him a sanctuary— if the French will let him go. The French view is that "legal difficulties" have arisen.

The Emperor himself was prepared for the emergency. He owns a fine house in Prince's-gate, in the West End of London. The deeds were signed not long ago on his behalf by Dr. Martin, the Abyssinian Minister in London.

Off the port of Djibouti lies H.M.S. Diana. She is Britain's only link with official Addis Ababa. Her wireless still transmits to and receives messages from the capital of Abyssinia.

The Diana's steam is up, and she is ready to take the Emperor on board—when France permits.

But Haile Selassie has not abdicated. He has just "handed over the reigns of office to his Ministers." The Ministers, however, have fled. He remains King, even at Djibouti.

Three hundred miles behind him is his capital . . . burning . . . a shambles of corpses.

Five miles out on the hills watchers in the British Legation saw, as the sun sank, a cloud of dust. It was the vanguard of the Italians, conquerors of the Lion of Judah.

They were hastening because the French Legation, besieged by Abyssinians, had wirelessed an SOS to Paris for help.

M. Flandin telephoned to Mussolini "Troops have been told to occupy the city as soon as possible," replied the Duce.

They will enter a heap of ruins. The Palace, all the shops, the public buildings, had blazed all day.

Abyssinians, determined to leave nothing for

(Continued on back page)

*Haile Selassie.*

*Dr. A. J. M. Melly.*

## SOS HE DID NOT SEND

### Captain Heard It on the Radio in His Cabin

FROM OUR OWN CORRESPONDENT
LIVERPOOL, Sunday.

WHILE his ship, the Rushpool, was making a record passage across the Atlantic to Liverpool Captain J. E. Jackson, sitting in his cabin listening to the wireless from Daventry, was astounded to hear the announcement that the Rushpool was reported to be in distress.

This was revealed when the Rushpool, a West Hartlepool steamer, arrived here to-night from New Orleans, U.S.A.

Captain Jackson said: "It flabbergasted me when I heard that we were supposed to be in distress. We were making a record passage in fine weather.

"I wirelessed my owners telling them that we were all right, and then tried to find the source of the information saying that we were in distress.

"We are thirty hours ahead of our time after experiencing a wonderful passage for this time of the year.

"We received the SOS from the St. Quentin, another British boat, but there were other boats nearer to her than us."

## Guard Chases His Train for Two Miles

FRANTICALLY waving his lantern, and with perspiration pouring from his brow, a guard stumbled up the slope on to Leytonstone (Essex) L.M.S. Station last night.

He had missed the train at Wanstead Park, and run nearly two miles along the line to catch up with it.

Excursionists from Southend witnessed the harassed guard's arrival.

### Cause of Delay

For more than twenty minutes the 8.30 train to St. Pancras had stood at Leytonstone station. Passengers alighted to see what was wrong. Then the cause of the delay hove in sight.

Owing to the exceptional length of the train several coaches had been left beyond the platform at Wanstead Park and the guard gave the signal for the driver to pull on a short distance.

But, mistaking the signal, the driver proceeded on his way, hotly pursued by the guard.

## 'REDS' FRENCH ELECTION GAINS

FROM OUR OWN CORRESPONDENT
PARIS, Sunday.

GENERAL election results made known to-night indicate a wholesale defeat of Ministers, ex-Ministers and well-known M.P.s.

The Radical Socialists (the equivalent of Liberals in England), chief supporters of the present Government, have been routed. Big gains have been registered by Communists.

Paris and its suburbs have a majority of Red members, and even respectable Cannes has sent a Red M.P. to the Chamber.

The parties are: Left, 376; Right and Centre, 238. Eighty-one Communists were returned.

## GIRL DESCENDS 400 ft. CLIFF FOR A WAGER

Miss Doreen Moorfoot, a sixteen-year-old Queensgate (Bridlington) girl, having climbing gear fixed to her by an expert before descending the 400ft. Bempton Cliffs and obtaining two guillemot's eggs.

It was the first descent made this year and was done for a wager. Miss Moorfoot wore an ordinary walking costume with a steel helmet to protect her from falling stones.

She told the "Daily Mirror": "I was wagered a cocker spaniel puppy that I would not go over the cliffs and get some eggs. I was nervous when the climbing gear and ropes were being put on me.

"I became rather nervous when I was going up, for I suddenly swung away from the cliff face and then back into it."

See also page 16.

## GRETA GARBO HAS BROKEN HER SILENCE

FROM OUR OWN CORRESPONDENT
NEW YORK, Sunday.

BREAKING her own rule by granting me an interview when she arrived here to-day from Sweden on board the Gripsholm, Greta Garbo registered many strange emotions and waved her hands dramatically, but did not say, "Ay tank ay go home."

Devoid of make-up and looking very pale, she registered mild horror at being interviewed.

"My next picture will be 'Camille,'" she said, and laughed mysteriously. As to rumours that she may appear on the stage, she said she could not, being too nervous.

"Have you bought a home in Sweden?" I asked. "Home!" she exclaimed. "I am just a wanderer."

THE DAILY MIRROR, Thursday, May 7, 1936.

# Daily Mirror

THE DAILY PICTURE NEWSPAPER WITH THE LARGEST NET SALE

Broadcasting · Pages 22 & 23

EUSTACE ...... P. 9
QUIET CORNER ... 16
DOCTOR'S DIARY .. 19
5-DAY SERIAL .... 21
DOROTHY DIX .... 26
BELINDA ....... 26

No. 10,119 registered at the GPO as a Newspaper. THURSDAY, MAY 7, 1936 One Penny

Amusements: Page 8

## 'CRAZY' STORMS FLOOD MANY TOWNS

### Lightning Kills Man in Heat Wave

**By A SPECIAL CORRESPONDENT**

TOWNS were flooded, rain lashed at window panes, hailstones—"as big as marbles"—fell, motorists were marooned and traffic was stopped in roads that were like rivers when great storms burst over Britain yesterday

Accompanied by vivid flashes of lightning and claps of thunder, tons and tons of rain fell in all parts of the country while the thermometer hovered round the seventies.

It was the hottest heat wave—and the craziest—this year.
A man was killed by lightning at Dagenham—George Bennett, sixty-five, of Station-road.

**GIRL RESCUED**

A cloudburst over Dunstable, Beds, flooded the streets to a depth of several feet. At the height of the storm a girl cyclist was rescued just in time from drowning when she fainted and fell into the deep flood waters of Watling-street, the main street in the town

She collapsed while cycling home, and Inspector Weedon, of the Beds County Police, saved her by plunging in the water and grasping her clothes.

At the Saracen's Head Hotel in the centre of the town three valuable fox terriers belonging to Mr. J. Hunt were drowned when the yard was flooded to a depth of more than 5ft.

Hailstones an inch in diameter smashed windows and skylights, and many shops and private houses were flooded. Drivers of motor-cars had to climb on to the roofs of their vehicles and await rescue by lorries.

A landslide on the L.M.S. branch line between Leighton Buzzard and Dunstable stopped the evening train service between the two towns. Workpeople were taken from Dunstable to Leighton Buzzard by bus.

Lightning cut off an overhead electricity supply in Leighton Buzzard for half an hour. The traffic lights at cross-roads were put out of action.

A garage was struck in St. Mary's-lane, Upminster. The lightning exploded the electric light bulbs.

Two houses were struck in St. John's-road, Walthamstow; five in the Dagenham district, one of which caught fire.

At Sittingbourne, half of the townspeople looked out of their homes to see the rain pouring down in the streets, while the other half were blessing the sun!

### THE KING WALKS IN SAVOY HILL

The King strolling yesterday afternoon up Savoy Hill off the Strand to the Savoy Chapel. It was an unprepared visit. Yet, as may be seen, he was quickly recognised.

Earlier in the day he had carried out a ceremony as formal as this was informal, inspecting the Irish Guards. Picture on page 5.

### He Forgot His Wife— She Died

LILLE, Wednesday.

A FRENCH butcher who "forgot" his wife, is in hospital here to-day suffering from injuries and shock.

Maurice Cartigny was returning from Donai when his car skidded on a bridge and plunged into the canal.

Rescuers got him out of the car, and in answer to their questions, he said he was alone in the car. Later he burst out: "I forgot, my wife was with me."

People hurried back to the car and found his wife drowned.—Exchange.

### Riddle of 2 Neighbours

FOR the second time in six days police are searching for a Chatham man who has mysteriously disappeared.

And—the homes of the two men are next door to each other in Hillcrest-road, Chatham.

One disappearance, which took place last Friday, has already had a tragic sequel in the discovery of the body of John Charles Kidwell master painter and decorator, by the river at Borstal, near Rochester on Sunday night.

The second man is Frederick William Salmon, aged about thirty-seven, an assistant clerk to the County Justices at Chatham.

A fellow clerk of his, Mr. E. T. Vaisler, said that apparently the last anyone heard of Mr Salmon was on Monday night.

Mr. F. W. Salmon

## CRIPPLE TRAVELS ROUND THE WORLD TO LISTEN TO OPERA

**By A SPECIAL CORRESPONDENT**

SHORTLY before the start of last night's opera at Covent Garden, London, a young man in a grey flannel suit elbowed his way through the crowded foyer. In his arms he carried a pale thin young man dressed in a dinner jacket.

Slowly he made his way with his human burden to a seat in the stalls, where he settled him comfortably and left him.

The man who was carried into the opera was a twenty-five-year-old American from Cincinnati. His name is Mr. L. B. McCallay.

His father is a wealthy American mill owner.

When he was at Yale University he had to have an operation which left him unable to walk.

Always his great passion in life has been opera, and now he spends his life travelling round the world listening to opera to every performance of which he has to be carried by a friend.

He has come to England for the Covent Garden season, and after that he is off to Germany to hear the performances at Bayreuth, the famous opera house dedicated to Wagner

### FAMOUS STORE CLOSING

Glave's the well-known New Oxford-street, W., drapery store, is to close.

After next Saturday only the restaurant, which is to be continued, will remain as a reminder of a concern founded by the late Henry Glave in 1847.

Most of the staff have received a week's notice; many of them are veterans of long service

### SLANDER AWARD ENDS A YEAR'S 'NIGHTMARE'

"THANK God it is all over"
That was the remark of Mrs Figgins, wife of Mr. Frederick James Figgins, builder, of Pilley, near Lymington, Hants, when she heard that her husband, a former churchwarden, had won his slander action against the Rev. Ivone Kirkpatrick Jones, vicar of Boldre.

Judgment for Mr. Figgins for £535 damages and costs was entered in the King's Bench Division yesterday

Stay of execution was granted pending possible appeal.

Mr. Figgins alleged that the vicar had used words imputing that Mr. Figgins was a rogue and a thief who had stolen money from the church restoration box.

The defence was a plea of justification and privilege.

"The past twelve months has been a nightmare," said Mrs. Figgins to the *Daily Mirror*.

"My husband has got a clear name; my children can hold their heads up, and that is all I want."

Court judgment on page 7

THE DAILY MIRROR, Friday, May 8, 1936

# Daily Mirror

**THE DAILY PICTURE NEWSPAPER WITH THE LARGEST NET SALE**

Broadcasting - Pages 22 & 23

EUSTACE- - - - - - - P. 9
DOCTOR'S DIARY - - 10
QUIET CORNER - - - - 14
SERIAL - - - - - - - - 21
DOROTHY DIX - - - - 26
BELINDA - - - - - - - - 26

No. 10,120 Registered at the G.P.O. as a Newspaper

FRIDAY, MAY 8, 1936

One Penny

Amusements: Pages 24 and 25

## CIDER TASTERS AT OVER SEVENTY

**The Best Ever . . .**

. . . was Mr. R. T. B. Kerslake's verdict at yesterday's cider-tasting at Long Ashton, near Bristol. He's seventy-four and should know.

**New Zealand Judge . . .**

. . . was Mr. A. J. West, who at seventy-eight came over from his 4,000-acre sheep farm to give his verdict. He got a good laugh, too.

# ROYAL OCULIST FOR BLIND BOXER

## Twin Children He Has Never Seen

BY A SPECIAL CORRESPONDENT

SIR Stewart Duke-Elder, the Royal Oculist, is to try to restore the sight of a poor, blind coloured boxer.

All boxing devotees knew Dixie Brown. He was eight years welter-weight champion of the West of England.

The sight of one eye went; he still fought. Gradually the other eye began to fail.

Now Mr. George Charles, for that is Dixie Brown's name in private life, is totally blind.

A Bristol sportsman, hearing of his plight, has now come to his aid, and has engaged Sir Stewart Duke-Elder to perform an operation. It will take place at St. George's Hospital, W., on Wednesday.

### Wife's Prayers

At their little home in Bristol, Charles's wife is praying that the operation will be successful, so that her husband may once more be able to see her and his six children. Two of his children, twins—a boy and a girl—Charles has not yet seen. They were born shortly after he lost his sight.

Charles, a handsome, well-built man, looked a pathetic figure when I saw him at St. George's Hospital. But he has not lost heart.

His white teeth flashed as he greeted me with a smile.

"Call me 'Dixie,'" he said. "Ah was known as Dixie Brown when ah was fighting. Ah sure feel strange being called Mr. Charles."

Then Charles told me the tragic story of the last few years.

"For seven years," he said, "Ah was fighting while Ah was blind in one eye. Only my

(Continued on back page)

### Film Director Wins Enticement Case

THE wife-enticement suit, brought by Mr. Edward Charles Rickard, of East Molesey, Surrey, against Mr. Norman Lee, the film director, failed in the King's Bench Division yesterday, judgment, with costs, being entered for Mr. Lee. (See page 9.)

Dixie Brown, in St. George's Hospital, smiles with delight at hope of having his sight restored.

## This Motorist Had Never Seen Traffic Lights or Used 'Phone!

BY A SPECIAL CORRESPONDENT

TRAFFIC lights? Highway Code? Jumping the red? Racing the amber? It's all news to me." Mr. Frank Lewis, a farmer in the little village of Willesey, near Sherston, Wilts, was speaking. He had the shock of his peaceful life yesterday when he was summoned at Chippenham for driving a motor-car without due care and attention.

And so did the magistrates. Mr. Lewis told them—London motorists please note—that HE HAD NEVER SEEN OR HEARD OF TRAFFIC LIGHTS!

Farmer Lewis also told them that he had been driving for twelve years. He was fined £1 and ordered to pay 18s. 6d. costs.

It was stated that he drove against the traffic lights at Chippenham and knocked a boy off a bicycle.

Sir John Gladstone, the chairman, told Mr. Lewis to have a good look at the Highway Code before he went on any more motor trips.

### 'Phone Talk by "Proxy"

It was difficult to tell Mr. Lewis how surprised everyone was to find that someone in our traffic-lighted, beacon-lined, pedestrian-crossed land had never been confronted with the colours of our robot traffic controls.

For Mr. Lewis, it seems, has never spoken on the telephone. "I ought to know, because when I telephoned to a neighbour last night to ask him to speak to me, my neighbour friend had to act as 'interpreter.'

It was a sort of interview by proxy. "No, he's not deaf," I was told, "only he has never spoken on the telephone before."

"Is it true about never having seen the traffic lights?" I asked.

Back came the answer: "Quite right. Never knew anything about it."

"Has Mr. Lewis ever been to London?"

"Not once."

"Would he like to drive in London?"

"He says: 'No thank you very much.'"

## CHILD SEES HIS SISTER KILLED

### Inseparable Playmates

BY A SPECIAL CORRESPONDENT

A NINE-YEAR-OLD boy, Michael Fox, was waiting for his twin sister, Eunice, outside his home at Brixton Hill, S.W., when he saw her knocked down and killed.

She was returning from the open-air school at six o'clock last night, and as she jumped off the tram, she was struck by a lorry.

Michael and his sister were inseparable, his mother told me.

"Eunice had ginger hair and hazel eyes. She was a happy child, though her whole life had been a long struggle for good health.

"She had had many operations, and no end of money had been spent on specialists.

"In the last month her health improved marvellously, and she enjoyed playing with the other children in the yard.

"Michael was devoted to her, and used to wait for her to come home every evening. The two shared each other's toys.

"When Michael saw the accident, he ran straight indoors, too overcome to say a word."

Eunice's other brother, Peter, aged seven, was nearby at the time of the accident.

Picture on back page.

## GROWING FEELING SANCTIONS SHOULD END

BY OUR POLITICAL CORRESPONDENT

NOW that the Italians have occupied the Abyssinian capital there is a growing feeling in political circles that the sanctions against Italy should be withdrawn.

Most of the 100 M.P.s who attended the Foreign Affairs Committee meeting at the House of Commons yesterday favoured this course, in support of which Mr. L. S. Amery and Mr. H. G. Williams spoke strongly.

Other members urged the reopening of conversations with Italy.

The general feeling of the meeting was that something must be done to reform the League.

In political circles importance is attached to the visit of Mr. Attlee, Leader of the Socialist Opposition, to Paris during the week-end.

He will meet leaders of the new French Socialist Government, and will discuss, among other things, the League's future and the French Government's line of policy.

The Opposition Liberals tabled a resolution in the House of Commons last night urging the Government to take the lead at Geneva in advocating the maintenance and intensification of sanctions "until a settlement is reached in accordance with the principles of the Covenant."

THE DAILY MIRROR, Thursday, May 14, 1936.

# Daily Mirror

THE DAILY PICTURE NEWSPAPER WITH THE LARGEST NET SALE

Broadcasting - Pages 24 & 25

EUSTACE ........ P.10
CALENDAR OF FATE 17
QUIET CORNER ... 18
5-DAY SERIAL ... 23
BELINDA ........ 30
RUGGLES ........ 32

No. 10,125  Registered at the G.P.O. as a Newspaper.   THURSDAY, MAY 14, 1936   One Penny

Amusements: Page 26

## THE HOUSE AT THE SEASIDE BOUGHT FOR MR. J. H. THOMAS

Front view. Mr. J. H. Thomas's house, Milberry, at Ferring-on-Sea, Sussex, which Mr. Alfred Bates stated yesterday he had bought for him in part-payment of his autobiography.

## FLAMING DANCER FIRES NIGHT CLUB

### 4 Killed in Panic Battle for Door

FROM OUR OWN CORRESPONDENT
NEW YORK, Wednesday.

GAY movements of a beautiful torch dancer ended in an inferno of flames with four dead and twelve injured in a San Francisco night club early to-day.

Laughter was transformed in a moment into screams of terror when one of two lighted torches carried by the dancer set fire to the decorations.

With her flimsy clothing alight, Peggy Blossom, the dancer, swirled through the hall as though in a mad dance of death, while in a wild panic the crowd rushed for the only exit.

Jo Dickenson, heroic little cloakroom girl, tried to calm the mob, but she was in their path and she was trampled to death in the mad rush.

Later, fighting their way into the smoke-filled club, firemen found the bodies of another woman and two men who had been suffocated.

The terror befell just when the most sensational item of the club's entertainment came on at 2 a.m.

A number of beautiful semi-nude girls clad only in gossamer-like dresses entered and danced their way round the club bearing torches, while the lights were put out.

According to the club manager, Miss Blossom was swirling torches which had been dipped in benzine when a diner tried to grasp one to light a cigarette.

There was a struggle round the torch. Peggy Blossom's skirt caught fire and her falling torch set fire to a table.

Miss Blossom ran screaming from the building, and passers-by outside extinguished her blazing clothing.

### Clawing Women

No one thought of turning on the lights and the flames spread rapidly to the curtains and rugs in the room.

Men and women in evening dress fought their way to the only exit, a small door through which only one person could pass at a time.

In their rush to escape men and women clawed and fought each other. The inside of the club was like an inferno, with more than fifty persons screaming and fighting to a flaming background.

Firemen, who dashed to the blaze, found three members of the orchestra huddled in an ice-box, where they had taken refuge.

The scene is now a pile of burned wood and twisted steelwork.

"I regard this as criminal," said Police-Inspector Dullia, after viewing the hall. "There was only one exit and all the windows were boarded up."

## BUDGET INQUIRY

## A RECEIPT FOR £15,000

### Mr. Thomas's Letter

BY A SPECIAL CORRESPONDENT

DRAMA came suddenly yesterday amid the rustling of papers, the monotonous tones of counsel and the slightly stuffy atmosphere of the Law Courts in the Budget leakage inquiry.

Into the witness-box there had stepped again Mr. Alfred Bates, the man who had insured heavily against a rise in the income tax.

His new evidence was that he had bought the life story of Mr. J. H. Thomas, the Colonial Secretary, for £20,000 when he retired, and had bought a house and cottage for £15,100 for Mr. Thomas as a set-off against this payment.

The even tones of counsel were heard reading the letters that had passed.

"My Dear Jim, . . ." It was Mr. Bates's letter confirming a conversation. "I am prepared to give you £20,000 for the exclusive literary rights of your life . . ." The letter went into details.

Then Mr. Thomas's reply.

"Dear Alf . . . I do not want you to think you have been too generous. . . . Many people have made offers to me of very substantial sums . . . you would be prepared to make an advance at once. . . . If you can get the house in your district. . . ."

There were some more questions on other matters, then Mr. Justice Porter, who is presiding at the inquiry, was asking Mr. Bates:

"Of the £20,000, you have paid something over three-quarters without any security. . . . Mr. Thomas might die to-morrow."

Mr. J. H. Thomas will give evidence to-day.

**Full report of the inquiry, pages 4 and 5.**

### SHIRLEY'S DOG VANISHES

SHIRLEY Temple's dearest friend, Corky, a Scotch terrier, has vanished.
Film stars joined police in the search.
"Shirley cried herself to sleep," said Mrs. Temple.

## WASP IN CAR— FAMILY IN RIVER

WHILE admiring the countryside round Winterbourne Abbas as they motored through Dorset, Mr. Mackay, a Londoner, and his wife heard a scream from the back seat of their car.

"O-o-o . . . A WASP!" one of their three children was shouting.

Mr. Mackay turned round in his seat, and the car, a baby saloon, ran off the road, over a little bridge into the river.

The car landed on its wheels. Mr. Mackay, his wife and the three children in the back seats, scrambled safely out.

While the others were wringing the water from their clothes, Mr. Mackay stood on the bank of the river, supervising the salvage of his car by men from a neighbouring garage.

And that was not all.

As soon as adjustments had been made and the car was in running order again, Mr. Mackay collected the family—and away they went to Devon.

This time they had the car windows CLOSED.

## WONDER CURES OF SCIATICA
—DOCTOR'S CLAIM

### New Hope for Thousands

BY A SPECIAL CORRESPONDENT

SCIATICA can now be cured, "almost immediately," by an inexpensive treatment, which has been successfully tried.

This consoling news for thousands of sufferers was given yesterday in an address by Dr. Gerald Slot to the International Congress of Physical Medicine in London.

"A cure is often effected overnight," the doctor claimed, adding that successful results had been obtained in twenty-three of the twenty-four cases treated at the Royal Waterloo Hospital, London, S.E.

The treatment, he explained, was painless and without risk.

First was a carefully made diagnosis, including X-ray examination. Next the patient was

(Continued on back page)

## BRITAIN WATCHES GIANT ZEPP

THOUSANDS watched the Hindenburg, Germany's giant Zeppelin, speed low over Britain last night after her record crossing of the North Atlantic.

After passing over the south coast of the Irish Free State in glorious sunshine, at 10.30 she was seen over Gloucester.

Crowds ran into the streets from cinemas to watch the airship.

Villagers north of Oxford, rushing from their beds, saw the monster immediately overhead.

The Hindenburg passed over Chelmsford just after midnight.

Dr. Eckener was hoping to reach Frankfurt-on-Main at 5 a.m. to-day.

THE DAILY MIRROR, Monday, May 18, 1936.

Broadcasting - Pages 24 & 25

# Daily Mirror

THE DAILY PICTURE NEWSPAPER WITH THE LARGEST NET SALE

**£100 IN PRIZES**
See Page 27

No. 10,128 Registered at the G.P.O as a Newspaper    MONDAY, MAY 18, 1936    One Penny

Amusements: Pages 18 and 24

# CLOUDBURST, FOG AND LIGHTNING

## Will-o'-the-Wisp Storm in South

### CLOUDBURST CAUSES A ROAD HOLD-UP

BY A SPECIAL CORRESPONDENT

WILL-O'-THE-WISP weather played pranks on the country round London last night.

**After the hottest Sunday in the year**

CLOUDBURST struck West Wycombe (Bucks), flooding the main London-Oxford road to a depth of 4ft., drenching motorists and holding up traffic for an hour;

LIGHTNING struck houses in Clapton and thunderstorms broke over several suburbs while their neighbours basked in sunshine;

FOG blotted out patches of South London and Surrey.

So fierce was the cloudburst at West Wycombe that tons of earth and rock were washed down from the hills and from the cutting through which the road runs, blocking it.

From Piddington to West Wycombe the water rushed downhill carrying rocks and small trees with it, and sweeping in its trail chickens and small pigs from a nearby farm.

Motorists were stranded and had to leave their cars. Others, caught as they sat, were drenched before they knew what was happening.

### Householders Had to Bale

In the only street of West Wycombe, which was recently taken over by the National Trust as a model English village, water rose to a depth of four feet, and householders feverishly baled out for more than an hour.

Rocks and earth were strewn in the ground floors of many houses.

High Wycombe—two miles away—had little or no rain.

The perversity of the thunderstorm was shown at Hampstead, N.W., where it broke heavily, while at Finchley, only two miles away, the sun shone brightly.

### Fuse Explodes

At Raynes Park, S.W., heavy rain flooded several roads, there was vivid lightning and the thunder roared, but at Wimbledon, S.W., little more than a mile away, there was light rain, and the thunder merely growled.

In Central London there was the threat of a big storm, but eventually light showers fell—and that was all.

Along the Portsmouth Road hundreds of cyclists were soaked to the skin by a rainstorm, and the bluebells hanging from their handlebars were sadly bedraggled.

Following a loud crash of thunder, two houses in Springfield, Clapton, E., were found to have been struck by lightning.

The main electric light fuse exploded, and the lights were thrown into darkness. Mrs. H. G. Clark, the occupant of one of the

(Continued on back page)

A long line of motor-cars brought to a halt on the main Oxford road when it was flooded by yesterday's cloudburst.

Wading waist-deep to the rescue of livestock on a farm flooded by the cloudburst at West Wycombe.

## TREE CAUGHT MAN 150ft. ABOVE RAVINE

### Held Until Rescued

AN unknown solitary climber fell 50ft. down Gimmer Cragg, which stands over 2,000ft. high, in the Langdale Valley, Westmorland, yesterday.

Members of the Preston Mountaineering Club saw his falling body; they saw it hit, and remain in, an ash tree; and they clambered with a stretcher to his aid.

They found him unconscious in the tree. Beneath the tree was a drop of 150ft.—and certain death.

A seventy-year-old doctor, Dr. George Johnson, of Ambleside, climbed up the fell side to apply first aid, and a stretcher party led by Mr. H. Grisdale carried the injured man to the New Dungeon Ghyll Hotel.

In the pocket of the climber, who arrived in the valley by cycle, was a slip bearing a Blackburn name.

## Oil-Blinded, but Landed 'Plane

ALTHOUGH he was almost blinded by hot oil which spurted in his face from a burst pipe, the pilot of a Flying Flea landed his machine safely in a field near Lympne yesterday.

He was Mr. Claude Oscroft, and he left the Aero Eight Flying Club, near Southend, with the intention of making a double Channel crossing.

Mr. Oscroft, on his return to his home at Ashingdon, said to the Daily Mirror:

"A burst feed pipe was the trouble.

"My goggles were smothered with oil, and I could barely see. When landing, I struck a wire fence, damaging both wings."

## SIGHTSEERS' DAMAGE AT £15,000 SEASIDE HOME OF MR. J. H. THOMAS

PART of the fence of Millbury House, the £15,000 Ferring-on-Sea home of Mr. J. H. Thomas, in Sussex, which was mentioned last week before the Budget Leakage Tribunal was broken down by sightseers yesterday.

The only reward the visitors gained was a view of lovely flowers in full bloom and carefully-tended lawns.

No one was in residence, and four men, guarding the approaches to the house, politely requested visitors to "move on."

Motorists and pedestrians approached the main entrance, up a private road; others peered through the gate leading from the grounds to the beach.

The custodians said they had received instructions that no one was to go in.

## BURNED UNDERGRAD: WATCH CLUE

REMAINS of the wristlet watch worn by Mr. Thomas Patteson Moss, the Oxford undergraduate whose charred body was discovered early on Friday between two blazing hayricks at Ascot Park Farm, eight miles from Oxford, were found by police searching the debris yesterday.

The watch had stopped at 2.10 a.m. The face was damaged and discoloured. The time at which the watch stopped is regarded as important by the police as it narrows down the period of inquiry into one of three hours twenty minutes.

House-to-house inquiries are being made.

THE DAILY MIRROR, Tuesday, May 19, 1936

# Daily Mirror

**THE DAILY PICTURE NEWSPAPER WITH THE LARGEST NET SALE**

Broadcasting - Pages 22 & 23

**£100 IN PRIZES**
See Page 14

No. 10,129 — Registered at the G.P.O as a Newspaper. — TUESDAY, MAY 19, 1936 — One Penny

Amusements: Page 22

# ITALIANS ARREST A BRITON IN ABYSSINIA

## Sick Man on Way to Hospital

### DISPATCHES MYSTERY

TWO startling Abyssinian developments involving Britain were revealed last night.

A diplomatic bag addressed to the British Consulate at Djibouti, in French Somaliland, has disappeared from the train between Addis Ababa and Djibouti.

Italian military authorities at Diredawa arrested a sick member of the British Ambulance unit—a Londoner—on his way to hospital—a delay which may endanger his life.

When the diplomatic bag was dispatched, it is stated, the Consul at Djibouti was warned by telegram to meet the train.

He did so, but when the train arrived the bag was not forthcoming and it has not since been discovered.

The arrested Briton is Mr. Bonner, a warrant officer attached to the British Ambulance Unit in Abyssinia.

Mr. Bonner was being rushed to Aden for treatment when he was prevented from catching the train at Diredawa on the Djibouti-Addis Ababa railway, by the military authorities.

Later he was arrested, and it is feared, says Reuter, that the delay may endanger his life.

### Worked with Dr. Melly

Mr. Bonner, who is reported to be suffering from rabies, left London with the first ambulance unit and worked with the late Dr. Melly in Ethiopia.

A member of the British Red Cross in London said last night:—

"Mr. Bonner was one of the orderlies with the first ambulance unit. He was being sent to Aden, suffering, I am told, from rabies. It is inferred that he had been bitten by a dog."

Another message from Djibouti states that the first train of deportees from Addis Ababa arrived there last night.

The travellers reported that 300 more Europeans are to be expelled.

## "NOT FAIR PLAY," SAYS PRELATE

A COMPLAINT that he believed he had not had "what you English call fair play," was made by the dismissed Archbishop of Rouen, Monsignor de la Villerabel yesterday.

This is the first time the Archbishop has broken his silence since his dismissal.

The Archbishop, who is tall and of commanding appearance, despite his seventy years, received Reuter's correspondent in his palace, where he is living with only one old faithful servant.

"I have had many letters of sympathy," declared the Archbishop, "including several from England.

"I feel convinced that the head of the Church, in coming to his decision, was not in possession of the facts."

### COME TO DADDY!

The warm weather gave her the chance to have her first bathe of the season. Hence this leap into her father's arms at Surbiton Lagoon.

## LIGHTNING FLASH KILLS ATHLETE

### Hottest Day of the Year

GUILDFORD police are investigating the death of a prominent Surrey athlete, whose body was found in a wood at Shere, near Guildford yesterday, by an old woman picking bluebells.

He had apparently been sheltering under a tree in Sunday night's storm and is believed to have been struck by lightning.

There is nothing to account for a large bruise found on the man's neck, and a post-mortem examination is to be held.

The man is Robert Crombie, aged twenty-five, commercial artist, of Figges-road, Mitcham, a member of Mitcham Athletic Club, and the Inter-county A.A. long-jump champion.

Crombie set out from home on Sunday morning with members of the club.

His sister, Miss J. Crombie, told a *Daily Mirror* reporter last night:

"My brother had been out several times before with the same party. They usually split up in twos on reaching their destination, but this time my brother was alone, as his friend was unable to go."

A fire, believed to have been started by the heat of the sun, yesterday destroyed the factory of Messrs. W. Diggins, piano part manufacturers, of Tottenhall-road, Edmonton, N.

R. Crombie.

The May heat wave is more than holding its own.

Yesterday was the hottest day of the year at Kew, where the temperature reached 75 deg.

The thermometer at the Air Ministry showed 74 deg.—the same as on May 6. Britain's hottest spots were Brighton, Bath and Cheltenham, where it was 79 deg.

A breeze is expected to keep the temperature a little lower to-day, and thundery showers are expected in the Midlands.

## NO SECRET TIMES FOR EXECUTIONS

THERE are to be no secret execution times in Britain.

In the House of Commons yesterday Mr. G. Lloyd (Under-Secretary at the Home Office), answering Mr. Bernays, who asked what steps it was proposed to take to prevent demonstrations outside prisons on the morning of an execution, said the power to regulate public meetings was limited to such steps as were necessary to preserve order and prevent obstructions.

Mr. Bernays: Is he not of opinion that these demonstrations would be avoided if the time and place of the executions were not announced beforehand?

Mr. Lloyd: No, sir, because it is necessary that the time and place of execution should be communicated to a considerable number of persons. It is our view that in these circumstances it is impracticable to secure secrecy.

### 'VARSITIES AID RECRUITING

Universities and colleges are co-operating with the War Office, which is taking steps to make further provision for the supply of officers to the technical branches of the Army, by forming new technical units in the senior division of the Officers' Training Corps.

An Army Service Corps unit with an establishment of 100 cadets is being formed in the University of London contingent and steps are being taken to form a unit for the training of ordnance mechanical engineers.

## Club-Foot Boxer Fights Ex-Champion

### RICK DEATH: SCOTLAND YARD AID

Thomas Patteson Moss, twenty-four-year-old Balliol (Oxford) undergraduate whose charred body was found beside two blazing hayricks at Stadhampton. Scotland Yard have been called in to assist Oxfordshire police. See story on page 3.

at work on the buses for seventeen hours on Sunday.

Arrived in London at 5 a.m. yesterday.

Beaten on points at the Stadium Club in a boxing match with Johnny Walters, the ex-amateur feather-weight champion, despite his handicap of a club foot.

THAT was the hectic start of the week for Al Capone, the West Hartlepool boxer.

Capone quickly showed that he is a plucky boxer. He happened to find Walters at the top of his form, and both men gave a clever display.

When the verdict of a win on points for Walters was announced there was equal applause for the winner and gallant loser.

52

# Daily Mirror

THE DAILY PICTURE NEWSPAPER WITH THE LARGEST NET SALE

Broadcasting-Page 20

EUSTACE------P. 9
QUIET CORNER----14
SERIAL---------21
BELINDA--------22
CALENDAR OF FATE 24
RUGGLES--------24

No. 10,133 Registered at the G.P.O as a Newspaper. SATURDAY, MAY 23, 1936 One Penny

Amusements: Page 20

# MR. THOMAS ON WHY HE RESIGNED

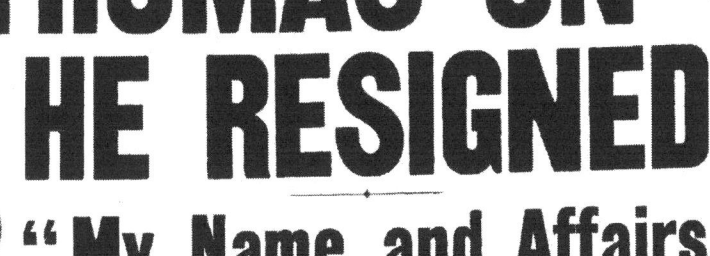

## "My Name and Affairs Have Been Bandied About"

Mr. J. H. Thomas.

MR. J. H. THOMAS, THE SECRETARY FOR THE COLONIES, RESIGNED HIS SEAT IN THE CABINET LAST EVENING. HIS RESIGNATION HAS BEEN ACCEPTED.

IN a letter to the Premier, Mr. Thomas said: "The way in which my name and affairs have been bandied about renders my continuation in the Government impossible. . . . I feel that instead of being a source of strength . . . . I shall be a drag."

The announcement was made from 10, Downing-street with the issue of the following letters:—

Colonial Office, May 20
My dear Prime Minister,
"I understand that the Tribunal has to-day finished its public sittings and will, therefore, proceed at once to consider its report.
"Before, however, the report is known, and without any regard to what it may contain, I feel that it is my duty, from reasons which I will state, to send you my resignation from the Government.
"You will be aware that immediately the announcement of the appointment of the Tribunal was made known, I wrote to the secretary and offered to give evidence before it.

### "PUBLIC PROPERTY"

"This I have done, and my evidence is public property. In addition to my evidence, all my private and personal transactions have been submitted to the Tribunal.
"I have come to my decision because the way in which my name and private affairs have been bandied about renders my continuation as a member of the Government impossible.
"You will know that my only object in joining the National Government was because I felt sure that the coming together of all political parties—regardless of past difficulties—was the only chance of pulling this country through its crisis.
"To-day I hold that opinion even more firmly than before, but as far as I myself am concerned I feel that instead of being a source of strength to your Cabinet I shall merely be a drag on it, and not in a position to pull my full weight.
"This will be inconsistent with my desire to serve my country which—I hope my past public life justifies me in saying—has always been my object.
"I ought, in fairness to all parties in the House of Commons, to emphasise that I feel no resentment at this demand for a full and impartial investigation, inasmuch as the absolute integrity of public life in this country was involved.
"It is well known that I have no political difficulties with my colleagues or with the policy of the National Government.
"I am fully conscious of the grave and diffi-

### HIS FUTURE

IT is probable, writes our Parliamentary Correspondent, that Mr. Thomas will choose to abandon politics and devote himself to literary work in the seclusion of his Sussex home. He is sixty-one.

cult problems—changing almost hourly—which have to be faced by the Cabinet and, in coming to this decision which means so much to me, I can only wish to you and all my late colleagues God-speed in leading the nation out of its present difficulties.
Yours very sincerely,
J. H. THOMAS."
Mr. Baldwin replied to Mr. Thomas's letter as follows:—

10, Downing-street, May 21.
"My dear Jim,—You have acted as I should have done in your place. I accept your resignation with deep regret, which I know will be shared by all my colleagues.
"The loyal support you have given through five strenuous years to the National Government will be always remembered by those who worked with you.
"With all good wishes, I am,
Very sincerely yours,
Stanley Baldwin.
(Mr. Thomas's Career: Page Five; Cabinet Reshuffle: Page Three.)

MR. J. H. THOMAS STAYED LAST NIGHT AT THE HOUSE OF HIS FRIEND, MR. BATES, IN FERRING-ON-SEA, SUSSEX. TELEPHONES A "DAILY MIRROR" SPECIAL CORRESPONDENT.

## FLOWERS FOR A GRAVE DROPPED FROM AIRSHIP

WATCHERS gasped as the giant Zeppelin Hindenburg, looming out of the dusk over the hills on the Lancashire border, dipped very low near the centre of Keighley, Yorks, last night.

Then, at the feet of two boys, gaping open-mouthed, there dropped from the airship a neatly-wrapped parcel. In it they found:—

A spray of freshly gathered carnations, a crucifix, a letter, a picture of a flying boat and some specimens of the Hindenburg souvenir stamp.

The letter, written on the official notepaper of the Hindenburg, read: "Mai 22, 1936. To the finder of this letter, please deposit these flowers on the cross on the grave of my dear brother, Lieut. Franz Schultz, 1 Garde Regiment. Prisoner of war in Skipton cemitary in Keighley, near Leeds
"Many thanks for your kindness, Johann P. Schultz, the first flying priest."

### "God Bless You"

Then followed the address—Aachen, Lotsfringenstrasze 62, Germany.
A postscript read:—
"Please accept the stamps and the pictures as a small souvenir from me. God bless you. The first holy man on the Hindenburg, 9 Mai, 1936."

The boys were taken by car to Morton Banks Cemetery, and in the fading light picked out the name of Lieutenant Schultz on the bronze tablet which is on the German memorial
The flowers were on the grave within an hour of leaving the airship.

**Tumbler and Juggler . . .**

. . . at Surbiton yesterday. C. E. Malfroy falling in his match with H. L. de Morpurgo. Above, Senorita Anita Lizana's racket flies out of her hand as she was being beaten by Dorothy Round.

THE DAILY MIRROR, Wednesday May 27, 1936.

Broadcasting—Page 21

# Daily Mirror

THE DAILY PICTURE NEWSPAPER WITH THE LARGEST NET SALE

£100 IN PRIZES: See Page 23

No. 10,136 Registered at the G.P.O as a Newspaper. WEDNESDAY, MAY 27, 1936 One Penny

Amusements : Page 16

## They're Off!—The Derby 3p.m. : The Queen Mary 4.15p.m.

# SENSATIONAL BACKING PUTS BOSWELL 8-1

## Pay Up the New Favourite

TWENTY-TWO horses will go to the starting-gate for the Derby this afternoon.

Sensational backing for Boswell—much of it money from America—has brought that colt down to 8 to 1. A fortnight ago he was a 35 to 1 chance.

And Gordon Richards will **not** be on the favourite if to-day's betting follows on the lines of the final call-over last night.

Pay Up—Guineas winner and Bouverie's choice—again headed the market as he did after his success in the first classic. His price is 6 to 1.

The best illustration of how intricate is the Derby puzzle this year is the fact that it is possible to back the first five favourites on a level stake and be a winner should any of them score.

A £1 stake on each of them would mean a profit of £2 on Pay Up; over £3 on Taj Akbar or Noble King; £4 on Boswell; and £8 10s on Bala Hissar.

Pay Up, Bouverie's selection.

The Hon. Mrs. David Baker.

## PEER'S SISTER DIES —HER TWINS LIVE

### Tragedy 18 Hours After Birth

THE Hon. Mrs. Eileen Sybil Mary Nelson Baker, beautiful sister of Lord Bridport, died in a West End nursing home last night, eighteen hours after she had given birth to twins.

The twins—a boy and a girl—are both doing well.

From the time her babies were born until she died she struggled pluckily to live.

Doctors and nurses unsuccessfully used all the skill of modern science to save her.

Mrs. Baker who was twenty-six, married Mr. David Lawrence Baker, of Church Farm, Minety, Wiltshire, three years ago after a romantic chase from London to Southampton.

Miss Hood, as she then was, had arranged to travel to Malta to see her brother, who was serving with the Fleet abroad.

Mr. Baker caught an express train to Southampton, found Miss Hood at an hotel, proposed, was accepted, and got her luggage off the boat.

A second romance followed the marriage. Lord Bridport, then serving in the Navy on board H.M.S. Nelson, was unable to be present at his sister's wedding, but when he returned to London he met Mr. Baker's sister, Pamela, who had been a bridesmaid.

They fell in love and were married a year later.

## RUNNERS AND JOCKEYS
(Race run at Epsom, 1½ miles 5 yards)

| | | |
|---|---|---|
| 2210 | ABJER (M. Boussac) .................. | C. Elliott |
| | (orange, grey cap) | |
| 1001 | BALA HISSAR (Aga Khan) .................. | R. Jones |
| | (green and chocolate hoops, chocolate cap) | |
| 011 | BARRYSTAR (Mr. Shenstone) .................. | J. Marshall |
| | (scarlet, royal blue belt, white cap) | |
| | BEL AETHEL (Duke of Norfolk) .................. | S. Donoghue |
| | (sky blue, sky blue and quartered cap) | |
| 3140 | BOSWELL (Mr. W. Woodward) .................. | P. Beasley |
| | (purple, cream sash, quartered cap) | |
| 0302 | CARIOCA (Maharajah of Rajpipla) .................. | A. Wragg |
| | (white, red spots, black cap) | |
| 010 | COUVERT (Mr Elsgrave) .................. | M. Beary |
| | (maroon and light blue hoops, maroon cap) | |
| 0032 | FEARLESS FOX (Mr. Gordon Smith) .................. | E. Smith |
| | (green, gold seal back and front, gold sleeves, tartan cap) | |
| 0001 | HAULTRYN (Mr. F. Minoprio) .................. | Lane |
| | (blue, white collar and cuffs, white cap and hood) | |
| 4003 | HIS GRACE (Lord Carnarvon) .................. | H. Wragg |
| | (scarlet, blue collar, white cap) | |
| 2012 | MAGNET (Lord Hirst) .................. | B. Carslake |
| | (Oxford blue, yellow stars, yellow cap) | |
| 1302 | MAHMOUD (Aga Khan) .................. | C. Smirke |
| | (green and chocolate hoops, chocolate cap) | |
| 4000 | MENDICANT FRIAR (Sir A. Bailey) .................. | T. Weston |
| | (black and gold hoops, gold cap) | |
| 1410 | MIDSTREAM (Mr. A. de Rothschild) .................. | F. Fox |
| | (dark blue, yellow cap) | |
| 311 | NOBLE KING (Sir A. Butt) .................. | R. Perryman |
| | (yellow, graduated blue hoops, blue cap) | |
| 2111 | PAY UP (Lord Astor) .................. | R. Dick |
| | (light blue, pink sash and cap) | |
| 0010 | RAEBURN (Mr. Hollingsworth) .................. | J. Sirett |
| | (crimson, silver braid) | |
| 2400 | SPINALOT (Mr. Ramsden) .................. | H. Jelliss |
| | (royal blue and white hoops, white cap) | |
| 0020 | SQUADRON CASTLE (Mrs. P. Ahern) .................. | Dines |
| | (sea green, mauve collar and cuffs, quartered cap) | |
| 3211 | TAJ AKBAR (Aga Khan) .................. | G. Richards |
| | (green and chocolate hoops, chocolate cap) | |
| 0032 | THANKERTON (Mrs. Shand) .................. | T. Burns |
| | (lavender and white stripes, white sleeves and cap) | |
| 3200 | WALVIS BAY (Major Courtauld) .................. | T. Lowrey |
| | (primrose, light blue striped sleeves, primrose cap) | |

## FAIR WEATHER FOR TO-DAY'S BIG THRILLS

DERBY Day—and the Queen Mary's day—will be fine, say the experts.

The Air Ministry gave this forecast last night for to-day's Epsom weather:—Light northerly winds, cloudy at first, becoming fair.

And here is "God speed" weather at Southampton:—Light north-easterly winds; bright periods, local mist in the morning.

## HERE IS THE LATEST BETTING

| | | | | |
|---|---|---|---|---|
| 6-1 | Pay Up | | 33-1 | Couvert |
| 100-14 | Taj Akbar | | 35-1 | His Grace |
| 15-2 | Noble King | | 40-1 | Raeburn |
| 8-1 | Boswell | | 40-1 | Fearless Fox |
| 100-8 | Bala Hissar | | 45-1 | Bel Aethel |
| 100-7 | Mahmoud | | 45-1 | Magnet |
| 25-1 | Barrystar | | 55-1 | Haultryn |
| 28-1 | Carioca | | 66-1 | Walvis Bay |
| 28-1 | Abjer | | 100-1 | Mendicant Friar |
| 28-1 | Thankerton | | 100-1 | Squadron Castle |
| 28-1 | Midstream | | 100-1 | Spinalot |

## DRAMA STAGED IN A GRASS RING

### By BOUVERIE

Who last year gave the Derby first and second—Bahram (5 to 4), Robin Goodfellow (50-1).

ADJOINING the judge's box at Epsom is a small enclosure packed full of racing history.

Inside is accommodation for three horses. On the right, looking from the course, is a ring carpeted with grass—the "place appointed for the unsaddling of the winner."

On the left are two stalls, marked "second" and "third." No grass there to be nibbled. The horses to occupy them are led in to face a wall, giving the impression of two naughty children.

Soon after three o'clock to-day three horses will walk through the iron gate, one to the right with his name newly written on the scroll of Derby winners—the others to be forgotten almost as quickly as the also rans that have been dismounted on the course.

Which will prove the "big three" to-day and how will they divide once inside?

Even these few hours before the race it is by no means certain what will start favourite. Never, surely, has a Derby crowd gone to Epsom without at least that knowledge.

Thousands will go to Epsom to-day fully convinced that it is Gordon's year. Tens of thousands more will listen-in fully anticipating the magic words "Taj Akbar wins".

(Continued on page 26)

Tips from the Pin's Point ...... Page 3
The £ s. d. of It ............... Page 10
Pictures ........................ Page 15
Listeners' Derby Plan ........... Page 17

THE DAILY MIRROR, Thursday, May 28, 1936

Broadcasting - Pages 22 & 23

# Daily Mirror

THE DAILY PICTURE NEWSPAPER WITH THE LARGEST NET SALE

EUSTACE - - - - - - - P. 9
SERIAL - - - - - - - - 21
CALENDAR OF FATE 25
BELINDA - - - - - - - - 26
RUGGLES - - - - - - 28

No. 10,137  Registered at the G.P.O as a Newspaper   THURSDAY, MAY 28, 1936   One Penny

Amusements: Page 18

# J. H. THOMAS SPEAKS

## Exclusive Talk to 'Daily Mirror'

### "BROKEN-HEARTED"

FROM OUR SPECIAL CORRESPONDENT

SOMEWHERE IN DEVON, Wednesday.

**What was the inquiry about? To find out what they could about Jim Thomas!"**

THIS sensational statement was made to me to-night by Mr. J. H. Thomas. He made it with many emphatic gestures, and labouring under deep emotion.

I found him at an hotel on the edge of a famous golf links. He is staying there with a few friends and members of his family. These include his wife and his son-in-law, Mr. Robert Fearnley Whittingstall.

To avoid undue publicity there appears in the register the entry: "Mr. R. Fearnley Whittingstall and party."

"I am a broken-hearted man," said Mr. Thomas.

I could well believe him, for the former Colonial Secretary was a shadow of his former jovial self.

"I have been in public life for forty-five years," he said, "and now they do this. It is shattering, and enough to break up anyone. You cannot blame me if I feel bitter."

Mr. Thomas indicated that he did not intend to make any full statement until the finding of the tribunal had been made public.

"Then," he said, "I may speak my mind. Now I am here to have a quiet holiday."

Mr. Thomas spoke of what he termed "persecution" of members of his family.

"There is my son Leslie," he said. "He is an innocent victim who has been put in the pillory. What has he done? You have heard that he has resigned from his firm. He is being hounded from public life, and he has had to resign from a town council where he was doing useful work."

Mr. Thomas and his party arrived at the hotel last night. This morning Mr. Thomas played a round of golf, rested in the hotel garden after luncheon, and later played another round of golf. After dinner he and his party settled down in the private sitting-room to play a game of bridge.

The hotel in which Mr. Thomas is staying has few guests, though, with the advent of the Whitsun holidays, there is likely to be a crowd of visitors there. It is the intention of Mr. Thomas and his party to stay at this hotel until the middle of next week.

### Furnishing Mr. Thomas's £15,000 Home

FROM OUR OWN CORRESPONDENT

WORTHING, Wednesday.

TWO large furniture vans drove yesterday into the grounds of Millbury House, Mr. J. H. Thomas's new £15,000 home at Ferring, which was bought for him by Mr. Alfred Bates in payment for the first rights of his autobiography.

The decorating of the house is now finished, and furniture is being put into the west wing.

Curtains could be seen in many of the windows for the first time yesterday.

I understand that no plans have yet been made for Mr. Thomas to take up residence.

### BON VOYAGE!

Full steam ahead! The liner Queen Mary, which left Southampton on her maiden voyage yesterday, out in the open sea speeding towards the West.

Mr. J. H. Thomas.

### PROCLAIMING THE CORONATION

PROCLAMATION at St. James's Palace of the King's coronation will be broadcast to-morrow in the National programme at 9.50 a.m.

The proclamation will take place at Temple Bar, Charing Cross, the Royal Exchange and St. James's Palace.

Thoroughfares to be closed to road traffic from 9.30 a.m. or 9.15 a.m. include:—

Aldwych; Approach-road, Temple; Arundel-street, Chandos-street, Charing Cross, Constitution Hill, Cockspur-street, Duncannon-street, Horse Guards approach road (north of Horse Guards Parade), King William-street, Kingsway (south of Great Queen-street), Marlborough Gate and Marlborough Yard,

Norfolk-street, Northumberland-avenue, Pall Mall East, Queen's Gardens, Spur-road (St. James's Park), Stamford-street, Strand, Surrey-street, The Mall, Trafalgar-square, Waterloo-road, Whitehall (north of Horse Guards-avenue), Whitehall-court, Whitehall-place.

Fleet-street, Ludgate-hill, St. Paul's Churchyard (south and east sides), Cheapside, Poultry, Mansion House-street, Cornhill, Threadneedle-street, Queen Victoria-street.

## THE QUEEN MARY MAKES MIDNIGHT MYSTERY STOP

There was a mystery pause in the Queen Mary's progress early to-day. Reaching Cherbourg at 8.50 last night—four hours and twenty minutes after casting off at Southampton—she left again early to-day to face the Atlantic rollers. Outside the harbour she unexpectedly stopped. No reason for the delay was given, but it was rumoured that she had dragged her anchors. Then, at 1.30, after nearly an hour's wait, came the flash: "She's off again."

BY A SPECIAL CORRESPONDENT

On board the Queen Mary,
Thursday Morning.

HER sailing from Southampton was an historic event which the King himself has signalised in a message to the Commander—"All good wishes to you for a successful maiden voyage—(Signed) Edward R.I."

Half a million voices on the shores swelled by fog horn and siren in the tribute of the seas gave the Queen Mary to-day the mightiest send-off a liner has ever known, and found an echo in the hearts of millions of listeners the world over who heard the scene broadcast.

The enthusiasm of the watchers found an answering thrill in the crowds clustered like flies at the rails. Only one man was calm in all that great throng—Sir Edgar Britten on the bridge, the man on whom 2,000 souls depend.

Overhead snarled a score of aeroplanes, a hundred sirens shivered the air, the band played "Rule Britannia" and, just as it always seems to do on great occasions, the sun threw back the clouds to reveal the liner in all her glory.

As we headed out for the Channel in the sunlight it was a spectacle of sheer beauty no showman could have better devised—a moment worthy of a big place in history.

### More Thrills on Board

With the cheers of our countrymen dying in our ears, the passengers recuperated among teacups and cocktails in the lounges and bars before retiring to our cabins to unpack. But our excitement was not yet ended.

At 6 o'clock, when the ship was leaving Cowes Roads, the stewards and stewardesses sounded the alarm for boat-drill.

Each of us dashed for our boat station. Lifebelts were adjusted over morning coats, lounge suits and fashionable summer frocks, while officers gave brief lectures on the correct behaviour in emergencies.

Duty over, we could turn to the beauties of

(Continued on back page)

THE DAILY MIRROR, Saturday, May 30, 1936.

# Daily Mirror

**THE DAILY PICTURE NEWSPAPER WITH THE LARGEST NET SALE**

Broadcasting - Pages 20 & 21

EUSTACE ......... P. 9
SERIAL ............ 21
CALENDAR OF FATE 25
BELINDA .......... 26
RUGGLES .......... 28

No. 10,139  Registered at the G.P.O as a newspaper    SATURDAY, MAY 30, 1936    One Penny

Amusements: Page 20

## SAVED BABY FROM LION

### Mother Sweeps Child to Safety in Dash from Escaped Beast

By A SPECIAL CORRESPONDENT

Clutching her three-year-old child in her arms, a woman holidaymaker fled terror-stricken before an escaped lioness among the uneven sandhills at Skegness yesterday.

THE lioness escaped from her cage at an amusement park and roamed the beach and dunes for an hour before she could be "arrested."

Several family picnicking parties broke up in confusion as it ran along the sandhills.

On her travels the lioness leapt on to the beach between two wooden sheds—to land within a few feet of where Patricia Sayles was playing in the sand.

#### "I Was Terrified"

"I was writing when I saw the lioness leap on to the beach in our direction," Mrs. I. Sayles, Patricia's mother, told me last night.

"Picking Patricia up, I fled across the sandhills, and each time I stumbled I was terrified. The ground was very bumpy, and as I scrambled away several men, also running away, overtook me and rushed on.

"I didn't stop until, exhausted, I got into the garden of the house where I am staying, and from there I saw the lioness still careering about."

Mrs. Sayles's home is at Manor-road, South Wingfield, Derby. Her husband is to join her for the rest of the holiday at Skegness.

#### Sitting on Verandah

Again in the course of her "outing" the lioness entered a beach cafe.

Mr. Brueton, the manager, told me: "I was wondering what all the excitement was about, and then I saw the cause of it.

"There was that lion, sitting calm and dignified on MY verandah! All my staff had fled. Customers locked themselves behind doors in the restaurant.

"Then some men from the amusement park, which was being made ready for the Whitsun holidays, cornered the lion, and took it back to a cage."

## MAN OF 69 SUED FOR BREACH BY WIDOW OF 39

A WIDOWER of sixty-nine is sued by a widow of thirty-nine in a breach of promise action which was mentioned in the Court of Session at Edinburgh yesterday.

Plaintiff is Mrs. Elizabeth Rae Bathgate, or Keast, of High-street, Montrose. She sues John Milne, retired farmer, of Lossie Bank, Montrose, for payment of £1,000.

Through her membership of the Old Church, Montrose, plaintiff says she made the acquaintance of Milne. In 1935 he proposed marriage and was accepted.

A few days later she was given a diamond engagement ring. They intended to be married in September, but the marriage was postponed, and in December last it was agreed that the marriage should take place in the first week of February.

They parted at that time on friendly and affectionate terms. The following day they met at the public library, Montrose, and Milne told her that their engagement was ended and that he did not intend to marry her.

Milne says that the proposal and acceptance were conditional.

He asked the plaintiff to marry him provided that his daughter was willing to leave his house and could get another home. The plaintiff, he said, agreed to this condition, stating that on no account would she marry him if his daughter was to remain in the house

During the second half of 1935 she adopted an increasingly overbearing attitude towards him.

Owing to her domineering character and readiness to take offence and interference with his business, he says, it was evident that it would be a mistake for them to marry.

The case has been sent to the procedure roll for debate.

## MAN WHO WAS ONCE A GIRL

**With His Girl Friend**

Mr. Mark Weston, who, before having two operations recently, was known as Mary Weston, walking at Oreston, his home near Plymouth, with Miss Alberta Bray, who for years has been his particular friend.

## Aged Woman Trapped at Window for 15 Hours

FOR fifteen hours a woman of seventy-five was suspended from the window of her flat, her hands caught in the window sash and her feet only partially resting on a pair of steps.

All through the night, unable to move, she cried for help, but her voice was too feeble to attract attention and, as the blind was partially drawn, she could not be seen from the street.

Not until another occupant of the house found that the woman's milk and newspapers had not been taken in was it suspected that anything was amiss.

Then a constable, finding the door locked from the inside, entered by removing a panel. The woman, whose hands were severely injured, was taken to hospital, where she died from blood poisoning.

She was Miss Emma Cardinal, of Carisbrook-road, St. Leonards, and the story was told at the inquest at Hastings last evening.

The constable told how he found Miss Cardinal in a fainting condition and how her hands were trapped when he released her.

In a very feeble voice she informed him that the previous evening, some fourteen or fifteen hours earlier, the sash slipped and caught her hands.

Death by misadventure was the verdict.

### GOLD MEDAL FOR AMY

In recognition of her many Empire flights, the Royal Aero Club last night awarded its gold medal to Mrs. Amy Mollison.

## The Queen Mary SMASHES 3 RECORDS

### Normandie's New Speed Challenge

THREE records have already been captured by the Queen Mary on her first full day's noon-to-noon run. They are:—

1. She did 747 miles, as against the Normandie's 744.
2. She did considerably more than the Normandie's 31.3 knots.
3. She averaged 29.88 knots for the day's run, against the Normandie's 29.76.

The French Line announced yesterday (according to the British United Press from New York) that in future the Normandie will cross the Atlantic in ten hours less than previous normal crossings.

In New York this is considered as an admission by the owners of the French liner that the Queen Mary will capture the record.

The general conviction seems to be that the Queen Mary could reach New York to-morrow evening instead of on Monday.

The Queen Mary cabled to New York yesterday for a fresh supply of picture postcards. Twenty-five thousand cards of the liner had been taken on board, but nearly all of them were sold yesterday.

One cable to the commander from a friend in New York (says Reuter) read:—"If you don't do thirty-five, don't come."

### Stowaway's Own Story

A stowaway was discovered after the ship sailed. His name is Frank Gardener, aged forty-one, of Taft street, Merthyr Vale, Glam.

"It all happened on the spur of the moment," he declared.

"I was standing on the docks at Southampton, where I was working as a navvy.

"I had not had regular work for seven years, and I was sick of it.

"Suddenly I thought, Why not try America? I took off my coat and went aboard in my shirt sleeves among the firemen. On Wednesday evening I had a good meal in the firemen's mess and went amidships.

"About ten o'clock on Thursday night hunger drove me to the firemen's quarters. Then someone spotted me and handed me over

"The cook in the third class kitchens gave me a good meal. Now I am working in the kitchen

### VICTORY AHEAD

By BASIL D. NICHOLSON
(Our Special Correspondent on board the Queen Mary)

FRIDAY NIGHT

WE are heading effortlessly towards the victory of a record crossing.

The engines have still plenty of power in hand, and our day's speed of 29.88 knots was achieved without a trace of vibration.

Thirty-four knots is said to have been maintained for some three hours last night, but the captain will neither confirm nor deny this.

A bet of £236 by a woman on the number 747 last night was rewarded with £837 to-day.

Shortly after the announcement of the day's run furious barking broke out in the kennels between a setter and a Bedlington. Gambling is suspected!

The weather is fine, the sea calm, and the outlook good.

A record in the volume of ship to shore calls has been set up.

Operators have had to work thirty-six hours at a stretch, and calls to New York have been delayed up to twelve hours.

# Daily Mirror

**THE DAILY PICTURE NEWSPAPER WITH THE LARGEST NET SALE**

Broadcasting - Page 20

£100 IN PRIZES FOR THE STORY OF YOUR ROMANCE SEE PAGE 10

No. 10,141  Registered at the G.P.O. as a newspaper.   TUESDAY, JUNE 2, 1936   One Penny

Amusements : Page 20

# THE QUEEN MARY DOCKS SAFELY

## Million Cheer Her in New York

TO the accompaniment of wild cheers from a million throats, of screaming sirens from scores of ships, of the pealing of bells and of the zooming of a hundred 'planes, the Queen Mary docked in New York just after 4 p.m. yesterday, four days, thirteen hours and twenty-three minutes after she left Cherbourg.

The Queen Mary took exactly twenty-five minutes to dock. There were no mishaps, but there was one anxious moment when a tug rammed her bows against the liner and nearly capsized.

The liner had failed by eighty-eight miles and 2h. 32m. to beat the record run of the Normandie, when it seemed that she had the record in her grasp.

Save for that eleven hours of fog she would have been three hours ahead.

But her run from Southampton to the Ambrose Lightship is a record for any ship—107h. 33m.

Her average speed for the record route was 29.133 knots. The Normandie's speed on her record trip was 29.68 knots. But at one stage of her trip the Queen Mary travelled faster than ever merchant ship has gone before.

Unprecedented scenes marked her arrival. As she passed the Ambrose Light and stood-by for the pilot.

Mr. Grover Whalen, former Mayor of New York, flew over her and broadcast the city's official greetings, on behalf of Mayor La Guardia.

### GREETING FROM THE AIR

Sir Edgar Britten, the Queen Mary's commander, replied from the bridge: "We deeply appreciate this official welcome by aeroplanes, yachts and all other craft from the port of New York."

The harbour presented an extraordinary sight.

From dawn scores of yachts and sight-seeing craft had wended their way down the stream.

They formed a lane miles long—like Henley Regatta day with the punts transformed into big craft.

Other liners from all over the world en—
(Continued on back page)

Miss Joan MacDonald, the dead girl, competing at Guildford Horse Show last month. She was second in the novices' jumping event.

## SHE RODE FOR HER FRIEND—AND WAS KILLED IN THE RACE

SEVENTEEN-YEAR-OLD Joan Macdonald took the place of a friend in a race at a holiday gymkhana at Witley Park, Surrey, yesterday—and was thrown and killed before a crowd of 3,000 people.

Her parents, Mr. and Mrs. H. Macdonald of Green Street Green, Farnborough, Kent, were present, and saw the horrified spectators rushing to the spot where the girl had fallen.

When they reached the tent to which their daughter was carried, they found she was dead.

The gymkhana was held at the country estate of Sir John Leigh. Mr. K. G. Poland, chairman of the gymkhana committee, told the *Daily Mirror*.

"Miss Macdonald was riding in place of a friend in the Victoria Cross race, in which the competitors have to take a flight of hurdles, pick up a dummy, and return to the winning post.

"At the second fence she appeared to slip out of the saddle and was thrown about twenty feet, on to her head.

"Ambulance men rushed to the spot, and Miss MacDonald was carried on a stretcher to a tent.

"Two doctors who were called found that she was dead.

"The rest of the gymkhana was cancelled."

Afterwards officials broadcast through loudspeakers an appeal for witnesses who were close to the hurdle where Miss MacDonald fell.

Miss MacDonald was a high school girl. All her leisure she spent riding her favourite pony in the Farnborough district.

### EX-PREMIER ARRESTED

SOFIA, Monday.
A former Prime Minister of Bulgaria, Alexander Tsankoff has been arrested, accused of anti-Government activities.—Reuter.

## ACTRESS DROPS DEAD ON THE STAGE

### Playing in Revue with Husband

FROM OUR OWN CORRESPONDENT
PORTSMOUTH, Monday.

DURING the revue "Streamline" at Portsmouth Hippodrome to-night, Connie Rhode, who was appearing with her husband Len Clifford in one of the sketches, collapsed on the stage and died.

It was announced at the fall of the curtain that she had fainted, and after a minute or so, the show proceeded, the audience being unaware of the tragedy.

Mr. Clifford and Miss Rhode were billed as "That Cheeky Pair," and were appearing together in a lovers' sketch.

"I have just bought you a diamond ring," he told her. "Are you surprised?"

"I am very excited," she replied, and fell backwards on the stage.

Clifford tried to lift his partner but failed to do so. As the curtain was lowered he was frantically rubbing her hands.

Other members of the cast and stage hands went to her assistance and Miss Rhode was taken to hospital, where she was found to be dead.

Miss Rhode celebrated her thirtieth birthday to-day.

## "Mutiny" Pamphlets for British Troops

PAMPHLETS seeking to incite mutiny among British troops stationed in Palestine are reported to have been found.

They are printed in English and signed by the "Central Committee of the Palestine Communist Party."

According to Reuter, the Mayors of Jaffa, Nablus, Ramleh, Lydda and Hebron have decided to discontinue municipal services such as the water supply, lighting and scavenging.

## ARAB RIOTERS FIRE ON BRITISH PATROL

RIOTERS in Palestine yesterday opened fire on a British military patrol, says the British United Press.

In the same district, says Reuter, rioters fired on a Jewish bus on the Jerusalem-Jaffa road. One Jewish passenger was killed.

### OWL ATTACKS P.-C.

WHILE patrolling his beat in Hornsey-lane, Highgate, London, yesterday, Police-Constable Trickett was attacked by a white owl.

The owl pecked his ear, and as a result he is now on the sick list.

It is believed the owl is responsible for the disappearance of chickens from gardens in the district.

Surrounded by tugs, speed-boats and sightseeing craft . . . the Queen Mary arriving at the quarantine station, New York. A picture taken from the air and received by wireless.

# Daily Mirror

THE DAILY PICTURE NEWSPAPER WITH THE LARGEST NET SALE

Broadcasting · Page 22

DREAM BEDROOM CONTEST WINNERS—P. 27

Amusements: Page 18

No. 10,145 Registered at the G.P.O as a newspaper. SATURDAY, JUNE 6, 1936 One Penny

# VICAR'S WHITE SLAVE WARNING TO PARENTS

## Reveals Two Cases in the Last Fortnight

IF you have a pretty daughter don't overlook the danger of white slave traffickers!

The warning is given by the Rev. George Potter, vicar of St. Chrysostom's Church, Peckham, London, S.E.

He has written an article in his parish magazine warning girls and revealing recent activities of these traffickers in London. Last night he told the "Daily Mirror," "They present a very real danger.

"Girls and their parents are apt to scoff at stories about white slave traffickers and in scoffing they lay themselves open as victims.

"I have had twenty-five years' experience in a poor London parish and I can instance more than a dozen cases in which girls have been carried off, never to be seen again."

### Favourite Methods

"The favourite methods of the traffickers are to lure girls away in motor-cars or to entice them from their homes by promises of marriage.

"Only in the last fortnight two cases have been brought to my notice.

"One girl was at the cinema with her boy. She suddenly felt faint. A well-dressed woman in the seat behind her took the girl to the ladies' room.

"The boy waited for half-an-hour and the girl did not return. He made inquiries and learned that the girl had been taken to a certain address.

"The address proved to be false and the girl has not been seen since."

### Man Was a Fraud

"In the other case the girl was going to be married to an Egyptian student. She had been enticed by nice clothes and jewellery.

"The father was suspicious. I made inquiries through the National Vigilance Association and the police learned that the man was a fraud."

Mr. Potter added that he had not the slightest doubt that scores of girls were shipped from this country to South America every year.

## SUNNY TO-DAY (OFFICIAL)

BY A SPECIAL CORRESPONDENT

OVERCOATS, umbrellas and scarves can be put away this week-end.

June weather (official) will arrive to-day and continue over the week-end, according to the Air Ministry weather experts.

Their report is: Light, variable winds, warm on Sunday. In fact, a real June day.

Temperatures showed a marked improvement yesterday afternoon. At 5 p.m. the thermometer on the roof of the Air Ministry's building in Kingsway recorded 61 degrees. Normal is 66 degrees.

## HUSBANDS BREAK STAY-IN STRIKE

### Wanted Their Wives Back— So They Fetched Them

FROM OUR OWN CORRESPONDENT

PARIS, Friday.

DISGRUNTLED husbands have given a lead to M. Blum, the French Premier—last night they broke one of the stay-in strikes.

Many wives are among the strikers in shops and offices. Last night one husband decided that this state of affairs was not good enough.

His wife was among the clerks in a railway administration office close to St. Lazare Station.

But he decided he wanted her at home, so he collected some more lonely husbands and marched around to his wife's office.

The picket on the door told him he could not take his wife away. The angry husband hit him and knocked him out.

Then he marched into the office, collected his wife and took her home.

In the confusion other wives among the strikers decided that perhaps they, too, would be better at home, and now only a handful of unmarried strikers are left in the building.

### Sleeping on Counters

With the spread of the strike to the big Paris stores, however, hundreds of girls are spending the night sleeping on the counters. There are 2,000 employees inside the Galeries Lafayette alone.

Hundreds of tourists are marooned in the Paris hotels. At the Hotel Majestic, one of the leading hotels in the city, guests had to work the lifts for themselves, tidy their own bedrooms and make their own beds.

Despite the efforts of the new Socialist Government, strikes are multiplying and slow paralysis is spreading over the country.

Last night 1,500 army mobile corps had been called out for duty at Les Halles—the Smithfield and Covent Garden combined—of Paris.

There were rumours shortly before midnight that there might be some attempt to interfere with the unloading of food supplies.

The Government at once rushed the guards to the market. They were taking no chances.

(Continued on back page)

## DIPLOMATS BOYCOTT THE EMPEROR'S RECEPTION

AMBASSADORS of France, Belgium, Poland and Brazil have declined invitations to attend the Emperor of Abyssinia's reception in London to-day.

Mr. Anthony Eden, the Foreign Secretary, will not be present owing to a previous engagement in his constituency.

He will, however, be represented by Lord Cranborne, Parliamentary Under-Secretary.

Mr. Eden paid a courtesy visit to the Emperor yesterday.

He stayed about twenty minutes. On leaving he was escorted to the door by Dr. Martin, the Abyssinian Minister.

### Sick Boy's Calls for Father Answered

A sick child and his father who had been missing for three weeks from his home at Sidney-road, Muswell Hill, London, N., will be reunited there to-day.

The father is Mr. Walter Theodore Robotham, whose five-year-old son, William, was taken seriously ill a few days after he vanished, and has been calling continually for him.

Now Mr. Robotham has been found at Brighton, and at his home a letter is waiting offering him immediate employment. He is to return to-day.

### Fearing Famine...

... as a result of the strikes in Paris, these housewives are laying in a good stock of bread.

And like women in every other country, they pause in their shopping to gossip.

## WANTS TO BE FATHER OF HIS TWENTIETH CHILD WHEN HE'S 100 YEARS OLD!

FROM OUR OWN CORRESPONDENT

NEW YORK, Friday.

"MY great ambition is to have my twentieth child when I am aged 100."

The speaker was George Isaac Hughes, aged ninety-six, whose seventeenth child was born to his wife Libby on Wednesday.

When I spoke to him to-day he and his wife, who is twenty-eight, were being overwhelmed with congratulations at their home in Newbern, North Carolina.

"I want three more children before I die," he announced in a strong voice. "Women must have children."

Hughes, who looks younger than ninety-six, married his wife Libby in 1933 after a short courtship. In December, 1934, he became father of son Franklin Roosevelt Hughes.

Of fifteen children by a previous marriage six are living. The eldest is sixty-one.

### KILLED BY CRICKET BALL

Albert Jones, aged sixteen, of Piercefield-street, Kentish Town, N.W., while playing cricket at Parliament Hill Fields last night, was struck on the head by the ball, and died on the way to hospital.

# Daily Mirror

THE DAILY PICTURE NEWSPAPER WITH THE LARGEST NET SALE

Broadcasting - Pages 22 & 23

**FELL IN LOVE WITH A VOICE** — SEE £100 ROMANCE CONTEST, PAGE 12

No. 10,149. Registered at the G.P.O. as a newspaper. THURSDAY, JUNE 11, 1936. One Penny. Amusements: Page 18

## A Miracle of Prayer

FROM OUR OWN CORRESPONDENT
Shoreham-by-Sea, Wednesday.

A SHOREHAM couple believe that they have witnessed a miracle in answer to prayers which have been offered up in Shoreham churches and and by themselves.

They are Mr. and Mrs. Lawrence Patterson, of Regina, Lower Beach-road, Shoreham. Their six-and-a-half-year-old son, Joseph, was run over by a lorry filled with bricks when on his way to school. He was rushed to Southlands Hospital with multiple injuries. A delicate emergency brain operation was performed.

*The parents were told that his life was despaired of.*

### Coincidence

Three days later an airman, suffering with similar injuries received when in a crash near Shoreham, Hugh Graham Aitchison, aged twenty-six, of Collington-grove, Bexhill, was placed in the bed next to Joseph.

During their periods of consciousness they struck up a friendship. Then the airman had a relapse.

Dr. Cairns, a brain specialist from the London Hospital in Whitechapel, where Aitchison's brother is a medical student, dashed to Shoreham.

When Aitchison recovered he pointed to the tiny, prostrate figure in the next bed and asked the specialist to take an interest in the case.

*The result was that when Aitchison was taken to the London Hospital by ambulance he was accompanied by his tiny friend. Now they are both recovering.*

### "A Miracle"

The father, Mr. Lawrence Patterson, said last night:—

"When my wife and I learned that our boy's life was despaired of we both knelt in prayer. We knew that everything was being done for him at the hospital.

"Prayers were also offered up in the churches of The Good Shepherd and St. Nicholas.

*The next we heard was that a London brain specialist had appeared as if from nowhere and had taken an interest in our boy. It has not cost us a penny.*

"My friends tell me that we are lucky. But my wife and I are convinced that this is a miracle in answer to our prayers."

## SAD BRIDESMAID FOUND DYING

FROM OUR OWN CORRESPONDENT
NEWHAVEN, Wednesday.

TWO days after being a bridesmaid at her younger sister's wedding, Miss Florence Gilbert, of Chapel-street, Newhaven, was found dying from throat wounds this afternoon.

Her employer, Mr. J. R. Akehurst, of First-avenue, Newhaven, told me that Miss Gilbert, who was about thirty-five, had served lunch at his home, afterwards returning to the kitchen.

A few minutes later he looked into the kitchen and found her dying on the floor.

She had not seemed happy about her sister's wedding.

Mr. J. Evans, of Saxon-road, Newhaven, husband of the dead woman's elder sister, described Florence as a "regular old maid." He, too, said she did not appear pleased about the marriage.

Miss Hilda Henrietta Gilbert was married at Newhaven Parish Church on Monday to Mr. Charles Lower, Jnr., only son of Mr. and Mrs. Charles Lower, of Glynde-road, Brighton.

# RESCUE SWIM AT 82

## Woman Fights River Current, Saves Her Friend's Life

SWIMMING against fierce currents, an eighty-two-year-old woman displayed amazing strength and courage in saving her girl companion from drowning in the River Hamble, near Bursledon, Hants.

She is Mrs. Mabel Constance Gaussens, of Holland-on-Sea, Essex, who, in spite of her years swims regularly.

Her prodigious feat in keeping afloat a woman many years her junior after they had been carried away down the river, was revealed last night by Mr. Frederick Evans, a Bursledon man, who saw them in distress and put out to the rescue in a rowing boat.

Mrs. Gaussens was on the verge of death when she and her companion were lifted on to the beach.

### "Amazing Feat"

For half an hour Mr. Evans applied artificial respiration and kept her alive until the arrival of a doctor.

Yesterday, at the Swan Hotel, Bursledon, both women were reported to be recovering.

The doctor who attended Mrs. Gaussens told the "Daily Mirror" last night: "She is a woman of magnificent physique for her years. It was an amazing feat. I have never heard of anything like it before."

Mr. Frederick Evans said that both women were almost unconscious when he reached them.

"Apparently," he said, "they had both been swimming strongly when the current carried them away. I reached them in the nick of time. They were both practically 'all in.'"

### On Holiday

Mrs. Gaussens had been spending a holiday on the yacht Almida, which belongs to her son, Mr. James A. C. Gaussens, of Hatfield, Hertfordshire.

"In her younger days she was a remarkable swimmer," Miss Gaussens, a niece, told the Daily Mirror.

"I knew that my aunt swam regularly until a few years ago, but I did not know she had been in the water recently. Perhaps the warm weather tempted her out. She really is a wonderful woman for her age."

*Joseph Patterson.*

## CHANCELLOR CONDEMNS SANCTIONS "MADNESS"

MR. Neville Chamberlain, Chancellor of the Exchequer, last night condemned the "madness" of continuing or intensifying sanctions against Italy.

"If we were to pursue it," he said, "it could only lead to further misfortunes."

Mr. Chamberlain was speaking at a dinner of the 1900 Club at Grosvenor House.

He referred to the action of Lord Cecil, president of the League of Nations Union, in urging a campaign with the idea that by pursuing sanctions it was still possible to preserve the independence of Abyssinia.

"That seems to me," he declared, "the very midsummer of madness."

## DR. SHANNON TO GO INTO WORKHOUSE TO-DAY

AFTER obtaining his discharge from bankruptcy yesterday Dr. Samuel Shannon, inhibited vicar of St. Luke's, Leicester, obtained an order for admission to the Public Assistance Institution, which he enters to-day.

He said that he had only sixpence left, and could not go on living on borrowed money.

## 103, AND SHE LIKES THE MODERN GIRL

FROM OUR OWN CORRESPONDENT
SITTINGBOURNE, Wednesday.

"The modern girl is all right."

THAT is the opinion of Mrs. Mary Dowler Penfold, of Bredhurst, near here, who was 103 to-day.

"A lot is said against the modern girl," she added, "but she can look after herself."

Mrs. Penfold, who attributes her longevity to "nothing in particular," is quite modern herself. She makes her own bed, does odd jobs, reads newspapers and novels—love stories for preference—and is fond of a glass of beer.

She often goes down to the village, a mile or so away. "I call in and have a drink when I am down there," she told me with a twinkle in her eye.

Mrs. Penfold now spends much of her time writing her own memoirs, and she claims that her memory goes back to the age of three.

"I officiated at the Jubilee celebrations in the village last year," she said, "and I hope to be asked to present the Coronation mugs next year."

## BABY LIKES THIS!

*A Ride for Baby..*
The Duchess of York trying out a new elastic swing bag, with baby inside, when opening the Silver Jubilee Building at the Girls' Heritage Craft Schools at Chailey, Sussex, yesterday. (Another picture on centre page.)

## ITALIANS FLY TO AID BRITISH PLANTER

WITH food and ammunition gone after a month's siege, four tea planters, one an Englishman named Henry William Harris, are holding a gang of bandits at bay among the plantations at Assala, near Lake Zwai, in Abyssinia.

Yesterday Reuter reported that in response to an urgent S O S brought in by runners, an Italian 'plane was sent out and located the farmers, but was unable to land.

Signals were exchanged and the Italians are now considering a motorised rescue expedition.

Harris is accompanied by two Dutch brothers named Lennartz, and one Czech planter named Franz, who has his wife and two children with him.

The runners report that the little stronghold had reached the end of its resources and did not expect to be able to resist much longer.

Until a rescue expedition is organised, Italian 'planes will fly over the spot frequently to frighten away the bandits.

THE DAILY MIRROR, Saturday, June 13, 1936.

# Daily Mirror

**THE DAILY PICTURE NEWSPAPER WITH THE LARGEST NET SALE**

Broadcasting – Page 20

SATURDAY MAGAZINE
—Pages 11, 12, 17 & 18

No. 10,151  Registered at the G.P.O. as a newspaper.  SATURDAY, JUNE 13, 1936  One Penny

Amusements: Page 16

## "SEND AN ARMY TO PALESTINE"

### Britain Warned by Ex-Official

"DAILY MIRROR" SPECIAL CORRESPONDENT

At least fifty battalions of soldiers are needed to quell the present Palestine riots instead of the eight battalions Britain has stationed there.

THAT was the opinion expressed to the *Daily Mirror* last night by Mr. J. F. Broadhurst, retired Chief of the Palestine C.I.D. This is the situation as he sees it:—

The anti-Jewish activity there is no longer confined to Arab ruffians but has spread to the wealthy and influential Christians;

Organised determination to prevent the continued influx of Jews is becoming intensified every day;

Arms are being carried into the country in vast quantities and frontier patrols are too small to cope with the smugglers.

Mr. Broadhurst returned to this country a year ago after thirty years' experience in the Holy Land.

His son Ronald is at present Assistant District Superintendent of Police in Nazareth, and is actively engaged in quelling the riots.

### Blood Money

Meanwhile, in Palestine twenty-nine men are hiding with a price on their heads for murder. Each is worth £500 to an informer —£14,000 in all.

Police posted the countryside with this offer last evening.

The wanted men have shot and killed P.-C. Bird, twenty-four Jews, three Arabs and an Austrian, says the British United Press.

The notice appeared after a fresh outbreak of shooting, which may cost the life of another official.

Assistant-Police-Superintendent Alan Sigrist, M.C., was shot and seriously wounded in the Garden of Gethsemane.

He and Police-Constable Doxate were returning from an inspection, when two men

(*Continued on back page*)

Mr. J. F. Broadhurst's son, Ronald, Assistant District Superintendent of Police in Nazareth, with Assistant Police Superintendent Alan Sigrist, M.C. (bareheaded), who was shot and seriously wounded in the Garden of Gethsemane.

## DEPORTED TO "CERTAIN DEATH"

FROM OUR OWN CORRESPONDENT
NEW YORK, Friday.

"I GO to certain death," said Otto Richter, a young anti-Nazi refugee, on leaving Ellis Island to be deported to Germany in the liner Western Land tomorrow.

With Richter went his American-born wife, weeping bitterly, and crying: "He will be killed. I am too young to be widowed."

Both wore placards round their necks. Richter's read, "Shoot me, for if they send me back to Hitler's Germany I will be murdered by Nazis."

They were followed to the Ellis Island boat by a procession of sympathisers, who circulated petitions for signatures in a last-moment effort to save the couple from deportation.

Richter said he was beaten by Storm Troopers on the night of the Reichstag fire, and, after hiding in Germany, escaped to America as member of a ship's crew. He has been threatened with arrest if he returns to Germany.

## QUINS IN £10,000 DAMAGES CLAIM

ALLEGED to have used the names and pictures of the Dionne quintuplets without authority, the Blossom Products Corporation, manufacturers of dolls, toys and children's clothes, is being sued by the Canadian Minister of Public Welfare.

The Minister, Mr. Croll, has filed a suit for £10,000 in the county court against the Corporation, claiming that the names and pictures of the quintuplets have been used in the promotion of the Corporation's products.

He declares that the quintuplets have the exclusive property right of their names and the "popularity phenomenon" of their birth. Anyone trading on this must pay for the privilege.—Reuter.

SUNSET LAME SOPHISTICATION

Renée de Marco wearing one of her 200 dresses. It is of sunset lamé. She says that lamés and heavy fabrics make her feel more sophisticated.

## 200 DRESSES FOR 200 MOODS

### One of Best Dressed Women in U.S. Here

BY A SPECIAL CORRESPONDENT

TWO hundred dresses—and a different mood for each—has Renee de Marco, one of the highest paid dancers in the world, who has just arrived in London.

With her husband, Antonio de Marco, she will dance at Grosvenor House, London, W., for a six-weeks' season beginning next Thursday, and during her seventy-two performances she will not wear the same frock twice.

Renee de Marco is a beautiful French Canadian brunette, and one of the three best-dressed women in the United States. She designs more than half her own dresses.

"I am intensely interested in clothes. I also brought thirty hats with me and quite fifty pairs of shoes," she told me yesterday.

"My forty trunks, though, have got me into a spot of bother with the Customs, at Southampton. They couldn't believe that I could possibly be going to wear all the clothing I brought.

"They seemed to think that I was going to set up as a modiste, and wanted me to pay duty of 43 per cent on a good deal of it."

### Her Favourite

"I told them everything was for personal wear, but they insisted on detaining a lot of my things, among them the dress I am most anxious to wear on my opening night.

"It is my favourite one—I feel happy in it—and as my mood changes with my dress I should like to face my first English audience in it.

"I feel a different person in a different frock, and as Tony and I dance just as we feel dresses are important to me.

"Chiffons make me feel light and airy, induce a certain mood, and I dance accordingly.

"Lamés, or heavy fabrics, perhaps drapes about me to bring out the lines of my figure, make me feel a little more sophisticated and influence my dancing."

## HE GAVE UP JOB ON THE QUEEN MARY TO WIN THIS BRIDE

BY A SPECIAL CORRESPONDENT

THE Queen Mary is so fast that Victor Charles Cook, aged twenty, a musician, gave up his job on her. Her speed means only a few hours at home each fortnight—and Mr. Cook is in love.

Such devotion won its reward yesterday when Eastbourne magistrates gave him permission to marry the lady of his choice, though his parents objected.

Cook lives at Upperton-gardens, Eastbourne, and his bride-to-be is Miss Hilda Evelyn Beare, of Vine-road, Shirley, Southampton.

Cook told how he had just left the Queen Mary, and said that he and Miss Beare had the offer of an engagement at a roadhouse

I called at Miss Beare's home in Southampton last night, and saw one of her two sisters. When I told her of the magistrates' decision, she said, "Oh! I am so glad!

"Neither my father nor mother nor any of the family have any objection to their marriage.

"Hoping that the Court would give their consent, Hilda and Victor had made all arrangements to get married, and notice was given to the Southampton Registrar. They will probably be married at Southampton Register Office on Tuesday.

## TORCHLIGHT SEARCH ON LAKELAND MOUNTAINS

SEARCH parties left Patterdale, Westmorland, late last night to look in the mountains for Mr. A. Lancaster, of Oaten Hill, Canterbury, who disappeared after setting out on a walk last Wednesday.

Mr. Lancaster left for Mardale. When he did not return yesterday and inquiries were made it was found that he never reached Mardale.

The only report to help the searchers was from a shepherd in Mardale Valley who thought he heard someone whistling in the hills.

Search parties, equipped with torches, were composed of shepherds and visitors.

# Daily Mirror

**THE DAILY PICTURE NEWSPAPER WITH THE LARGEST NET SALE**

Broadcasting - Pages 22 & 23

**WEEK'S WEATHER CHART** —Page 10

No. 10,156 Registered at the G.P.O as a newspaper.  FRIDAY, JUNE 19, 1936  One Penny

Amusements: Pages 24 and 25

# QUADS TO BE ON SHOW—6D. A LOOK

## Only Way to Balance Budget

### PUBLIC FUND FAILS

FROM OUR SPECIAL CORRESPONDENT
St. Neots, Thursday.

Britain's famous quads—Ann, Paul, Ernest and Michael Miles—are going to start earning their own living when they are eight months old—in three weeks.

THEY are to be put on public exhibition in the new sun nursery that is being built on to the country house, The Gables, the new home of their parents.

By paying 6d. visitors will be able to walk up a staircase on to a balcony surrounding the nursery and look through windows into the room where the quads will lie in their cots.

This course has been decided upon as the only possible way of raising the money.

So far, the bulk of the cost has been borne by Dr. Harrisson, who brought them into the world and who has been the means of keeping them alive—"one chance in ten thousand that came off through the doctor's constant care," say the experts.

It was hoped that the public would contribute by supporting a fund that was opened, but that has been a failure.

### Already Cost £2,000

The only way left of meeting the steadily rising bills for their upkeep, Dr. Harrisson thinks, is to copy the idea of the Canadian Quins and put the Quads on exhibition.

Their parents have no option but to agree. Mr. Miles is still working as a lorry driver.

He earns no more than £3 a week, and as the cost of upkeep of the new house will be heavy, apart from maintaining his wife and two-year-old son, he will be unable to contribute much towards the rearing of the Quads.

Already over £2,000 has been spent upon them. For the first few weeks of their lives they were costing £15 a day, as four nurses were engaged.

Since then, Dr. Harrisson has managed to raise £750 to buy The Gables, but he has himself had to guarantee the £450 needed to build the new sun nursery.

Even now, one nurse, Miss Murrant, will have

(Continued on back page)

## A Day with Shirley

WHAT is Shirley Temple really like? This question is answered by Reginald Whitley, the "Daily Mirror" film expert, who has just returned from Hollywood.

Turn to page 12 and read what he says about a day he spent with the charming, unprecocious little girl who, at seven years of age, is the sweetheart of the world.

## GIRL PAT IS "SIGHTED" AGAIN

### Mystery Deepens

MYSTERY OF THE GIRL PAT, TRUANT GRIMSBY TRAWLER, DEEPENED LAST NIGHT.

Two days after being reported wrecked with three white men dead on board in the Bahamas, she was "sighted" off Georgetown, British Guiana, nearly 2,000 miles away.

And her skipper, George Osborne, was reported to have been taken from Inagua, Bahamas, to Haiti in the sloop, Malake, and to be now in Jamaica.

The vessel off Georgetown, says Reuter, answered closely to the description of the Girl Pat. She anchored two miles off the town.

A seaplane flew out. The white crew on board seemed to signal for help.

A police launch then left port, but the vessel made off after claiming that her name was the Kiaora.

On Wednesday Mr. J. H. Jarrett, K.C., Colonial Secretary of the Bahama Islands, sent the chief magistrate of the Mayaguan Island to Atwood Cay, sixty miles away.

Yesterday, over the long distance telephone at Nassau, the capital of the Bahamas, Mr. Jarrett said:—

"Not having heard from Mr. Forbes, the Justice of the Peace at Mayaguana, I have now sent an aeroplane from Nassau to Atwood Cay.

"If the wreck is that of the Girl Pat I shall know within the next few hours."

## RIFLE AND GAS "WAR" ROUND U.S. FACTORY

FROM OUR OWN CORRESPONDENT
New York, Thursday.

FOURTEEN people are stated to have been shot or gassed in a fierce battle at Kent, Ohio, between pickets and strike breakers.

Eye-witnesses compared the fighting to wartime scenes in France. There was a constant crackle of rifle fire and bursting of gas bombs.

The trouble started when lorries containing forty strike breakers drove through hostile pickets into a factory yard behind a barrage of tear gas.

The women of the district are in a state of hysteria.

## "DEAD SOLDIERS" IN CARNIVAL

A tableau depicting two dead soldiers entangled in barbed wire and wearing gas masks appeared in a carnival procession at Carlisle last night.

It was entered by the Carlisle Peace Council, and caused considerable adverse comment.

### Milady in a Fix

Victorian crinoline and modern car set a problem for little bridesmaid bound for the wedding at Christ Church, Didsbury, Manchester, yesterday of Captain S. Whipp and Miss Noreen Carlyle.

## The King George—Sister Ship for the Queen Mary

THE Queen Mary, Britain's wonder liner, is to have a sister ship—and M.P.s think she will be named King George. Mr. Neville Chamberlain announced in the Commons yesterday that he had received an application from the Cunard-White Star Company for authority to use the sum available under the North Atlantic Shipping Act for the construction of a sister ship.

The Chancellor said the company had obtained preliminary tenders from various yards and he understood that, after considering them, they would negotiate in the first instance with Messrs. John Brown and Co.

The Government, however, still reserved the right to further consultation before any contract is signed.

It is believed that John Browns are practically certain to secure the contract (writes our Political Correspondent), since the stocks on which the Queen Mary was built are available, and the present ship is said to be highly satisfactory.

The order will mean work for nearly 200,000 men, in many cases for three years, and Clydeside is delighted. It is suggested that a start will be made in August.

Meanwhile the Queen Mary is making excellent progress on her second trip across the Atlantic. By noon yesterday she had covered 566 miles since leaving Cherbourg breakwater, at 5.30 a.m. on Wednesday.

## LIFE AMBITION TO KILL A GIRL

WHEN the twenty-eight-year-old son of a wealthy real estate operator confessed, according to the San Francisco police, that he strangled a girl of twenty-four and then assaulted her, he said:

"I have done everything possible to hurt women since I was fourteen. I have ruined as many as I could. An incident which occurred when I was fourteen turned me against them.

"This killing is no surprise to me. I knew that eventually I would achieve my supreme vengeance—that I would kill a woman."

The police say the man's story is that he met the girl a fortnight ago and made violent love to her, which she repulsed. Two nights ago he went to her apartment.

Again he made love to her and she rejected his advances. He then caught her by the throat and tied a silk stocking round her neck. Most of her clothes were stripped off.

Walter left the apartment and walked the streets "for twenty-four hours" before going to the police, says the British United Press.

He told the police: "I don't want a lawyer. I want to plead guilty and get it over as soon as possible." He is living apart from his wife, who, when informed of his confession, exclaimed: "Oh, what can I do to help him?"

THE DAILY MIRROR, Monday, June 22, 1936.

Broadcasting—Page 21

# Daily Mirror

THE DAILY PICTURE NEWSPAPER WITH THE LARGEST NET SALE

CLARK GABLE TALKS Page 10

No. 10,158 Registered at the G.P.O. as a newspaper.  MONDAY, JUNE 22, 1936  One Penny

Amusements: Pages 16 and 21

# 11-FT. FLOOD'S HAVOC

## Homes Ruined— Trains Held Up

### ABBEY STRUCK

LIGHTNING struck an abbey and a church, and floods, in places 11ft. deep, wrecked homes and held up crack trains in Britain's third night of tropical storms last night.

Greatest havoc was wrought in the Hadley Wood district of Middlesex, where two hours of rain falling " like a cascade " produced floods that rose to the level of station platforms and caused all north-bound trains from King's Cross to be diverted through Hertford.

A raging torrent poured from the surrounding hillsides into Hadley Wood and parts of Barnet. It swept across fields and roads, raced through the cutting in which stands Hadley Wood Station. The main L.N.E.R. line from King's Cross was blotted out for a quarter of a mile.

As the water thundered down it uprooted a lamppost on the station, tore up the platform paving and smashed down fences. Then it spread along the lines and roared through two tunnels on either side of the station, where it formed an impassable barricade.

In less than an hour the flooding in the neighbourhood was eleven feet deep.

Cottages on low ground by the side of the road were inundated. The inhabitants were cut off. They rapidly gathered their belongings and took refuge in the upper stories.

### Window Escape

The floods followed them up the stairs and had reached the top when passers-by noticed their plight and informed the fire brigade.

Escapes were quickly run up and they and their belongings carried down to safety.

Mr. W. Tillock, of East Barnet-road, said: "The brook was a raging torrent. Struggling in the water were chickens and pigeons."

In Brookhill-road, East Barnet, a family of five, Mr. and Mrs. Humphries and their three children, were marooned for three hours at the top of a house.

Firemen made a temporary bridge with their escapes to reach them and get them to safety. Afterwards the firemen returned and rescued a dog and canaries.

### Jumped Train

The 11.15 a.m. train from Edinburgh reached King's Cross nearly four hours late.

After passing Welwyn Garden City it stopped, under leaden skies, for nearly two hours.

Two girl passengers who wanted to be home punctually decided to jump the train.

In the pelting rain they climbed down on to the line with their luggage, jumped across a wide ditch, clambered with difficulty through two barbed-wire fences and, with sodden skirts and stockings struggled across a muddy, slippery field towards the road, where they caught a bus.

L.M.S. main line service was interrupted by parts of the embankment between Harpenden and St. Albans (Herts) being washed on to the line.

The storm was also very severe over St. Albans.

St. Albans Abbey was struck twice by lightning during the annual Rose Day service, attended by hundreds of children.

Children were walking through the great building to place roses at the shrine of St.

(Continued on back page)

Hadley Wood Station last night. Other flood pictures pages 17 and 28.

### MONDAY MORNING TONIC

There is always something in the news to cheer, to encourage, to rid you of the Monday morning feeling. Follow this prescription:—

IF fame still escapes you—there's always to-morrow (when the King's Birthday Honours will be published). If you're not feeling fit, read about the boy who could hardly walk five years ago and to-day is a champion sprinter. If you want something to argue about, there's England's choice of a Test team. Turn to page three.

\* \* \*

DON'T BE ENVIOUS.—You may not like your job—but how would you like to broadcast at 300 m.p.h.? On page 7 you will learn of a man who will.

\* \* \*

BE ENTERPRISING.—Let the stories of a girl (page 7) and a gardener (page 13) inspire you.

\* \* \*

FIND ENJOYMENT—by turning to the new serial, "Desire," beginning to-day on page 18.

\* \* \*

LOOK YOUR BEST.—" No one need look fat " is Margaret Curzon's message to women on page 23.

### HUGE TRAM HOLD-UP

Trams jammed in one direction from Westminster to Blackfriars and in the other from Westminster to the Elephant and Castle were seen late last night when a tram broke down in the centre of Westminster Bridge.

The hour was the peak one for homeward-bound trippers, and buses and tubes were overwhelmed. Thousands of travellers were delayed.

## TROOPS' VAIN BATTLE FOR BRITISH SERGEANT'S BODY

### Palestine Terrorists Defy Bombs in Cave

TROOPS and police fought vainly yesterday to bomb Arabs out of a cave into which they had dragged the body of Sergeant Henry Sills, Seaforth Highlanders, killed in the biggest battle since the Palestine riots started.

Eleven Arabs had been killed in the battle, which took place near Nablus, says Reuter.

### Snipers Attack Convoy

Meanwhile a private of the Scots Fusiliers was shot dead, three Britons wounded, and two Arabs killed in a major engagement in which troops, 'planes and police routed a strong force of armed rebels near Tulkarem. After an all-day fight the Arabs, hotly pursued, dashed for the shelter of their mountain caves.

Three out of the four 'planes co-operating with the military were hit by Arab bullets, but managed to land safely at Tulkarem Aerodrome.

One of the machines was hit three times in the engine. The others were struck in the wings. Before the battle terrorists had fired on a military convoy at Tulkarem.

Scaling a mountain in the dark, a party of Seaforth Highlanders rounded up and captured a gang of Arab snipers.

In the pitch dark the Seaforths deployed and clambered up the mountain-side towards the snipers' stronghold.

As they climbed they peered through the darkness to track the spots from which the flashes came.

Then, at a given signal, the party closed in and engaged the gang in battle.

### TO-DAY AT WIMBLEDON

Fred Perry, Bunny Austin and J. F. Crawford are among those who will play on the Centre Court at Wimbledon to-day. Play will begin at two, and the order of the matches is:

F. J. Perry v. G. D. Stratford, followed by B. M. Grant v. H. Henkel, P. D. B. Spence v H. W. Austin, D. Prenn v. J. F. Crawford

2 p.m., Wimbledon Zero Hour.—Page 26

THE DAILY MIRROR, Wednesday, June 24, 1936.

Broadcasting - Pages 22 & 23

# Daily Mirror
**THE DAILY PICTURE NEWSPAPER WITH THE LARGEST NET SALE**

## CLAUDETTE GRUMBLES
Page 10

Amusements : Page 16

No. 10,160 Registered at the G.P.O as a newspaper. WEDNESDAY, JUNE 24, 1936 One Penny

# MAN DIVES FROM EXPRESS TO ESCAPE ESCORT

## Caught in Tree After 6-Hour Police Hunt

FROM OUR OWN CORRESPONDENT
CARDIFF, Tuesday.

Six hours after diving through the window of a moving express train near Severn Tunnel Junction to escape from an escort of two detectives, a man was recaptured at Crick (Monmouth) at midnight.

POLICE of two counties—Monmouthshire and Gloucestershire—had joined in the search for the man amid the culverts and ditches with which this marshland is honeycombed. Several hundred civilians joined in the hunt.

Police had one clue to work on. After the escape a finger was found on the track. It was believed that it had been torn from the man in his leap for safety.

The man was Evan John Jones, of Tonypandy. While on remand at a London prison he had made a statement to the authorities in connection with the death of Stephen Gilbert, the grocer, whose body was found in his Cardiff shop on June 6.

Chief Detective-Inspector Lewis and Detective-Sergeant Bradley travelled to London to escort him back to Cardiff, so that he could make a fuller statement.

On the return journey the train pulled up after emerging from the Severn tunnel. It had just restarted as Jones, accompanied by his escort, left the lavatory. The three were walking along the corridor when the escort had to step aside to allow a woman passenger to pass. Jones jumped through an open window.

With the detectives holding him by his legs, he hung head downwards arms outstretched. Then the detectives could hold him no longer. He crashed on to the track.

The communication cord was pulled.

The police hunt began. Jones was eventually seen hiding in a tree at Crick by some boys.

They told a householder, police were immediately informed and when they arrived at the scene the man was persuaded to leave his hiding place. Onlookers thought he had a broken arm. He appeared to be in great pain.

### R.A. AND HIS BRIDE-TO-BE

Mr. Henry Macbeth-Raeburn, seventy-five-year-old R.A., and his thirty-five-year-old fiancee, Miss Marjorie Mary Bacon, in his studio. Miss Bacon has worked as his pupil and assistant.
Mr. Macbeth-Raeburn specialises in engravings.

## Golf "Open" Records and Shocks at Wimbledon

WOMEN'S Surprise Day at Wimbledon; "Record" Day on that hot Golf Open course at Hoylake.—This was yesterday in sport.

Wimbledon's first big surprise was the defeat of Mrs. Sarah Palfrey Fabyan, heroine of America's Wightman Cup victory, and seeded player No. 3 who went out in the first round to the German girl Fraulein M. Horn, 6—3, 7—5.

Next surprise was the defeat of Peggy Scriven by Joan Saunders 6—4 1—6, 6—2. Peggy was far from her best.

Countess de la Valdene—better known as Senorita de Alvarez—showed all her old vivacity in disposing of Mrs. J. S. Kirk in straight sets.

Kay Stammers had a comfortable victory. Dorothy Round beat Betty Nuthall 9—7, 6—3.

Henry Cotton shattered Hoylake's record in the qualifying round of the open championship with a devastating 68, after Percy Alliss had startled the natives with 69.

The course has been stretched to 7,100 yards to prevent anybody doing a score in the sixties.

Before Cotton and Alliss returned 68 and 69, Gene Sarazen, the American, and Alan Dailey, formerly a Yorkshire professional, who is now at Wanstead, had set the Hoylake record at 71.

## FUTURE OF THE VICTORIA AND ALBERT

### The King to Decide After Navy Visit

FROM OUR OWN CORRESPONDENT
PORTSMOUTH, Tuesday.

DECISION on the future of the royal yacht Victoria and Albert will probably be taken after the King has inspected her during his first official visit to the naval establishments at Portsmouth next Tuesday.

The last active service of the royal yacht was in July, 1935, when King George spent two days afloat in her for the Silver Jubilee Review. King Edward, then Prince of Wales, occupied a small cabin.

### Royal Suites

No changes have been made in the royal apartments since, and little was done to the yacht during her annual refit.

There are suites on board for the use of the King, Queen Mary and other members of the Royal family if necessary, and his Majesty will have the opportunity next Tuesday of saying whether he wishes any alterations to be made.

The King will stay at Adsdean House, near Chichester, the home of Lord and Lady Louis Mountbatten, on Monday night, and will motor to Portsmouth on Tuesday morning.

He will be received by the Lord Mayor and aldermen of the city of which he was made the first freeman when he was Prince of Wales.

### Marines to March Past

Visits will be made to the Royal Naval Barracks, H.M.S. Vernon Torpedo School, H.M.S. Excellent Gunnery School at Whale Island, and the Royal Marine Barracks at Eastney, where the Royal Marines will march past.

The King will lunch at Admiralty House in the Dockyard with Admiral Sir J. D. Kelly, Commander-in-Chief.

Trooping the Colour—page 5: Pictures—pages 14 and 15.

## RUSH FOR ROYAL YACHT SOUVENIRS TO-DAY

The gear and equipment of King George's racing yacht, Britannia, is being sold by auction at East Cowes to-day. A rush of buyers is expected.

The sale will offer as much to the landsman as the seaman, for the cabin furniture and galley inventory alone takes up about 100 of the 300 lots.

Orders were received at Cowes last night for Britannia to be launched for the last time between July 7 and 9.

Admiralty officials will then tow the Britannia to deep water and sink her.

## LIGHTNING HITS BALLROOM ROOF

DURING a thunderstorm at Ongar, Essex, last night, lightning struck the Budworth Hall, Ongar's public hall, making a great hole in the roof of the ballroom, which was flooded. Shops were flooded and all traffic, including coaches and buses, were held up.

A house at Oxney Green, near Chelmsford, was struck by lightning and a wireless set was shattered. Mrs. P. Terry, occupant of the house escaped with a severe shaking.

A goat tethered in the meadow near the house was killed.

Several houses in Springfield-road, Chelmsford, were flooded to a depth of two feet when a terrific thunderstorm burst over the town.

Mr. D. K. Brown of Rosebury-road told the Daily Mirror:—

"Thunderclaps were like heavy gunfire, and for more than an hour torrential rain fell."

THE DAILY MIRROR, Thursday, June 25, 1936.

Broadcasting - Page 20

# Daily Mirror

THE DAILY PICTURE NEWSPAPER WITH THE LARGEST NET SALE

JANE - - - - - - - - P. 7
USELESS EUSTACE - 8
QUIET CORNER - - - 14
DOCTOR'S DIARY - - - 17
DOROTHY DIX - - - 22
RUGGLES - - - - - - 24

No. 10,161 Registered at the G.P.O. as a newspaper.   THURSDAY, JUNE 25, 1936   One Penny

Amusements : Page 16

# R.A.F. 'PLANES 'TO BEAT WORLD'

## Second Test Triumph in a Week

### RECORD BID

Within a week Britain has shown that her Royal Air Force possesses the fastest military fighter and the most formidable bomber in the world.

A WEEK ago the Vickers supermarine Spitfire was put "through its paces" at Southampton. Yesterday experts watched the new Handley Page bombing land 'plane show what a terrifying opponent it will make in war.

Grey and sinister, it soared into the air above Radlett (Herts)—Britain's latest triumph in air design.

At the same time a new attempt to establish a new air record for Britain was revealed.

Inspired by a challenge at a London dinner party, Lord Sempill aims at flying to Australia and back, 25,000 miles, in six days. The present one-way record is held by H. F. Broadbent, the Australian, with 6 days 21 hours.

### One Condition

At the dinner an Australian friend said that Britain had no machines capable of beating the Americans. "Done," said Lord Sempill, and got on the 'phone to his friend, Major Anson, who had just bought a New Monospar S.T.18 'plane, first to be built of its class, and fastest of Britain's commercial 'planes, with a top speed of 210 m.p.h., and room for ten passengers.

Major Anson agreed to lend him the 'plane, and with it Pilot H. Woods, his private pilot. But on one condition.

The 'plane would be ready by July 7. And it must be back in England by July 27.

Pilot Woods told the *Daily Mirror* last night that he sees no difficulty in this.

"We shall reach Australia in three days," he said, "which means that Lord Sempill will be able to stay there for a fortnight before we need to return.

"I have no doubt that we shall show the Australians that British machines are second to none in performance."

The Handley Page bombing land 'plane demonstrated at Radlett is a monoplane. It will be seen by the public for the first time on Saturday, when it will be flown in the R.A.F. display.

The new Handley Page day-and-night bombing aeroplane demonstrated at Radlett, Herts, yesterday.

She whipped her rival with a dog-lead after a road chase. Mrs. Elise Ives, who was granted a decree nisi yesterday.

She is seen here with her husband on their wedding day.

## SONG OF THE HANDCUFFED POLICEMAN

IT were down at the Races at Brighton,
    When P.C. (we won't give his name)
Was shown a nice new type of handcuff,
    And tried 'em on—just for a game.
They were smart, they were cute, they fit tightly,
    They locked with a crisp-sounding "clack,"
And he muttered to Sergeant, "They're beauties!"
    But Sergeant said, "Let's have 'em back."
"All right," says the Bobby, "unlock 'em,
    I'm sure I'll be glad to get free."
But Sergeant were looking dismayed like,
    And hunting around for the key.
He feels in his trousers, his tunic,
    While bystanders laugh and look on,
And grumbling into his whiskers,
    "Now where can the d—— thing have gone?"
He finally shouted, "I've got it!
    I never came out with the key—
I've left it locked up in the station . . .
    Tha'd better come back there wi' me."

        *  *  *

'Twere a sad, disappointed procession
    That dashed off, wi' never a stop,
To free the P.C. from his handcuffs—
    By gum, lads, that WERE a fair cop!
                                    G. B.

### Wife Who Whipped Her Rival Says—

## "THRASHING 'OTHER WOMAN' WOULD SAVE MARRIAGES"

FROM OUR SPECIAL CORRESPONDENT
NORWICH, Wednesday.

"I THINK if more wives whipped the 'Other Woman' there might be less matrimonial unhappiness in the world. Some husbands might learn a lesson from such action."

In these words a beautiful twenty-six-year-old brunette—formerly a stage dancer—explained to me to-night why she whipped with a dog lead "the other woman" and threw a pot of paint over her husband.

She is Mrs. Elise Ives, of the Mount, Thorpe St. Andrew, near Norwich.

She was granted a divorce decree nisi to-day against her husband, Mr. Reginald Ives, of Sandringham-court, Ipswich-road, Norwich.

The co-respondent was Miss Eva Elaine Cowling, who lives with her uncle and aunt at Christchurch-road, Norwich.

### Stage "Come Back"

Mrs. Ives arrived home late to-night with her parents, travelling by car from London. She was tired out after the ordeal of the five-day trial of her action.

She told me she hoped to resume her career as a stage dancer.

"I am hoping to make my stage come-back with the Tiller School of Dancing, with whom I started in my 'teens," she added.

"I performed under their control at the Folies Bergere, at the Globe Theatre, New York, and in Chicago and other parts of the U.S."

(Divorce Court Story on page 2.)

## DO YOU KNOW . . .

WHAT noise can make a deaf man hear?
    —Answer, Page Two.
WHAT was the bravest deed of 1935?—See Back Page.
THAT women may soon dress in "steel" fabric to be popularised by the "Daily Mirror" Eight?—Page Five.
THAT one firm alone can supply 4,000 suits on hire to Ascot racegoers?—Page Five.
WHO challenged Fortune with £5 to become a successful playwright?—Page Ten.
WHICH nation has to use a foreign flag on its ships?—Page Four.

## "Strong Navy Can Avert War"
—*Sir Samuel Hoare*

"IF the British Army, Navy and Air Force are adequately strengthened and are strengthened in time, there is going to be no world war."

SIR Samuel Hoare, First Lord of the Admiralty, speaking at a Royal Empire Society dinner at the Hotel Victoria, last night, made that declaration.

"If a new war were to break out in the immediate future," he declared, "there would be no breathing space as there was in the past when a predominant British Navy held off the attack and gave us the chance of setting our house in order. Our house must be put in order before the crisis.

"If a well-balanced fleet, capable of defeating the enemy and keeping the seas open, equipped to go anywhere, whether it be in the wide oceans or the narrow seas, in the blue waters or the grey, concentrated upon its three essential duties of cover, cruising and convoy, if such a fleet can be built in time, there is going to be no world war.

"My advisers . . . are determined to make the fullest possible use of air power."

# Daily Mirror

**THE DAILY PICTURE NEWSPAPER WITH THE LARGEST NET SALE**

Broadcasting - Pages 22 & 23

**MORE HOLLYWOOD SECRETS** — Page 12

No. 10,162   Registered at the G.P.O. as a newspaper.   FRIDAY, JUNE 26, 1936   One Penny

Amusements : Pages 24 and 25

## STEEL "HAND" TO CAPTURE BANDITS

### Invention of Sir M. Campbell

GREATEST STEP FORWARD IN BRITAIN'S WAR ON MOTOR BANDITS, THE INVENTION OF A GIANT STEEL "HAND" THAT SHOOTS OUT FROM A POLICE CAR TO CAPTURE A PURSUED CAR AT SPEED WAS REVEALED LAST NIGHT.

IT is the work of Sir Malcolm Campbell, world's speed record-holder.

Already preliminary tests have been made at the Police College, Hendon. Cars dodged and twisted all over the road trying to evade this new arm of the law. But they failed.

Sir Malcolm was led to think of his gadget by the death, in Ealing (London), of a pedestrian when a police car, trying to edge a stolen car into the kerb, skidded and hurled the civilian against a wall, killing him.

"I thought," Sir Malcolm said, "that the first thing you do when you are running after a thief is to grasp him by the neck. I thought the same might be done with a car."

A TELESCOPIC STEEL ARM WITH STRONG CLAWS A FOOT WIDE IS FITTED TO THE FRONT OF THE POLICE CAR.

ON MAKING CONTACT WITH THE REAR BUMPERS OF A CAR THE CLAWS BECOME FIRMLY LOCKED. BY BRAKING THE POLICE CAR, THE PURSUED CAR IS BROUGHT TO A STANDSTILL.

### Sir Malcolm Tries It Out

To demonstrate his device to a reporter Sir Malcolm fitted it to one of his own cars, and with the assistance of two of his mechanics staged a police chase in his grounds.

The "bandit" made off and Sir Malcolm set off in pursuit. He caught up with the car and out came the arm. Its movement was controlled by a small hydraulic pump operated with a hand lever by a mechanic sitting in front next to Sir Malcolm.

A few turns of the lever and it opened out like a penknife and pointed in the direction the car was going. A few more turns and it protruded still further by telescopic action.

The steel claws then opened and as soon as a metal disc in the centre pressed against the bandit's bumper the claws closed and the "bandit's" car was brought to a standstill.

"Once it has taken hold," said Sir Malcolm, "anyone with experience of towing will realise that merely by slowing down and applying its brakes the police car must force the car in front to come to a standstill."

### THE GRABSTERS

What will Sir Malcolm Campbell's new Arm of the Law come to be called? Suggestions:—

    Claw of the Law.
    Car-grabber.
    Grab-a-car.
    Bandit bagger.
    Bandit-clutch.
    Car-clutcher.

And what will the police who "grab a car" be called? Suggestion: Grabsters.

But what would the grabsters do if the bandits' car had neither rear bumpers nor luggage grid?

"Here Is How It Works,"

... Sir Malcolm Campbell is saying. Above: The claw normally stays open. When, however, something touches the buffer on which he has his finger, the claw snaps to; for instance (left), over the back fender of the car pursued, and (below) draws back.

## MRS. DIONNE WON'T HAVE DOCTOR: CALLS IN PRIEST

FROM OUR OWN CORRESPONDENT

NEW YORK, Thursday.

MRS. Dionne, mother of the world-famous "quins," who is expecting another child is reported to be spurning medical aid.

Believing that the survival of the quintuplets was a divine miracle, she wants to rely solely on religion. Last night she sent for a priest.

### Clasping a Crucifix

All day the priest and two men, who declined to reveal their names, remained with Mrs. Dionne. She spent hours in prayer, clasping a crucifix.

Although another doctor is believed to have seen her, she has sought no aid from Dr. Dafoe, who brought the quintuplets into the world.

Dr Dafoe has waited vainly for a call to her.

## GRIEF FOR FRIEND WHO SWINDLED THEM

### His "Fatal Fascination"

FROM OUR SPECIAL CORRESPONDENT

EXETER, Thursday.

BROUGHT from independent means almost to the verge of pauperism by a man who defrauded them for five years two elderly daughters of a former Devon clergyman feel only grief that they have lost a friend.

Sentencing Cuthbert Raymond Newton, aged thirty-nine, salesman, Judge Goddard said at the Assizes here to-day:

"You had a fascination, a fatal fascination, for these two old ladies, a fascination that some animals have for others.... I can hardly trust myself to speak with the calm that is desirable to a person occupying a judicial position."

To-night the two old ladies, the Misses Henrietta Sophy Wrey and Evelyn Maria Wrey, kind-hearted and generous, are penniless and are dependent on the help and care of friends and relatives.

Sad, and greatly disillusioned, they are living in secret seclusion in a small Devon village. Their home at Kingskerswell is closed and the future of it is not yet known.

Even now, after months of investigation by the police into the frauds of Newton, who was a salesman and as such first made the

(Continued on back page)

## 20,000 CHILDREN TO GREET THE KING

TWENTY thousand schoolchildren will line Southsea's three and a half miles of sea front when the King drives from the Royal Marine Barracks at Eastney on his way to Portsmouth Dockyard next Tuesday.

All the city's schools will be closed for the day. The sea front is the only part of the King's route which is being made known. It will be decorated and lined with police and representatives of the Army, Navy, Boy Scouts and Girl Guides.

The King will leave Eastney Barracks at a quarter past one.

While at Portsmouth, his Majesty will also pay visits of inspection to the Royal Naval Barracks, the Vernon Torpedo School, the Naval Gunnery School at Whale Island, and the royal yacht, Victoria and Albert.

THE DAILY MIRROR, Tuesday, June 30, 1936.

# Daily Mirror

THE DAILY PICTURE NEWSPAPER WITH THE LARGEST NET SALE

Broadcasting - Pages 20 & 21

## SUMMARY GUIDE TO ROMANCE
—Page 10

No. 10,165  Registered at the G.P.O as a newspaper    TUESDAY, JUNE 30, 1936    One Penny

Amusements: Page 16

| NEVER-NAG WIFE SAYS | ## "NOW I CAN SMOKE WHEN I LIKE" | RECORD AIRMAN'S BRIDE WIDOWED |

### Women's Right to Use Make-Up

BY A SPECIAL CORRESPONDENT

WITH a cigarette between her lips, Mrs. Diana Mary Cummings, the twenty-three-year-old wife who signed a written promise "never to nag," smiled last night and declared:

"Now I can smoke when I like . . . and use a lipstick if I want to."

She was sitting in a cafe opposite Kingston Police Court, where earlier in the day she had been granted a separation order from her husband.

"I have little to say except that I'm glad the case is over and I am free at last," she declared. "The conditions I have been living under I found intolerable. I was only twenty-one when I signed the document . . . and I was very much in love.

"I did not realise at the time how much it would mean. To be restricted to three or four cigarettes a week, to be unable to use lipstick, was terrible for a young woman.

#### In Love

Mrs. Cummings passed a hand wearily over her eyes

"Before I was married I always made up," went on Mrs. Cummings. "In fact I was in the business. I was a manicurist and hairdresser. I was made up when my husband met me and I did not realise at the time he objected to it so much."

"When I knew my daughter had signed that document I was very perturbed," said Mrs. Cumming's father. "It seemed all wrong for these days. But I couldn't do anything. She was very young. She was in love."

"Every wife has a right to smoke as many cigarettes as she likes," said Mrs. Cummings, "as long as she doesn't waste money or injure her health. No woman should be dictated to by a man . . . especially about make up. Why, women make up to please men!"

"There is no reason why a woman should not make up," said her mother. "I think it enhances her appearance."

Mrs. Cummings was granted a separation order against her husband, Sydney Edward Cummings, of Coombe-lane, Kingston on the ground of persistent cruelty. Mr. Cummings was ordered to pay £2 a week.

The case for Mrs. Cummings was that four days before their marriage in August, 1934, Cummings told her that it was necessary to

(Continued on back page)

#### £2-a-Week Order

Mrs. Diana Mary Cummings.

Mrs. Rubin, whose husband, Mr. Bernard Rubin (left), airman and racing motorist, has died. They were married less than sixteen months ago. Mr. Rubin took part in record flight to Australia in 1934.

## LIGHTNING STRIKES WOMAN HOLDING CARVING KNIFE

A WOMAN who was struck by lightning while carrying a carving knife in a house on the seafront at Aldeburgh (Suffolk) yesterday, was hurled through the hall into the kitchen wall.

She was Miss Bedwell, who keeps a boarding house. She was knocked unconscious, besides receiving severe burns on the arm.

Almost all the street lamps in Wimbledon went out shortly after 10 o'clock last night when more heavy rain fell and the water, entering an electricity conduit, affected a cable.

Houses, factories and hospitals continued to receive their supplies as usual, but early to-day the streets were still in darkness.

At Gills Green, Hawkhurst (Kent), Sidney Rivers, a bricklayer, ran into a house on which he was working for shelter.

What is described as "a ball of fire" struck the house; Rivers was killed; his mate, who remained outside, was uninjured. Rivers was found doubled up near the fireplace, with his clothing smouldering.

During the height of the storm at Bristol part of the ceiling of the Royal Infirmary collapsed and the X-ray department was flooded to a depth of nearly 2ft.

At West India House, typists had to scramble on to their desks until they were carried to safety.

At Ashton Court, where the Royal Show opens to-day, damage was done to stocks, machinery and goods.

### GIRL PAT MEN FLYING TO NEW YORK

Two of the crew of the Grimsby trawler Girl Pat—Hector Harris, thirty-one, and Howard Stephen, seventeen—have arranged to fly from Georgetown, British Guiana, to New York, says Reuter.

Captain George Black Orsborne and his brother Jim are in Georgetown Gaol, charged with the larceny of the Girl Pat.

## Vicar Clears Church of Strikers

BECAUSE Riviera "stay-in" strikers occupying his church began to smoke, the Rev. A. Palmer, vicar of the English church at Mentone, ejected them single-handed yesterday.

### NORMANDIE DAMAGED

Crashing into a steel girder, the Normandie's bridge was damaged as France's giant liner was trying to dock on an ebb tide in New York yesterday, says Reuter.

She was swung by the wind too close to the pier, but eventually berthed safely.

"I believe in a living wage, but the House of God is no place for a stay-in strike," he declared afterwards, says the British United Press.

The men went on strike while redecorating the church and announced that they would "occupy" the building.

The strikers were allowed to sleep in the vestry.

## FELL 1,500ft. ON GLACIER

### Comrades' Vain Search

TRYING to retrieve his glasses, which had slipped from his nose, a twenty-three-year-old Londoner lost his foothold and fell 1,500ft. to his death from the summit of the Slingsby Glacier in the Skagastoelstindene Mountains of Norway yesterday.

He was Mr. Hubert Douglas Sweeney, and had made the ascent with two fellow-members of the Cambridge University Alpine Club.

His comrades, Mr. Nigel Beaumont-Thomas, son of Major Beaumont-Thomas, M.P. for the King's Norton Division of Birmingham, and Mr. A. Hamilton Robins, of Edinburgh, vainly hunted for his body.

Four search parties, led by guides, also braved the wilderness of ice—in vain.

Eight of the Cambridge University mountaineers left London for Norway a week ago.

# Daily Mirror

**THE DAILY PICTURE NEWSPAPER WITH THE LARGEST NET SALE**

Broadcasting · Pages 22 & 23

LIVE-LETTER BOX P. 12
CASSANDRA - - - - 14
USELESS EUSTACE - 15
DOCTOR'S DIARY - - 15
DOROTHY DIX - - - - 26
THE RUGGLES - - - - 28

No. 10,168   Registered at the G.P.O. as a newspaper.   FRIDAY, JULY 3, 1936   One Penny   Amusements: Pages 16 and 18

## "ESCAPED" PRISONER FOUND ON ROOF OF GAOL

### His 2-Day Ordeal While Police Combed All London

AFTER ONE OF THE GREATEST MAN-HUNTS LONDON HAS KNOWN, ERNEST FREDERICK MORRIS, TWENTY-ONE-YEAR-OLD PRISONER WHO ESCAPED FROM HIS CELL IN WANDSWORTH PRISON ON TUESDAY, WAS FOUND LATE LAST NIGHT—ON THE ROOF OF A BUILDING IN THE PRISON.

FOR two days he had stayed on the roof without food, without shelter. Immediately he was found Morris was taken to the prison hospital in a state of exhaustion.

Only a few hours before Flying Squad men and detectives had been searching hundreds of lodging houses and cafes in South London for Morris.

All along the authorities had been puzzled how it was possible for Morris to make a getaway when it would be necessary for him to scale a 30ft. wall and walk through the streets in prison garb.

#### 18 Months' Sentence

The escape was made on the same day as Aircraftman F. H. C. Field was executed in the prison. The following day an inquiry into the escape was opened at the prison.

Morris was missed about 3 p.m. on Tuesday, when it was noticed that he was not on parade.

His description was circulated to flying squads, plain-clothes detectives and policemen on their beats shortly after the escape was discovered.

Morris, who is a batman, is serving a sentence of eighteen months.

The authorities, while perplexed as to how Morris could have got out of the prison, were apparently satisfied that he was not inside, because since Tuesday police officers had visited addresses in the Balham district where he was known.

### RETURNED 23 YEARS AFTER HE WAS "KILLED"

FOR twenty-three years Mrs. Warren, of Fleet-road, South Benfleet, Essex, has mourned her son, John Evans, a petty officer stoker in the Royal Navy.

She last saw him in 1913 and believed him to have been killed in the Battle of Jutland.

Yesterday eighty-five-year-old Mrs. Warren went to her door, and on opening it saw a man standing there who said his name was John and that he was her son.

"I thought he was dead." Mrs. Warren said last night. "I can still hardly believe he is with me now."

John Evans told the Daily Mirror that he was discharged from the Navy in the ordinary way in 1919. He is now fifty-three.

The Emperor of Abyssinia.

## EMPEROR RETURNING TO LEAD ARMIES AGAIN

### Asks League for £10,000,000

FROM OUR OWN CORRESPONDENT
GENEVA, Thursday.

HAILE Selassie, ready to face death rather than defeat, is planning a secret flight to Abyssinia to lead his armies again.

To-day he has asked the League for a £10,000,000 defence loan, and, I learn, is once more plotting to outwit the Italians by a return to his country.

There was a dramatic scene at the hotel where the Emperor—and Mr. Eden—is staying.

Seeing his cause hopelessly lost—the Negus was seized by a violent fit of temper. Pacing feverishly through the fifteen rooms of his splendid apartments, he said:—

"I will leave for Ethiopia, I shall march again at the head of my warriors, and either I shall be killed fighting or I shall show the world that there can be still an independent Government in Ethiopia."

One of his sons, who was playing in the gardens, came to his father, and said: "I shall do the same, daddy."

#### Britain Criticised

The Negus is making very sharp things about France and even Britain, and repeated bitterly: "Italy is not the only one responsible for my present difficulties."

Britain, I understand, is opposed to his return to Abyssinia.

The Emperor's appeal for a loan has been made in a resolution laid before the Assembly calling on members of the League to act under the terms of the Covenant granting assistance to Ethiopia "to defend her territorial integrity and political independence."

A large box containing new Savile-row lounge suits and a number of silk-lined overcoats were conveyed by air from London to Geneva to-day. They were addressed to the Emperor.

Sanctions will be lifted and definitely abandoned by all the nations of the League on July 15.

This date has been virtually accepted by Mr. Eden and M. Blum, the French Premier, because it will make it easier for Italy to participate in the conference of the Locarno Powers, which will be held in the second half of July at Brussels.

*Grown-up Role . . .*

*. . . for Nova Pilbeam, with Lilian Braithwaite in last night's new play, "The Lady of La Paz," at Criterion Theatre, W.*

*See review on page 7.*

George Henry

## A PENNY BROUGHT THIS BOY HIS DREAM—AND THEN TRAGEDY

NINE-YEAR-OLD George Henry had only one wish. He longed to go to the baths with his friends to learn to swim like other boys.

Day after day he worried his parents for permission, and little did he listen or understand when they told him it would be dangerous for him to go.

His parents, who live in Westmoreland-road, Hoxton, London, E., knew that George suffered from an ear complaint.

Yesterday George saw his great opportunity. He saw it in the shape of an empty mineral water bottle.

This he took to a shop and sold it for a penny—his entrance money to the forbidden baths. Then, as though to make his longing come true all the sooner, the Hoxton children were given a holiday.

* * *

Soon after George entered the water at Pitfield-street Baths he collapsed. One of his pals brought him to the side, but he was dead.

### MILLION CATTLE STARVING IN U.S. DROUGHT

One million cattle are starving and 100,000 families are in need of aid as a result of the great drought in U.S. prairies.

In some places, says Reuter, crops are reported to have failed.

Wheat prices are rising in the world's markets.

## SURGEON NEVER FLINCHED AS HE FOUGHT FOR LIFE

"I SAW no flinching as we walked with him to the operating theatre."

In these words Dr. Francis Roles, writing in the "British Medical Journal," describes the bravery of Mr. H. P. Nelson, the brilliant young surgeon, for whose life the best brains of St. Bartholomew's Hospital fought in vain.

As Mr. Nelson lay dying he turned to his wife, who had been almost continuously with him during his illness, and said: "It will have to be a different sort of struggle now, won't it?"

"No one who had been near him during the last month had any but the highest respect for his bravery," writes Dr. Roles. "When his resistance was at its lowest, he had to be told that his arm was to be taken off forthwith.

"On recovering consciousness that evening he had to face the loss of his career and the end of his ambition. But he uttered no word

THE DAILY MIRROR, Monday, July 6, 1936.

Broadcasting - Page 24

# Daily Mirror

THE DAILY PICTURE NEWSPAPER WITH THE LARGEST NET SALE

CASSANDRA - - - - P. 12
LIVE-LETTER BOX - - 12
USELESS EUSTACE - 13
HOLIDAY SHORT
   STORY - - - - - - 19
DOROTHY DIX - - - - 22
THE RUGGLES - - - - 24

No. 10,170    Registered at the G.P.O as a newspaper.    MONDAY, JULY 6, 1936    One Penny

Amusements: Pages 16 and 20

# CRASH KILLS AIR HERO OF 22

## Belief in Fate Deceived Him

### FEARLESS MELROSE

TWENTY-TWO-YEAR-OLD Jim Melrose — the man who beat the Australia-England flight record with only £10 in his pocket and glided five miles to second place when his petrol gave out in the London-Melbourne air race—was killed yesterday in an air taxi.

As he was flying near Melbourne his machine developed an uncontrollable spin and broke up in the air.
Bad luck had ended the career of the man who once said: "Flying is my lucky pastime. I do not think I am fated to die flying."

The tragedy which robbed Australia of the man who was rapidly assuming the place of the late Sir Charles Kingsford-Smith also took one of its foremost mining experts. Lieutenant-Colonel A. G. Campbell, D.S.O. He had chartered Melrose's air taxi. Both were killed instantly.

Mr. N. Pemberton-Billing, a former M.P. for East Herts and an uncle of Melrose, when told of the crash, said: "I don't know what his mother will do now. She and Jimmie were devoted to each other."

### "From Australia"

Melrose, always distinguished by his unruly shock of flaxen hair, was an intrepid young airman who knew no fear of danger.
His record-breaking flight from Australia to England in September, 1934, brought him into the public eye. He arrived at Croydon after flying from Australia in eight days and nine hours, beating the then existing record set up by Mr. J. A. Mollison in 1931.

His arrival was unheralded and unexpected. When he landed an aerodrome official asked, "Where have you come from?" "Australia," was Melrose's laconic reply.

Melrose flew solo in the London-Melbourne air race, and won the second prize of £1,000 in the handicap section.

Melrose made four England to Australia flights in fourteen months.—British United Press and Central News.

Mr. C. J. (Jim) Melrose.

## THREE MEN DROWN IN HUMAN CHAIN TO SAVE GIRL

THREE men in a human chain formed to save a girl who got into difficulties while bathing at Tregantle, near Plymouth, last night were drowned.

The girl, Miss Eileen West, of Upper Tooting, London, S.W., who was staying at Looe, was unharmed.
The victims were:—
Isaac Edwards, aged twenty-one, of Herbert-place, Devonport;
Private W. Lowe, of the King's Regiment, undergoing training at Fort Tregantle;
H. Williams, Album-road, Torpoint, Cornwall.

### Swept Away by Wave

Miss West was bathing with Mr. Douglas Heaton, also of Upper Tooting, when she got out of her depth and was swept by the heavy rollers some distance from the shore.

A sixteen-year-old lad, Roy Horsham, of Paisley-street, Devonport, swam to the rescue with a life line, but had to be dragged from the water suffering from shock.

Spectators at once formed a human chain and waded out to sea, but they, too, were swept away.

Ambulance men applied artificial respiration for two or three hours and oxygen was administered, but they failed to recover.

### HIS LAST TEXT

"For Thy sake we are killed all the day long."

When Mr. Frederick John Mason, aged sixty-four, of Coverley-way, Worcester Park, Surrey, came to these words while reading the lesson from the 8th Chapter of Romans at the Baptist Mission Hall, Longfellow-road, Worcester Park, yesterday, he faltered and fell dead.

### TO-DAY'S TONIC NEWS

MONDAY MORNING. Let your tonic be the news that—

ALTHOUGH handicapped by blindness, a twenty-year-old Egyptian-born pianist, George Themeli, who learned by the Braille method—"reading" with one hand and playing with the other—has made history by winning the first prize of the Paris Conservatoire of Music.

    * * *

Mr. Wallace Ford, the British film star, who is now on his way home to do a picture for Gaumont-British, and has insured his life for £20,000, was once in Dr. Barnardo's Home for Boys at Stepney, London.

    * * *

The marvellous optimism that breaks the spell of gloom over the unemployed will be one of the things the Duke of Kent will see on his two-day Lancashire tour beginning to-day.

    * * *

Four famous men had helpful words for youth this week-end. (See page 13.)

Mr. Victor Clarke and his bride, Miss Edith Thwaits, cutting their wedding cake at the reception in the flat of Mrs. Scott-Gatty, to whom the bride has been housemaid for several years.

## SOCIETY WOMAN'S HOME FOR HOUSEMAID'S WEDDING

### BY A SPECIAL CORRESPONDENT

AFTER driving her twenty-year-old housemaid to St. Saviour's Church, London, S.W., for her wedding to a fruiterer's assistant, a society woman turned over her luxury flat to them for the reception.

The bride and bridegroom were Miss Edith Thwaits and Mr. Victor Clarke, twenty, of Clapham Park-road, S.W.

They were driven to the church by Miss Thwaits's employer, Mrs. Scott-Gatty, of Cadogan-gardens, S.W., at the week-end.

The wedding had been kept secret, and only a few friends of Mrs. Scott-Gatty and relatives of the couple were present. One of the bridesmaids was the cook.

At the reception a friend of Mr. Clarke—a jazz pianist—entertained the party on a grand piano.

The bridegroom's father proposed the health of the couple in the kitchen, where the wedding breakfast—attended by thirty-six relatives—was held.

### Left to Themselves

When I called at Mrs. Scott-Gatty's flat, the bride, in white satin and wearing a wreath of orange blossom, answered my knock.

"I have been employed by Mrs. Scott-Gatty for several years, and she has been wonderfully kind to us," she told me.

"She has gone away for a few hours, and is leaving the entire flat to us for my reception."

Mrs. Clarke, looking radiantly happy, introduced me to her husband.

"We cannot go on our honeymoon yet," she said, "but will leave for a holiday somewhere in August.

"It has been a wonderful day—the happiest of my life."

# Daily Mirror

**THE DAILY PICTURE NEWSPAPER WITH THE LARGEST NET SALE**

Broadcasting - Page 24

CASSANDRA..... P. 12
USELESS EUSTACE - 13
HOLIDAY SHORT
    STORY ....... 19
DOROTHY DIX..... 22
THE RUGGLES..... 24

No 10,171 Registered at the G.P.O. as a newspaper. TUESDAY, JULY 7, 1936. One Penny

Amusements: Page 16

## Britain Better Off Than for 6 Years

BRITAIN'S UNEMPLOYED TOTAL, LOWEST FOR SIX YEARS, GOES ON FALLING. FIGURES FOR JUNE, ISSUED LAST NIGHT, SHOW A DROP OF 2,366 ON MAY. PRESENT TOTAL IS 1,702,676.

In Britain there are now 10,832,000 people in work—441,000 more than a year ago. Thousands more will find work this month at holiday resorts. Millions more in money will be spent—millions that will give even more work to the growing Back-to-Work Brigades.

Shipbuilding, engineering, iron and steel, public works, transport and distributive trades all shared in last month's improvement. More work poured into these factories. More men were needed to cope with it. More wages were paid out. Prosperity's return made itself felt in thousands more homes.

Black sheep of Industry's Family was coalmining. Numbers temporarily stopped increased. This was attributed largely to the suspension of work on June 22 at a number of pits in Yorkshire for the annual demonstration of the Yorkshire Miners' Association.

## SEX POSTCARDS CLEAN-UP URGED

### Seaside Censor Plan

NATION-WIDE campaign for a censorship to clean-up "sex postcards" at seaside resorts is advocated by a Margate curate.

"Obscene," is the description applied by the Rev. J. W. Garnett, senior curate of the Parish Church to nine out of every ten of the postcards sold in Margate shops.

Margate postcards, he declares, are the worst in Britain for their "disgusting portrayal of sex subjects," but he is not so sure that the postcards at Blackpool and Scarborough are all they ought to be.

For twenty years there has been a censorship of postcards in the Isle of Man. Out of 8,000 designs submitted to the censors last year ten per cent. were rejected as vulgar or ridiculing religion.

Mr. Herbert W. Holt, secretary of the Stationers' Association of Great Britain, told the *Daily Mirror* last night: "Our Association would welcome such a censorship scheme for the rest of Britain."

### Sense of Humour

Mr. Garnett, explaining his proposed campaign, said:—

"I find that the Mayor of Scarborough made some outspoken comments on the postcards on sale in his resort the other day.

"He would find that those in the Margate shops are worse, and I am anxious to see a nation-wide 'cleaning-up' campaign started here.

"I have not begun this agitation because there is anything wrong with my sense of humour. On the contrary, I always make a point of sending funny postcards to my friends.

"But when I go around the shops in Margate I find that 95 per cent. of the postcards are filthily indecent—far worse than those I have seen in North Wales, Blackpool and other resorts in the north.

"The only body that can stop it is the Watch Committee, unless the authorities stepped in and prohibited such cards being printed.

### Making a Start

"It is not easy to get the authorities to move, but I am trying to rouse public opinion here to demand some sort of censorship.

"I have no doubt that if we make a start in Margate, other resorts will soon follow. Already I have had dozens of letters supporting me in my stand. But not a single shopkeeper has come forward to defend the obscene goods he sells.

"If they really have to sell that class of postcard to live, then they had better close.

"In fact, in all other respects, Margate I consider is the happiest and homeliest resort in the country... So it's a real pity that we can't sell witty postcards too!"

Miss Constance Hayde, beauty culture expert of twenty-four, who broke into tears when giving evidence yesterday in a suit for breach of promise she is bringing against Mr. E. J. Hawes. Story is on page 5.

## FAIRIES AT BOTTOM OF HIS GARDEN!

A COALVILLE tradesman, who through pressure of work had done nothing in his garden at the back of his house, awoke yesterday to find the garden, fifty yards by five, dug and set with a variety of plants.

It was bare when he went to bed on Sunday night.

He is now wondering whether someone dug the wrong garden in the early hours of the morning, or if he has a friend in need.

## LIGHTSHIP MAN COLLAPSES

Taken seriously ill with internal trouble on board the East Goodwin lightship, Mr. T. Hermanson, a member of the engine crew, was brought ashore yesterday in a Ramsgate motorboat.

On arrival at the harbour he was taken by taxi-cab to the station and placed in a train for London.

## KEEP SLIM—AND LIVE LONGER

"Keep slim if you want to keep young. I can tell you when a man is going to die by one look at his paunch.

"At City banquets I pick them out. 'You will last about eight years,' I say to myself—and I am always right."

—Sir William Arbuthnot Lane, who is eighty, speaking yesterday.

## 8,000 TO SEE WOMAN HANG NEGRO KILLER

### She Feels It "Her Duty"

FROM OUR OWN CORRESPONDENT
New York, Monday.

A woman sheriff hanging a negro before 8,000 men, women and children....

THIS will happen at Owensboro, Kentucky, on July 31 unless the pressure of decent opinion holds up plans for one of the most spectacular executions in American history.

The condemned man, Rainey Bethea, aged twenty-two robbed, assaulted and killed a woman.

### "It Is My Duty"

Deputy Sheriff Simon Smith plans to build a high scaffold for Bethea in a garage lot to accommodate 2,500 spectators. But he boasts that 5,500 more people can obtain a good view from nearby vantage points.

I have just talked on the telephone to Mrs. Florence Thompson, aged forty-two, Sheriff of Davies County and mother of four children who "feels it her duty" to be executioner.

I asked her why.

"Because I am Sheriff," she drawled. "I was appointed in place of my husband when he died. I guess it's my duty to do what he would have done."

### "Mustn't Shirk"

"My view? I haven't altogether made up my mind about it, but I guess I mustn't shirk in a case like this. Yean, 3,000 folks, at least, will see the execution."

"Why make it public?" I asked.

"Because he killed a very fine lady. Those who see him die will know murder doesn't pay. Yes, sir."

### HE WANTS DIVORCE

## BECAUSE HIS WIFE ATTACKS ROOSEVELT

BECAUSE his wife made caustic remarks about President Roosevelt, ex-Senator C. Dill has brought a suit for divorce against her.

"When the President visited a dam in Washington State I was afraid to have my wife at my side for fear of what she might say about him," Mr. Dill said in Court yesterday, says Reuter.

Mrs. Dill is the former American suffragette leader, Rosalie Jones.

## THIEVES RANSACK KNIGHT'S HOME

SERVANTS returning yesterday to Queen's-gardens, Osborne-road, Windsor, the home of Sir James and Lady Bell, found that the place had been ransacked and furniture and bedding thrown about.

Silver plate and jewellery are missing, but the full extent of the loss will not be known until to-day, when Sir James and Lady Bell return.

Apparently the intruders had forced an entry at a back window 12ft. from the ground.

THE DAILY MIRROR, Saturday, July 11, 1936.

Broadcasting - Page 24

# Daily Mirror

THE DAILY PICTURE NEWSPAPER WITH THE LARGEST NET SALE

USELESS EUSTACE P. 10
CASSANDRA - - - - 11
GREAT LOVE STORY 19
DOROTHY DIX - - - 22
THE RUGGLES - - - 24

No. 10,175  Registered at the G.P.O. as a newspaper  SATURDAY, JULY 11, 1936  One Penny

Amusements: Page 16

# 300 DIE AS GREAT DROUGHT PARALYSES U.S.

## £60,000,000 Loss in the Middle West No-Man's-Land

FROM OUR OWN CORRESPONDENT
NEW YORK, Friday.

WITH MORE THAN HALF THE COUNTRY PARALYSED BY DROUGHT, AMERICA'S HEAT WAVE DEATH ROLL TO-DAY TOPPED 300.

Realisation of what is happening in the no-man's-land of the Middle West, where 5,000,000 people are ruined, has reached New York, for the city has been struck by terrific heat and humidity that had already killed twenty-two and prostrated hundreds.

As I write, amazing stories reach me from all parts of New York City and State.

Latest comes from West Eighteenth-street, where seventy-five women collapsed from heat in one building.

From Troy, New York State, comes the report that twenty-five women collapsed at one meeting.

But America's real tragedy lies in her "heart," the middle west.

President Roosevelt has acted quickly. He offered immediate Government work to 75,000 of the ruined families to-day and promised millions for relief.

But no Government can alleviate the tragedy of vast areas, many times the size of Great Britain, reduced by lack of rain and a blazing sun to deserts of dust.

### Homes of Dead

An airman who flew over Montana farm lands to-day described them as "homes of the dead." He added:—

"I saw monotonous acres of barren soil and farmhouses that seemed deserted. Now and then I saw a few cattle. They looked like walking skeletons. On the roads were bands of refugees with all their belongings piled in ramshackle cars and carts. Heaven knows how they could stand the intense heat. Once the sun was blotted out by millions of grasshoppers searching in vain for food."

In Michigan and Wisconsin there are big forest fires with hundreds fleeing before them. The Middle West's loss is estimated at £60,000,000. Several towns there have been invaded by religious cranks, who, calling the drought a judgment of God, asked people to repent.

Brilliant sunshine will not harm your neck if you wear the Nina Batchelor creation shown above. It is of linen with a frill of stiffened organdie.

A "squashed trilby," shown on the right, resembles the hat of a drunken man, but it is more becoming than you imagine.

High hats will be the fashion for the autumn. Tall, upstanding ornaments will be worn. Berets will have a forward tilt, often showing a peak. Other ideas are small Breton brims, swathed turbans and trimmings of suede and kid.

HOLIDAYMAKERS at Tynemouth show what you may try to do also when you go to the seaside. It's quite easy—when you have the knack!

## ARCHBISHOP GAOLED FOR "IMMORALITY"

FROM OUR OWN CORRESPONDENT
WARSAW, Friday.

ARCHBISHOP Kowalski, head of the Margavit Church in Poland, was thrown into prison to-day following his two-year sentence for immoral relations with young and beautiful girls, members of his church and choir.

The Archbishop, who is sixty, had thousands of followers all over Poland.

Recently he was tried for sensual behaviour and for insults to the Roman Catholic Church. He was then sentenced to two years' imprisonment, but the sentence was not at once carried into effect.

To-day, however, the Archbishop was ordered into prison on the special instructions of the Polish Minister of Justice.

The Archbishop was taken by several policemen to the prison at Rawicza, in Western Poland. His clerical dress was taken off and he was given a prison uniform. His hair was cut short. The only concession was that he was allowed a separate cell.

Thousands of the Archbishop's followers are making a pilgrimage from all parts of the country to Warsaw.

Many of them are young girls from remote parts of the country, who announce that they will walk to Warsaw to expiate the sins of their Archbishop and beg for mercy.

## £156 A SQUARE INCH PAID FOR A PICTURE

A drawing measuring five-and-a-half inches by five inches realised 4,100 guineas, or £156 per square inch, during the sale of art treasures from the Oppenheimer collection at Christie's yesterday.

It was a drawing by Leonardo da Vinci of a rider on a rearing horse and was bought by Colnaghis.

Twenty years ago the little picture was valued at only £300.

## JULY DAY OF HAIL AND FLOOD

TOWNS swept by floods three feet deep, motorists held up by hailstones, schoolboys throwing snowballs, and houses and a ship struck by lightning were incidents of yesterday's storms.

Eastbourne is a town of flooded basements and ground floors following the most amazing storm the town has ever experienced—thunder accompanied by torrential hail, which continued for an hour.

Water ran down the streets like mountain torrents sweeping pedestrians from their feet and cyclists from their machines.

At the east end streets and houses were flooded to a depth of three feet.

At the height of the storm the pleasure steamer, Brighton Belle, was approaching the pier with passengers from Hastings for the cross-Channel steamer, when her wireless aerial was struck by lightning.

Mr. W. Cuthill, of Bristol, the radio operator, who was in the wireless room when the flash occurred, was badly burned, and Captain E. R. Smith, who was on the bridge, was temporarily deafened.

Both had to be treated by a doctor.

For a long time after the storm, hail lay on the ground like snow in parts of the town and was used by schoolchildren for snowballing.

A house in Sunnyhill-road, Herne Bay (Kent), was struck by lightning.

(Flood Picture: Page 15.)

## £10,000 MYSTERY GIFT TO HOSPITALS

KING Edward's Hospital Fund for London yesterday received a gift of £10,000 from an anonymous donor towards the general support of the London hospitals.

This sum will be included in the grants made by the King's Fund to the hospitals at the next distribution.

The donor, whose anonymity is strictly preserved, has now given in the course of the last thirteen years the large sum of £88,500, all of which from time to time has been distributed to the London hospitals.

## "HITLER MEANS WAR"
—Says a German

"BEHIND the peace speeches of Hitler, war is being prepared," said a German speaker whose name was not announced, at the International Trades Union Congress in London yesterday.

"Preparations for war in Germany are very much further advanced than is generally supposed," he said.

THE DAILY MIRROR, Thursday, July 16, 1936.

Broadcasting - Page 24

# Daily Mirror

THE DAILY PICTURE NEWSPAPER WITH THE LARGEST NET SALE

USELESS EUSTACE - P. 6
CASSANDRA - - - - - 12
GREAT LOVE STORY - 19
DOROTHY DIX - - - - - 21
THE RUGGLES - - - - - 24

No. 10,179 Registered at the G.P.O as a newspaper. THURSDAY, JULY 16, 1936 One Penny

Amusements : Page 16

# BRITISH BABIES BEING SOLD ABROAD

## 300 Victims Are in Holland

BY A SPECIAL CORRESPONDENT

UNWANTED BRITISH BABIES ARE BEING SOLD INTO HOLLAND, WHERE THEY ARE BROUGHT UP AS DUTCH CHILDREN.

DUTCH law forbids any parents legally to adopt a child. English children therefore are entirely at the mercy of the people with whom they live, without any right of supervision by proper authorities.

Cases are known of "fees" being paid by people to gain possession of a child and exploit it. "I can point to cases where 'fees' have been taken," the secretary of an adoption society told the "Daily Mirror" last night.

Complaints by authorities in Holland about the way in which "imported" English children are looked after by Dutch foster-parents have caused alarm both there and in this country.

### Starving Child

Dr. H. Sark, honorary general secretary of the National Federation for the Unmarried Mother in the Netherlands, is appearing to-day before the Home Office Committee appointed by Sir John Simon to inquire into the traffic in children.

He will give evidence on the way in which English children are brought up in Holland without any possibility of proper supervision.

Dr. Sark, speaking at a meeting of the National Council for Unmarried Women, in London, yesterday, said that 300 children had been received by people in Holland, and it was felt by the authorities in both countries that steps should be taken to limit the numbers of these children, 90 per cent. of whom were children of unmarried mothers.

The first complaint was made by an Englishman, who found a child starving in Amsterdam last night. Daily Mirror was told in Amsterdam last night.

Alarmed by reports of the ill-treatment of children, chosen by foster-parents who travel to England for this purpose and take the child back with them, many English adoption societies refuse to allow "adoption" of British children by people of Dutch nationality. Others reserve the right of supervision of the child by one of their inspectors.

### Untraced Mother

In spite of the precautions taken by reputable adoption societies to see that no child goes to Holland without supervision, the numbers of English children "adopted" there continues to increase.

"One tragic case was of a child whose Dutch foster-parents lost their money, and insisted on returning the child to England. The real mother could not be found, and the child who had been brought up as Dutch, and who could speak only Dutch, had to go to an institution," the secretary of one well-known society told the Daily Mirror.

The National Children's Adoption Society, which does not allow adoption by Dutch parents, has had eighteen applications in the last twelve months.

"English children are very popular for adoption," they say.

Every baby loves a merry - go - round and every mother shares her child's fun.

So it is in this picture, where the baby is Princess Margaretha, of Sweden, and the mother is Princess Sibylla, wife of Prince Gustaf-Adolf.

## BISHOP DEPRIVES "LOST" RECTOR OF HIS LIVING

THE Rev. J. W. H. Nankivell, rector of Hatford, Berkshire, who disappeared mysteriously from home nearly five weeks ago and was found later by his wife, has been deprived of his living by the Bishop of Oxford.

"Certain charges" have been made against him, but the nature of them is not disclosed.

After Mr. Nankivell's disappearance, police and bloodhounds searched for him for two days before he was found.

His wife went to Oxford to look for him after she had received a 'phone call saying he had slept under a haystack and was then at an Oxford hotel.

Mr. W. H. Chadune, rector's warden at Hatford, said last night that the rector and his wife were not at their home.

"The pronouncement of the Bishop," he said, "comes under a ruling made by the Church Assembly a short time ago, but I am not in a position to say what the reason is at the moment.

Mr. C. A. Chilton, registrar of the Oxford Diocese, said that he could not say where Mr. Nankivell were staying.

"Proceedings under the Clergy Discipline Act of 1892 the living is vacant. "Proceedings under the Act were instituted by the Bishop of Oxford," he added. "In accordance with the Act, Mr. Nankivell exercised his right to admit the charge and to ask for the Bishop to pass sentence without further proceedings.

"This was done. Because it was done in this way there was no need for a public hearing.

"The sentence means that he has been deprived of holding preferment. He has not been unfrocked."

The Rev. J. W. H Nankivell

### Wettest July Ever!

With torrential rain falling throughout the country yesterday—St. Swithin's Day—and no sign of settled weather ahead, this month promises to be the wettest July on record. Yesterday was London's eleventh wet day this month.

Already the total rainfall for the first fourteen days is higher than that of the whole of the month last year.

The rainfall recorded for July last year was just over two inches, the total for this month so far is over two inches—and there are sixteen days to go.

## POLICE CLIP IVY FROM MURDERED WOMAN'S HOME

DETECTIVES investigating the murder of Mrs. Mordaunt-Chapman last night made a surprise visit to her home in Hampton-road, Twickenham, London, and clipped off the whole of the thick growth of ivy from the wall running outside the house.

The leaves were put into a sack which, it is understood, is to be taken to the police laboratory at Hendon, where the ivy will be scientifically examined.

A statement on the business affairs of the dead woman was taken from a woman who visited Twickenham Police Station last night.

## MODERN GIRLS' "BIT OF FUN" A DANGEROUS FORM OF PLEASURE

—WARNS K.C.

MODERN girls of adventurous spirit who seek a little more fun in their unexciting lives were warned at Lewes Assizes yesterday that it is "a dangerous pleasure."

Four men, whom the Judge said had acted as though they were uncivilised, were sentenced to eighteen months each for criminally assaulting a girl in a car near Brighton.

They were Leonard Gooding, twenty-three, John Anderson, nineteen, Alfred Thomas Ochiltree, twenty-four, and William Jack Arthur Munro, twenty-three.

The sixteen-year-old girl involved in the case, whose name was not disclosed, was found stripped at the roadside after leaving a dance-hall with the men in a car.

### "Adventurous Spirit"

In his closing speech for the prosecution Mr. St John Hutchinson, K.C., said :—

"Although some of you may think that this girl is a somewhat brazen person, I thank no one can entirely withhold sympathy from her.

"It is quite likely she was at Sherry's for the purpose of meeting young men with whom she could dance.

"Quite possibly she was there in an adventurous spirit away from her home, and adding a little bit more fun to her not too exciting life as a chambermaid, but it is a very long stretch from that to think that this girl was the absolutely abandoned creature that, if the defence is true, she must be.

"She may be one of the many girls who go out, perhaps, not realising what the world is, hoping to have a bit of fun by picking up young men, and possibly drinking.

"I hope other young girls may learn that this sort of thing in these days is a somewhat dangerous form of pleasure."

### "Shocking Act"

Passing sentence, Mr. Justice Hilbery said:

"The act which you men did on this night done as it was—was a shocking, disgusting, and anti-social act. It was criminal in the real sense of the word.

"You treated that young woman as though this were not a civilised country at all."

There were special circumstances in this case and he hoped that people outside, when they saw the sentences he was pronouncing, would not misunderstand his opinion of the crime of rape.

### Equally Guilty

In his summing up the Judge pointed out that if four men in a case like the one before the court acted in concert and assisted one another, then those who did not actually commit the acts were equally guilty.

"Not one of the defendants has told us how her clothes came to be torn off.

"If they were torn off does that look to you like a case of a girl who was apparently willing?"

The Judge went on to say that Gooding's case was different from that of the others. He was said to have assisted in what he knew was an unlawful act which was going on and to have kept a look out.

Yesterday's evidence on page 6

THE DAILY MIRROR, Friday, July 17, 1936.

Broadcasting - Page 28

# Daily Mirror

THE DAILY PICTURE NEWSPAPER WITH THE LARGEST NET SALE

CASSANDRA - - - - P. 12
USELESS EUSTACE - 13
GREAT LOVE STORY 15
DOROTHY DIX - - - - 22
THE RUGGLES - - - - 24

No. 10,180  Registered at the G.P.O. as a newspaper.   FRIDAY, JULY 17, 1936   One Penny

Amusements : Pages 26 and 27

## ATTEMPT ON THE KING'S LIFE

# HERE IS THE MAN WITH LOADED PISTOL

## And The 'Special' Who Saved The King

George Andrew McMahon under arrest in Constitution Hill yesterday after an attempt on the life of the King. Helping to hold him is Special-Constable Dick (wearing peaked cap), of Hackney, whose prompt action saved the King's life. He was on duty for the day only. His eye caught the glint of metal in the sunshine, and he saw a man on the outskirts of the crowd holding a revolver. He threw himself between the revolver and the King, and, pouncing on the man, knocked the revolver into the roadway. He then arrested McMahon. Full story on pages 2 and 3; the King's speech page 4; world opinion page 5; other pictures on pages 12, 14, 16, 17 and 19.

THE DAILY MIRROR, Monday, July 27, 1936.

Broadcasting—Page 20

# Daily Mirror

THE DAILY PICTURE NEWSPAPER WITH THE LARGEST NET SALE

EUSTACE - - - - - - - P. 9
SERIAL - - - - - - - - 21
CALENDAR OF FATE 25
BELINDA - - - - - - - 26
RUGGLES - - - - - - 28

No. 10,188  Registered at the G.P.O. as a newspaper.   MONDAY, JULY 27, 1936   One Penny

Amusements: Pages 8 and 14.

## MOTHERS WEEP AS THE KING GREETS BLIND HEROES AT VIMY

**FROM OUR SPECIAL CORRESPONDENT**

ARRAS, Sunday.

WOMEN wept and knelt in prayer while aeroplanes dived and screamed overhead during the King's unveiling of the Canadian war memorial at Vimy Ridge to-day.

While young French soldiers held back the crowds with locked rifles, Canada's legions—armless, legless, shocked, blinded—stood in a natural bowl below the twin columns of Canada's memorial to her 12,000 missing, and in a semi-circle three miles in diameter stood thousands of the women of Canada.

Throughout the King's speech a grey-haired woman, with a bunch of sweet peas in her hand, stood pressed close against the stark white stone which will carry in perpetual memory the spirits of those who fought on this blackened hill nearly twenty years ago.

This woman, Mrs McKenzie, had with her her husband, grey-haired, nearly blind, and they had made a special pilgrimage of over 3,000 miles only to touch the memorial once with their fingers.

### Barriers Collapse

Barriers went down when the King, his fair hair ruffled by the wind, appeared among the crowd for a brief handshake and a chat with one or two, who symbolised by their presence here to-day that the women of Canada will never forget and will never break faith with those who died for the Empire.

Police cried "Stand back" as the ranks of grey-haired women broke and closed about the King, anxious only to touch his coat and to hear a word of comfort from his lips.

Chief among them was Mrs. C. M. Wood, who on her breast wore twenty-one medals won by the twelve sons who had fought for Canada in the war. The names of five of them are engraved in stone upon the white base of the memorial.

He touched her arm in silent solace and passed on, leaving a broken-hearted, grey-haired woman in tears.

### Sun Shines

The sun shone as the King stood in front of the dignitaries and warriors then banked behind him on the memorial as he made his simple speech (reported on page 5).

Almost fainting as she heard the King's words of comfort was the Princess Marie Croy, who in her Chateau de Bellingie, rescued hundreds of Canadians, men who wandered wounded and alone through the woods.

Nursing them back to health, she earned a place in our national histories almost equal to Edith Cavell's.

As the scarlet and blue flags fell from the mourning figure of Canada, symbolised by a woman standing with bowed head looking over the carved names of the men whose bones lay beneath the green grass, Mrs. Cleopatra Christian, coloured wife of a coloured man who had lost both hands and both feet in the Vimy offensive, clasped her little son tightly to her breast.

### Returned Maimed

"That stands for the thing for which your father so nearly laid down his life," she said into his ear. "I will never let you go into a war so long as I am alive."

Mrs. Christian married in 1920.

Curly Christian, her husband, who was sitting to-day on the identical spot under which he was buried for two days and two

(Continued on back page)

### A MOTHER'S PRIDE

The King shaking hands with Mrs. C. S. Woods, who represented the Mothers of Canada, at Vimy Ridge. She had twelve sons in the war and lost five. Left: The medals on Mrs Woods's blouse.

## NEW YORKERS STAYING UP TO GREET THE RECORD-BREAKING QUEEN MARY

**FROM OUR SPECIAL CORRESPONDENT**

NEW YORK, Sunday Night.

AS the Queen Mary races towards New York with the record well within her grasp, thousands of enthusiastic Americans are preparing to sail out in the night to greet the winner of the Blue Riband of the Atlantic.

She has until 2.30 a.m. (7.30 a.m. British Summer Time) to reach Ambrose Light and beat the Normandie, and it is expected that she will better this by at least two hours.

Shortly after the Queen Mary had passed Nantucket Lightship, a seaplane, believed to have gone out to greet the liner, crashed into the sea. At least eleven passengers were in the 'plane. One is dead, another is dying.

New York is staying up to celebrate the event in a big way. Even her first crossing welcome may be overshadowed by the scenes on the quay.

British societies here have chartered a vessel in which to go out together at midnight and greet the liner as she approaches the city.

Up to noon to-day the Queen Mary had covered 2,708 miles, leaving only about 450 miles to go.

Despite patches of fog her day's distance up to noon was 734 miles at an average speed of 29.36 knots. That figure is sixty-six miles better than the fourth day's journey of her maiden voyage.

With her engines overhauled since the last time she made the transatlantic trip, she has been steaming along consistently at around thirty knots.

### SEE HOW THEY RUN

This is how the Queen Mary's speeds compare with the record-breaking trip of Normandie:—

| | QUEEN MARY | NORMANDIE |
|---|---|---|
| 1st day, | 476 m., 29.32 kts. | 228 m., 26.30 kts. |
| 2nd day, | 738 m., 30.51 kts. | 744 m., 29.76 kts. |
| 3rd day, | 760 m., 30.40 kts. | 718 m., 28.72 kts. |
| 4th day, | 734 m., 29.36 kts. | 748 m., 29.92 kts. |
| 5th day, | | 754 m., 30.37 kts. |

## HER BABY BORN AFTER 1,000 MILE CYCLE TOUR

RATHER than spoil her husband's leave, a British sailor's wife completed a 1,000-mile cycling tour on a tandem, then did some washing and cleared up their home—only a few hours before giving birth to a baby girl.

And her youngest sister had her first baby within two hours of the daughter's arrival.

A keen cyclist all her life, twenty-nine-year-old Mrs. Kitty Warren, of Batterbury-avenue, North End, Portsmouth, spent her honeymoon on a tandem tour.

Her husband, an electrical artificer on board H.M.S. Porpoise, which has been in the Mediterranean for some time, was recently drafted home on leave.

He was not aware that his wife was so soon to have a child.

### Shared Her Secret

"I was the only one who knew my sister's secret," Mrs Wilkin, of Manor Park, told the Daily Mirror.

"When her husband wrote home and said he had been granted an unexpected month's leave and made such wonderful plans for a cycling tour, she hadn't the heart to spoil them.

"After riding the 1,000 miles they arrived home at tea time, and my sister prepared the meal.

"She then did some washing and cleared up the home. At midnight she was taken ill, and, for the first time, a doctor saw her. Then, of course, the husband heard the amazing story.

"Three hours later the child was born. Both mother and child are progressing famously.

"My youngest sister, whose first child arrived within such a short time of the other birth, is twenty-five."

Mrs. Kitty Warren, whose baby was born after she had ridden 1,000 miles on a bicycle.

## LAWYER WILL DEFEND—A DOG

**FROM OUR OWN CORRESPONDENT**

NEW YORK, Sunday.

FRENZIED thousands, moved to fever heat of emotional sympathy, are fighting for the life of—

A MONGREL DOG.

He is Idaho, a big, gawky, half-grown puppy, and he is accused of murdering a boy.

His defenders have engaged a first-class lawyer and a stenographer, sent telegrams to the President, demanded that Idaho should be released "without a stain on his character."

Owned by Victor Portune, Idaho is believed to have caused the drowning of Russell Breeze, aged fourteen, on July 4, by jumping into a canal and leaping on the boy's back while he was swimming.

Magistrate Benedict, who called the dog and owner to his office "for trial" will decide on August 5 whether Idaho must die.

Meanwhile Dr. Mahoney, apparently for the defence, says he is "going over the dog from head to tail, taking blood tests and studying reactions to see if he becomes unusually excited under certain conditions."

THE DAILY MIRROR, Tuesday, July 28, 1936.

Broadcasting—Page 24

# Daily Mirror

THE DAILY PICTURE NEWSPAPER WITH THE LARGEST NET SALE

CASSANDRA · · · · P.12
USELESS EUSTACE · 13
GREAT LOVE STORY 19
YOUR FATE TO-DAY 22
DOROTHY DIX · · · 22
THE RUGGLES · · · 24

No. 10,189 Registered at the G.P.O. as a newspaper. TUESDAY, JULY 28, 1936. One Penny

Amusements : Page 8

# EX-WIFE MANAGED HUSBAND'S MONEY

## Peer's Sister Tells of Her Devotion

BY A SPECIAL CORRESPONDENT

"We were still devoted to one another, though he had fallen in love with another woman.
"Even after he married her, we often dined together, and I managed all his money matters for him."

A SLIM, dark-eyed woman, sister of a peer, dressed in deepest mourning, wept as she told me last night of her love for her former husband.

He was Charles Barry Domvile, forty-two, living at Hans-crescent, Chelsea, London, S.W., and formerly of Loughlinstown House Co. Dublin. He took some sleeping tablets when he went to bed on Friday, was taken ill and died on Saturday.

Mrs. Ada Domvile, whose marriage to him was dissolved on June 25, and his widow, Mrs. Miriam Barbara Domvile, whom he married only three weeks ago, gave evidence at the inquest which opened yesterday.

### Married 20 Years

I met Mrs Ada Domvile as, with her fifteen-year-old son, she was exercising her two Corgi dogs.

"I was married to him for twenty years," she said. "We were happy and devoted to one another. He was the kindest and the bravest man I have ever known.

"Though the marriage was dissolved, he asked me to continue looking after his business affairs, and I agreed.

"He had been very much richer, and he still owned a good deal of property in Killiney and in Kingstown. But he did not know the value of money. I lived near him so that I could help.

"We dined together on Thursday. He was not unhappy, but he was worried by sleeplessness. All his life he had had to take tablets to sleep, because although he had tremendous vitality, he was a sick man.

"At 1.20 on Saturday morning he rang me up—as he often did—and told me he had taken enough tablets to make sure of sleep. I am sure he took them only to sleep.

"I am sorry for his young wife, whom he married on July 6. But it is terrible, too, for me, who was married to him for twenty years and loved him still."

### Inquest Adjourned

Mrs. Domvile is sister of Lord Bellew.
At the inquest she told the coroner: "I did not take it he was suicidal, and I think he wanted to take a thoroughly big sleeping dose. He had no real trouble." "I do not think he took his life intentionally."

Sir Bernard Spilsbury said the man was suffering from chronic alcoholic poisoning, but that would not account for his symptoms in view of the fact it was suggested that he had taken those tablets.

The inquest was adjourned till August 20.

---

**THE KING and the Prime Minister cancel their holidays in France.**
—See Page 3

*Lasting Friendship*

Mrs. Ada Domvile, Mr. Domvile's first wife. They often dined together even after his second marriage.

# WOMAN FIGHTS BULL WITH A FORK IN VAIN ATTEMPT TO SAVE HUSBAND

HOW a woman went to the rescue of her husband who was being gored by a bull was described at a Grantham inquest yesterday on William Henry Outram, of Frieston-lane Farm, Caythorpe.

Mrs. Outram said she was in the farmyard when she heard a moan.

She went to a gate leading into a field and saw a bull standing over her husband, who was on the ground.

"I got a hay fork and tried to drive the bull away," she said. "I shouted for help and two boys kept the bull off while I stood by my husband."

Outram died before a doctor arrived.

Returning a verdict of Death by misadventure, the coroner, Mr. Theodore Nocton, described the wife's action "as a great act of bravery."

### WON PROSPERITY WITH 2s. 6d.

With half-a-crown as his capital, Thomas Bloxsom began farming, and by dint of hard work became one of the most successful farmers in the Midlands.

When he was buried yesterday at Thornton, Leicestershire, wheat straws which he grew fifty years ago, and which were exhibited in the House of Commons, were placed in the coffin.

Mrs. William Outram, who, with a hayfork, drove the bull away from her gored husband.

# FORGOTTEN LAWS MAKE FREEMASONS LIABLE TO SEVEN YEARS IN PRISON

BY A SPECIAL CORRESPONDENT

IT was disclosed yesterday that thousands of Freemasons in the Kingdom—

Take part in an unlawful assembly every time they go to their lodge, and are liable to be sentenced to seven years' penal servitude or a minimum of two years' imprisonment.

It is because of the Unlawful Societies Act, passed in 1799 and never repealed.

The Act requires that Masonic lodges shall provide certificates annually containing their names, addresses and descriptions, for enrolment in the records of the courts of Quarter Session.

Originally, the penalty for non-observance of the Act was transportation for seven years.

### "Dangerous People"

Yet few Freemasons now even know of the existence of a law which could make them "long-term" men.

It came, too, as a surprise to a Recorder when Masonic certificates were mentioned for enrolment in his court yesterday.

"When the Clerk of the Peace wrote to me on the matter I wondered what it was I had to deal with," Mr. John Wylie, Deputy Recorder, stated at Burton Quarter Sessions. "Then I resorted to the statute and found that in 1799 Freemasons were considered dangerous people.

"I was surprised to learn that Lodges of Freemasons are apparently illegal assemblies unless they present certificates before a Court."

Few Freemasons to whom I spoke yesterday knew of the necessity to provide certificates, but Sir Algernon Tudor Craig, librarian at the Freemasons' Hall, London, said : "Certificates certainly should be provided, though doubtless in many Lodges all over the country the old statute is more recognised in the breach than in the observance."

### Members' Surprise

Certificates of the Abbey, St. Modwen's and the Old Denstonians' Lodges were enrolled in the records of the Court at Burton yesterday. And most of the members will be surprised to hear it.

"I have been connected with the Abbey Lodge for twenty years," Mr. B. A. D. Tunnicliffe, a past master, said to me when I told him what had happened at the court, "and I have never heard of the existence of certificates. I expect someone has delved into that old statute and taken steps to regularise the situation."

# BOBBY HOWES SAW HOME BLAZE

WITH tears in their eyes, Bobby Howes, famous comedian, his wife and two children saw their beautiful new cottage home at Essendon, Herts, destroyed by fire yesterday.

They had only occupied the thatched, oak-beamed house since last Saturday.

With help of villagers Mr. and Mrs. Howes and their son, Peter, aged nine, managed to save most of the furniture, entering the burning cottage time after time until the roof threatened to collapse.

Mr. and Mrs. Howes and the children were having lunch when they were told by a passer-by that the thatch had been on fire several minutes.

THE DAILY MIRROR, Thursday, July 30, 1936.

# Daily Mirror

THE DAILY PICTURE NEWSPAPER WITH THE LARGEST NET SALE

Broadcasting—Page 24

CASSANDRA - - - - P. 12
USELESS EUSTACE - 13
GREAT LOVE STORY 19
YOUR FATE TO-DAY 21
DOROTHY DIX - - - - 22
THE RUGGLES - - - - 24

No. 10,191  Registered at the G.P.O as a newspaper.  THURSDAY, JULY 30, 1936  One Penny

Amusements: Page 18

# THE KING TO GO ON SECRET CRUISE

## £300,000 Yacht Chartered

FROM OUR SPECIAL CORRESPONDENT
SOUTHAMPTON, Wednesday.
**King Edward has chartered Lady Yule's £300,000 luxury yacht Nahlin for a secret cruise with a party of friends.**

THE captain of the Nahlin has not yet received his sailing orders, but he is to have the yacht ready by Saturday, and the King will probably go aboard on Sunday.

The Nahlin is lying here, moored at the mouth of the Itchen River. She was due to leave shortly on a Mediterranean cruise, but that has been cancelled.

Her skipper, Captain N. P. Doyle, was told only this morning that the King—his visit to Cannes having been cancelled—had chartered the yacht. Immediately preparations for the royal party were begun.

Lady Yule removed her personal belongings from the yacht this evening.

To-morrow the Nahlin will be bunkered with oil fuel. The Nahlin is one of the biggest and most luxurious yachts afloat.

She carries a crew of fifty, but although so large, she has only room for eight guests. She was planned for comfort.

### Eight Staterooms

There are eight large state-rooms on board, each with its own bath-room. There are also quarters for maids and valets attending the guests.

The crew only yesterday finished repainting her hull a beautiful cream colour with a Cambridge blue water-line.

More than twice the size of the ordinary seagoing private steam steel yacht, the Nahlin was built to travel anywhere in the Seven Seas, and has already cruised from New Zealand and the South Seas to the frozen coast of Alaska.

Lady Yule, the richest woman in Britain, inherited £9,000,000 on the death of her husband, Sir David Yule, the Anglo-Indian merchant. Sir David left about £20,000,000, and £8,000,000 was paid in death duties.

Mrs. Wildman holding her baby, Ian, awarded first prize at Bedford baby show, and the cup which she won as beauty queen of Northamptonshire for 1934.

## Beauty Queen's 6-Weeks-Old Son Wins Baby Show Prize

A BEAUTY queen, Miss Northamptonshire for 1934, gave birth to her second son six weeks ago—and, following in his mother's footsteps, he has won first prize at the Bedford Baby Show.

The mother is Mrs. Freda Wildman, wife of a Bedford bus driver.

A lovely brunette of twenty-seven, she has only one regret—that the child is not a girl. . . .

"If only he had been a girl," she said to a "Daily Mirror" representative yesterday, "she could have gone in for beauty competitions."

It was only at the last moment that Mrs. Wildman entered the baby for the competition. Her husband tried to persuade her not to do so.

"My husband was driving his bus when I told him the good news," declared Mrs. Wildman. "He was so delighted—he waved his cap in the air."

The baby, who was christened Ian on Saturday, like his mother is a brunette. And despite her views on his sex, his mother says he is "the world's best baby."

When she was chosen Beauty Queen of Northamptonshire Mrs. Wildman won a hundred-guinea cup.

### B.B.C. HAS A SECRET

Sir Stephen Tallents, B.B.C. Controller of Public Relations, asked at a conference at Bristol yesterday how the B.B.C. would prevent enemy radio propaganda to Empire countries in war, said: "That is easily answered; that is secret."

Asked if there was an answer to the question, he replied: "The question whether there is an answer or not is also secret."

The twin-screw yacht Nahlin, 1,574 tons, owned by Lady Yule.

## MORE PEOPLE ARE WORKING NOW THAN EVER BEFORE

UP and up and up still mounts the scale of Britain's returning prosperity.

The number of insured workers now in employment in this country is 10,832,000—the highest ever achieved in the fourteen years during which records have been kept.

It is 1,500,000 more than in 1932.

When Mr. Ernest Brown, Minister of Labour, gave these figures in the Commons last night he added that—

Figures to be published next Tuesday would show a further reduction of unemployment in the neighbourhood of 50,000.

The biggest reduction in unemployment had been on the north-east coast. This is one of the areas which has been most hard hit by the depression.

### £500,000 More Wages

And wages are going up, too!

Mr. Brown said that since 1932 changes in the rates of wages reported to his department had shown an increase of over £500,000 a week.

More schemes for finding work are also in prospect.

The Minister explained that schemes in hand would result, it was hoped, in the settlement of 2,000 families on the land by next summer, mostly in groups of about forty.

A planting programme of the Afforestation Commission would give employment to 2,000 people and permanent settlement to 1,000 families on various holdings.

Other commitments by the Special Commissioner for England on work schemes amounted to about £4,000,000.

## AGED 76, DROVE CAR CARELESSLY FROM HIS WEDDING

A SEVENTY-SIX-YEAR-OLD motorist who had an accident while driving back from his wedding, was fined 15s. at Scunthorpe yesterday for driving a car without due care and attention.

He was Henry West, a retired farmer, of Burringham, near Scunthorpe.

It was stated that West collided with a wagon and told the police he did not see it.

"He was just returning from getting married, and I hope you will not impose a heavy penalty to mar his new-found happiness," pleaded West's solicitor.

### FOUR MORE TEST MEN

Four more players to accompany the England cricket team to Australia in quest of the "Ashes" were announced by the M.C.C. last night.

They are: Duckworth (Lancashire), Worthington (Derbyshire), Fagg (Kent) and Copson (Derbyshire). Eleven players have now been invited. No further names are expected to be issued before August 9.

Details on Page 26.

THE DAILY MIRROR, Friday, July 31, 1936

Broadcasting - Page 24

# Daily Mirror

THE DAILY PICTURE NEWSPAPER WITH THE LARGEST NET SALE

CASSANDRA - - - - P. 12
USELESS EUSTACE - 13
GREAT LOVE STORY 19
YOUR FATE TO-DAY 21
DOROTHY DIX - - - - 22
THE RUGGLES - - - - 24

No. 10,192  Registered at the G.P.O. as a newspaper.    FRIDAY, JULY 31, 1936    One Penny

Amusements: Page 16

# WOMEN AS PILOTS OF R.A.F. BOMBERS

## Fit to Fight, Says Peer

"Women might just as well be up in the air fighting as staying at home being bombed in their houses."

WITHIN three hours of declaring in the House of Lords that women pilots should be allowed to join the new Royal Air Force Reserve, Lord Strabolgi—Socialist peer, who, as Commander Kenworthy, had a distinguished war record—made that statement to the *Daily Mirror*.

"If we are fighting for our lives and women want to fight, many of them make excellent aeroplane pilots and could do it," he added.

Lord Strabolgi stressed the fact that he was not speaking for the Labour Party, but was expressing his own personal views.

"Morally, I cannot see that it is any more wrong for a woman to drop an aeroplane bomb than to make it.

"Civil aviation and air race experience proves that many women make excellent pilots because of their delicate touch, especially flying fast machines."

Lord Strabolgi raised the question of women joining the Air Force Reserve when Viscount Swinton, Minister for Air, made an announcement on the Reserve in the House of Lords last night.

### "Take Lot of Training"

Lord Swinton—described by Lord Strabolgi as "old fashioned"—stated that 800 pilots would be required annually for the Reserve.

He said that women's place was not in the fighting line, but they would get their chance in air defence as nurses in flying ambulances.

Opposite views on women as air pilots came from experts on both sides of the Atlantic. This is what they said:—

Captain H. M. Schofield, King's Cup winner, 1934: "There are only a few good women pilots of the type that could be useful in war.

"Unlike men, they take a lot of training and the expense and the time taken up would not be worth it to the Government.

"But a development that must come is aerial ambulance work. This is definitely a chance for the women, and a corps could now be formed."

Clyde Pangborn, famous American flyer:—"I have seen many women pilots, and I know that if they receive proper training they're just as competent as men.

"When women receive as much training as men pilots they're equal to them.

"I am sure women could face the terrors of aerial combat so long as they were well trained."

## Front-Line Girl

BY OUR WOMAN CORRESPONDENT

BOSCOMBE DOWN, Thursday.

AS the first girl ever to take part in a night bombing raid over England, I say immediately that, had it been real warfare in the skies to-night, I should have been shot down.

Flying in darkness above a sleeping country, the sudden leap of a searchlight, the vicious stab of a fighter, are only the

(Continued on back page)

Lovely Marlene Dietrich of the languorous glance and enigmatic smile at yesterday's reception

## MARLENE'S DAUGHTER WILL BE "SAFE" HERE

BY A SPECIAL CORRESPONDENT

FOND mother as well as glamorous film star, Marlene Dietrich is sure her eleven-year-old daughter, Maria, will be safe in England.

"I must find a school for Maria, who is now in Paris," said Marlene when she arrived in London last night with her husband Rudolf Sieber.

"She must always go to school wherever I am. . . . I don't like her to be away from me for long.

"I have come here for conferences about the Korda film that I'm to act in at Denham. It's called 'Knight without Armour' and is about the Russian Revolution. I play a White Russian and Mr. Robert Donat appears as an Englishman.

"I've only been here once before—for a single day. This time I hope to see something of the English country and of your theatre. If I've time I may also visit Austria.

"Germany? No. They do not like me now. They think I should have stayed there. But I was not a success in Berlin, so why should I stay?

"Shall I settle here? I don't think so. I have to make a film with Lubitsch in Hollywood."

## THE KING TELLS HIS YACHT CAPTAIN AND CHEF PLANS FOR HIS HOLIDAY CRUISE

FROM OUR SPECIAL CORRESPONDENT

SOUTHAMPTON, Thursday.

THREE British sailors went from Southampton to-day to see the King at St. James's Palace.

They were Captain N. P. Doyle, of Lady Yule's yacht Nahlin, in which the King is going for a holiday cruise, Chief Steward Penny and Chef Ennew.

These are the three men who will watch over the comfort of the King and his guests and see that he has a good holiday.

With Captain Doyle, the King discussed plans for his cruise, and to Chief Steward Penny and Chef Ennew he gave instructions for special stores to be taken aboard the Nahlin for the voyage.

With the chef, he discussed the meals during the holiday and told him his favourite dishes.

All three returned to Southampton this evening to make last minute preparations for the cruise.

To-morrow morning, the Nahlin will leave her moorings at the mouth of the Itchen River at 8.30, and go to the Empress Dock to take on board heavy stores by crane.

After that a compass adjuster will probably go on board and the Nahlin will come down to Stokes Bay to adjust her compasses and to see that everything is in order before she leaves with the royal party.

She is expected to set sail on Saturday.

Captain Doyle has the reputation in Southampton as a skipper who will sail a ship anywhere in the world.

### Sailed All the Seas

Short, spare, with very pale blue eyes, he served in minesweepers during the war, and has sailed in all the seas of the earth.

He has been six years in the Nahlin, and was formerly chief officer. He has been in command for the last two years.

When King Edward goes on board it will not be the first time that he has been in the Nahlin.

Last year, as Prince of Wales, he was entertained on board by Lady Yule for a week during the Jubilee Naval Review at Spithead.

Meanwhile, there is great activity on the Nahlin as she lies at her moorings opposite the Vickers Supermarine Aviation Works.

### "Fleet of Foot"

The word Nahlin is a Red Indian word for "fleet of foot," and the yacht has a large Red Indian chief as her figurehead.

It was officially announced from the Palace to-day that the King's cruise will be along the Dalmatian coast and in the Eastern Mediterranean.

In accordance with the usual custom, two destroyers will escort the yacht.

The King will be away for about three or four weeks, and it is expected that he will land at various points along the coast during his cruise.

Captain N Doyle going aboard

## QUEEN MARY'S HOLIDAY

Queen Mary went to Sandringham yesterday. It is her first visit since King George died there.

She will remain at Sandringham for a few weeks' holiday and will afterwards visit her daughter, the Princess Royal at Harewood House.

THE DAILY MIRROR, Wednesday, August 5, 1936.

# Daily Mirror

**Broadcasting - Page 24**

THE DAILY PICTURE NEWSPAPER WITH THE LARGEST NET SALE

CASSANDRA .... P. 12
USELESS EUSTACE - 13
GREAT LOVE STORY 19
YOUR FATE TO-DAY 21
DOROTHY DIX .... 22
THE RUGGLES .... 24

No. 10,196  Registered at the G.P.O. as a newspaper.  WEDNESDAY, AUGUST 5, 1936  One Penny

Amusements: Page 16

# ENGLISH WIFE TREATED LIKE ORIENTAL

## Shot Gambler of 70 —Now Freed

AN Englishwoman faced a jury at Nice Assizes yesterday and told them how she shot her seventy-year-old Syrian husband because he treated her like an Oriental girl in a way that was intolerable to a woman of Western race and culture.

Within twenty minutes of their retirement, the jury found her not guilty of murder, and she left th court with her sister, a free woman, to start life again in England.

"I am so happy I can hardly believe I am free," she said tearfully as she stood once more in the street.

She is Mrs. May Kemeid, who, before her marriage to Joseph Kemeid, a wealthy whisky merchant, in London thirty-two years ago, was Miss May Duggan, of Ipswich.

She was charged with murdering her husband by shooting him as he lay in bed in their villa at Vence, near Nice, last November. After the shooting Mrs. Kemeid attempted to commit suicide, and seriously wounded herself.

In answer to the opening questions of the President of the Court she said that she had shot her husband because he had caused her moral suffering.

"He treated me like an Oriental girl," she said.

"Why did you return to him?"

### "I Told Him"

"I saw him again at Monte Carlo in 1929, and went back. We had a daughter who was then fifteen, and who became a nun in 1931. From that time life became intolerable."

Her husband was a terrible gambler and lost heavily. She had asked him for a separation, but he refused.

When Mrs. Kemeid was brought before an examining magistrate at Grasse it is alleged she made a statement which said:—

"I intended taking my husband's life and my own, too, as I have been suffering morally for several years.

"The idea of putting an end to it all occurred to me in the morning. I picked up a revolver I had in my room and went to my husband's bedroom He was asleep.

"I woke him up and told him of my intentions and my reasons for it.

"For over an hour we argued the matter over. As he refused to listen to my argument and turned his back on the pillow I fired twice.

"His head dropped without his uttering a word. I thought he was dead and turned the weapon against myself, but I was in such a state of excitement that I missed blowing my own brains out."

The medical expert, Dr Cottin, testified that at the time of the shooting Mrs. Kemeid was in such a state of neurasthenic depression that she was not fully responsible for her actions.

A letter from her daughter, then a nun in the Sacred Heart Convent, Newcastle-on-Tyne, was read by Mrs. Kemeid's lawyer.

The girl exhorted her mother to place her trust in God and all would be well.

*Messages from British United Press, Exchange and Central News*

Mrs. May Kemeid.

## CAN YOU DO THIS ↓ OR THIS? ↓

Kathryn Garrett, Oklahoma typist, never lacks a hug or a squeeze even if she has to give it to herself.

If she bangs her funny bone on a door she can kiss it well, —and (left) how's this for a waist reducing exercise? With both arms twisted across her back, Kathryn can shake hands.

## AREN'T YOU GLAD YOU LIVE IN ENGLAND?

*Aren't you glad you live in England? Read this and you'll know why.*

MILLIONS of you are enjoying holidays. Did you say weather?

Think of nearly 5,000 dying in America's heatwave, whole towns forced to move by drought, the maize crop reduced by more than 600,000,000 bushels and spring wheat by 25,000,000.

* * *

YOUR holiday is over, and you have to go back to work? Well, another 50,000 who haven't had a job for months are going with you. Unemployment figures are rising abroad, but look at our record:—

July's decrease of 50,604 is the sixth consecutive drop in the monthly figures this year.

The July total of 1,652,072 is the best return for well over six years.

Insured persons in employment on July 20 were approximately 10,895,000, exclusive of agricultural workers. This is 63,000 more than a month before and 481,000 more than a year before.

* * *

THAT makes pretty good reading, but if you are still not convinced, take another look abroad.

Spain's rebellion has already cost thousands of lives and shows no signs of ending

Greece is faced with a general strike called by the unions against a new wage law.

Poland is beset with political riots, and 10,000 Ukranian Nationalists were reported yesterday to have lynched two Communists tearing their bodies to pieces.

Abyssinia is still torn by war. Yesterday Reuter reported a furious battle raging round Lake Tana between Italians and Ethiopian warriors. Heavy losses have been suffered by both sides.

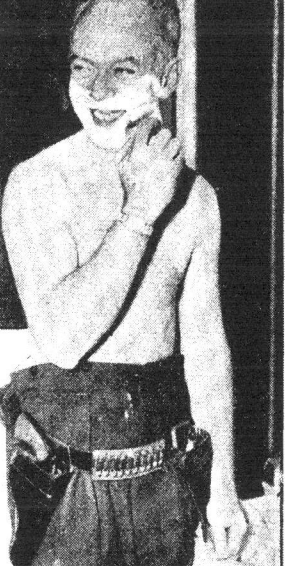

He's always expecting a close shave is Thomas Manville, jnr., heir to the Asbestos millions.

As soon as he gets up in the morning he straps guns round his hips, because of threats against his life.

## BRITAIN SENDS "NO BARGAIN IN SPAIN" ULTIMATUM TO THE DUCE AND HITLER

**"DAILY MIRROR" EXCLUSIVE NEWS**

THE British Foreign Office yesterday told Herr Hitler and Signor Mussolini that Britain could not permit the establishment of a Fascist Government in Madrid:—

if such a Government received support from Germany and Italy in return for a promise to concede Ceuta and a port in Minorca to Italy.

Ceuta, in Spanish Morocco, is immediately opposite Gibraltar; Minorca, second biggest of the Balearic Isles, lies in the centre of the western Mediterranean.

It is believed that Mussolini wishes to establish naval bases in both these centres

### France Also Warned

At the same time Paris has been informed that Britain will be no party to the establishment of a Communist regime in Spain, and will give no assistance to France in any steps she may contemplate taking in that direction.

France is urged to fall in line with Great Britain in impressing on Germany and Italy the fact that there will be no interference in Spain unless a bargain with the Spanish rebels threatens British security in the Mediterranean.

In their reply to the French Note regarding non-intervention in Spain, the British Government state that they are prepared to agree to the suggested issue of a neutrality declaration if France delays the adherence of Italy.

### Italy Delays

Baron von Neurath, it is understood, has informed the French Ambassador in Berlin that Germany is prepared to agree to a neutrality accord if the U.S.S.R. agrees similarly.

When Italy was asked for an assurance, France is believed to have been told: "Italy needs time to consider this."

Fears of European complications developing from the civil war in Spain were emphasised by events yesterday.

Spanish rebel headquarters have, it is reported, ordered the closing of the Franco-Spanish frontier.

British travellers arriving at Gibraltar from Tangier report that nine Italian 'planes and three German seaplanes are at Ceuta, rebel headquarters in Morocco.

## SHE IS TELEVISION MAKE-UP EXPERT

MISS Mary Allan has been appointed assistant in charge of make-up and wardrobe in the television department of the B.B.C., it was announced last night.

She joins the Corporation on August 10. Miss Allan has been fifteen years in stage and film work, specialising in make-up, dress design and wardrobe in association with leading theatrical producers

THE DAILY MIRROR, Thursday, August 6, 1936.

# Daily Mirror

**THE DAILY PICTURE NEWSPAPER WITH THE LARGEST NET SALE**

Broadcasting - Page 24

CASSANDRA .... P. 12
USELESS EUSTACE - 13
GREAT LOVE STORY 19
YOUR FATE TO-DAY 21
DOROTHY DIX .... 22
THE RUGGLES .... 24

No. 10,197. Registered at the G.P.O. as a newspaper. THURSDAY, AUGUST 6, 1936 One Penny

Amusements: Page 18

# AIR MINISTRY CHIEF DISMISSED BY PREMIER

## Inquiry Says "Own Interest Pressed"

Sir Eric Geddes, chairman of Imperial Airways.

### A BRILLIANT CAREER

Sir Christopher Llewellyn Bullock, K.C.B., was born in November, 1891. He was captain of the running eight at Rugby and a scholar of Trinity College, Cambridge. He took first place in the open competitive examination for the Home and Indian Civil Services in 1914.

During the war he served with the Rifle Brigade and the Royal Flying Corps.

Sir Christopher was the son of the Rev. L. C. W. Bullock, rector of Wigborough, Essex.

## BRITON FALLS 3,000 FEET ON MATTERHORN

ROPED to a local guide, Mr. George Restall, aged twenty-four, connected with a well-known Birmingham furniture company, fell 3,000ft. with his companion to a terrible death on the Matterhorn, in the Alps, yesterday.

The manager of his hotel at Zermatt told the *Daily Mirror* last night that three parties, including Mr. Restall and a guide called Perron, started to climb at 9.30 in the morning and all reached the top.

The first party came down, and ten minutes later were followed by Mr. Restall and his guide. When the third party reached the first waiting at a boulder on the mountain it was discovered that Restall and his guide had failed to turn up.

### Trapped on Cliff

On the precipitous rocks of the Avon Gorge at Bristol, near the spot known as Fairyland, where a man fell to his death on Monday, two children who had become trapped were rescued yesterday while crowds watched 250 feet below.

Mr. Albert Bidwell, of Grosvenor-road, Bristol, rescued the children with the help of another man as his wife and two children were watching below.

Motorists used their car lamps and searchlights along the embankment at Putney to guide a man to the rescue of two boys who fell into the Thames from a home-made raft last night.

The boys were Michael Daniels, nine, and Edward White, eleven, both of Upper Richmond-road, Putney.

THE PRIME MINISTER HAS DIRECTED THAT SIR CHRISTOPHER BULLOCK, PERMANENT SECRETARY OF THE AIR MINISTRY, BE DISMISSED THE SERVICE.

THAT was the sensational announcement made last night

A Board of Inquiry set up by Mr. Baldwin had, it was revealed, found that Sir Christopher had acted "improperly" in discussing with Imperial Airways the possibility of his becoming a director, and that he had pressed on the company "unwelcome suggestions."

The findings have ended one of the most brilliant careers at the Air Ministry. At forty-four Sir Christopher, son of a country rector, had for five years held the £3,000-a-year Permanent Secretaryship.

His rapid promotion from the time when, in 1917, he joined the staff at the Air Ministry to the day when he became a civil head was recognised as the outcome of outstanding ability.

Sir Christopher first sprang into prominence when in 1919 he was made Principal Private Secretary to Mr. Winston Churchill, Secretary of State for Air.

From 1923 to 1930 he acted in the same capacity to successive Ministers—Sir Samuel Hoare and Lord Thomson.

Last month it was announced that he had been appointed a member of the Executive Committee of the Coronation Committee of the Privy Council.

Sir Christopher, who was made a Knight Commander of the Bath in 1932, married in 1917 Barbara May, daughter of Henry Lupton, of Torquay. They have two sons.

### Sir Christopher's Statement

In a letter to the Editor of the *Daily Mirror* last night, Sir Christopher said:—

"I do not seek to burke responsibility for consequences which have flowed from my own actions.

"But it is easy to be wise after the event; and fortunate is he who can honestly say that, if every private and informal conversation he has held were sifted and resifted months, even years, afterwards in the rarefied atmosphere of a solemn and formal inquisition, no passing phrase uttered in an unguarded moment could be held injudicious, no word or deed be called in question in some degree by absolute standards of taste or propriety."

**Board of Inquiry's Findings—Page Five**

Sir Christopher Bullock, Air Ministry Permanent Secretary, dismissed the Service.

## 'PHONE CALL TO WIFE ON HOLIDAY TELLS TRAGEDY OF HER HUSBAND

### By A SPECIAL CORRESPONDENT

SCOTLAND Yard telephoned to Felpham Sussex, police late last night to break the news to a mother enjoying a happy holiday with her two little girls that her husband had been found dead in London.

The body of Mr. Arthur E. Wheeler, thirty-eight-year-old City insurance agent, was discovered eight hours before in their ivy-covered villa in Winscombe-crescent, North Ealing.

Police officers who went to the house yesterday found him lying outside his bedroom. He was dressed in red silk pyjamas.

There was a gaping wound in the back of his head.

Mrs. Wheeler, an attractive woman of thirty-five, and her two daughters, Carol, aged ten, and Barbara two years younger left Ealing by car on Saturday for a holiday with Mrs. Wheeler's mother in Sussex.

Yesterday, just before noon, a man walked into Ealing police station and made a statement. Immediately officers went to the house in a flying squad car.

Inside they found signs of a struggle. Mr. Wheeler was lying on the second floor landing.

Inquiries last night were concentrated on a mystery car which was seen parked outside the house.

A man will appear at Ealing Police Court to-day charged with the murder of Mr. Wheeler.

## QUEEN OF NETHERLANDS ABDICATION RUMOURED

REPORTS reached Stockholm last night hinting at the possible abdication of the Queen of the Netherlands and of a pending marriage between Princess Juliana of the Netherlands, the Queen's only daughter, and Carl, Prince of Sweden, son of the Duke and Duchess of Vestergotland.

Similar rumours have been circulated several times during the last few years, the last occasion being about six months ago, when a semi-official denial was issued, says Exchange.

Last night, however, it was impossible to get any comment on the rumour in the absence from Stockholm of King Gustaf, the Crown Prince and Princess, the Duke and Duchess of Vestergotland, and Prince Carl himself.

# Daily Mirror

THE DAILY PICTURE NEWSPAPER WITH THE LARGEST NET SALE

Broadcasting—Page 20

CASSANDRA — P. 12
USELESS EUSTACE — 13
GREAT LOVE STORY 19
YOUR FATE TO-DAY 21
DOROTHY DIX — 22
THE RUGGLES — 24

No. 10,199  Registered at the G.P.O. as a newspaper.  SATURDAY, AUGUST 8, 1936  One Penny

Amusements : Page 16

## RICH ISLAND QUEEN MARRIES FISHERMAN

### Was Her Devoted Servant

Island "Queen" of Thorn, off the Pembrokeshire coast, a rich heiress has secretly married the twenty-nine-year-old fisherman who has been her devoted servant, rowing her from the mainland across the dangerous channel to her lonely castle.

THE wedding took place in Monkton Priory Church, Pembroke, by special licence. Three large motor cars drove quietly to a side entrance of the church and from the first descended the bride, Miss Lena Adela Mary Pearson, twenty-five-year-old daughter of Mr. George Sherwyn Hooke Pearson, a retired Civil Servant, of Baynton Hall House, East Coulston, Westbury, Wiltshire.

The bridegroom was Mr. Sydney James Hicks, son of Mr. and Mrs. William Cecil Hicks, of Bay View, Angle.

The bride's father and brother witnessed the ceremony in addition to the father, mother and sister of the bridegroom.

Villagers knew nothing of the wedding. None of them was aware of the romance in their midst.

### Island Fort

This is how the beautiful bride came to marry the man who for the past three years has been her boatman, chauffeur and electrician.

She was intrigued by the beauty of an obsolete fort standing on the crest of the island of Thorne.

She bought it from the Government and at great expense converted it into a magnificent residence at which, in the summer time, large parties of guests were entertained.

She is a keen yachtswoman and motorist and has a fleet of motor-boats anchored in Angle Bay.

### Met Three Years Ago

A friend of the bridegroom told the *Daily Mirror* last night:—"Mr. Hicks met Miss Pearson about three years ago, when she first came to live on the island.

"They became close friends, and I understand they became engaged twelve months ago.

"They had kept their wedding a close secret, and no one in the village of Angle knew anything about it until to-day.

"Miss Pearson used to leave the island at the end of each summer, and lived with her parents at Westbury, Wiltshire, in the winter.

"We often saw Miss Pearson and Mr. Hicks together, and last year he drove her home in the car to Westbury. They seemed very much attached."

The bridegroom's parents, who have a family of twelve, were surprised when they heard the wedding was to take place on Tuesday.

(Continued on back page)

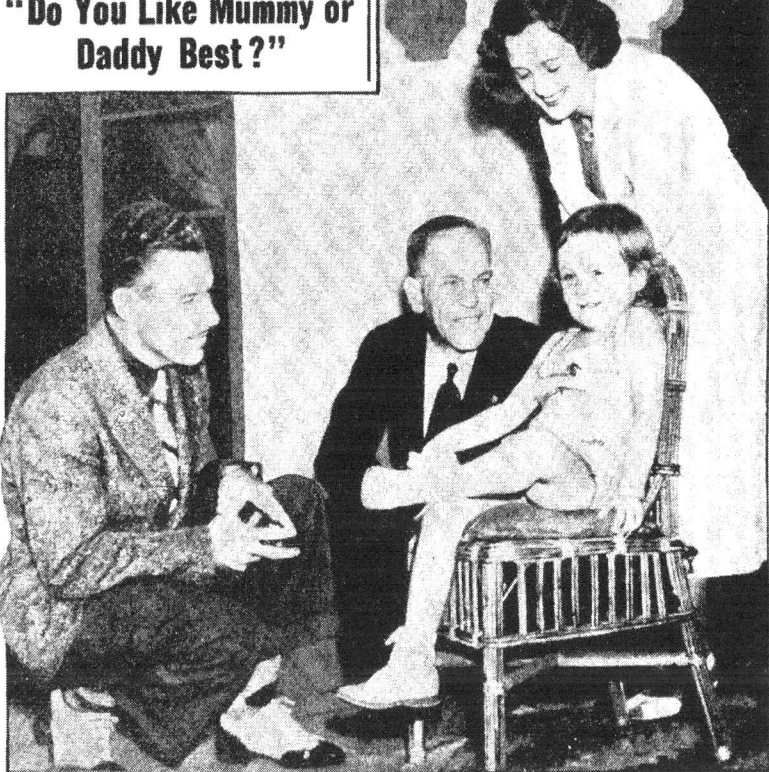

"Do You Like Mummy or Daddy Best?"

Equal to rank with painting, "When did you last see your Father," is this picture of Mary Astor, Dr. Thorpe and Marilyn, for whose custody each is fighting. Judge Knight (centre) sought the child's solution. "I love Mummy; I love Daddy," she said

### TERRITORIALS FIRE — CATTLE FALL, PLOUGHMEN FLEE

WHEN two shells fired by Territorials on Salisbury Plain fell into a field at Redhorn Hill, four miles from Devizes—

Two cows and two sheep were killed outright;

Seven other cattle had to be slaughtered;

Farm labourers unyoked their horses from ploughs and fled.

And a farmer leading a horse a mile away complained of being struck by shrapnel.

A soldier at look-out post was surprised when he looked through the window to see a hail of shell splinters and mangled animals.

A fragment of shell penetrated a shepherd's hut. Local people also complain that shells fell on the public path which is much used.

## JUDGE WILL IGNORE FILM STAR SCANDAL STORIES IN ASTOR SUIT

Los Angeles, Friday.

JUDGE Goodwin J. Knight, presiding in the Mary Astor action, warned the parties and their lawyers to-day that love-life scandals of film stars that may emerge in Monday's hearing will not affect the issue.

Custody of the four-year-old Marilyn Thorpe, daughter of the film star and her divorced husband, Dr. Thorpe, will be decided solely on the issue of the child's welfare, he said

"It will not be awarded in revenge or as a prize in the family row," said the Judge.

"My decision will not be swayed by the lawyers or the principals in the case using the mistakes of either Dr. Thorpe or Miss Mary Astor.

"The welfare of this wee, healthy, happy, dimple-faced child is the only issue in which I am interested."

Judge Knight added that he would decide the question of the custody of the child only on this basis—which of the two parents was the more certain to rear Marilyn properly— says British United Press.

Miss Astor is seeking the custody of the child from Dr. Thorpe, who alleged that the star is not a fit and proper person to have the custody.

Besides her suit for the child's custody, Miss Astor is seeking the annulment of her marriage to Dr. Thorpe—the marriage that was afterwards dissolved—on the ground that Dr. Thorpe was already married when he eloped with her.

### HE IS ENGLAND'S NEW MILLIONAIRE

THE *London Gazette* announced last night that Mr. Whitney Willard Straight, the young American millionaire racing motorist, has been granted a certificate of naturalisation by the Secretary of State.

Mr. Straight was educated in England, and his marriage in July, 1935, to Lady Daphne Finch-Hatton, daughter of the Earl and Countess of Winchilsea, was one of the social events of the season.

# Daily Mirror

**THE DAILY PICTURE NEWSPAPER WITH THE LARGEST NET SALE**

Broadcasting—Page 24

CASSANDRA - - - - P. 12
USELESS EUSTACE - 13
YOUR FATE TO-DAY 17
GREAT LOVE STORY 19
DOROTHY DIX - - - - 22
THE RUGGLES - - - - 24

No. 10,202 Registered at the G.P.O as a newspaper. WEDNESDAY, AUGUST 12, 1936 One Penny

Amusements: Page 16

## LOVERS IN CHILDHOOD WED AT 75

### 'We're So Happy' —3-Day Courtship

BY A SPECIAL CORRESPONDENT

A newly-married couple of seventy-five, who were childhood sweethearts sixty years ago, at Rothwell, Northants, spoke to me last night of their new-found happiness as the Empress of Britain bore them towards Canada.

THEY are Mr. J. T. Tebbutt, a Canadian gold-mine owner, and his bride, formerly Mrs. Kitty Brown, a Leicester widow.

Over the wireless telephone from the liner, Mr. Tebbutt's voice came to me strong and clear: "We're very happy."

"I was very fond of Kitty when we were both young together in Rothwell, where we were born. We taught in the same school together. Then I emigrated to Canada to seek my fortune. I've done very well.

"I never lost touch with the old country, though I married in Canada and had five children—they'll be meeting me at Quebec on Thursday to meet their new mother for the first time. I visited Leicester some years ago, after my wife's death and found Mrs. Brown a widow.

"We corresponded, and I came back to Leicester to propose. She accepted me, and we're going to spend the rest of our lives together at Three Rivers, Quebec, where I live.

#### Children's Congratulations

"We've had cables of congratulation from my five children."

Mrs. Tebbutt's voice came more faintly over the line. "I can't hear you very well, darling," she said to her husband, and then, to me: "All I can say is, I'm very happy."

Mrs. Brown's only son, Mr. Walter B. Brown, of East Park-road, Leicester, said last night:—

"Mr. Tebbutt proposed to mother and they were married by special licence three days later.

"This is a happy ending to a broken romance of Victorian days. My mother was courting Mr. Tebbutt then, but they had a little tiff and they parted.

"No one was more surprised than I when they shyly told me they had decided to pick up the threads of their old romance, but I am glad now. Mother looks twenty years younger.

"Mr. Tebbutt insisted on buying mother a beautiful diamond engagement ring for their three days' engagement.

"They kept their wedding very quiet. I gave mother away, and my little girl acted as bridesmaid.

"Then they rushed off to Buxton for a few days' honeymoon, both of them as happy as schoolchildren."

#### NANNIE HANDS ROUND 'BONNET'

The King George National Memorial Fund has received a cheque for £3 7s. with the following note:—

"This amount has been collected by my nannie, Miss Keightley, from her various nannie friends in the park."

**SOUNDING THE ALARM . . .**

**. . . AND THE RETREAT**

Two-year-old Dafila Wilson was the bridesmaid who didn't want to be photographed, which isn't usual. When she saw the camera she went like the top picture—and fled. The elder bridesmaid just stopped her from running out of the picture. The wedding pair were Miss Dorothea Nance and Mr. H. A. Whittemore, and the ceremony at Bebington, Cheshire.

### Panic as Leopard Roams a City

Panic spread throughout Zurich yesterday when a leopard escaped from the city Zoo and roamed the streets.

The animal was at large for a considerable time while guards tried to trap it or drive it back to the Zoo.

Eventually when there was no hope of getting the leopard back to his cage the guards killed it.—Central News.

## JUDGE THREATENS TO 'STREAMLINE' ASTOR CASE: MORE DIARY REVELATIONS

FROM OUR SPECIAL CORRESPONDENT
LOS ANGELES, Tuesday.

WHILE Judge Knight was telling lawyers in the Astor case here today that "mud-slinging" will not help them, more entries from Mary Astor's diary revealing her love for George Kaufman were made public.

"This child custody case is not a divorce action, so I must 'streamline' this trial," said the Judge.

"The case is very simple, and I am about ready to give a decision."

### "Rosy Glow"

The excerpts from the diary start with October 1, 1934, on Mary Astor's return from New York, where she saw Kaufman. She wrote:—

"I'm still in haze—ice-rosy glow. If I thought this business with George was half-hearted I'm crazy. It's beautiful, glorious—and I hope it's my last love—I can't top it with anything in my experience or do I want to."

On December 1, 1934, she contrasted her husband with the man she loved:—

"Franklyn, who loves me, needs me, leans on me, whom I like to be with sometimes because of that love, because of certain niceness, warmth and used-to-ness, who loves me to death most of the time, but who has no sense of humour whatsoever. . . .

"George Piece Mercury, a completely fascinating, elusive person who has the power of making me so happy when I'm with him that I want to laugh from sheer joy."

### Sacredness of Marriage

Later Mary tells of a call her husband made on Kaufman:—

"Franklyn called on him. . . . He told George he knew he couldn't completely fill my life, that I needed other interests, but the sacredness of marriage and the child were at stake, and George must be willing to take a share in the responsibility involved.

"What he meant by that . . . George couldn't find out. George knows I love him—we kid a

*(Continued on back page)*

## LORD HAREWOOD BANS BATHERS

LORD Harewood, whose Yorkshire estate includes a stretch of the River Wharfe eight miles in length, has banned bathers from using it.

"There is not the remotest chance of the ban being lifted," an official of Lord Harewood's estate office said yesterday.

"We have had a great deal of trouble with bathers," he added. "They go down to any part of the river, whether it is private or not, undress on the bank, sun bathe and generally do just as they please.

"Our farmers have complained repeatedly of broken bottles and other litter being left in the fields by the riverside. Broken bottles are a real danger to cattle."

One of Lord Harewood's tenant farmers expressed his pleasure at the decision to ban bathers.

"Some people," he said, "actually drive their cars into the fields, use the cars as dressing-rooms and after bathing play football or cricket or have a picnic, leaving all their litter behind them."

Yorkshire bathers complain that they are being blamed for the carelessness of ordinary picnickers and anglers.

THE DAILY MIRROR, Thursday, August 13, 1936

Broadcasting - Page 24

# Daily Mirror

THE DAILY PICTURE NEWSPAPER WITH THE LARGEST NET SALE

USELESS EUSTACE P.12
CASSANDRA - - - - 13
GREAT LOVE STORY 19
YOUR FATE TO-DAY 21
DOROTHY DIX - - - - 22
THE RUGGLES - - - - 24

No. 10,203  Registered at the G.P.O. as a newspaper.  THURSDAY, AUGUST 13, 1936  One Penny

Amusements : Page 20

# GAMES STAR GIVES UP FAME—
## TO BE 'JUST A WIFE'

Phyllis Harding.

By McKENZIE PORTER
"Daily Mirror" Special Correspondent at the Olympic Games
BERLIN, Wednesday.

IT was not Phyllis Harding, England's famous swimmer, who spoke from the heart to-day—it was her other self, Mrs. Turner, charming little wife of a Coventry solicitor.

Phyllis Harding, or Mrs. Turner, is to retire after she has competed in the back-stroke final at the Olympic Games here.

"And at last I shall know what it is to be called by my married name and to live the life of a normal woman," she said.

Although not yet twenty-nine, Phyllis, holder of several world's records, is the only woman in the world to have swum in four consecutive Olympics.

"Yet, I have paid a great price for my athletic distinction," she said.

### Early to Bed

"From the moment I was recognised as a swimmer twelve years ago, I have been deprived of many things which the true woman should enjoy.

"Other girls can go off to play tennis or golf, but if I had done this my trainer would have objected.

"My muscles have to be soft, and any other form of sport would have hardened them. I have not been allowed to run, not even for a tramcar! Running is bad for a swimmer.

"If occasionally I have gone to a dance, I have had to miss many numbers and refuse cigarettes, and every time I have had to leave early to get to bed."

Phyllis described how every day in the year, with the exception of Sundays, she has had to spend an hour in the bath training, and once each week has had to drive 118 miles to see her coach.

### No Regrets

Then there were always galas in which she had to appear, and international contests all over the world she had to attend.

"All that takes a big slice out of a woman's life. And then it is hard to be away from my husband for such long stretches.

"I have given the best years of my life to sport, and I don't regret it. After all, it has taken me to many different countries and has always thrilled me, but now I am going to settle down to family life.

"Some people are pressing me to train for the next Empire Games, but it is no use . . . I am going to enjoy those things I have missed during the past twelve years. I am going to be Phyllis Harding, the famous swimmer, no more. . . . I am going to be just Mrs Turner, of Coventry."

## GIRL SEES FIANCE DIE

COLLAPSING as he came out from a bathe during Sandown Bay (Isle of Wight) Regatta yesterday, a man was helped by his fiancee to a chair, but died at her side within ten minutes.

He was Douglas Boar, aged twenty-four, of Broomhall-road, Ipswich, who was on holiday with Miss Hilda Croft, of Norwich-road, Ipswich.

UNVEILING of Vimy Memorial made this romance. That brought Mr. Samuel Emerson to Europe. He met this girl, with whom he had already been exchanging letters. She was Miss Lily Bell, of Darlington; here she is Mrs. Emerson. Story page 4.

## 14,000 CHILDREN KILLED ON ROADS IN TEN YEARS

FOURTEEN thousand children were killed and 400,000 were injured on the roads of Great Britain in the last ten years.

This is one of the "grim and challenging reminders" of the road accident problem given by Lieutenant-Colonel J. A. A. Pickard, general secretary of the National "Safety First" Association, in an appeal to motorists to help in minimising the danger to children during holidays.

In London, one in every twelve boys meets with a traffic accident during his school life, he said.

"Ship Ahoy!" Crew and passengers of the yacht, Mary, being taken on board the pleasure ship, Essex Queen, after their yacht had sunk, following a collision off Margate.

## "MY FIRST SWIM"—BY WIFE SAVED FROM SINKING YACHT

FROM OUR OWN CORRESPONDENT
MARGATE, Wednesday.

NEVER once using the word Fear, two women—one aged forty-five, a non-swimmer, the other seventeen—told me to-night of the "minutes that seemed years" when a yacht sank beneath them after a collision at sea.

The yacht was the Mary, owned by Mr. J. W. Snell, of Seal, Sevenoaks, outward bound from Ramsgate. It was sunk in collision off Margate with the pleasure steamer Essex Queen, which had 250 passengers on board.

Mr. Snell, sixty-year-old Albert Matthews, the skipper, Mrs. Snell and her seventeen-year-old niece, Beryl Thompson, of Dovercourt, Essex, were on board.

In a blouse and pair of black trousers borrowed from Margate Hospital, where she had been taken, Mrs. Snell gave me this account of her adventure:—

"I have never had such a time in my life. I was shot overboard, and, not being able to swim, I sank.

"When I came to the surface, however, I had the presence of mind to remember that as a child I had always been told that in the case of emergency always try to get on my back and keep my head down

"To my surprise I succeeded, and then began twisting my hands in the water in the form of a ship's propeller, as I had seen others do.

"I did this for some time, and later was rescued from the water—I seem to have been floating about for a long time. I dare not attempt to look round or even anywhere

Beryl, her dark hair still wet, told me:—"I was not afraid. Even when I saw the steamer almost on top of us I was only thrilled.

"The Mary sank beneath me, and I found myself in the water. There was a piece of wreckage near at hand, and I grabbed hold of it and hung on."

## "SIZZLING LOVE-LEDGER"

LOS ANGELES, Wednesday.

WHAT a New York paper calls "Mary's Sizzling, Scarlet-Bound Love-Ledger," is believed to have prevented a settlement between Mary Astor, the film star, and Dr. R. F. Thorpe, her ex-husband, in the suit over the custody of their child.

Dr. Thorpe is reported to have refused to relinquish the "love-ledger" because "it is worth a million dollars."

After spending half an hour with the respective attorneys the Judge summoned witnesses to the court, thus indicating that the negotiations for a settlement had failed.—Reuter.

# Daily Mirror

THE DAILY PICTURE NEWSPAPER WITH THE LARGEST NET SALE

Broadcasting—Page 20

YOUR FATE TO-DAY P. 9
USELESS EUSTACE - 9
GREAT LOVE STORY 14
CASSANDRA - - - 16
DOROTHY DIX - - - 17
THE RUGGLES - - - 20

No. 10,205 Registered at the G.P.O. as a newspaper. SATURDAY, AUGUST 15, 1936 One Penny

Amusements: Page 8

## R.A.F. CAMP RAIDED—AS JOKE

### Stink Bombs Used in "Reprisal" —Night Chaos

FROM OUR SPECIAL CORRESPONDENT

FOLKESTONE, Friday Night.

SMOKE bombs and home-made stink bombs were dropped on the mess tents and equipment belonging to No. 600 City of London Auxiliary R.A.F. Squadron in camp at Hawkinge near here to-night.

The raid, carried out by members of No. 601 City of London Auxiliary Squadron, now in camp at Lympne, was an act of retaliation for a raid earlier in the week.

Bomb after bomb was dropped with deadly accuracy. Officers of the squadron in full evening kit were beginning dinner in mess tents when the attack occurred.

As the bombs, dropped from machines, skilfully and daringly piloted, thick white smoke covered the aerodrome.
Chaos reigned for a while. It was impossible to see.
Numerous motor cars, belonging to members of the squadron, parked nearby were hit.

#### Stunt-Flying

No machines from the aerodrome took to the sky to battle with the attackers.
After the supply of bombs had been exhausted, the attacking pilots let off crackers, and performed stunt flying over the encampment before disappearing across the horizon.

The attack was not an authorised one. It was, the "Daily Mirror" understands, carried out without the knowledge of the Commanding Officer of 601 squadron.
Many of the pilots and members of this squadron possess privately owned machines These were used for the attack.

To-night, an officer, speaking on behalf of the C.O. denied the attack.
"We have no official knowledge of it here," he said. "As far as I know no machines, either R.A.F. or privately owned have taken to the air."

#### No Sherry

Speaking to an officer at Hawkinge, the Daily Mirror was told that the "attack" had taken place.
"They surprised us," he said. "Their bombing was deadly and accurate.
"We had not started dinner when we first heard the zoom of machines.
"Foul-smelling bombs dropped all round us. Cars that were parked nearby were hit. There was complete chaos for a time.
"It was a grand leg-pull. We all enjoyed it, but could do nothing in retaliation. There was no danger to anyone. The raid was carried out in good fun and with complete sportsmanship.
"In fact, it was so awful that it was impossible to drink our sherry before dinner. That was the biggest catastrophe."

It is understood, however, that an inquiry into the unofficial raid will be made by officials of the Air Ministry to-morrow.

### DUKE AND DUCHESS OF KENT IN CRASH

VIENNA, Friday.

THE Duke and Duchess of Kent, who have been staying with the Count von Hoffmannsthal, at Kamner on the Attersee, had a narrow escape to-day when their host's car, in which they were travelling, came in collision with a car from Vienna on a narrow road at the edge of the Atter Lake.

The other car overturned and fell into the lake, the four occupants being slightly injured.

Neither the Duke and Duchess nor their host was hurt.

In spite of the accident, the Duke and Duchess left Kammer Castle this afternoon and motored via Salzburg and the Gross Glockner mountain road to Yugoslavia, where they are to stay

The driver of one of the cars in the Duke and Duchess of Kent's party said:
"When we stopped, all the men passengers, including the Duke, ran to help the four occupants of the overturned vehicle.
"We all feared the worst, but by a miracle they had only received slight bruises and shock."

The driver of the wrecked car was Dr. Schultz, a merchant from Vienna.—Reuter.

The happy parents.

### DAUGHTER FOR PRINCESS PEARL AND HARRY ROY

A DAUGHTER was born last night to Princess Pearl, wife of Harry Roy, the dance band leader, in a West End nursing home.

Princess Pearl's mother, the Ranee of Sarawak, told the "Daily Mirror," "It's a beautiful girl! Harry will be delighted.

"He doesn't know yet, because he's been at St. Juan-les-Pins under medical advice.
"I'm delighted it is a girl. Daughters are more companionable than sons."

#### Glad It's a Girl

And Mrs. Litman, Harry Roy's mother, learning that she had become a grandmother when she returned from holiday to her Park-lane flat last night, said:

"No, I don't mind the baby being a girl, nor will Harry. He will be simply crazy with delight. I know he will want to rush back to London.

"I have not yet seen the baby, or my daughter-in-law, but will do so to-morrow."
Princess Pearl, who is twenty-three, married Harry Roy in August last year.
Her father, Sir Charles Brooke, the white Rajah, was unable to attend the wedding at the Caxton Hall Register Office, owing to Government duties.
Sir Charles is ruler of an area in North-West Borneo almost as big as England and with 500,000 inhabitants.

### "READY TO BOMB BRITAIN" DECLARES I.R.A. GENERAL

An amazing plot to "rain bombs on England" in an attempt to establish an Irish Republic is revealed in the following statement issued and signed by "General" Sean Russel, Quartermaster-General of the Irish Republican Army, in New York last night.

FROM OUR OWN CORRESPONDENT

NEW YORK, Friday.

IN a slow, deliberate voice General Russel told me to-night that the I.R.A. had aeroplanes in Ireland with skilled pilots ready for action at the word of command.

He told me of large stocks of arms and ammunition hidden in Ireland and England, and of bodies of loyal Republicans drilling secretly in various parts of the British Isles.

#### Hide-and-Seek

The interview ended with a calm expression of his belief that Admiral Somerville was "executed" at Cork by Republican order Then came a warning to Britain that any of her nationals guilty of meddling in Irish affairs might meet with a similar fate
Sean Russel has arrived in America to raise a 1,000,000 dollar fighting fund to finance the Republican forces. He slipped quietly from Ireland after playing a dangerous hide-and-seek game with the Free State authorities
Sean Russel says they want to imprison him too. But he added that he had no hatred for the people of Britain.

He said, however, that his compatriots would "stop at nothing" to obtain the "complete independence they deserve."

"You know, of course," he said, "that De Valera has betrayed the trust of the Irish nation by becoming the tool of Great Britain.
"Instead of fighting, as he promised, for the Republic of Ireland, he has been content to allow her to be a nation subject to a foreign King

"Republican forces await an opportune moment to fight with all their might for the nation's freedom.
"When the moment will come I do not know. It may come when the British become embroiled in a European conflict. But our plan of campaign is ready.

"Then, over in England, where we shall also take the offensive, we have another secret army of Irishmen, who meet quietly for drill and target practice.

"We have also quantities of ammunition and other war material in England.
"Our Air Force may be small but it is reasonably efficient.

"When hostilities start we shall certainly send 'planes to bomb England.
"It is a very definite plan in our scheme for an offensive.

"Admiral Somerville was recruiting for the British Navy, and we won't tolerate a foreign Power recruiting for its navy or army.

"I plainly warn the British people not to interfere with Ireland."

(World Copyright reserved.)

### 200 PASSENGERS IN LINER COLLISION

AFTER coming in collision with the British liner Corinaldo (7,131 tons), owned by the Donaldson S. American Line, the French liner Eubee was badly damaged and transferred 200 passengers to the British ship.
The collision occurred ninety-five miles north of Rio Grande while the Corinaldo was bound from La Plata to Liverpool.
Immediately on picking up the passengers she turned back and is expected at Montevideo to-morrow, says Lloyds.
Damage to the Corinaldo is confined to the starboard bow above the water line.

# Daily Mirror

THE DAILY PICTURE NEWSPAPER WITH THE LARGEST NET SALE

Broadcasting - Page 24

CASSANDRA - - - - P. 12
USELESS EUSTACE - 13
GREAT LOVE STORY 19
YOUR FATE TO-DAY 21
DOROTHY DIX - - - - 22
THE RUGGLES - - - - 24

No. 10,208 — WEDNESDAY, AUGUST 19, 1936 — One Penny

Amusements: Page 20

## MONTH OF WAR COSTS SPAIN
## £125,000,000; 20,000 MEN

In its first month the civil war has cost Spain 20,000 lives. The bill for damage to property and loss of trade is put at £125,000,000.

THE figures are based on reports of British United Press correspondents throughout the country. These are the details:—

- 8,000 killed in battle, shot after surrender, or after court-martial.
- 12,000 killed in street fighting, massacres and house-to-house man-hunts.
- 14,000 wounded in battle and in street fighting.
- 8,000 civil and military prisoners in gaol.
- 10,000 people held as "hostages."

These "hostages" are chiefly non-political and non-military people such as wealthy business men, sons and daughters of aristocratic families, priests and nuns.

Extremists have voluntarily set fire to more than 200 churches since the start of the revolution and have wilfully destroyed priceless art treasures contained in Spanish churches and convents.

### Britain's "Push"

Mr. Eden's return to the Foreign Office yesterday coincided with what is regarded on the whole as a rather encouraging improvement in the international situation as far as non-intervention in Spain is concerned.

As deaths and destruction increase, Britain is urging the need for speedy agreement on the French suggestions for neutrality, and this view is being conveyed to Signor Mussolini, who is not in Rome at present.

Last night the Belgian Government decided to allow only under licence the export of aeroplanes, ships and the transport of all kinds of war material.

### "Poison Gas"

Allegations that Government forces are using poison gas, in violation of international law, were made by the rebels yesterday, and it is reported that protests will be lodged at Geneva.

Discontented because they had not been fully paid, Moorish troops in La Linea brought over by the rebels have been given permission to loot when engaged in "mopping up" operations in the small villages of the region.

San Sebastian was again shelled by the rebel warship Espana yesterday afternoon. Many casualties are reported.

One shell hit the maternity hospital, fortunately in an untenanted wing.

Final arrangements were being made yesterday for the first medical aid unit to leave London for Spain this week-end. The unit will comprise four doctors, eight technical assistants, six nurses and three administrative staff.

### 12 Children Stung— by the Same Wasp

Twelve children in a motor-coach returning from Littlehampton, Sussex, last night were stung when a wasp flew in at the window and could not get out again.

The children, who belonged to a party of 1,400 enjoying an annual outing from Morden, Surrey, were given first aid and taken home.

### TWO SAD MEN

... at the funeral of a third, friend of their happy days — Sir Harry Preston, aged seventy-six.

Mr. J. H. Thomas is sixty-two (and the last few months seem to have aged him years); Mr. Bertram Mills is sixty-three.

All three rose to be famous each in his own sphere. Bonhomie common to all bound them together in comradeship—and farewell.

## EARL'S AEROPLANE DASH TO BEDSIDE OF INJURED SON

EARL Beauchamp and his youngest daughter, Lady Dorothy Lygon, made a dash by aeroplane from Venice to the bedside of the Earl's second son, the Hon. Hugh Lygon, who is dangerously ill at Rothenburg Hospital, near Munich, Germany.

Late last night Lady Sibell Lygon, another sister of the sick man, arrived from London. Viscount Elmley, M.P., Mr. Hugh Lygon's eldest brother, said:—

"I gather that my brother got out of his car to inquire the way to Rothenburg when he fell to the ground in a fainting fit and fractured his skull.

"He was taken to hospital, and I fear that he has not yet regained consciousness. I am mystified by this attack, as he has never had one before."

## SHE SYMPATHISES WITH LOVER WHO CHEATED HER OF LIFE SAVINGS

FROM OUR SPECIAL CORRESPONDENT
WINDSOR, Tuesday.

"There is still secret sympathy for him in my heart, though in the street we shall meet as strangers."

A WOMAN who had lost all her savings entrusted to a man on a promise of marriage saw him sentenced to twelve months' hard labour for the fraud here to-day, and walked out of the court with tears in her grey eyes.

But Miss Ada Sarah Crow, of Bexley-street, Windsor, still has a fighting smile to show her friends.

Her fiance was Kenneth Walter Merry, aged thirty-nine, of Harmondsworth, Middlesex, where he has a wife and child. In sentencing him, the chairman of the bench said it was one of the meanest and cruellest frauds ever heard in that court.

Years of work as a lady's maid and as a housekeeper have stamped tolerance and humour on Miss Crow's thin, pale features. The disastrous end to her short happiness has not robbed her of her old trust in men.

### "Ideally Happy"

"He said he loved me, that he was a widower with one child. I had no reason to doubt his word," she told me.

"After a fortnight—I know it was a hurried courtship—we became engaged. We were ideally happy. We toured the surrounding country in his car looking for a house to live in. I thought life held everything for us.

"I cannot go on . . ." She pressed her needle-pricked fingers to her eyes. "I cannot go over the next dreadful month.

"He talked of getting more money for us to live on," she went on after a pause.

"He said he wanted money for a wireless business that would enable us to live comfortably on profits. His first figure was £100, which I gave him without question. Later he said the price was £150; in all I parted with £198—almost my life savings.

"I never saw the wireless shop, I never saw a receipt for my money. I never saw his child. Why should a woman like me fail to trust him implicitly.

As she showed me to the door Miss Crow squared her spare shoulders and flung back her proud little head. To-day she will be at work once more—one of Britain's million of spinsters—as though nothing had happened.

"It is all past and gone. Let us forget. I am only sorry for his wife and child," were her parting words.

Merry was said to have been sentenced in Belfast in 1930 to three years for bigamy and fraud upon a woman.

## EUROPE REPORT ENDS ROOSEVELT'S HOLIDAY

FROM OUR OWN CORRESPONDENT
NEW YORK, Tuesday.

PRESIDENT Roosevelt has drastically curtailed his plans for a Mississippi cruise to be near his advisers.

This follows news that the President has received secret reports from American diplomats in Europe revealing startling facts.

He is remaining at his desk.

On Friday Mr. Roosevelt warned the nation against becoming embroiled in a war of greed. Yesterday he discussed the need for armed neutrality and more anti-aircraft guns.

Confidential dispatches are believed to be responsible for this alarm.

THE DAILY MIRROR, Monday, August 24, 1936

Broadcasting—Page 20

# Daily Mirror

THE DAILY PICTURE • NEWSPAPER WITH THE LARGEST NET SALE

USELESS EUSTACE P.12
CASSANDRA - - - - 13
GREAT LOVE STORY 19
YOUR FATE TO-DAY 21
DOROTHY DIX - - - 22
THE RUGGLES - - - 24

No. 10,212  Registered at the G.P.O. as a newspaper.  MONDAY, AUGUST 24, 1936  One Penny

Amusements: Pages 14 and 16

# SEIZED BRITISH SHIP— THEN APOLOGISED

## Repulse Clears Decks for Action in Chase

PURSUED BY TWO BRITISH DESTROYERS AND THE BATTLE CRUISER REPULSE WITH HER DECKS CLEARED FOR ACTION, THE SPANISH CRUISER, MIGUEL DE CERVANTES, WAS STOPPED AND HER CAPTAIN APOLOGISED LAST NIGHT FOR HAVING BOARDED AND SEIZED A BRITISH MERCHANTMAN.

THE captain of one of the destroyers, H.M.S Codrington, boarded the cruiser and protested against interference with British shipping outside territorial waters.

While the discussion was going on the Repulse—with Captain J. H. Godfrey in command—steamed past, her crew standing by the guns.

After the apology had been made the ships went on their ways and the master of the seized British merchantman, the Gibel Zerjon (1,535 tons), was told that he could proceed as he thought fit.

### PATROL'S ROUND-UP OF OFFICERS AND MEN ASHORE

Prompt action by the British Navy had followed the official reports that the Gibel Zerjon, which plies between Gibraltar and North Africa, had been stopped off Melilla (Spanish Morocco).

Within half an hour H.M.S. Repulse, accompanied by H.M. Flotilla Leader Codrington, were steaming out of Gibraltar.

Many of the officers and men of the Repulse were on shore when orders were given her to leave immediately. Naval patrols, assisted by civil police, "rounded up" those not on board, and told them to report immediately.

H.M. Destroyer Wolsey also sailed from Malaga.

Although the Spanish Government gave a categorical assurance to the British Government this week-end that such incidents would be avoided, it is recognised that instructions on the subject might not have reached the Miguel de Cervantes.

An official protest is likely to be made

H.M.S. Repulse to the rescue.

In Germany, which has not yet made known her reply to the French appeal for non-intervention, the Spanish civil war is still being made the excuse for an elaborate newspaper campaign against Soviet Russia.

### BARRACKS BOMBED IN MADRID AIR RAID

A renewed bombardment of the Government positions between San Sebastian and Irun by insurgent warships, an air raid on Madrid, and the gutting of a big petrol depot of Malaga, were features of the civil war over the week-end.

The petrol depot, which was hit by several incendiary bombs dropped by insurgent aircraft in a raid on the city yesterday, is understood to have held a million gallons of spirit.

Insurgent 'planes are said to have bombed heavily districts where the militia barracks are situated in their raid on Madrid.

Captain J. H. Godfrey.

British cargo steamer Gibel Zerjon.

## THE QUEEN MARY IN FOG ON RECORD DASH

WITH a new Atlantic record for the westward crossing within her grasp, the Queen Mary early this morning was driving on through patches of fog.

Before reaching the fog she had touched 30.5 knots, her average speed for the first four days of the crossing being 30.08 knots, as against 29.94 knots averaged by the Normandie.

Speaking by telephone from the Queen Mary, Charles MacArthur, husband of Helen Hayes, told the Daily Mirror New York Correspondent: "Officers seem optimistic that we shall reach Ambrose Light about midnight local time. This will surpass the Normandie's record by from two to three hours.

"We are planning all-night celebrations."

Meanwhile the Union Castle liner Stirling Castle was ahead of schedule on her bid to reduce the England-South Africa voyage by three days.

THE DAILY MIRROR, Tuesday, August 25, 1936

Broadcasting - Page 21

# Daily Mirror

THE DAILY PICTURE NEWSPAPER WITH THE LARGEST NET SALE

CASSANDRA - - - - P. 12
USELESS EUSTACE - 13
GREAT LOVE STORY 19
YOUR FATE TO-DAY 21
DOROTHY DIX - - - - 22
THE RUGGLES - - - - 24

No. 10,213  Registered at the G.P.O. as a newspaper.  TUESDAY, AUGUST 25, 1936  One Penny

Amusements: Page 18

# HITLER DOUBLES ARMY—DUCE INCREASES AIR FORCE

**By a stroke of the pen Adolf Hitler virtually doubled Nazi Germany's conscript army last night.**

THE period of compulsory military service in Germany has been increased by a new decree to two years, and it is estimated that as a result Germany will have an Army of 1,000,000 men by the end of the year.

At the same time Mussolini was authorising the increase of the regular Italian Air Force to:—

3,200 officers and non-commissioned officers.
34,000 men on the ground staff (personnel 1934-35 was about 24,000).

He also decreed that all Italian scientists must take an oath of allegiance to the King, his successors and the Government if they wish to hold their posts.

The measure is described as "absolutely urgently necessary," and it is interpreted as an effort to maintain inviolable secrecy regarding important scientific discoveries

### Reply to Russia

The promulgation of Hitler's decree, says Reuter, was accompanied by pointed references to Soviet "militarism," and it comes as a dramatic reply to Soviet Russia's recent decision to reduce the age for beginning military service from twenty-one to nineteen years, which will increase the strength of the Soviet Army by 250,000 during the next four years.

The change means that each German reaching the age of nineteen will start a minimum of two and a half years of service, counting the six months he must serve with the Labour Corps before entering the Army itself.

All over the country new barracks will have to be built. One side-issue of the new law will be, of course, a further reduction in the German unemployment figures.

### Week-End Talks

The decree was dated from Hitler's summer residence at Berchtesgaden, Bavaria, where he received Admiral Horthy, the Hungarian Regent, at the week-end.

The Nazi Party correspondence in a comment on the new measure makes it plain that the increase is definitely an answer to Soviet Russia's lowering of the army age.

"Since a Bolshevist Power has declared openly and cynically that it would also be the task of the Bolshevist Army in certain circumstances to support the revolution in other countries by the intervention of the Red Army," it declares, "then National Socialist Germany will no more give way to such announcements than it gave way to the agitators in Germany itself who were paid by Moscow."

## ON THE LAST DAY OF THE HOLIDAYS!

No bathing cabins left for my last bathe. "Rubbish!" she said, and that one word solves her problem.

Now look at Young Disconsolation down below. He wanted to go bathing too—with the lads of the village, but a round of "eeny-meeny-miny-mo" left him in charge of the boots.

Age follows youth into the news. On page 17 are seventy-nine-year-old Mr. Parren playing bowls; and eighty-two-year-old Miss Gold, sixty-three years in the service of one family

## 'WE PASS THE LIGHTS, ALIVE OR DEAD...' RUNAWAY 'SUGAR BOX' FLASHED PAST RED

TWO Battersea boys, Ronald Williams, aged eight, and Billy Davenport, aged twelve, built a sugar-box car, and on the side in red letters, they wrote:—
"We pass the lights, yellow, green or red, for we must get there, alive or dead."

Last night they went for a ride down Battersea Rise. The brakes failed, and as they shot down the hill a motorist saw them coming, and stopped his car in the middle of the road.

### Crashed Into Car

Ronald fell out, but Billy held on to the wheel, flashed past the lights, and then fell out, too, just before the "car" hit the side of the motor and was smashed to pieces.

Both the boys were bruised, but they picked up the remains and went sorrowfully home.

## 3 MYSTERY TRAGEDIES IN BRITISH SHIP

STRICKEN by some mysterious sickness as they crossed the Atlantic, the crew of the British steamer Sea Rambler (2,327 tons) is reported by Lloyd's to have arrived in Madeira for medical aid.

As soon as the boat touched port a doctor was called in and advised the captain that it was probably fever.

But a later diagnosis revealed ptomaine poisoning, and eleven men, including the captain, were hurriedly landed. Three have since died.

Lloyd's report that it is impossible to say when the ship will sail.

The Sea Rambler is owned by the Dover Navigation Co., Ltd. Her port of registry is Dover.

## THE KING VISITS DELPHI

THE King made a surprise visit to the village of Delphi, on Mount Parnassus, yesterday.

Accompanied by Mr. Duff Cooper, the War Minister, his Majesty landed at Itea, in the Gulf of Corinth, states Reuter.

Delphi is famous as the site of the Ancient Oracle of Apollo. The town was associated with that of Dionysus, and every four years was the scene of the celebration of the Pythian Games.

## "GRANNIE TOO OLD" NOTE ON BABY

"Please take care of him. Grannie too old to have the worry. Fifteen days."

THIS appeal was pinned on the clothing of a baby found in the Embankment Gardens, Charing Cross by an L.C.C. park-keeper yesterday.

The baby, a bonny, well-nourished boy, was in a perambulator.

The child was taken to Cannon-row Police Station and later to Fulham Hospital.

# Daily Mirror

THE DAILY PICTURE NEWSPAPER WITH THE LARGEST NET SALE

Broadcasting—Page 17

**LISTEN IN TO BERNARD BUCKHAM** —PAGE 16

No. 10,218. Registered at the G.P.O. as a newspaper. MONDAY, AUGUST 31, 1936 One Penny

Amusements: Page 20

# THE QUEEN MARY WINS RIBAND FOR BRITAIN

## Atlantic Crossed in Under 4 Days

FIRST SHIP EVER TO CROSS THE ATLANTIC IN LESS THAN FOUR DAYS, THE CUNARD WHITE STAR LINER QUEEN MARY LAST NIGHT REGAINED FOR BRITAIN THE BLUE RIBAND.

THE Queen Mary's average speed between the Ambrose Light and Bishop's Rock was 30.63 knots, compared with the Normandie's 30.31 knots on her best west-to-east run which gave France the Riband more than a year ago.

She has now broken the record in each direction with consecutive trips.

On the return journey she took three days 23 hours 57 minutes, three hours and 31 minutes less than the Normandie's best.

The Queen Mary is expected at Southampton about noon.

### To-day's Pilgrimage

A pilgrimage of honour will start this morning from London and south coast resorts.

Coastal bus and motor-coach services have made arrangements for taking holidaymakers to the Ocean Dock, Southampton, to welcome the Queen Mary and special trains are running from London.

The Southern Railway has arranged for a half-guinea return excursion from Waterloo, taking passengers from the railway out to Southampton Water in a steamer to greet the liner.

The price has been arranged to give the "small man" a chance to join in the rejoicing.

The big stand will be used at the Ocean
(Continued on back page)

Side by side on the bridge of the Queen Mary—Sir Edgar Britten, her captain, and Mr. S. J. Piggott, managing director of John Brown, her builders.

### PROGRESS

THE Santa Maria, in which Columbus sailed on his voyage of Discovery, took seventy days to reach the West Indies.

The Mayflower, with the Pilgrim Fathers aboard, took sixty-six days to reach Massachusetts.

### "ITALY'S 8,000,000 ARMY IN FEW HOURS"

"Italy could mobilise 8,000,000 men within a few hours."

SIGNOR Mussolini, in a speech to the Italian Army and the nation at the conclusion of the big army manoeuvres in the south, made this statement at Avellino yesterday.

"The armaments race," he added, "cannot now be checked."

The speech, says the British United Press, was broadcast by all Italian wireless stations.

The crowd which listened to the speech in the square greeted the address with wild enthusiasm.

When Mussolini asked the crowd: "Have all accounts been settled?" they yelled the answer: "No."

"Have we gone straight ahead?" asked the Duce.

"Yes," chorused his listeners.

Amid cheers, Mussolini said that Italian war manoeuvres had started and ended with the troops vitally enthusiastic.

He spoke in praise of Italy's "just war" in Abyssinia, adding that "Italy will now be able to work there for several decades. Our Empire was not born on the green tables of diplomacy, but out of five victorious battles."

FULL SPEED AHEAD.—How the Queen Mary brought to England the Blue Riband of the Atlantic. Her triumph wins the trophy (on the right) insignia of the fastest passenger ship afloat.

### THE KING'S YACHT FORCED TO SLOW UP IN STORM

ATHENS, Sunday.

THE King's holiday yacht, Nahlin, which left Phaleron Bay last night for the Island of Skyros, where the poet Rupert Brooke is buried, is encountering bad weather and rough seas.

Both the yacht and the Greek destroyer flotilla which was escorting her were forced to reduce speed considerably.

The King sent a wireless message, suggesting it was not necessary for the destroyers to accompany the Nahlin any further. The escort was accordingly withdrawn.—Reuter.

### DRIFTED ON AIR MATTRESS—DROWNED

A GIRL who drifted more than a mile out to sea on an ebbing tide lying on an air mattress, was drowned off Shoeburyness, Essex, last night.

She was Katherine Ivy Dodkin, aged twenty, a wireless assembler, of Ingleton-road, Fordstreet, Edmonton, London, N., who had been camping at Shoeburyness.

The girl had become panicky when she found herself drifting, and in her vain efforts to get back to the beach overturned into deep water near a cabin cruiser.

One of the occupants at once dived in and dragged her on board, unconscious.

As the tide was going out two policemen waded out to the cruiser—sometimes waist deep in water—with oxygen apparatus to give artificial respiration.

Unknown to each other, a brother and sister took part in two heroic rescues at Flamborough, Yorkshire, yesterday.

Miss Betty Salmon, of Bridlington, whose photograph appears on the front of the resort's official guide, with two men swam a quarter of a mile and rescued two boys trapped below cliffs by the tide.

Her sixteen-year-old brother Robert brought ashore a boy suffering from cramp.

THE DAILY MIRROR, Tuesday, September 1, 1936

Broadcasting - Page 17

# Daily Mirror

THE DAILY PICTURE NEWSPAPER WITH THE LARGEST NET SALE

LISTEN IN TO BERNARD BUCKHAM —PAGE 16

No. 10,219  Registered at the G.P.O. as a newspaper.  TUESDAY, SEPTEMBER 1, 1936  One Penny

Amusements: Page 18

# BRITON OF 21 SHOOTS DOWN ENEMY DURING AN AIR DUEL

A young Englishman who is lying wounded in a Madrid hospital is the hero of the Air Force of the Spanish loyalists.

HE is Mr. John Wilson, described as a student of Oriel College, Oxford. He is one of two Londoners injured in events connected with the Spanish Civil War yesterday.

Mr. Wilson, who, at twenty-one, is the baby of the volunteer pilots fighting for the Spanish Government, was wounded by three bullets in the right side when he gave battle to three rebel 'planes.

He was flying a three-motored Junker bomber with an observer.

He went up at a moment's notice, although it was his day off, because a colleague who should have piloted the machine was shaving when the enemy 'planes were sighted. Straight at the enemy machines he flew with his machine-gun blazing.

Two of the rebel Capronis flew on either side of him and a fighter came at him from above. All three opened fire with their machine-guns, riddling his fuselage and puncturing his petrol tank.

## Operation Horror

Mr. Wilson managed to shoot down the fighter, which hurtled headlong to the ground. He managed to land his machine in a ploughed field, and as he climbed out in great pain some loyal militiamen covered him with rifles and took away his revolver.

After that Mr. Wilson remembered nothing. He was brought to hospital in Madrid where three bullets were extracted from his side.

He was given chloroform but not enough, and his nurse told the British United Press he yelled in agony during the operation. Afterwards he told her he was so conscious that he could hear the knife cutting through his flesh.

The other Londoner injured was Mr. William Belcher, who received facial cuts when a lorry, forming part of the British medical aid unit for Spain, crashed into a tree at Brive, France.

An official of the unit said last night that Mr. Belcher, who has red hair and a red beard, is aged about thirty, an engineer, and a bachelor. He lives at Gloucester-crescent N.W.

## Castor-Oil Torture

Castor-oil torture for women is being practised.

Anyone found guilty of smuggling clothing to insurgents trying to flee the country is forced to swallow half a pint of castor oil.

Thirteen women paid this penalty at La Linea yesterday.

## THESE "CAME IN" AT MIDNIGHT—

**New stamps, oysters, and partridges.**

AND the King Edward stamps were soon in demand.

As twelve o'clock chimed crowds besieged the London post offices which remain open all night. A picture of the scene in Fleet-street office is on page 3.

At the counter of the General Post Office dealers purchased sheets of the new issue.

To-day is the great day for gourmets. With an "R" in the month once more, oysters and partridges are in season. Partridge shooting begins.

### MURDERED AS A FAVOUR

Lovely, isn't she? Her mother thought so . . . wanted to see her in pretty clothes . . . worked her fingers to the bone trying to earn the money. . . .

Hopelessly.

She gave up in despair, took an axe and killed the child.

"I thought I was doing her a favour," she said. Now Mrs. Olson, tragic mother of Seattle, U.S., is being tried for murder.

## "COULD NOT BUY PRETTY CLOTHES, SO I KILLED HER," SAYS MOTHER

FROM OUR SPECIAL CORRESPONDENT

SEATTLE (U.S.), Monday.

A SEATTLE mother hit her daughter on the head with an axe, cut her throat with a butcher's knife and then buried her.

Three days later she confessed to the police: "I thought I was doing her a favour. . . . I hadn't got the money to buy her pretty clothes like other girls, so I killed her."

She is Mrs. Esther Hilda Olson, aged thirty-two, soon to come up for trial for the murder of her daughter, Rose, in what is known as the "mercy axe case."

Mrs. Olson lived with her daughter in a small shack in the woods near here. Rose was a very beautiful girl and although still at school was making plans to get married shortly. Then she vanished.

For three days the police searched for her, and then Deputy Sheriff O. K. Bodia, who was in charge of the case, began to have his suspicions.

"I questioned the mother," he told me to-day, "and she confessed to the killing of the girl and took us to the spot in the woods where she had buried the body.

"I think the defence will be insanity."

## BULLOCK JUMPED OVER BANISTERS— MAID RAN AWAY IN HER "UNDIES"

BY A SPECIAL CORRESPONDENT

THIS is the story of the boisterous bullock who preferred the butcher's bathroom to his slaughterhouse; and the half-clothed maidservant who went to the bathroom to wash.

A bright young bullock made a dash for the side door when it was unloaded in the slaughterhouse yard of Mr. E. J. Elton, a High-street, Orpington, butcher.

Within a few minutes the bullock had:—

Rushed upstairs;
Became wedged in the bathroom;
Stuck his head out of the window;
Put his foot through the bath;
Knocked over a wash-basin;
Broke pipes and caused a flood.

### Ran to Balcony

Mrs. Elton's twenty-five-year-old maid, Mary Gibson, who did not hear the hue and cry, was changing. She was in her underclothes when she left her bedroom to go to the bathroom.

Faced with the hind-quarters of the bullock instead of the bathroom door, she screamed and climbed out of a window on to the roof of a conservatory.

"When the bullock put his head through the bathroom window, one of the slaughtermen rushed up a ladder and tried to push him back," Mrs. Elton told me last night.

### House Flooded

"Then when the men managed to get him down the stairs again—he crashed through the banisters!

"The house was in a dreadful state—floods of water streaming into the rooms below, a smashed bathroom and staircase, and a frightened maid.

"I have been a butcher's wife for forty years and have known beasts break loose before—but never a bullock who was so insistent on having a bath!"

## 39 YEARS' MOTORING WITHOUT MISHAP—MUST NOW PASS TEST

AFTER driving for thirty-nine years without an accident and doing pioneer work in aviation, as well as motoring, Sir Walter George Windham, of Berkeley-square, London, W.—retired naval commander and former King's Messenger—must now put up an "L" sign and pass the driving test.

He was disqualified for a month, fined £1 and ordered to pay £2 costs at Marylebone Police Court yesterday for dangerous driving, the magistrate (Mr. Harold McKenna) ordering him to pass the test before he drove again.

It was quite obvious, he said, that Sir Walter's eyes and ears were not what they were.

It was stated that Sir Walter zig-zagged along High-street, Camden Town, and caused a slight collision between his car and a 'bus.

Survivor of one of the first 'plane crashes—at Brooklands in 1910—Sir Walter sent a letter by 'plane from France to England in 1909 and helped in the rescue when the machine crashed in the water at Dover Harbour.

Sir Walter said last night:

"I have driven some hundreds of thousands of miles, and only yesterday drove two hundred miles from Wales without mishap.

"It is very annoying, after all these years, to go through a test of the elementary principles of driving and to have to have 'L' plates on my motor."

# Daily Mirror

**THE DAILY PICTURE NEWSPAPER WITH THE LARGEST NET SALE**

Broadcasting—Page 17

USELESS EUSTACE P.12
CASSANDRA - - - - 13
GREAT LOVE STORY 19
YOUR FATE TO-DAY 21
DOROTHY DIX - - - - 22
THE RUGGLES - - - - 24

No. 10,220 Registered at the G.P.O. as a newspaper WEDNESDAY, SEPTEMBER 2, 1936 One Penny

Amusements: Page 18

## 3½ LB. "COTTON-WOOL" BABY BECOMES A CHAMPION

### ON A STEAMER COMING OVER..

... was this Hungarian actress, Vilma Hertha Holenia.

And now she's claiming £6,000 damages from the ship's owners and Captain H. Vogt because, she says, the captain tried to monopolise her company and finally used force to drag her into her cabin, with the result that her arms and legs were bruised black and blue.

*He's a Big Noise Now*

After spending the first three months of his life wrapped in cotton wool and being kept alive on oxygen, a nine-month-old baby boy who weighed 3½lb. at birth has won a baby championship.

Twin boys of five who always have the same aches and pains are both suffering from swollen eyes after only one of them had injured his eye.

THESE two remarkable stories of children reached the "Daily Mirror" office last night.

The baby is Anthony Ian Simmonds, son of Mr. and Mrs. Louis Simmonds, of Stamford Hill, London, N. The championship he won was at Hastings yesterday.

### Father Dance-Band Leader

Anthony's present weight is 19lb. 10oz.

Bonny and happy, no one could believe that when the "champ" was born he was not expected to live. His birth was two months premature.

Anthony was entered by his mother, who is on holiday there.

His father is the leader of the dance band at Prince's Brasserie, Piccadilly, and a telegram was sent to him telling him of his son's success.

Anthony is the fourth child. His brother and sisters, aged twelve, nine and seven, are all at Hastings.

His mother, who is thirty-two, stated: "When Anthony was born at the Mothers' Hospital, Clapton, he weighed only 3½lb., and was on oxygen for fifteen and a half hours. Until he was three months old he had to be kept wrapped in cotton wool and olive oil.

### Doctors Amazed

"Now, although he is only nine months old, he weighs 19lb. 10oz., and the doctors to-day were amazed at his progress. I only decided at the last moment to enter him for the show and now he is a champion.

"It is the most thrilling thing that has ever happened to me.

"My sister and I were so excited that we just had to stop in to-night to calm down. Anthony is a perfect baby, and gives no trouble."

... But—he was 3½lb. nine months ago and lived in cotton wool. He's a credit to mother, seen with him.

## SIX SOLDIERS INJURED IN BOOBY TRAP

SIX Cameron Highlanders were injured when a "booby trap" exploded during an ambush by snipers between Jerusalem and Nablus yesterday.

Lance-Corporal D. Prowse, who was injured seriously, and Private A. Taylor are now in hospital.

The buses in which troops were travelling ran into an ingenious booby trap arranged in the roadway.

Simultaneously firing started.

The soldiers dismounted, and while deploying the two Cameron Highlanders kicked the trip wire of another booby trap, which exploded, injuring them both.

### Eight Cities Bombed

Terrors of air raids were suddenly released yesterday in a great wave of bombing in many parts of Spain. Eight key cities were raided, including Madrid, where the insurgents claim that 400 people have been killed by bombs.

Irun, the Government stronghold near the French frontier, was also bombed by rebels.

Five cities held by the insurgents were bombed by Government 'planes. They are Burgos (the northern headquarters), Seville, Granada, Cordoba and Cadiz.

Senorita Ibarruri, known in Spain as "The Passion Flower," is in Paris on a mission which appears to be designed to influence the French Government to depart from its non-intervention policy.

The Spanish Embassy in Paris, however, denied that the Spanish Government has for more than a month been asking the Powers to mediate in the war.

*Messages from Reuter and British United Press.*

### SYMPATHETIC TWINS

THE twins, who no matter how far they are apart do the same things at the same time and contract the same aches and pains, are Thomas and William Stockie, aged five, of Gower-street, Patricroft, Lancs.

During last week-end Thomas was playing with some friends near his home making a tent. One of the boys was hammering with the wrong side of an axe, and Thomas, who was standing behind him, was pierced on the left eye. He was removed to the Royal Man-

*(Continued on back page)*

## 'PLANE CRASHED ON HOLIDAY FLIGHT, BUT MAJOR KEPT HIS MONOCLE IN!

FROM a 'plane that made a forced landing and "crashed" at Barn Hill, Wembley, last night stepped the pilot—still wearing his monocle. His wife stepped out after him. They were Major Herbert Musker and Mrs. Musker, flying from home at Rushford Hall, Thetford, Norfolk, to the Isle of Wight on holiday.

Owing to engine trouble over the wooded Barn Hill district, Major Musker had to land in a field.

A landing wheel came off and crashed through the rear fuselage.

The Major and his wife later continued their holiday journey by car.

"We have had the plane three years, so I suppose we cannot grumble," said Mrs. Musker.

## COUNTY CRICKET CAPTAIN KILLED IN CAR CRASH

MR. D. A. C. Page, the Gloucestershire County cricket captain, died in Cirencester Hospital early to-day following a car crash.

He was returning to his home last night at the end of the match between Gloucestershire and Nottinghamshire with a friend, Mr. W. Herbert, of Cirencester, when Mr. Page's car skidded and crashed into a wall.

Both men were injured and Mr. Page died of his injuries.

Mr. Herbert was stated early to-day to be in a satisfactory condition.

Mr. Page, who was twenty-five, was killed on the last day of the county championship season, and in the match at Gloucester which had just ended he led his county in a fine victory by an innings and 70 runs.

## CHANNEL ATTEMPT ON AIR MATTRESS

*FROM OUR OWN CORRESPONDENT*
DOVER, Tuesday.

LYING on his back on an air mattress, forty-five-year-old Mr. C. W. Mason, of Dover, set out from Western Beach here, intending to cross to Calais, using only his hands as paddles.

After paddling 5h 40m and reaching the East Goodwin lightship—a distance of thirteen and a half miles—he had to give up owing to pains in his legs.

These were caused by his cramped position. The mattress was 6ft. long—and Mr. Mason's height is more than that!

He returned to Dover to-night in the rowing boat which had accompanied him, with his daughter Florence on board.

On coming ashore he said he was satisfied that the trip across the Channel could be made on an air mattress.

He felt neither cold nor tired. The only trouble was the pain in his legs, he added.

Mr. Mason is a non-smoker and total abstainer.

THE DAILY MIRROR, Monday, September 7, 1936.

Broadcasting—Page 17

# Daily Mirror
THE DAILY PICTURE NEWSPAPER WITH THE LARGEST NET SALE

5-DAY SERIAL —Page 19

No. 10,224  Registered at the G.P.O as a newspaper  MONDAY, SEPTEMBER 7, 1936  One Penny

Amusements: Pages 8 and 16

# REDS PREPARE TO BLOW UP 1,200 TRAPPED IN FORTRESS

With Madrid in fear of a gas attack, a serious last warning was given last night by Mr. G. A. D. Ogilvie-Forbes, Counsellor-in-Charge of the British Embassy in Madrid, when he called a meeting at the Embassy of the 130 Britons still in the capital.

"There is a possibility that the rebels may drop mustard-gas bombs on Madrid," he declared, "and those staying in Madrid do so at their own risk."

AFTER six weeks siege Spain's Red Government, is now prepared to blow up the Alcazar citadel in Toledo, and every one of the twelve hundred people in it. Enough high explosives will be used to complete the job with one blast. While mining under the foundations at various points the Government forces have kept up a steady shelling of the walls and towers so as to keep the rebels occupied

Women and children are among those besieged in the Alcazar. They have sought refuge in the cellars of the citadel, the stone walls of which are 9ft. thick.

The last offer of mercy has been made to all who surrender but there is no sign of the spirit of the defenders weakening.

From inside its walls the insurgents have been sniping the militiamen and soldiers. It is this persistence of defence which has forced the Government to reconsider their decision not to blow up such an historic building.

## Stifled by Bombs

One of the four great towers has been completely destroyed by bombardment and another is on the verge of collapse.

When the military governor's palace close to the Alcazar was stormed, the building was set on fire. The miners hurled dynamite at the walls as they advanced.

Squads of bomb-throwing specialists have started a number of small fires inside the Alcazar which are stifling the insurgents.

Moors and foreign legionaries who form the backbone of the forces of General Franco, the insurgent leader, are preparing for a new advance in the Estremadura towards Toledo

But the insurgents have a long way to go before they reach Toledo, and then they would still have about fifty miles to go before they got anywhere near Madrid.

Mass executions of workers have been held in Tetuan, in Spanish Morocco, according to Sergeant Julio Vasquez, formerly of the Spanish Foreign Legion, and stationed in Tetuan, where the revolt of the army generals began

Communists who gathered in Trafalgar (*Continued on back page*)

*Cricketer Into Baseball . . .* player: how Patsy Hendren will appear to the fans when he stands on the plate next season.

# PATSY HENDREN AND TATE ARE READY TO SIGN UP FOR A LONDON BASEBALL TEAM

Exclusive "Daily Mirror" News
By AL MALE

PATSY Hendren and Maurice Tate, famous England Test cricketers, are to turn baseball players.

Hendren, idol of the Middlesex cricket crowds for thirty years, has agreed to sign baseball forms and will play for White City next season.

In order not to interfere with existing cricket contracts Hendren will play in Sunday matches only for the first season, but after that, baseball will be his full-time summer occupation.

Tate, Sussex bowler, has agreed to sign on similar conditions to Hendren.

Baseball is sweeping the country. Thirteen thousand fans watched West Ham and White City play at West Ham yesterday.

The game has gripped the imagination of boys as well as their parents. There are thirty boys' teams in Manchester alone and over 200 boys' team in the country.

They all look forward to next season with the prospect of the Junior Baseball Trophy (presented by the *Daily Mirror*) being their first national prize.

Baseball has come to stay.

## COLOUR CURE FOR MONDAY "BLUES"

Have you got the Monday morning "blues"?

Then try sitting in a blue light.

Dr. H. Riley Spitler, of Eaton (Ohio) who, after six years' research, has described his "colour cure" to the American Academy of Optometrists, says blue light makes you happy.

The treatment is indirect, Dr. Spitler adds (according to Reuter), correcting the physiological symptoms by either stimulating or relaxing the nerves of the eye.

Each colour has its individual effect. Blue or violet light stops headaches by relieving distress due to ocular reflex.

Red increases blood pressure and stops the type of dizziness which occurs when an individual rises from a sitting position.

Yellow, green or blue - green relieves stomach trouble and other digestive ills.

# CHANNEL STEAMER RIDDLE OF VANISHED HUSBAND

BY A SPECIAL CORRESPONDENT

SAYING he was going to have a chat with the wireless operator, a husband walked away from his wife along the deck of the steamer, Isle of Guernsey, during the voyage from Southampton to Jersey this week-end—and vanished.

He was Mr. George Sawyer, of Harvist-road, Willesden, N.W.

When the vessel berthed in Jersey, Mrs Sawyer searched for her husband, but could find no trace of him.

She reported the matter to Mr. Gale, checker, of the Southern Railway, and went to the police station.

Mr. Poole, of the Southern Railway Co., appears to have been the last person to have seen Mr. Sawyer, and states that he saw him walking on the upper deck off the Needles.

The strange part of the mystery is that when the passengers disembarked a man gave up two tickets, and stated that one was for his wife and she was lying down

## Tickets Riddle

This passenger was the only one to yield up two tickets, but unfortunately the officer cannot remember his appearance.

At their Willesden home last night Mr. Sawyer's aged mother and younger brother were frantic with anxiety.

Sound asleep, unaware that her father was missing, lay Mr. and Mrs. Sawyer's daughter, Dorothy.

Mr. Sawyer's description is: Aged forty-one, 5ft. 4in., dressed in grey flannel trousers with check lounge coat, no hat, very fair hair, clean shaven.

Mr. George Sawyer with his wife.

**Mrs. Markham, first woman to fly the Atlantic east-to-west, may fly back.—See Back Page.**

# Mothers Boycott National Baby Show

BECAUSE they object to babies being put on exhibition, and to the possibility of them being crowded together, Croydon Mothers' Infant Welfare Centre executive have declined to support the National Baby Show to be held at Crystal Palace on September 19.

In a letter to the organiser, Mr. A. E. Fruitnight, they state:—

"The executive committee is opposed to the whole idea of baby shows.

"Infant welfare work is intended to help mothers to bring their children up as, as possible, whatever the home conditions, and the mother most deserving of a prize would be the mother who obtained the best result possible in difficult circumstances."

"The idea of making a show of a baby is sufficiently objectionable to justify our attitude."

Mr. Fruitnight has replied that the National Baby Show was only to be regarded as an experiment, and 60 per cent of the doctors to whom the suggestion had been made, approved of it.

It was certain that 2,000 babies would be on show from Aberdeen to Land's End.

# Daily Mirror

THE DAILY PICTURE NEWSPAPER WITH THE LARGEST NET SALE

Broadcasting - Page 17

CASSANDRA - - - - P. 12
USELESS EUSTACE - 13
GREAT LOVE STORY 19
YOUR FATE TO-DAY 21
DOROTHY DIX - - - - 22
THE RUGGLES - - - - 24

No. 10,228 Registered at the G.P.O as a newspaper — FRIDAY, SEPTEMBER 11, 1936 — One Penny

Amusements: Page 16

# POUND-NOTE WOMAN'S TOUR OF MERCY SECRET OUT

### BY A SPECIAL CORRESPONDENT

MYSTERY of the "Pound-Note" Lady Bountiful has been solved.

While poor people of Wandsworth, London, S.W., waited anxiously in their homes last night wondering if the thin, pale, fair-haired little woman who, for nearly a week has been knocking on doors and distributing pound notes, would call on them, she was lying at her home in West Hill-road, not far away, exhausted and distraught, a nervous wreck.

No more will she call on them; lay her hands on them and their children to cure their ills and then hurry away leaving a pound note behind.

This is her story.

She is thirty-four-year-old Miss Alice Laker, who lives with relatives in West Hill-road, Wandsworth.

On Monday she stole out of the house taking with her her Post Office Savings Bank book, and set out on her mission of charity in the poor districts of Wandsworth. The police were informed that she was missing but they could not trace her.

Then yesterday afternoon she called on a woman in Iron Mill-place to see her little boy who suffers with his heart.

She had no money left. She looked tired and ill. Suddenly there came a knock on the door. It was her brother. He saw her and took her home.

## Lost Her Job

Last night I spoke to her sister, Miss Mary Laker.

"When she came home she was too exhausted to tell us anything," she said.

"She has been under treatment for nervous trouble for some time and I think she lost her memory. The trouble dates from last Easter when she lost her job."

**The poor of Wandsworth will not forget her kindness.**

On entering a house she always washed her hands and then had a drink of water.

People whom she visited believe that she had some power to cure illness and relieve pain.

A girl in Iron Mill-place told me how she massaged her leg and the pain ceased. In another house she put her hands on a man who had cut his hand and had splinters of glass still in it. After she had gone the splinters came out.

## STAR OF SCIENTISTS' WHOOPEE PARTY AT 72!

Re-living his childhood's joys—white-bearded Professor Edridge-Green (he is seventy-two) sharing a miniature speed-boat with Mr. Maurice Blood, M.A., when the Professor led the revels of scientists at Blackpool Fun Fair during break in British Association Conference.

Then the party tried that sinking feeling on the downward rush of the "Big Dipper." See story on page 24.

## SHE BIT HER WAY INTO B.B.C.—AND STAYED WITH CONTRACT FOR A YEAR

### BY A SPECIAL CORRESPONDENT

TWICE yesterday when he was rehearsing Mr. Lou Preager turned her out of his B.B.C. studio. The third time she was carried biting and kicking down the stairs.

But last night blue-eyed, golden-haired Molly O'Connor gave her first broadcast. She is fourteen.

"I said I had no time to see her, and when she appeared a second time with her mother, I repeated it," Mr. Lou Preager told me last night.

"But while her mother was pleading with the commissionaire in the entrance hall, she eluded the staff and managed to climb two flights of stairs before officials caught her.

"As she was carried down again, she bit one of the men and kicked the shins of another.

"At this moment Mr. O'Connor, my manager, came in at the main door, found her weeping.

"When he heard that she also was an O'Connor and that she came from the same part of Dublin as he did, he brought her up. And when I heard Molly sing I decided to put her in my programme to-night.

"I have given her a contract for a year."

Miss Molly O'Connor

### RADIO BLUNDER

After stating in the first news bulletin that the world speedway championships at Wembley had been postponed the B.B.C. last night interrupted the programme to state that a mistake had been made, and that the championships would be held as arranged.

The first correction was made shortly after the first news bulletin at 6.30 p.m.; another announcement was made at eight o'clock.

## STAY-IN STRIKERS' FOOD HELD UP

RIOTS were feared following the refusal of the management of a Blantyre (Lanarkshire) colliery last night to allow food to be sent down to fifty-one men who earlier in the day started Scotland's first stay-in strike.

After sending a telegram to the T.U.C. at Plymouth seeking advice on the question of food supplies.

Lanarkshire Miners' Union decided early to-day to post pickets and call a sympathetic strike of 3,500 men in six neighbouring pits.

Wives and mothers of the stay-in strikers took baskets and boxes containing thermos flasks and sandwiches to the colliery, but officials refused to permit them to go near the pithead and all the food had to be left in a hut. Cheering crowds greeted the women. Hundreds had gathered at the pithead, and strong police reinforcements were drafted in.

Twenty-three-year-old John Carson, who came up with two other men (one had influenza and two were "fed up") told the Daily Mirror:

"Our only trouble was food. We finished our supplies at five o'clock, and the men below are waiting for more.

"We have been singing songs and playing dominoes and cards.

"Even when the electric light was switched off it did not matter much. We were ready for it with thirty-eight spare lamps."

The dispute—at the Blantyre Colliery of Messrs. William Dixon, Ltd.—started on Monday over wage rates. But yesterday's development was a complete surprise to the union.

THE DAILY MIRROR, Saturday, September 12, 1936.

Broadcasting - Page 15

# Daily Mirror

THE DAILY PICTURE NEWSPAPER WITH THE LARGEST NET SALE

USELESS EUSTACE P.12
CASSANDRA - - - - 13
GREAT LOVE STORY 19
YOUR FATE TO-DAY 21
DOROTHY DIX - - - - 22
THE RUGGLES - - - - 24

No 10,229  Registered at the G.P.O as a newspaper  SATURDAY, SEPTEMBER 12, 1936  One Penny

Amusement : Page 14

# FAMOUS SPORTS CUP STOLEN
## UNDER EYES OF CROWD

BY A SPECIAL CORRESPONDENT

WHILE 250 people were having a last drink and a sandwich in the club restaurant at Wembley Stadium five minutes before the start of last night' greyhound racing, thieves stole the Greyhound St. Leger Gold Cup, which was exhibited in a glass case in the restaurant.

Uniformed attendants and a boy selling programmes were standing within a few yards. It was one of the most daring and skilful robberies of recent years.

The Gold Cup, eighteen inches high and valued at £50, was in a glass case standing against the wall just outside the secretary's office.

This is what the thieves did:—
Pulled the four-foot high case away from the wall,
Forced the door at the back of the case,
Took the cup and put the case back against the wall, so that when the cup was missed nobody could tell that the case had ever been moved.

*And all the time 250 people were present !*

The cup was placed in its case by the secretary, Mr. F. Jackson, a few minutes before eight o'clock.

"On coming out of my office just before racing was due to commence, only a few minutes later," he told me, "I nearly fainted. The cup had disappeared."

Police were at once informed and a squad of plain-clothes detectives hurried to the stadium

While thousands watched the racing last night they searched the stadium from end to end They inspected every cloakroom, mingled with the crowd in all the enclosures, and scrutinised every person as he left at the end of the meeting

### Got Clean Away

But the thieves got clean away.
The cup had only been made a fortnight ago ready to be handed to the winner of the Greyhound St. Leger final on Monday night at Wembley.

Last night Mr. A. J. Elvin announced that he was determined that a replica should be presented to the winner at 9.10 on Monday evening, and goldsmiths had been instructed to work "all hours necessary" to reproduce it in time.

Long before the days of greyhound racing two other famous trophies were stolen.

In 1895 the original Football Association Cup, which had been won by Aston Villa, vanished from a shop window in Birmingham. Then in 1907 someone (the thief was never captured) took the Ascot Gold Cup from the table where it was on view.

And two policemen were on duty all the time to guard the treasured trophy !

### SUMMERY WEEK-END

Weather experts predict a fine week-end. It is probable, they say, that yesterday's summery conditions will continue.
Southend and Ramsgate had about eleven hours of sunshine each yesterday.

**Gladys Cooper**
... with her daughter Sally—
a picture taken recently.

## SIR NEVILLE PEARSON BRINGS DIVORCE SUIT AGAINST GLADYS COOPER: PHILIP MERIVALE CITED

SPECIAL "DAILY MIRROR" NEWS

THE *Daily Mirror* understands that Sir Neville Pearson, Bart., has instituted divorce proceedings against Lady Pearson (Miss Gladys Cooper, the famous actress). They have been living apart for more than a year.

The suit will be heard during the forthcoming legal term.

Mr. Philip Merivale, who has for some time been acting with Lady Pearson in America, is being cited as co-respondent.

Sir Neville was married to Miss Cooper in 1928. Their daughter, Sally, is six years old

### Both Previously Wed

Both Sir Neville and Miss Cooper had been previously married. Sir Neville's first marriage with a daughter of the late Lord Melchett was dissolved in 1928.

Miss Cooper has a son and a daughter by her marriage to Mr. H. J. Buckmaster, which was dissolved in 1923.

Her son, Mr. John Buckmaster, is twenty-one years old and recently took up a stage career

## DIED SAVING WIFE AND SON AS CAR FELL IN HARBOUR

FROM OUR OWN CORRESPONDENT
WEYMOUTH, Friday.

WITH his last action to-day Mr. Laurie McGinn, aged thirty-two, saved the lives of his wife and little son—and lost his own.

Mr. McGinn, who was employed at a Weymouth brewery, was driving a small saloon car round a bend on the quayside here when, it is believed, he swerved to avoid a child.

Realising the car was going into the harbour, Mr. McGinn pushed open the door for his wife and child to jump out.

Before they could do so, however, the car had dived into the river. Mrs. McGinn and her son were forced out by the pressure of water.

Three or four men jumped in and rescued them.

"I helped Mrs. McGinn to a house near by," said another man. "She kept crying, 'My husband, my husband.'"

Half an hour later the car was raised and McGinn's body recovered.

A few yards away Mrs. McGinn and her children were being comforted by friends.

### BRITON SHOT BY ARABS

JERUSALEM, Friday.

SERGEANT Sweeny, of the Loyal (North Lancs) Regiment, was killed in an engagement with Arabs near Haifa to-day.

In addition to the military a force of police and aeroplanes were engaged

The Arabs are known to have had at least five casualties.—Central News.

Philip Merivale, with his daughter, on their arrival in the Aquitania at Southampton on August 25.

### DOCTOR SENT DOWN TO FASTING MEN

MORE than 30,000 men, all the miners in Lanarkshire pits, will come out on strike on Monday in sympathy with the forty-eight stay-in strikers who have been underground in the No. 2 Blantyre pit since early on Thursday.

The management of the colliery still refuse permission for food to be sent down to the men.

Three county councillors, after visiting the men, asked for a doctor to go down and examine the strikers. Dr. George Hutchison went down late last night

THE DAILY MIRROR, Tuesday, September 15, 1936.

# Daily Mirror

THE DAILY PICTURE NEWSPAPER WITH THE LARGEST NET SALE

Broadcasting - Page 17

CASSANDRA - - - - P. 12
USELESS EUSTACE - 13
5-DAY SERIAL - - - - 19
YOUR FATE TO-DAY 21
DOROTHY DIX - - - - 22
THE RUGGLES - - - - 24

No. 10,231  Registered at the G.P.O. as a newspaper.  TUESDAY, SEPTEMBER 15, 1936  One Penny

Amusements: Page 16

# HUSBAND'S DEATH MAY END NORMA SHEARER'S FILM CAREER

FROM OUR OWN CORRESPONDENT
HOLLYWOOD, Monday.

HOLLYWOOD'S "perfect romance" ended to-day with the ⁓ of Irving Thalberg, famous producer and husband of lovely Norma Shearer.

**Within a few hours all Hollywood was saying that Norma Shearer will never act again.**

Thalberg, for love of whom she abandoned the Anglican Church for the Jewish faith, was the inspiration of her art.

Norma called him the directing genius of her career. It was her love for him that fired her to give such memorable screen performances in "Smiling Through" and "The Barretts of Wimpole-street."

Her love had been likened to that of Juliet, the part in which she has scored her latest film triumph.

### Specialist's Dash

As dawn broke to-day Norma sat in her home in Santa Monica, while nurses and a specialist, brought from New York, fought to save her thirty-seven-year-old husband.

A slight cold contracted a week ago had developed into pneumonia.

Norma's children, Irving and Katharine, were taken to the bedside, but Thalberg did not recognise them.

A smile shone on Norma's face. Thalberg stirred, smiled back. Then suddenly he fell back dead.

Parents strove, in vain, to console the sobbing Norma.

Hundreds of flowers from a mourning Hollywood soon filled the house.

### "Kindest Man She Met"

But Norma still wept—and thought of the days of 1924 when she was terrified of the new producer Thalberg.

She remembered how when she met him off the "set," she found him the kindest man she had met.

Before her marriage she vowed to him that if her career as an actress interfered with her marriage she would abandon it.

"Couples must have no separations," she said, "because these make them believe they can get along without one another."

Thalberg, who was production manager of Metro-Goldwyn-Mayer, began work as a clerk at £3 a week.

He was the greatest brain in the film industry. Almost every big picture that has been made had his name behind it.

He was dynamite when working—and he was always working.

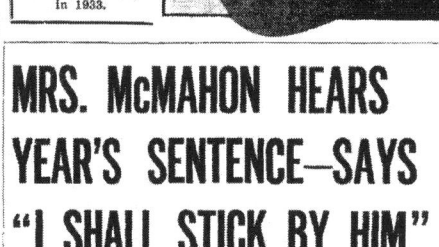

**"Perfect Romance"**

Mr. Irving Thalberg with his wife, Norma Shearer, and their little boy in 1933.

---

| **CROWD LAUNCH LIFEBOAT** : **50 WAIST-HIGH IN SEA** |

FIFTY people waded into the sea up to their waists, and some so far that waves broke over their heads, to launch Hythe lifeboat on a rescue dash last night. And it was all unnecessary.

After putting to sea the lifeboat was recalled without having reached its objective.

When the call was received it was low water and the boat had to be hauled over a shingle bar to reach the sea.

One hundred and fifty people volunteered to help the crew and, seizing the ropes, dragged the lifeboat to the water.

Both Hythe and Dover lifeboats were called out to the assistance of three men in a small boat off Sandgate, but both were recalled before reaching it as the men had been rescued by a motorboat.

The rescued men were Tunbridge Wells anglers named H. Welch, T. Levett and G. Costick, who were towed to the shore by two Sandgate men, Mr. T. Moore and Mr. L. Catt.

### ATLANTIC "DOUBLE"

ATLANTIC flyers, Merrill and Richman, crash in a Newfoundland marsh after breaking the record for the westward crossing.—Back page.

---

# MRS. McMAHON HEARS YEAR'S SENTENCE—SAYS "I SHALL STICK BY HIM"

BY A SPECIAL CORRESPONDENT

"Whatever it means to me I shall stick by my husband."

WITH that resolution helping her to fight back the tears from her eyes, brunette Rose McMahon heard last night that her husband, George Andrew McMahon, had been sentenced to twelve months' hard labour for producing a pistol with intent to alarm the King.

Yesterday she sat alone in her home in Westbourne-terrace, London, W., while her thirty-four-year-old Irish husband was acting the chief part in one of the most sensational court dramas ever heard by a British jury.

From the lips of the quietly-spoken, quietly-dressed Irishman, 200 people sitting in the Old Bailey, scene of so many famous trials, had heard a story which McMahon's own counsel described as "Oppenheim at his best."

They heard a story of agents of a foreign Power in London plotting to assassinate King Edward as he rode at the head of his troops on Constitution Hill, offering McMahon £150 if he would be the assassin.

Then came the cold, relentless voice of the Judge telling McMahon he did not intend to let him become a "fancied hero."

The name of the Foreign Embassy in London, written down by McMahon in court, it is understood, was that of the German Embassy.

When the report was referred to an authoritative quarter, the only comment was, "Does anyone really take this seriously?"

Report of the trial begins on Page Five.

---

# LIGHTNING HITS CYCLISTS AND KILLS ONE

TWO cyclists sheltering under an ash tree during a heavy storm at Higham Ferrers, Northants, last night, were struck by lightning.

Albert Richardson, twenty-nine, of Marshall's-road, Raunds, was killed outright.

His companion, a man named Wheatley, of Chelveston, was paralysed from the waist downwards.

Wheatley was taken to his home and is in a serious condition.

Richardson and Wheatley were returning to their homes from a Higham Ferrers boot factory when they were struck.

The tragedy was discovered by Wheatley's half-brother.

THE DAILY MIRROR, Wednesday, September 16, 1936.

Broadcasting - Page 17

# Daily Mirror

THE DAILY PICTURE NEWSPAPER WITH THE LARGEST NET SALE

CASSANDRA - - - - P. 12
USELESS EUSTACE - 13
5-DAY SERIAL - - - - 19
DOROTHY DIX - - - - 22
THE RUGGLES - - - - 24

No. 10,232  Registered at the G.P.O as a newspaper.  WEDNESDAY, SEPTEMBER 16, 1936  One Penny

Amusements: Page 16

# BRIDE SEES HUSBAND AND TWO OTHERS DIE IN AIR WRECK

## FIRE DESTROYS CRASHED 'PLANE

Watching the man she married only five weeks ago take the night mail 'plane for Hamburg into the air from Gatwick (Surrey) Aerodrome last night, a wife was horrified to see the machine crash and burst into flames, carrying her husband and two of his crew to their deaths.

SHE was the wife of Captain Walter Fraser Anderson, chief pilot of British Airways, holder of the D.S.O. and D.F.C.

As the 'plane took off she saw it head for a bank of trees and skim the top. Branches ripped the bottom from the machine. Mrs. Anderson collapsed with shock.

She was taken to her home in Foxley-lane, Purley, Surrey, and was comforted by her parents. Through her father, Mr. de Reding, Mrs. Anderson gave her account of the tragedy.

"Since we returned by air from our honeymoon in Paris a week or two ago I have gone down to Gatwick every time my husband has flown the mail.

"We went down together last night and I was standing on the tarmac when the machine moved off after I had said good-bye to him.

"It taxied along the ground and rose. I glanced away and then I heard the engine making a most peculiar noise. My attention was then riveted to the 'plane. I saw it above

In the grip of consuming flames. The blazing wreckage of the crashed 'plane. On left is the dead pilot, Captain W. F. Anderson.

The three men killed in the crash were Captain Anderson, Engineer Slack and Operator J. Jackman, of Pembroke-road, Seven Kings. Captain Anderson and Engineer Slack were killed instantly. Operator Jackman died in hospital at Horley.

Second Officer Scorgie, of Lime-avenue, Horley, escaped with only slight injuries. This was his second escape in a 'plane crash within a week.

The machine, which belonged to British Airways, was not carrying passengers.

### Three Women Help

Three women from Rowley Farm helped heroically in the rescue efforts, together with the butler from the farm named Barrett.

Barrett said: "I do not know how I managed to get one of the men out, but the women helped me to drag him away despite the fierce blaze."

Captain Anderson, who was forty-six, was one of the best-known pilots in British aviation. He flew the first Continental air mail from London to Scandinavia—the same task which he was setting out to perform when he met his death.

After a thrilling war-time career flying over the Western front, Captain Anderson went to South Russia in 1919 to fight the revolutionaries.

**He was such a formidable enemy that the Russians put a price on his head.**

Captain Anderson's first marriage was dissolved two years ago.

Mrs. Anderson.

the trees and then there was a crash and the vivid burst of flame.

"It was ghastly. I wanted to rush to the spot. Other women who were standing beside me got hold of me and restrained me. Later I learnt he was dead."

Mr. De Reding said: "My daughter is stunned by the calamity. It is tragic. They were married quietly but a few weeks ago, went off on their honeymoon and were so happy."

## TRAVELLED 1,000 MILES, BRAVED SEA IN OPEN BOAT AND WENT MAD WITH THIRST—FOR A JOB

BY A SPECIAL CORRESPONDENT

Alone in a 30-ft. open boat, with only a 2s. 6d. cracked compass and a tattered map of the English coast as his guides, Leslie Hansen sailed out from Sunderland for London—and a job.

FOR four days and nights he braved tempest and suffered hunger and thirst. He was picked up by a steamer, landed at Penzance and sent by train to London last night.

And squaring his jaw Hansen told me on his arrival: "I've travelled more than 1,000 miles to get to London, and now I'm going to look for a job."

Hansen went on to describe his adventure.

"I was out of work," he said. "I made up my mind to get to London and look for a job there.

"I estimated that the trip would take me three weeks."

The weather was fine when he set out, but on the second day a storm arose and upset the stone jug in which he had stored his drinking water.

"For four days I was pitched and tossed like a cork. Gradually I lost sight of the coast in the mist that had arisen.

"I began to suffer agony with thirst.

"On the fourth day without water I tied my shirt to the mast.

### 12 Miles Out

"Towards evening a heavy swell rose and the small boat began to ship water.

"I just about made up my mind to give up. My clothes were soaked and I was mad with thirst.

"I lay down in the bottom of the boat and then half-unconscious I heard a shout."

The steamer Eskwood had seen the pitching boat and two seamen carried Hansen on board.

"I know that if they hadn't found me, I wouldn't have seen the dawn," Hansen added.

"The skipper of the Eskwood told me that I was twelve miles from the coast."

The crew of the Eskwood made a collection for Hansen and paid his fare from Penzance to London.

THE DAILY MIRROR, Thursday, September 17, 1936.

Broadcasting - Page 19

# Daily Mirror

THE DAILY PICTURE NEWSPAPER WITH THE LARGEST NET SALE

USELESS EUSTACE P.10
CASSANDRA . . . . 14
5-DAY SERIAL . . . . 21
DOROTHY DIX . . . . 26
THE RUGGLES . . . . 28

No. 10,233 Registered at the G.P.O. as a newspaper. THURSDAY, SEPTEMBER 17, 1936 One Penny

Amusements: Page 18

# RANDOLPH CHURCHILL DASHES TO U.S. ON TRAIL OF HIS SISTER

**HE WANTED HIS DADDY**

Mr. Randolph Churchill, son of Mr. Winston Churchill, and (right) Mr. Vic Oliver, the American comedian.

Twenty-three hours after his actress sister, Sarah, had left in the Bremen for America, Mr. Randolph Churchill, son of Mr. Winston Churchill, left England in the record-breaker, Queen Mary.

HE went in such a hurry that his name did not appear in the passenger list.

In a letter to her parents his sister had stated, it is understood, that she would join friends in New York and that her engagement to Mr. Vic Oliver, the American comedian, might be announced in the future.

Yet in New York yesterday, wires the *Daily Mirror* correspondent there, Mr. Vic Oliver said: " I wish to repeat I am not marrying anybody.

" I don't think I will even be in New York when Miss Churchill's boat docks. I simply can't believe the girl said she would marry me.

" When I met her in London she said she wanted to come to America, so later my secretary wrote offering her training in a dancing school and the possibility of a ten dollar-a-week chorus job in a show of mine.

" I know hundreds of girls in the show business and Miss Churchill is just one of them."

While the family and friends tried to get in touch with her on board the Bremen in mid-Atlantic yesterday, few of the passengers knew that they had in their midst a daughter of an ex-Cabinet Minister.

### No Messages

The quiet, red-haired girl, who spent her time walking on deck and reading, refused all telephone calls. Miss Churchill had made up her mind; she was not coming back.

" Nothing short of an earthquake would move Sarah when she had once determined on a thing; she said that at all costs she was going to America—and she went."

Those were the words of the only girl who was in the secret of her departure, who had seen her friend off on the boat-train and had the task of breaking the news to her parents.

She is Miss Jenny Nicholson, daughter of the poet Robert Graves.

Miss Nicholson yesterday rang up Mrs. Churchill to explain her part in the affair, but was unable to get into touch with her, and late last night her 'phone call to the Bremen was refused by Miss Churchill.

Then she sent a cable:—

" Wish you would reply. What do I say to people ? So far so good, or is it bad ? Cannot get in touch with your family. Randolph following. Vic again reported denial."

" I do hope they don't think I have done any harm. Miss Nicholson said tearfully to a *Daily Mirror* representative.

" Sarah told me I must keep the secret until after she had gone, and I did not tell a soul until the boat had sailed."

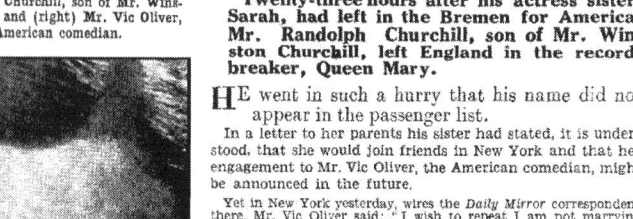

Miss Sarah Churchill, Mr. Winston Churchill's actress daughter.

This is David Selway, aged three. With him is his mother, Mrs. Ivy Selway, of Campsbourne-road, Hornsey, who was granted a maintenance order at Highgate yesterday against her husband (left). Mr. Selway was persuaded to let her have custody of the child, and told the boy to go to his mother, who held out her hand. But David clutched at his father and refused to leave him.

Mr. Selway was then advised to take the boy home with him, but eventually, as seen above, David and his mother were happily re-united.

## GRACE MOORE FAINTS SINGING AT FUNERAL

**FROM OUR OWN CORRESPONDENT**

LOS ANGELES, Wednesday.

GRACE Moore, famous opera singer and film star, collapsed in the arms of friends after singing the burial psalm, " The Lord Is My Shepherd," at the funeral of Irving Thalberg in Los Angeles yesterday.

Norma Shearer twice burst into tears as Hollywood paid its last tribute to her brilliant director-husband.

Freddie Bartholomew was present in a black " Little Lord Fauntleroy " suit, and other mourners were Myrna Loy, Douglas Fairbanks, Senior, Clark Gable and Fredric March.

## £4,000 FOR A LIFE

FRANCE has demanded a full apology and £4,000 compensation from the Spanish rebel authorities by to-morrow for the execution of a Frenchman in Spanish Morocco.

In case of a refusal the frontier between French and Spanish Morocco may be closed, states Central News.

## BLAZING GIRL FALLS FROM THEATRE BOX INTO CIRCLE

LIKE a " human torch " a young girl, with her dress in flames, fell screaming out of a box into the dress circle at the Gaiety Theatre, Dublin, last night.

**She was taken to hospital suffering from severe burns to the chest and body and from severe shock**

The accident occurred while a crowded audience was listening to Roy Fox and his band. The girl had been sitting in the box with two men.

Women screamed. In a moment the theatre was in an uproar. But the band went on playing.

Men rushed with coats which they threw around the girl.

She is believed to have been a member of a wedding party at the theatre.

Her name is Miss Birchill, of Stillorgan, near Dublin.

## M.P. IN LIFEBOAT DASH

Captain Derrick Gunston, M.P. for Thornbury, Gloucester, was among the volunteers on board when Bembridge (Isle of Wight) lifeboat went out last night to save a yacht.

**DRIVER WAS UNHURT : EXPRESS HIT HIS WAGON**

A FARM labourer and his horse had a miraculous escape from death yesterday when an express train travelling at sixty miles an hour smashed into the wagon the horse was pulling.

The man, Mr. R. Wilson, aged fifty-three, was driving his wagon over a railway crossing near Hemingbrough on the Leeds-Hull line, when the express approached.

The train struck the cart, tore it from the horse, swept off the animal's harness, and carried them away.

It threw Mr. Wilson safely on to the horse's back before it knocked the horse over, thus breaking Mr. Wilson's fall.

It scratched Mr. Wilson's elbow and didn't hurt the horse.

Then the train dropped the cart off its buffers.

And Mr. Wilson, returning to the farm, got another wagon and went back to the harvest.

THE DAILY MIRROR, Thursday, September 24, 1936.

Broadcasting - Page 17

# Daily Mirror

THE DAILY PICTURE NEWSPAPER WITH THE LARGEST NET SALE

CASSANDRA ----- P. 12
USELESS EUSTACE --- 13
SHORT STORY --- 19
DOROTHY DIX --- 22
THE RUGGLES --- 24

No. 10,239  Registered at the G.P.O. as a newspaper.  THURSDAY, SEPTEMBER 24, 1936  One Penny

Amusements: Pages 16 and 17

# 17 DIE AS PILGRIM TRAIN IS WRECKED BY EXPRESS

FROM OUR OWN CORRESPONDENT
TARBES (France), Wednesday.

SEVENTEEN people were killed and thirty injured when a train which had just left Lourdes full of pilgrims was smashed to pieces by an express to-night. The collision occurred two miles from Lourdes Station

**The impact was terrific and a third-class coach in the rear of the express was completely telescoped.**

Passengers who were unhurt and motorists waiting at a level crossing near by for the train to pass rushed to the rescue. From the wreckage arose screams of pain.

Among the first to arrive on the scene was Monsignor Gerlier, Bishop of Tarbes, who, owing to his experience in the Great War, was able to organise rapid first aid for the injured in addition to administering the consolation of religion.

The bodies of four children, three women and two priests have already been extricated from the wreckage.

All the bodies were terribly mutilated and one woman, who had been decapitated, still clung to the body of a child.

Lourdes ambulance corps, which is normally used for sick pilgrims, rushed the injured to Tarbes Hospital

Ann Sothern, the film star, who, states Reuter from Hollywood, is to marry Mr. Roger Pryor, actor and band leader, on Saturday.
The honeymoon is to be spent in Chicago, where Mr. Pryor's band has been engaged to perform next week.

## DIVORCE PLEA: "AM I HUBBY'S (FALSE TEETH) KEEPER?"

FROM OUR OWN CORRESPONDENT
NEW YORK, Wednesday.

Because her husband tantalised her with his false teeth, Betty Rice, of Los Angeles, is suing him for divorce.

The trouble is, says her petition, that he will pass his teeth to her to mind at unexpected moments—even in public.

The last straw was when, during a baseball game, he actually took out his teeth and passed them to her to guard while he batted.

# RANDOLPH CHURCHILL MEETS OLD GIRL FRIEND—BUT SAYS THAT'S NOT WHY HE'S STAYING ON IN AMERICA

FROM OUR OWN CORRESPONDENT
NEW YORK, Wednesday.

MR. Randolph Churchill has decided to lengthen his stay in America—but he denies that the reason is his meeting again with Miss Catherine Halle, to whom rumour engaged him five years ago, when he was twenty.

Yesterday Randolph had tea with Catherine.

When he was asked why he had decided to stay on he replied: "To study the political situation."

Admitting that Miss Halle and he had renewed acquaintance, he said: "We are old and very good friends."

The first time he met her (she is the daughter of a Cleveland department store owner) he was studying the international situation—making a lecture tour of the States in 1931 to give the views of youth on problems of the day.

It was his refusal, either to confirm or deny the reports of their engagement then that set American society tongues wagging.

At the time Mr. Samuel Halle said in an interview: "I am quite positive there is no truth in the report. Churchill is just a friendly young man and he and my daughter have many interests in common."

Randolph's official mission to New York as family ambassador when his actress sister, Sarah, dashed over to meet Vic Oliver, the comedian, is apparently ended.

It is stated that Sarah and Vic may soon make a stage appearance together in a vaudeville act at Schenectady.

## 31-OUNCE BABY IS BORN TO A MOTHER AGED 46: FIGHT FOR LIFE

BY A SPECIAL CORRESPONDENT

Happy that her tiny one-pound-fifteen-ounce baby boy came into the world before an operation could be performed to sacrifice its life and save her own, a forty-six-year-old mother lies in St. Pancras Hospital making a good recovery.

THE mother, Mrs. Selina Miller, of Haverstock Hill, Hampstead, London, N.W., went into hospital, a fortnight ago, agreeing to have the pregnancy terminated

They told her that the alternative might be that her other six children would be left motherless.

But on Sunday evening Baby Anthony was born, eleven weeks before he was due.

Anthony—eleven and a quarter inches in length—lies in a specially-prepared cot heated by lamps, and is fed hourly with his mother's milk and a milk food administered through a fountain-pen filler.

He cries surprisingly loudly when they bathe him in olive-oil and wrap him up again in cotton wool.

### Nurses' Pet

"He's the pet of all the nurses," I was told. "They chuckle admiringly at his little cries. It will be a hard fight to keep him alive, but we're making that fight."

Mrs. Miller had her last child eight and a half years ago, and her eldest daughter is aged twenty-three.

Mr. William Henry Miller, the father, who looks fifteen years younger than his forty-nine years is on sick leave from his work as a postman.

"I had a dekko at the boy before she did —on Monday—and I'm feeling so proud that I'm a father," he told me.

## MRS. FEARNLEY WHITTINGSTALL TO MARRY AGAIN

TWO days after the dissolution of her marriage had been made absolute, it was announced last night that Mrs. E. O. Fearnley-Whittingstall, formerly Miss Eileen Bennett, the tennis star, is to marry Mr. Marcus Marsh, the racehorse trainer, next Monday at Chelsea Register Office.

Mr. Marsh, speaking from his home at Lambourn, Berks., said that their future home would be at Lambourn, where he would continue to train horses.

Asked if Mrs. Fearnley-Whittingstall was likely to continue in competitive tennis, Mr. Marsh said that he thought it fairly certain she would retire.

Mr. Marsh is the son of Mr. Richard Marsh, who was King George's racehorse trainer. Mr. Marcus Marsh trained Windsor Lad, winner of the 1934 Derby.

**WHILE SWEDEN WENT SOCIALIST**

While the Government was falling in Swedish election that brought defeat of Agrarians and victory of Socialists. King Gustave duck shooting on the lakes surrounding his castle

THE DAILY MIRROR, Wednesday, September 30, 1936.

Broadcasting - Page 17

# Daily Mirror

THE DAILY PICTURE NEWSPAPER WITH THE LARGEST NET SALE

CASSANDRA .... P. 12
USELESS EUSTACE 13
SERIAL ........ 19
DOROTHY DIX .... 20
QUIET CORNER .... 23
THE RUGGLES .... 24

No. 10,244  Registered at the G.P.O. as a newspaper.  WEDNESDAY, SEPTEMBER 30, 1936  One Penny

Amusements: Page 8

# HIGHEST-EVER PILOT SAVED

## LIFE WITH KNIFE

BY A SPECIAL CORRESPONDENT

**DAPPER THIRTY-THREE-YEAR-OLD SQUADRON-LEADER F. R. D. SWAIN, R.A.F., TOLD ME LAST NIGHT HOW HE WON FOR BRITAIN A WORLD ALTITUDE RECORD — AND SAVED HIS OWN LIFE WITH A PENKNIFE.**

HIS most perilous moment came when he was coming down after reaching the height of 49,967 feet (nearly nine and a half miles) — highest ever flown by man in a heavier-than-air machine.

These are Squadron-Leader Swain's own words describing his ordeal:—

"After gliding down for about 5,000ft the window on the helmet of my suit hazed completely over.

"I could see neither the land nor my instruments. I was unable to read my compass.

"I continued losing height because I could see nothing, and then I started to feel that I was being suffocated.

### Fresh Air

"I pressed the release lever which should have opened the cockpit cover, but it would not function, then I tried to get hold of the zip-cord which was fitted to my suit for use in an emergency in order to get my head clear of the helmet.

"But I could not find the zip-fastener because over my suit I was wearing fighting harness and parachute harness.

"I was gradually getting weaker and I thought that the only thing to do was to get hold of a knife which I had taken with me for emergency and try to cut open the celestroid window in my helmet.

"I had great difficulty in doing this because I was feeling so very much exhausted. With a final effort I managed to slit the window of the helmet and was able to get in fresh air."

Picked a few months ago for the record attempt, Squadron-Leader Swain — neither married nor engaged — has taken his task as part of the day's job.

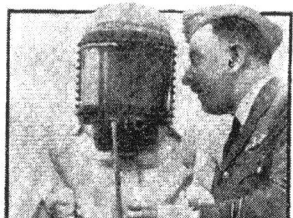

In his windowed oxygen helmet, Squadron-Leader F. R. D. Swain being wished good-luck before the start of his record altitude flight over Farnborough yesterday.

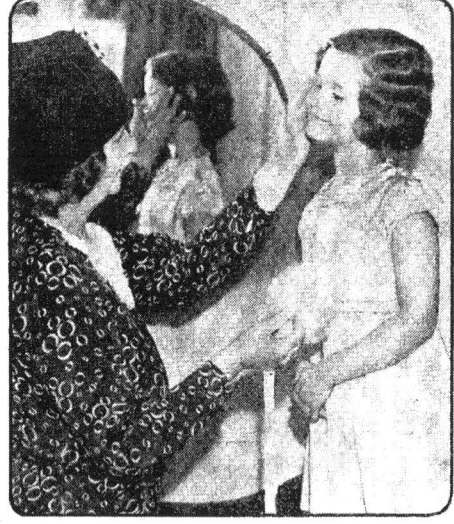

### OTHER BRITISH RECORDS

Other world records held by Britain are:—
Motor-car:—Sir Malcolm Campbell 301.129 m.p.h.
Rail:—Silver Jubilee, 113 m.p.h.
Ocean:—The Queen Mary, 30.63 knots (average for Atlantic crossing).

As mascot he carried with him a silver image of St. Christopher, patron saint of travellers. "I did this for the first time on this record-breaking flight," he said.

To face conditions nearly ten miles up he wore a special air-tight sealed flying suit, blown up to ordinary air pressure.

Roaring through the rarefied air of empty space at tremendous speed, climbing higher and higher, at the rate of 1,000 feet per minute, the newest explorer of the upper air looked like some figure from another planet.

### All-British

He accomplished his feat in a Bristol 138 machine fitted with a special "Pegasus" engine. The equipment was all-British.

The total flying time for the record was 3h. 20m.

"When I knew from my altimeter that I had broken the record," said Squadron-Leader Swain, "I was not exactly exhilarated, but just disappointed that my engine would not allow me to climb any higher."

He said that he took up flying because one of his brothers who has since died was a member of the Royal Flying Corps, and he himself was very keen to fly.

### His Mother Worries

Asked whether his mother worried when he made hazardous flights, he said: "She certainly does, particularly because two of my brothers are dead, but now she is resigned to it all."

And one of the first things that Squadron-Leader Swain did after he had completed his record-making ascent was to rush off to see his mother and invalid father, who live at Eastern Villas-road, Southsea.

"And," Mrs. Swain said, "we celebrated. I was perfectly certain that my son would do it if it were humanly possible."

The previous holder of the altitude record was M. J. Detre (France), who reached 48,698 feet on August 14.

## MAKE-UP COST WENDY, AGED SEVEN, A BEAUTY PRIZE, BUT SHE'S NOT WORRYING

BY A SPECIAL CORRESPONDENT

ROUGE and powder prevented seven-year-old Wendy Mary Skellon from winning the prize for the most beautiful child between seven and nine at the Hair and Beauty Fair at the Empire Hall, Olympia.

Mr. J. Foster, who has been one of the judges since the competition was founded in 1927, was hesitating whether to award her the prize when he noticed traces of make-up.

"I had never seen make-up on a child of that age before," he told me, "so I asked her gently if she had rouge on.

"She at once admitted she had. There is no rule against the use of rouge and powder, but the prize is awarded for the natural beauty of the child.

"The five finalists were all on a level for good looks, so I had to look for something to differentiate them."

★

Wendy Mary Skellon. Mother is "painting the lily" on the left. But powder and rouge lost Wendy a beauty prize. Below is Wendy — beauty unadorned.

### "Powder Puff" Dance

"Wendy is a very beautiful child, and if she had not worn make-up she would probably have won first prize."

Wendy Mary is the daughter of Mr. and Mrs. Frederick C. Skellon, of Decoy-avenue, Golders Green. She won first prize at the last exhibition.

It was Wendy's bath-time when I visited her home, and she received me in her dressing-gown with the self-possession of a debutante.

"Yes, I was disappointed," she admitted "but I have got over it now.

"I think dancing is the best fun in the world. My favourite dance is 'The Powder Puff' dance, which I have danced at public displays.

### Wants To Be Film Star

"I want to be a film star, but it will have to be in England I do not want to go to Germany; they have wars there.

"Shirley Temple is my idol I wish I had lovely ringlets like her."

Before I left Wendy bared her arm and showed me half way up a large blue W clearly etched by a network of blue veins

"That's W for Wendy," she explained. "If you look at it the other way round it is M for Mary."

## PALESTINE FIGHT AS MARTIAL LAW ORDER IS ISSUED

AS martial law measures for Palestine giving Lieutenant-General Dill almost dictatorial powers were announced last night four battalions of British troops went into action against Arabs.

An Order in Council provides that powers to be delegated to General Dill shall include—

Making of regulations for public safety, which will not be open to challenge in courts of law; and

Power to set up military courts for trial of offences against regulations.

Arrests, detention and deportation also come within the regulations covered by the Order.

General Dill will have control of harbours, forts and movement of vessels, aerodromes and all other services connected with transportation.

Trading, appropriation control forfeiture and disposition of property come under his command and he will be able to impose communal fines and the forfeiture and destruction of property as punitive measures.

It is expected that the proclamation bringing the new Order in Council into force will be issued by the High Commissioner to-day.

Not until a second proclamation has been issued delegating the powers to General Dill will the new measures come into actual operation.

An interval of some kind thus remains available to those among the Arab leaders who are trying to organise a peace movement.

Yesterday's fighting, in which four British battalions took part, was at Jaba. As dusk was falling, a converging movement was carried out upon an armed Arab band. Many Arab casualties are expected.

THE DAILY MIRROR, Friday, October 2, 1936.

Broadcasting—Page 17

# Daily Mirror

THE DAILY PICTURE NEWSPAPER WITH THE LARGEST NET SALE

USELESS EUSTACE P. 6
CASSANDRA .... 12
SERIAL ....... 19
DOROTHY DIX ... 20
QUIET CORNER ... 23
THE RUGGLES ... 24

No. 10,246  Registered at the G.P.O. as a newspaper.  FRIDAY, OCTOBER 2, 1936  One Penny

Amusements: Pages 20 and 21

# BIG BRITISH ARMS SPEED-UP:
## EXTENSION OF DEFENCE PLAN

### ONE REJOICES: THE OTHER MOURNS

FROM OUR POLITICAL CORRESPONDENT

MARGATE, Thursday.

**Britain is planning a big extension in her arms programme and a speed-up in arms production. Nothing will be allowed to stand in the way.**

TO-DAY the Imperial Defence Committee met in Whitehall to discuss the increase. Taken in conjunction with Sir Samuel Hoare's strong speech to the Conservative Conference here, the meeting is highly significant.

"The Government means business," was the summing-up of the delegates who heard th First Lord's statement. National defence dominated the day.

This was emphasised the more by the absence of Sir Thomas Inskip, Minister of Defence; Lord Swinton, Secretary for Air, and Mr. A. Duff Cooper, Secretary for War. Sir Samuel Hoare himself revealed that they were engaged in the bigger conference in London

"I must," he said, "emphasise the gravity of th international situation, and the urgent, insistent need of British rearmament.

"The Government is very far from complacent. Definite progress has been made in recent months, and the rate of advance will be greatly accelerated in the future."

Although recruits are coming forward in large numbers for the Navy and Air Force, Army enrolment still causes anxiety.

Employment exchanges will, in future, direct the attention of the unemployed to the need of a stronger Army. Ministers will shortly start a recruitment propaganda campaign. Special literature will be issued.

There will, however, be no coercion and nothing in the nature of conscription.

### Rebuffs for Government

The Government are hoping that the trade unions will co-operate with them in accelerating the output of arms and munitions and the encouragement of recruitments, especially in the Army.

Mr. Baldwin and his Ministers suffered three rebuffs to-day.

Delegates demanded a resolute non-surrender policy on mandates. They voted for agricultural tariffs and then almost unanimously decided that the House of Lords must be reformed.

Mrs. Gunning, a homely Conservative housewife, who has three sons in the Territorials, introduced the feminine note in the discussions on tariffs by saying:—

"One of my boys went away for a week-end camp. Each morning he had for breakfast a not very nice egg with Belgium written across it."

She urged the need for strengthening Britain's agricultural defence front.

Sir S. Hoare's speech: Page 6

### SIGNOR GRANDI TO LEAVE LONDON?

ROME, Thursday.

It is learned on reliable authority that Signor Grandi, the Italian Ambassador in London, will shortly be transferred to another post.

It is believed he will be replaced by Signor Guariglia, Italian Ambassador at Buenos Aires.

Signor Guariglia, in turn, will be replaced by Prince Colonna.—Reuter.

## GRIEF-STRICKEN WIDOWS OF AIR RACE VICTIMS MAY GET £6,000 PRIZE MONEY

TWO tragic women—one a bride of only six months—widowed by the crash of 'Plane No. 13 in the £10,000 Portsmouth-Johannesburg air race yesterday, will not suffer financially by their bereavement.

They are Mrs. Findlay, of Newhall, Surrey, whose husband, Captain Max Findlay, was piloting the 'plane, an Airspeed Envoy, at the time, and Mrs. Morgan, of Wallington, Surrey. Mr. A. H. Morgan was wireless operator on the ill-fated machine, which crashed at Abercorn, Northern Rhodesia, on the last lap of the flight.

Mr. J. W. Schlesinger, the sponsor of the air race, cabled from Johannesburg last night that, as the winning 'plane—that flown by C. W. A. Scott and Giles Guthrie—was the only one to finish, the remaining prize money, £6,000, should go to the dead airmen's dependents. In any case, he said, he would see that the two widows did not suffer more than they had done already.

Mrs. Morgan, the bride so tragically widowed, lay sobbing last night at her new home, unable to see anyone.

Margaret Findlay, little daughter of the dead pilot, does not yet know that her father lost his life in the crash.

She smilingly posed for a photographer yesterday while her grief-stricken mother stood at her side trying to hide her tears lest the child should guess something was wrong.

The companions of Findlay and Morgan, Ken Waller, co-pilot, and Mr. C. D. Peachey, who financed the venture, escaped

The flyers were warned at Abercorn Aerodrome not to take off, as the wind had changed, but decided to "risk it." The 'plane did not rise sufficiently and hit some trees.

Mr. Scott, winner of the race, covered the 6,154 miles in 52h. 56m. 48.2s., an average speed of 123 m.p.h. (See page 5.)

While Mrs. Max Findlay mourns her husband, killed in the crash of Entry No. 13 in the England-Johannesburg air race, Mrs. C. W. A. Scott (above left) hears over the telephone of her husband's arrival at Johannesburg, winning the race.

Beside Mrs. Findlay in the picture above, taken just after she had learned the tragic news, is her little daughter, Margaret, who was playing with her greyhound, Jock. She has not been told of her daddy's death.

## 'PLANES SAVE AMBUSHED TROOPS

CALLED by wireless, two R.A.F. aeroplanes last night rushed to the assistance of a Seaforth Highlanders' patrol ambushed by armed Arabs on the Acre-Safad road, says Reuter from Jerusalem.

The troops returned the Arab fire with a naval pom-pom gun and also went into action, inflicting casualties among the Arabs. The aircraft on arrival bombed the vicinity of the ambush, a hillside olive grove.

British casualties in Palestine from April 19 to the end of September totalled thirty-five dead and 162 wounded.

The first casualty to the British reinforcements who have just arrived in Palestine also occurred when Fusilier G. Turner, of the 2nd Battalion Northumberland Fusiliers, was seriously wounded in an ambush on the Jerusalem-Jaffa road.

### TRAIN KILLS WEALTHY MAN

A wealthy, well-dressed man, aged about forty-five, who is not yet identified, was killed by a train at Queen's Park Station, Kilburn, N.W., just before midnight last night.

He had a cheque book in his possession, and on the track station officials found a pocket book.

THE DAILY MIRROR, Saturday, October 3, 1936.

Broadcasting—Page 17

# Daily Mirror

THE DAILY PICTURE NEWSPAPER WITH THE LARGEST NET SALE

**PUT YOUR CLOCKS BACK TO-NIGHT**

No. 10,247  Registered at the G.P.O. as a newspaper.  SATURDAY, OCTOBER 3, 1936  One Penny

Amusements: Page 16

# CHAIN CAFES WANT MORE FOR CUP OF TEA: IS IT JUSTIFIED?

By A SPECIAL CORRESPONDENT

On Monday the price of a cup of tea in nearly every chain cafe in the country will be raised from 2d. to 2½d. The "Daily Mirror" considers this increase unjustified

THOUSANDS of pounds profit is made every year out of the "cup of tea" business. It has always been the most profitable trade of the large-scale restaurant and cafe combines.

Now the price is to be raised by 25 per cent. and the excuse is that prices of other commodities than tea are rising.

And so, those who drink tea have got to pay more so that the price of sausage and mash shall not be changed.

What does this mean to the tea shops?

It is said that 160 cupfuls can be made from one pound of tea. In places where this is done, it means from Monday onwards 160 more half-pennies for every pound of tea—which works out at an extra 6s. 8d.

At the end of a year the extra halfpenny will represent an increase of many thousands of pounds.

This is set against the recent 2d. per pound increase in tea duty imposed in the last Budget.

For years the price has been universally 2d. a cup, although from 1922 to 1928 the price of tea was far higher than it is to-day.

In those days, with tea at 2d. a cup, one company made profits which rose in 1927 and 1928 to well over three-quarters of a million.

This is not a sudden decision on the part of the teashop magnates. The idea has been brewing in their heads for some time.

The case for the rise in price was put by Sir Isidore Salmon, M.P., the chairman of Lyons, at the annual meeting last June, when a net profit for the company of over a million pounds was declared.

In the course of his speech he told of an increase in the cost of raw materials, and said that there had had to be compensation to enable the company to obtain the results they had shown

### "Mathematical Operation"

Then he went on to say that it would soon be necessary to extend the list of products to be raised in price.

Butter, eggs, lard, flour, milk, cream, potatoes and sugar, he said, had risen in price, and it was difficult to assess these costs in an equal manner over the various items of a menu.

"Many items cannot be raised without disturbing their relation to others," he said. "The adjustment of these figures to cover increased costs is a mathematical operation, yet immediately any small change is made, someone who presumably feels he knows much more about our business than we do, suggests it is iniquitous and accuses us of profiteering.

### "When Prices Rise"

"For example, if we were to put ¼d. on a cup of tea, it would at once be pointed out that a ¼d. on a cup of tea, with so many cups to a pound, means so many shillings, and that the only additional cost we have to pay is a few pence additional duty on tea, altogether overlooking the fact that there may be other reasons for the increase than the mere duty or even the cost of the tea itself.

"When prices are rising it is an impossibility to raise every item on the menu even by so small a sum as ¼d.

"That, indeed, would bring in a return,

*(Continued on page 2)*

---

**A CUP OF TEA**
will cost you 2½d. at:—
LYONS
A.B.C.
EXPRESS DAIRY,
MECCA,
W. HILL & SON
J.P. RESTAURANTS

---

The man who could not get into the jury box . . . 20-stone Mr. Albert Gordon, of Brighton.

## LIVES—AND LAUGHS—ON BEER AND JELLIED EELS

TWENTY-STONE Mr. Albert Gordon, who was unable to get into the jury box at Brighton Quarter Sessions, yesterday, laughed as he talked to the *Daily Mirror* about his experience.

Summoned to serve on the jury, he tried to enter the box but his girth prevented him. So he tried the other side of the box. No success.

Then he was advised to try and get in sideways.

"I am not a contortionist," was Albert's reply.

Roars of laughter re-echoed round the court, and Albert, who is known locally as "Happy," laughed loudest of all.

Finally Albert was told by the clerk that he was released, and he went home—still laughing.

"Happy Albert," who is a boarding-house proprietor in Brighton, said to the *Daily Mirror*:—

"Despite my size I am as fit as a fiddle. I attribute my good health to my diet, which is not a slimming one.

"For years I have pretty well lived on jellied eels and beer, and if they are fattening I guess it doesn't worry me very much."

He told me he was so fond of jellied eels that ten years ago he opened a stall on Brighton beach. Now he has ten stalls.

"They call me the jellied eel king," he said.

---

## RUGBY PLAYERS CONDEMN CLUB BAN ON MARRIAGE

FAMOUS Rugby players do not agree with an order issued by Mr. L. W. S. Howard, President of Windsor Rugby Club, that members must not marry until the end of the season.

Last year's England captain, B C Gadney, said last night: "I think the question of marriage during the season is entirely a personal matter.

"I do think that marriage in the middle of a football season might prove disturbing. But one must not be too arbitrary, and if the bride-to-be prefers to be married in December, I should think the wishes of the president would have to go by the board."

Mr. C. D. Aarvold (former England and Cambridge three-quarter) said: "Such a ban is, I think, rather foolish. One man played for England on his honeymoon—and played a very good game.

"Marriage means that players stay at home more, and that helps to keep them in good training."

### Eight This Summer

Seventeen players out of the two fifteens organised by Windsor Club are married. Eight of them were married this summer.

"In the interests of the club, I must ask single members not to consider matrimony until the end of the season," Mr. Howard declared at the annual meeting.

"I think we ought to tell Windsor girls, too, that they had better look elsewhere.

"Even if they do not retire, married members seem to lose their form," Mr. Howard told the *Daily Mirror* after the meeting.

### CHINA MOBILISING

PREPARATIONS are being made by the naval authorities for the evacuation of British women and children in the Yangtse ports following a report of the massing of Chinese troops.

The possibility of a Japanese blockade of Yangtse ports to enforce compliance with Japan's demands is being widely discussed in Shanghai.

British sea captain seized by Japanese.—Page 5.

## COMEDY OF MAN WHO GOT INTO "PROM" CHOIR BY MISTAKE

A GOLDERS Green man last night presented London with its best joke of the season. He went to the 'Prom' Concert in the Queen's Hall to hear Beethoven's Choral Symphony and expected to have to stand in the promenade.

### PAM BARTON IN U.S. FINAL

NEW YORK, Friday.

Miss Pam Barton, the British woman golf champion, to-day beat Miss M. Miley, American Curtis Cup player, by 3 and 1 in the semi-final of the American women's open golf championship (as reported on page 26).

She will meet Mrs. Maureen Orcutt Crows in the final at New Jersey.—Central News.

Instead, he had a seat—a seat in the choir. All during the first half of the performance he had to hold a piece of music and pretend to sing.

This is how it happened.

As he intended to go to a dance after the concert, he was in evening dress. As he came out of the cloak-room he was mistaken for a member of the choir. No one else in the audience was in evening dress.

Attendants ushered him upstairs, and before he could make his protests heard he was given a piece of music, and found himself among the members of the B.B.C. Choir.

# Daily Mirror

THE DAILY PICTURE NEWSPAPER WITH THE LARGEST NET SALE

Broadcasting - Page 17

CASSANDRA - - - - P. 12
USELESS EUSTACE - 13
NEW SERIAL - - - - - 22
DOROTHY DIX - - - - 26
THE RUGGLES - - - - 24

No. 10,248    Registered at the G.P.O. as a newspaper.    MONDAY, OCTOBER 5, 1936    One Penny

Amusements: Pages 18 and 21

# 84 ARRESTS AS THOUSANDS STAMPEDE IN LONDON RIOTS

## Stones Meet Police Batons: 268 Injured

### By A SPECIAL CORRESPONDENT

BATON CHARGES . . . RIOTING CROWDS . . . LORRIES OVERTURNED . . . PAVING STONES TORN UP . . . GIRLS AND MEN CRASHING THROUGH PLATE GLASS WINDOWS . . . DEMONSTRATORS WIELDING TRUNCHEONS BOUND IN BARBED WIRE . . . 5,000 FASCISTS MASSING TO PARADE HEMMED IN BY A CROWD OF 100,000, INCLUDING THOUSANDS OF ANGRY JEWS AND COMMUNISTS SHOUTING, "THE FASCISTS SHALL NOT PASS."

EIGHTY-FOUR arrests and the last-minute calling off by the police of the Fascist parade and meetings followed these wild scenes in the East End of London yesterday.

The injured totalled 268, and sixty-four had to be treated in hospital.

Violence and bloodshed began before the procession had even formed. Baton-law ruled for several square miles near the Tower.

Screaming women were dragged through the streets after their arrests; crying children were rescued from the mad rush of panic-stricken mobs in the nick of time.

Fascists had assembled at Royal Mint-street and Mark-lane, and the counter demonstra-

### RIOTS IN PARIS

More than 2,300 people were arrested during riots at a Paris stadium yesterday.—See page 2.

tion, which grew to 100,000, centred in Aldgate and Cable-street.

Sir Philip Game, Police Commissioner, and other high officials in plain clothes, were on the spot, and immediately Sir Oswald arrived he was told the meeting and parade could not be held.

Sir Philip took this action, according to a Scotland Yard statement, to "prevent further breaches of the peace" after many people were injured.

About 3,000 extra police were on duty. But despite a police guard standing shoulder to shoulder, the crowd managed to pelt Sir Oswald Mosley's car with stones.

Eventually the Fascists marched to the Embankment near Charing Cross Bridge with Sir Oswald at the head. There they were halted and dismissed.

### Marbles on Roads

According to the Scotland Yard statement, however, "a portion of the Fascist procession re-formed and caused minor disorders in Trafalgar-square and the Strand."

In the East End before the time fixed for the procession I saw, from a position at the junction of Cable-street and Leman-street, a pretty girl throw a piece of wood through a plate-glass window. Her action started a stampede.

Lighted fireworks were thrown at the hoofs of charging police horses.

Hundreds of persons were crushed against the walls of buildings and forced into door-

(Continued on back page)

SIR OSWALD MOSLEY . . .

. . . his black shirt for yesterday's East End march blossomed out into a new and military-looking uniform, with silver buttons in sets of three—a feature of Guards officer tunics—with riding breeches and peaked cap like a police-inspector's Brodrick. The badges on the cap are the Fascists' "flash of lightning," and, below, the axe and fasces of the ancient Romans, adopted by Mussolini.

The woman is Mrs. Anne Brook-Briggs, organiser of the southern command.

### QUADS' MOTHER REFUSES £10,000 OFFER FOR ANN

"I WILL give you £10,000 if you will let me adopt baby Ann."

This offer was made to Mrs. Miles, mother of the famous St. Neots' Quads, by a little grey-haired woman who refused to give her name.

The woman had come from her home in Scotland to the Huntingdonshire town specially to see the Quads.

When she saw them she was so infatuated with the smiles of baby Ann, the only girl in the four, that she made the offer—in vain.

She was carried away by her enthusiasm—with the result that she was carried away like this. The end of a struggle between a woman demonstrator and police in yesterday's East End battle between Blackshirts and Anti-Fascists. More pictures on pages 16 and 17.

## JEAN PACKS LOTS OF DRESSES FOR HER 12,000-MILE FLIGHT

WITH a full wardrobe of dresses in her plane, Miss Jean Batten, twenty-six-year-old New Zealand airwoman, arrived at Lympne, Kent, yesterday evening in readiness for her 12,000-mile flight to New Zealand, which she hoped to start at 4 o'clock this morning.

In addition to a sun-helmet and numerous patent foods, she busily packed away a number of sets of dainty underwear.

Miss Batten was specially concerned about the frocks and "undies," taking care to stow them away from any danger of being smeared with oil.

She was wearing a smart grey flannel suit with a green jumper.

"Are you going to wear green to-morrow?" I asked her.

"Certainly, why not?" she replied. "Green is my lucky colour."

Discussing the prospects of her flight, she told me: "I think I shall be able to get away about 4 a.m. I shall get a final weather forecast at three o'clock, and unless this is very bad I shall take off.

"I shall make my first stop Marseilles, and there I shall take on a load of 155 gallons of petrol.

"I hope to cut my Australian record in half, that is, by a week, and I think I can."

The machine is the same one in which she flew the South Atlantic last year.

THE DAILY MIRROR, Tuesday, October 6, 1936

# Daily Mirror

### THE DAILY PICTURE NEWSPAPER WITH THE LARGEST NET SALE

Broadcasting - Page 19

USELESS EUSTACE - P. 8
CASSANDRA - - - - - 14
NEW SERIAL - - - - - 21
DOROTHY DIX - - - - 24
QUIET CORNER - - - - 27
THE RUGGLES - - - - 28

No. 10,249  Registered at the G.P.O. as a newspaper   TUESDAY, OCTOBER 6, 1936   One Penny

Amusements: Pages 18 and 19

# GIRL TO MARRY MAN OF 78

## SHE WILL NEVER SEE

FROM OUR SPECIAL CORRESPONDENT
OXFORD, Monday.

ROMANCE has come into the life of a blind girl whose cheery smile and happy heart have carried her through pain, difficulties and affliction.

She is to marry a seventy-eight-year-old City Alderman, who is an ex-Mayor of Oxford.

**Miss Emily Allen, whose home is at Fritwell, Oxfordshire, lost her sight when she was four years old. She can just remember colours, and can just picture what a tree looks like.**

Standing in her fiance's garden now, with its banks of nasturtiums, beds of roses, and its old fruit trees, she can almost imagine herself a child again.

It is seven years since Miss Allen came to the Institute for the Blind at Oxford. With many other girls she has sat day in and day out doing circular knitting on a machine —socks and jumpers.

To these blind people, the periodical visits of those interested in their work were red-letter days. To Miss Allen, the deep, kind voice of Alderman Charles Brown, his firm hand-shake, and his cheery good-bye came to mean more than that.

### "I Enjoy Life"

"Mr. Brown is seventy-eight, and I am well . . ." Miss Allen lifted her face to the light. She looked twenty-one—is probably in the thirties.

"My friends have told me that it is madness to marry a man so much older than I am, but if I can bring him a few years' happiness, I will consider my life worth while," she said.

She had just helped him on with his overcoat, and with a soft "Good-bye, little missie," he had let himself out by the front door to go to a meeting.

I offered her a cigarette. She took one and lit it with enjoyment.

"Oh, yes, I enjoy life," said Miss Allen with a smile. "I go to the theatre and to the pictures, but dancing is my one passion. I love dancing."

### Happy Home

"I love housework——." She waved her hand around the room. It was spotless.

"I have an electric stove—no fiddling about with gas and matches for me. I can cook well, and we shall have a happy home.

"Mr. Brown wants to sell his house and move into a smaller one. The wedding is to be at Fritwell as soon as it can be arranged.

"I should like my people—I have five sisters and three brothers—to be near me when I am married," said Miss Allen. "It will make my happiness complete."

At the gates Mr. Brown was waiting.

"For myself, I will only say that I am terribly happy," he said—and disappeared up the road with the walk of a young man of forty.

---

Alfred Stratford and Mary Ann Flynn, charged with being concerned together in murdering Mrs. Elizabeth Ada Fortescue in her basement flat at Shepherd's Bush.

They were remanded for a week at West London Police Court yesterday. (See story on page 7.)

### L.I.G. TO REST

MR. Lloyd George has handed to his publishers the manuscript of the sixth and last volume of his war memoirs—a work of over a million words, written in just under two years—and is to take a complete rest.

Part of it will be spent abroad.

He is anxious to extend the scope and work of the Council of Action with a restatement of policy and an extensive series of demonstrations, but he has been advised that to embark on such a strenuous programme immediately after completing so formidable a task would be over-taxing his vitality.

With his sightless fiancée — Alderman Brown and Miss Emily Allen, to be married next month.

## REDS THREATEN TO SPLIT THE SOCIALIST PARTY

BY OUR POLITICAL CORRESPONDENT
EDINBURGH, Monday.

CRACKS—big ones—are appearing in the structure of official Socialism.

There are growing indications that disunion will before long split the party from top to bottom.

The left wing of Labour is becoming much more formidable. Since the formation of the French Government, the developments in Spain and the growth of Fascism, Communism is having a greater appeal to the rank and file.

The Socialist executive have won their victory on the question of non-intervention in Spain.

### Union Leaders Shy

They will win again when the National Defence policy is certain to be endorsed by the conference.

Their task will not be so easy when a proposal to affiliate with the Communist Party is discussed on Wednesday. The majority of Socialists and Trade Union leaders do not want to link up with the Communists.

There is, however, a growing belief that sooner or later the Communists will have to enter the Socialist fold.

When that time comes—and many say it is near at hand—the Reds are bound to cause trouble.

Because of this "red light," Socialism is now fighting its most critical battle in Edinburgh. Party leaders know well that unless they keep the extremists at bay, they would be in a hopeless position if they came into office.

Comedy Brightens Conference—page 5.

### THE DUCHESS OF KENT

THE following official announcement was issued from No. 3, Belgrave-square, S.W., last night:—

"Her Royal Highness the Duchess of Kent has cancelled her forthcoming engagements, and she is not undertaking any further functions this autumn."

## POLICE WHISPER TO HECKLERS AND "PRESERVE THE PEACE"

BY A SPECIAL CORRESPONDENT

DIFFERENT methods were adopted by the police to restrain interrupters at last night's meetings of the Fascists in the East End of London.

Bethnal Green and Aldgate, the scene of Sunday's disturbances, were again the meeting places of Fascist and Communist demonstrators, but instead of dragging hecklers through the crowds, police officers were detailed to speak quietly to them and to advise them to leave the demonstration.

On three occasions at Victoria Park-square last night I saw the effect of this new procedure.

Instead of a hostile crowd gathering to watch a number of policemen struggling with an interrupter, one officer would touch him on the arm, beckon him to the edge of the crowd, and warn him.

Following the banning of their procession on Sunday, when it was about to start, the Fascist headquarters issued last-minute orders for yesterday's demonstrations in the East End.

The biggest meeting was held at Victoria Park-square. Others were held in different parts of Bethnal Green and Stepney.

Crowds waiting for Sir Oswald Mosley to appear were disappointed. The meetings ended before ten o'clock with the Fascist song and the National Anthem.

Every man in the crowd took off his hat when the first strains of the Anthem were broadcast from the amplifiers.

"Free Speech Without Riots."—Page 5.

# Daily Mirror

THE DAILY PICTURE NEWSPAPER WITH THE LARGEST NET SALE

Broadcasting - Page 21

JANE .......... P. 7
QUIET CORNER .... 18
SERIAL ......... 23
DOROTHY DIX .... 27
THE RUGGLES .... 32

No. 10,258 — Registered at the G.P.O. as a newspaper. — FRIDAY, OCTOBER 16, 1936 — One Penny

Amusements: Pages 20 and 21

## JEAN ON PERILOUS 1,100 MILES' DASH OVER TASMAN SEA

She wouldn't take "No" for an answer when they tried to prevent her from crossing the perilous Tasman Sea—Jean Batten (right), daring New Zealand air girl. Above is her aeroplane, single-engined and without radio.

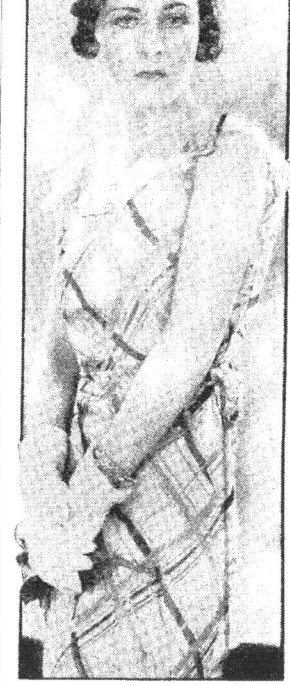

WITH A RUBBER BOAT ON BOARD IN CASE OF DISASTER, JEAN BATTEN SET OFF FROM AUSTRALIA LAST NIGHT ON THE PERILOUS LAST LAP OF HER FLIGHT TO NEW ZEALAND —1,100 MILES ACROSS THE TASMAN SEA.

IT has never yet been flown by a woman. And the London-Auckland flight which it completes has never been achieved by a man.

Her 'plane carries no radio, and before she left all shipping in the line of her route was warned to keep a look out.

In a radio conversation with her father at his Auckland home a few hours before she was due to start, Miss Batten gave a definite promise not to attempt the crossing unless the weather conditions were satisfactory.

"I am feeling in the pink," she said. "I am getting my machine ready. Bye, bye, daddy. See you about four o'clock to-morrow afternoon."

At Richmond, forty miles from Sydney, where she had gone for the sake of the longer runway it afforded, it was early morning when her 'plane left the ground.

She hoped to cover the 1,100 miles in eight hours, which would bring her home in less than eleven days since her departure from Lympne, Kent.

*Messages from Reuter and Exchange*

## SCOTLAND YARD RADIO FOR MAN WHO BOUGHT OVERCOAT

SCOTLAND Yard wants to trace a man who bought an overcoat in North - street, Edgware - road, London. The following message was broadcast last night:—

"Will the man who, at 2 p.m. on October 9, purchased a gentleman's blue, half-belted overcoat from a wardrobe dealer in North-street, Edgware-road, please communicate with New Scotland Yard?"

The message, which was broadcast at the request of the Lancashire police, relates to the inquiries into the death of Mrs. Mary Holden, of Manchester, who was found strangled by the roadside near Leigh (Lancs) on October 8.

Superintendent McHardy told the "Daily Mirror" last night that the police want to submit the coat to a microscopic examination.

The coat was sold to the wardrobe dealer by a man who is known to the police and has already given them important information. He sold it on Thursday, and next day the dealer sold it to another man.

## MOTHER'S PRAYER TO KEEP CHILD

"IF I have no child to go home to, what is life to me? For God's sake let me take her home."

This impassioned plea of a young mother was granted at Islington Juvenile Court yesterday.

It was proposed that the child should be sent away to an approved school, because her home influence might be undesirable.

The mother, it was stated, was deserted by her husband, and afterwards adopted a certain mode of life.

"I have seen that the child knew nothing of the matter," said the mother.

An official stated that the child had a good school character and there was no evidence of her being morally affected.

### LORD NUFFIELD PROMISES £80,000 TO HOSPITAL

Lord Nuffield has undertaken to be responsible for the £80,000 mentioned in Guy's Hospital appeal for extensions to the nurses' home—when the total balance of the appeal for £500,000 has been subscribed from other sources.

Lord Nuffield's £1,250,000 to aid doctors—see page 2.

### K.C'S £2,250 A YEAR POST MEANS BIG SACRIFICE

BY his appointment at a salary of £2,250 a year to the chairmanship of London Sessions, announced yesterday, Sir Henry Curtis Bennett, K.C., will sacrifice a considerable income.

He succeeds the late Sir Percival Clarke.

Sir Henry will have to give up almost entirely his extensive criminal court work as a barrister.

Murder trials in which he has been briefed included those of Ronald True, Armstrong (the poisoner), Mrs. Thompson, Field and Gray (the Crumbles murderers), Patrick Mahon and Vaquier.

### Peeress Patient...

... in a West End nursing home is Marchioness of Queensberry. She underwent an operation for appendicitis yesterday.

Only person allowed to visit her was Lord Queensberry. He saw her just before the operation and was allowed to greet her after it had been performed.

Latest bulletin says she is "making a splendid recovery."

## PUPILS AGED 10 TAUGHT SEX IN THIS SCHOOL

SEX instruction is given to children at the age of ten at Berkhamsted School, Herts.

This was stated by the headmaster, Mr. C. M. Cox, at the Peterborough Diocesan Moral Welfare Association Conference at Northampton yesterday.

"Young people of to-day think and talk of sex as though restraint is unnatural," he said.

"This state of mind is largely due to the films, plays and books of to-day. The only way to correct that state of mind is through education.

"I advocate sex instruction at an early age. At my school I begin sex instruction with children at the age of ten, and as far as I can see it is having a very good effect."

An ex-headmaster of a prominent English public school said to the *Daily Mirror* last night: "While I admit that many films and books to-day do concentrate on sex, I am afraid I cannot altogether agree with Mr. Cox.

"The danger of such instruction at too early an age is that an unhealthy curiosity might be aroused.

"It is the wrong kind of sex knowledge that they have. The minimum age for sex instruction should be fourteen."

## "FIRE" CRY IN CINEMA— OPERATOR INJURED

WHILE a film was being shown at the Pavilion Cinema, Chelmsford, last night a cry of "Fire" was heard.

Three hundred people in the cinema were asked to leave, and did so in perfect order.

The assistant operator, Mr. G. Storey, was re-winding a film when it burst into flames. The chief operator, Mr. F. Smith, in attempting to smother the blazing film with a blanket was badly burned on his arms.

Both men pluckily used fire extinguishers until the arrival of the fire brigade.

THE DAILY MIRROR, Saturday, October 17, 1936.

# Daily Mirror

**THE DAILY PICTURE NEWSPAPER WITH THE LARGEST NET SALE**

Broadcasting—Page 17

USELESS EUSTACE - P. 10
QUIET CORNER - - - - 11
DOROTHY DIX - - - - 18
SERIAL - - - - - - - - 19
THE RUGGLES - - - - 24

No. 10,259. Registered at the G.P.O. as a newspaper. SATURDAY, OCTOBER 17, 1936 One Penny

Amusements: Page 16

# BLOOD RITE AT A GIPSY WEDDING

## CUT WRISTS BOUND WITH 7 KNOTS AT CAMP FIRE

### BY A SPECIAL CORRESPONDENT

A WEDDING with no confetti, no ring, no bridesmaids and no veil—but a million witnesses—a gipsy wedding under a night sky and in the red glow of a camp fire.

The bride was attractive, dark-eyed Nellie Gray, and the groom Johnnie Lee, aged twenty-two, a tinker. They were married in Turner's Dell, Kingsbourne Green, near Harpenden, by Gipsy Petulengro with all the rites of Romany tradition, last night. The ceremony was broadcast.

Gipsy Petulengro faced the members of his clan and cried aloud: "If there is anyone who says that Nellie and Johnnie should not be married let them throw a piece of wood into the fire!"

No wood fell into the glowing embers of the camp fire.

So Gipsy Petulengro cut the wrists of Nellie and Johnnie. The two bleeding hands were tied together with a cord made fast with seven knots, each one woven by a gipsy virgin.

Then, released from the knotted cord, Johnnie leaped high over the bonfire, followed by his bride. Hand in hand, they leaped back over the embers.

The "minister" handed a twig to Nellie, which she broke—and Johnnie did the same. Two twigs were handed to Nellie, but she could not break them.

"One can be broken, but not two," chanted Gipsy Petulengro.

There came a cry from the assembled gipsies, for Johnnie and Nellie were man and wife according to gipsy law.

### "Promised" Since Babies

After the ceremony, Nellie told me, "I was ever so nervous. I love Johnnie very much. Ever since we were babies we have been 'promised' to each other.

"We do not have a honeymoon. Johnnie has a caravan of his own, and to-morrow we will go to it and start life together."

Johnnie cannot speak English—only Romany—but Nellie has travelled all over the world.

"We will be married to-morrow before a registrar, as gipsy marriage is not legal. But to us the ceremony this evening is far more sacred. The one by the registrar can be ended, but the Romany marriage lasts for ever," she said.

A rare picture is this of the solemn, ages-old ritual of a Romany wedding. This wedding took place in a dell near Harpenden (Herts). Gipsy Petulengro is opening a vein in a wrist of the chal and chi (bride and bridegroom), so that their blood shall mingle. The lower picture shows the bleeding wrists being tied together.

## ONE MINUTE RAID

At 1.5 p.m. yesterday a car drove up to A. Goldstein and Co.'s, glass merchants, Westminster Bridge-road, London, S.E.

At 1.5½ Goldstein's cashier got out of the car with £650—wages money—and turned towards the offices.

At 1.5¾ the cashier was on the ground and a thick-set man was racing with the money-bag towards a car a few yards away.

At 1.5⅞ the man was on the running-board of the already moving car.

At 1.6 the car and its £650 cargo was out of sight.

"Mr. A. Gold, the general manager, had driven me to and from the bank as usual," Mr. Ernest Leaf, the cashier, told the Daily Mirror.

"He was still at the wheel when I got out and I was pushed in the back and tripped up, falling heavily. My assailant was a thick-set man, but I did not see his face."

Mr. Gold said: "We just went back to the bank and drew another cheque for the wages."

## BABY CATAPULTED OVER WALL BY CAR

CATAPULTED from its perambulator over a 4ft. wall, a three-month-old baby hurtled into a bed of nettles when a car—which did not stop—came into collision with the child's parents on the main London road at Froyle, near Alton, Hants, last night.

Police are hunting for the car.

Covered with stings, but otherwise unhurt, the baby, with its mother, who was wheeling the perambulator, received attention at the neighbouring house of Sir Hubert Miller, Bart.

The father, Arthur George Upton, of Froyle, was rushed to Alton Hospital, and placed on the danger list.

Mrs. Upton, who escaped with bruises and shock, told the Daily Mirror:—

"My husband was walking with his bicycle a few yards behind me. Suddenly I heard a crash from that direction, and almost at the same moment the perambulator was wrenched out of my hands."

Mr. John Hanna, of Tangate-road, Guildford, said: "I was driving from the direction of Alton when I was pulled up by Mrs. Upton, who was standing in the road, frantically waving her arms.

"She said, 'I have lost my baby, I have lost my baby.'"

## DRIFTING COLLIER'S S O S

DRIFTING in a north-westerly gale with a damaged propeller, the Newcastle collier Hauxley, with seventeen men on board, sent out a dramatic SOS as she was being forced aground on the Dogger Bank last night. It read: "Require urgent assistance."

A tug stood by in the hope of taking the men off.

## WARRIOR CHIEF DEAD

Ras Nasibu, the Ethiopian warrior chief, survivor of Italy's Abyssinian campaign, died of consumption at Davos, Switzerland, last night, says Reuter.

He was the principal delegate of the Ethiopian Government at the League Assembly in July, and was then a very sick man.

# Daily Mirror

**THE DAILY PICTURE NEWSPAPER WITH THE LARGEST NET SALE**

THE DAILY MIRROR, Tuesday, October 20, 1936

Broadcasting - Page 19
USELESS EUSTACE P. 15
SERIAL ........ 21
DOROTHY DIX .... 24
QUIET CORNER .... 27
THE RUGGLES .... 28

No. 10,261  Registered at the G.P.O. as a newspaper.  TUESDAY, OCTOBER 20, 1936  One Penny

Amusements: Page 18

# BOY SENTENCED OVER AN EGG

## IS CLEARED ON APPEAL

FROM OUR SPECIAL CORRESPONDENT

SANDIACRE (Derbyshire), Monday.

AFTER six months of what he described as "torture," a youth who had been sentenced to three years at Borstal had his name cleared in five minutes by the Lord Chief Justice, Lord Hewart, to-day.

**AND THE CAUSE OF ALL THE SUFFERING WAS AN EGG.**

The youth was Samuel Carr, eighteen-year-old ironworker. After his appeal had succeeded he turned to his mother in the Strand, London, and said: "Come on, Mum—let's go home."

So Sam and his mother came back to their cottage here to-night.

They had heard Lord Hewart declare at the Court of Criminal Appeal that Sam had been convicted "on an indictment which should never have been permitted."

Five minutes after he stepped into the box, Sam stepped out again—free. It was the first time Mrs. Carr had been to London in her life, but that did not frighten her.

"I knew all along—and so did everybody in Sandiacre—that it was all wrong, and that Sam was innocent. And if I had not felt so faint, I should have got up in court and cheered," she told me as we travelled back home together.

Well she might have done, for Mrs. Carr went to London with the knowledge that her son had already spent nine weeks in prison for an offence he did not commit; had lost his job, and the only thing that would enable him to get another—his character.

Curly-headed Sam, Sandiacre's footballer with the permanent smile, told me all about it as we journeyed home.

Sam still believes that the affair which blew up over a boiled egg is a first-class comedy—he never once felt that it would end up at Borstal.

"It was ridiculous. Just imagine—I came back from a football match last May and a fellow I know came and asked me to spend the evening reading at his home.

"I knew that he had a bad leg, so I went.

"When I got there he put three boiled eggs on the table and asked me to have one. I told him I had had my tea, but to be friendly said I would have one. He put one on a plate before me, but before I could start on it, two detectives came in.

"They said they were going to arrest (Continued on back page)

## MIZLER FIGHT SECRET

LEAVING a sick bed last night, Harry Mizler's father surprised the rest of the family by joining them in their little drawing-room in St. George's, London, E., where the telephone brought the news that Mizler had lost his fight with Jimmy Walsh for the British light-weight boxing title.

News that his father was ill had been kept from Mizler.

Story of the fight—Page 30.

### A Romance Ended

Miss Patricia Bland, whose intended marriage with Mr. Thomas Oliver Neville Clarke this month will not now take place. She is the daughter of Mrs. Ernest Bland, of Colsterworth House, Grantham.

### THE KING MAY VISIT INDIA AFTER THE CORONATION

THE King is expected to visit India to be crowned Emperor in the year after the Coronation.

This statement was made last night by Lord Clarendon, Governor-General of South Africa, in a speech at Bloemfontein.

Lord Clarendon added that he hoped it would be possible for the King also to visit South Africa after his Coronation, says Reuter.

### Orsborne's Children

## MOTHERED BY GIRL OF 15

A GRIMSBY girl, aged fifteen, is acting as "mother" to the eight young children of Skipper George Orsborne, now on trial at the Old Bailey (see page 7), while Mrs. Orsborne is in London, to be near her husband.

She is Peggy Greenwood, daughter of a friend of the family, who is looking after the children from early morning to bed time.

### "I Control Them"

"I can manage them all right, she told the *Daily Mirror* last night. "I have given Dorothy, who is fourteen, the job of looking after Bobby, the baby, aged eighteen months, and she does it very well. The rest I can keep in control myself."

To demonstrate her qualities she soon settled a noisy argument between some of the children as to who should operate the gramophone.

"Mother has brought me up to do housework," said Peggy, "and I can do anything in the home.

"I wash the children and cook and bake for them, and put them to bed at night—the youngest first and the older ones a little later."

Five of the children, who are of school age, are staying at home during the trial.

### BAND LEADERS' "EQUITY"

AIMS similar to those of the theatrical profession's Equity will be served by the new organisation of dance orchestra chiefs, the *Daily Mirror* learned last night from Bert Ambrose, well-known band leader.

The Musical Directors' Federation, formed after a meeting which lasted well into the early hours of yesterday morning, will officially protect band leaders in their dealings

## DENTIST AND MAID ATTACKED BY MYSTERY MAN

AS an Edgware dentist stepped into the darkened hall of his home after returning from his West End surgery last night, he was attacked by an unknown man, who beat him savagely about the head with a fire-iron.

Then the man raced down the garden path of the little suburban villa and disappeared into the darkness.

Neighbours attracted to the scene by shouts for help found the dentist lying gravely injured in the hall.

Hearing moans coming from the garden, the neighbours ran through the house and found the dentist's twenty-one-year-old pretty maid lying bleeding from severe head wounds.

The man, it is believed, attacked the maid, knocked her unconscious with a blow on the head, carried her into the front garden and left her where she would not be seen. He then hid in the house.

The dentist, Mr. Harry Fry, aged about thirty-six, of The Drive, Edgware, and the maid, Annie Moran, an Irish girl, were rushed to Redhill County Hospital, where early to-day their condition was critical.

The attack on the dentist was witnessed by an eighteen-year-old youth who was passing the house.

Mr. Fry had been living apart from his wife for the past six months.

He has one child, a girl of nine, who is away at a boarding school.

Relatives of the injured man were at his bedside.

## ENGAGEMENT IS BROKEN ON BEAUTY'S WEDDING EVE

Mr. T. O. N. Clarke

BY A SPECIAL CORRESPONDENT

BEAUTIFUL Miss Patricia Bland, one of the most attractive debutantes of 1934, and Mr. Thomas Oliver Neville Clarke, handsome young film actor and producer, of Welbeck-street, W., had planned to be married in a few days' time. Yesterday it was announced that the wedding would not take place.

Miss Bland, whose home is at Colsterworth House, Grantham, Lincs, told me last night that she and Mr Clarke were still the best of friends.

"We decided mutually to break off the engagement," she said, "but there is no ill feeling on either side."

Mr. Clarke, who played in "The Barretts of Wimpole-street," "Clive of India," and "The Lost Patrol," said:—

"We were to have been married in London at the end of this month. Now, on the day I should have been married, I shall be up to my neck in work on a new film."

This is the seventy-first broken engagement announced this year.

## MANSION RENT FREE

REDGRAVE Hall, Suffolk, near Diss, with a park of about 300 acres, is to be offered, rent free for two years, to a good tenant who will take the property on a long lease at a nominal rental.

# Daily Mirror

**THE DAILY PICTURE NEWSPAPER WITH THE LARGEST NET SALE**

THE DAILY MIRROR, Friday, October 23, 1936.

Broadcasting—Page 19

USELESS EUSTACE P. 15
QUIET CORNER - - - 16
SERIAL - - - - - - - 21
DOROTHY DIX - - - 26
THE RUGGLES - - - 28

No. 10,264 Registered at the G.P.O. as a newspaper. FRIDAY, OCTOBER 23, 1936 One Penny

Amusements: Pages 18 and 19

## PRETTY GIRLS EJECT MEN IN WILD FIGHT AT MEETING

BY A SPECIAL CORRESPONDENT

**Pretty girl Fascists ejected interrupters when wild hand-to-hand fighting broke out at a Fascist meeting at Hampstead Town Hall last night.**

SCREAMING women and men shouting anti-Fascist slogans were carried from the hall by girl and men stewards.

Mounted police and a large force of foot police kept a crowd of 2,000 anti-Fascists moving on the pavements outside during the meeting.

Inside the hall men and women fought on the floor.
Several of the women could be seen using their fists and exchanging blows. It was over a woman that the trouble started.

Heckled and interrupted continually, Mr. William Joyce, director of propaganda of the British Union of Fascists, called upon stewards to eject a woman interrupter.

Pandemonium reigned. Chairs were overturned. Then the hand-to-hand fighting began.

About twelve people were ejected from the meeting and, it is understood, the names and addresses of eight or nine of them, including two women, were taken by the police.

Mr. Joyce appealed to those who had witnessed the ejections to give evidence of what they had seen.

Four people were later arrested and charged, two with using insulting words and behaviour, one with assaulting a police officer and one with obstructing the police.

### Cordon Across Road

They will appear at Marylebone Police Court to-day.

When the meeting was over police reinforcements moved along the crowd which had gathered in the main road.

Further disorder broke out when the Fascists marched from the Town Hall to their local headquarters a few hundred yards away.
They were surrounded by a crowd yelling: "Down with the black rats."
A cordon of police was drawn across Belsize-lane to stop the demonstrators. All traffic was diverted and the road was blocked for nearly a quarter of an hour.

### BIG BRITISH ORDER FOR U.S. WAR 'PLANES?

FROM OUR OWN CORRESPONDENT
NEW YORK, Thursday.

AMERICAN aircraft stocks rose on Wall Street to-day following a report that the British Government has decided to place a huge order for aeroplanes in the United States.

An official of the Curtiss Wright company mentioned in connection with the deal denied to-night that they were negotiating with the British Government for the sale of war 'planes, but the "World Telegram" quotes a reliable source as saying:

"Many important contracts are on hand and many more forthcoming, but I understand the negotiations were being made in greatest secrecy."

Lord Nuffield replies to Air Ministry—page 3.

OH! OH! OH! IT'S A LOVELY WAR!...

Chic and charming, well-dressed, you wouldn't think this party of girls had been in the wars would you? Yet the scene is Oviedo—the town where, for thirteen weeks, the populace were reported starving, ravaged by Spain's Reds, until General Lombarte, the merry old gentleman in the centre of the bevy, relieved it.

### TWO 'PLANES IN NIGHT CRASHES: FOUR INJURED

FOUR people were injured when two 'planes crashed in the South of England last night.

An R.A.F. Army co-operation 'plane made a forced landing at Warminster (Wilts) last night, and hit the side of a hayrick on the military camp ground.

The two occupants, Pilot Officer R. N. Keeble and Second Aircraftman Charles Moorhouse, both of No. 15 (Bomber) Squadron R.A.F., stationed at Abingdon, were unconscious when dragged from the cockpit by members of the Royal Engineers staff engaged on the Warminster Barracks scheme.

After circling four times round Horsham, Sussex, in a vain search for a landing place, a private 'plane from Redhill Aerodrome struck a tree and crashed into a field.

The Swiss pilot, M. Georges Ernest Guye, of Brixton Hill, London, and his passenger, Thomas Albert Edward Craven, of Shawberry-avenue, East Dulwich, were extricated from the wreckage by workmen.

Both men were taken to Horsham Hospital.

### EDNA BEST AND HERBERT MARSHALL REUNION AT PARTY

BY A SPECIAL CORRESPONDENT

EDNA BEST, the actress, and her film star husband, Herbert Marshall, have been brought together again as a result of a meeting at a party given by a friend.

Their meeting at the party was their first for nearly three years. During that time Herbert Marshall has been working in Hollywood.

The party was given by Mr. W. J. O'Bryen, husband of Elizabeth Allan and well-known film agent, at the Cafe de Paris.

Since Herbert Marshall arrived in England on Tuesday many rumours have been circulated about his own and his wife's future plans.

Their parting was rumoured in London and Hollywood.

Herbert Marshall had not seen his three-and-a-half-year-old daughter since she was about a year old.

### "SIN TO URGE MARRIAGE WHERE THERE IS NO LOVE"—ARCHDEACON

ARCHDEACON Newman, of Preston, put forward outspoken views on sex in a speech at Blackburn last night.

Referring to the "misuse of God-given gifts," he said:—
Marriage is even insisted upon in the case of sin, but where there is not love and affection between two partners it is a great mistake.

"Indeed, I regard it as a sin against God that two people should be urged to enter into a loveless marriage simply because there has been sin.
"It is no use saying, 'It puts the thing right.' It does not do so. This sort of marriage is wrong, and is likely to prove disastrous in the long run."

Referring to the blessings of parentage, the Archdeacon said: "Where there are no children by the will of God there is something lacking. Where there are no children by the will of man it is deplorable.
"Sex instinct is often fickle, and by itself frequently leads to infidelity."

### KILLED HOLDING BOUQUET

TEN minutes after receiving at a church mission a bouquet for his aged, ailing wife, a seventy-six-year-old agricultural labourer, James Herridge, of Windsor-lane, Cippenham, Slough, was killed in a collision with a motor-cycle on the Bath road and was picked up with the bouquet still in his hand.

THE DAILY MIRROR, Saturday, October 24, 1936.

Broadcasting - Page 17

# Daily Mirror

THE DAILY PICTURE NEWSPAPER WITH THE LARGEST NET SALE

USELESS EUSTACE P. 10
QUIET CORNER - - - 14
SERIAL - - - - - - - - 19
DOROTHY DIX - - - - 22
THE RUGGLES - - - - 24

No. 10,265  Registered at the G.P.O. as a newspaper.   SATURDAY, OCTOBER 24, 1936   One Penny

Amusements: Page 16

# HUSBAND DIES ON DAY WIFE'S BODY IS EXHUMED

## SOPHIE 'STONED'

SOPHIE Tucker, America's "Red Hot Momma," left the Troxy Cinema, Commercial-road, in London's East End last night, to go to the chemist's.

While she was crossing the road from the stage door two youths hiding in a dark alley threw stones at her.

One hit her on the arm. Another whizzed by her head. Frightened, Miss Tucker ran back to the stage door and told the keeper what had happened. He and two boys searched the neighbourhood without finding the youths.

Later Miss Tucker said: "I can't understand why anyone should want to do a thing like that—to me of all persons.

"Just before I got to the corner I was hit on the arm, and another stone missed my face by inches. Luckily I had my furs on.

"I turned round in time to see two youngsters running away down an alley."

### FROM OUR SPECIAL CORRESPONDENT
DERBY, Friday.

AFTER hearing of an order for the exhumation of his wife, who died sixteen months ago, George Minion, aged thirty-eight, of Mignonette, Field-lane, Alvaston, Derby, was found dead to-day with his head in a gas oven. To-night the exhumation took place.

This day of drama in this working class suburb of Derby ended shortly before midnight when, digging by the light of a hurricane lamp on a grave behind the centuries old church of Harington's Estate, three men exposed a coffin.

A few minutes later Sir Bernard Spilsbury, famous Home Office pathologist, arrived with the coroner, Mr. T. H. Bishop.

The coffin was opened and an elderly man was led forward to identify the body. It was the dead woman's father, Mr. George Kitchen, a Derby road sweeper. He almost collapsed as he was brought beside the grave, and below in the eerie light cast by the lamp saw the remains of his daughter.

Mrs. Minion, the mother of five children, died in the Derbyshire Royal Infirmary in June, 1935.

Mr. Minion knew that the exhumation was to take place, and that he was to have been called as one of the principal witnesses at the inquest.

He was interviewed by Detective-Inspector James Bray, chief of the Derby C.I.D., at his home on Thursday night.

### Daughter's Evidence

At the inquest on Minion to-night the fourteen-year-old daughter, who has been "mothering" the other children, said she was in bed at 9.30 on Thursday night when her father called to her to say he was going out.

He returned at 10.30, kissed her sister and herself and said: "Are you frightened?"

He then went into the next bedroom, kissed two of her three brothers who were asleep there and asked the same question.

"It was a long time before I went to sleep," she said, "because he had asked me if I were frightened. He kept coming upstairs and going down again, and when I asked him who was downstairs, he said: 'Nobody.'

"I did not hear him again."

When she got up yesterday she noticed a smell of gas in the scullery. She found a note and summoned a neighbour.

The inquest was adjourned.

Mr. and Mrs. Minion with one of their five children. Mrs. Minion died in June last year in Derbyshire Royal Infirmary.

## THE B.B.C. PUT A BAN ON 'BREWERY' IN THE BAND

### FROM OUR OWN CORRESPONDENT
WOKING, Friday.

CRITICISM of the B.B.C. was made by Captain C. A. Master, High Sheriff of Surrey, at a complimentary dinner to the Friary Brewery Band at Woking to-night.

Captain Master said the B.B.C. would not give the band its full title, but called it the Friary Band. Other bands were known by their vocation, and theirs was the only brewery band.

Mr. Denis Wright, of the B.B.C., who was present, said in explanation that the B.B.C. received many letters from all sorts of people.

After the band had been in the programme as the Friary Brewery Band they received many letters from listeners that they were not going to pay 10s. a year to hear beer advertised.

As far as it rested with him the band should be given its full title in the next programme, but he did not know whether the higher powers would be afraid of the criticism of teetotallers.

## A YACHT AS WEDDING GIFT

A YACHT, a motor-car and a magnificent carpet made by the women of Rotterdam will be among the wedding presents of Princess Juliana and Prince Bernhard Von Lippe Zur Biesterfeld, says Reuter.

## LORD NUFFIELD'S FACTORY MAY BE USED: SIR THOMAS INSKIP

REFERRING to the dispute between Lord Nuffield and the Minister of Air, Sir Thomas Inskip, Minister of Defence, last night said:—

"It may even in the end prove advantageous to the Government to have the capacity represented by Lord Nuffield's aero engine works available for the execution of another part of the Government's programme in the near future."

He added that everybody would regret the difference of opinion which had unfortunately taken place between two public men.

"I regret still more the inevitable publicity which this difference of opinion has obtained," he continued.

"I say emphatically that Lord Swinton has left nothing undone either in the way of enterprise, or research, or of making use of the resources of the aircraft manufacturing firms. It was hoped that part of the aircraft programme would have been carried out by Lord Nuffield's organisations.

"It was difficult to see an end to the services which the Morris organisation was in a position to render to the nation."

Sir Thomas said he wished to correct the misapprehension which might easily have been caused by statements that Lord Nuffield had broken away from the Government and was declining to put at the service of the nation his great resources.

Premier May Reply—Page Four.

## ITALY MAY FOLLOW SOVIET AND DROP NON-INTERVENTION

GRAVE developments are threatened in Europe by Russia's announcement yesterday that she will no longer hold herself bound by the agreement for non-intervention in Spain to any greater extent than other States.

It is reliably reported in Rome that at end of the visit of Count Ciano, Italian Foreign Minister to Berlin, Germany and Italy will renounce their refusal to tolerate any further Soviet provocations in European affairs, or the existence of a Soviet State in Spain.

Signor Grandi (Italian Ambassador in London) will undoubtedly receive instructions to-day to hand in Italy's resignation from the Non-Intervention Committee it is stated.

At the same time the Spanish rebel authorities have decided, according to a radio message from Salamanca, to search and detain any Russian ships entering Spanish waters, and if they are found carrying arms or munitions, to sink them.

This sensational decision has been taken following the reported arrival at Santander of a Soviet ship laden with arms for the Government forces, and of fifty Soviet 'planes, which, it is alleged, are to be followed by sixty more.

Doubts as to Russia's position arose when the announcement that she will no longer be bound by the Pact was followed by a statement that she will not withdraw from the Non-Intervention Committee.

Last night, however, it was officially stated in Moscow that Russia has simply denounced the nullification of the non-intervention agreement accomplished by other Powers, and there-

(Continued on back page)

THE DAILY MIRROR, Monday, October 26, 1936.

# Daily Mirror
THE DAILY PICTURE NEWSPAPER WITH THE LARGEST NET SALE

Broadcasting - Page 19

USELESS EUSTACE P. 15
QUIET CORNER - - - 16
SERIAL - - - - - - - 21
DOROTHY DIX - - - 26
THE RUGGLES - - - 28

No. 10,266  Registered at the G.P.O. as a newspaper.  MONDAY, OCTOBER 26, 1936  One Penny

Amusements: Pages 10 and 24

## BOY OF 4 INHERITS £500,000 FROM AUNT HE SAW 6 TIMES

FROM OUR SPECIAL CORRESPONDENT
LYMINGTON, Sunday.

A CHUBBY four-year-old lad with brown eyes, fresh complexion and curly, golden hair, Charles Andrew Morrison, has inherited a fortune of more than £500,000—and he has not been told about it.

When he is twenty-one Charles Andrew will be the possessor not only of this wealth but also one of the loveliest estates in Hampshire—Walhampton.

ALL THIS HE WILL OWE TO A GREAT-AUNT WHOM HE SAW ONLY HALF A DOZEN TIMES IN HIS LIFE.

The great-aunt was Viscountess St. Cyres, daughter of a multi-millionaire, Mr. John Morrison, who died last month. She has left, it is revealed, £923,525.

Charles Andrew is the second son of her nephew. But Viscountess St. Cyres did not overlook the elder boy, James Ian Morrison, aged seven.

For James will, in due course, inherit another part of the Morrison millions acquired on the death of Mr. John Morrison by his father, who married the daughter of the second Lord Hambleden, of W. H. Smith and Sons, Ltd., newsagents and booksellers.

The two brothers spend most of their time at their parents' beautiful Wiltshire home, Fonthill Bishop, near Wilton, or on Mr. Morrison's extensive Scottish estates.

A friend of the family told me that Charles Andrew is 'quite an unspoilt little fellow who loves best of all to roam about his father's Wiltshire estate and to play "Red Indians and cowboys" with his brother."

In her will Viscountess St. Cyres has provided for every one of her staff and workpeople, many of whom she had never seen.

From the youngest hall boy to the old woodman on the estate, everyone will receive a bequest, and many of them a life annuity.

### Fairy Godmother

"From the day she came here until the day she died she has been a fairy godmother—not only a millionairess, but a woman in a million," was the way one of her servants described her late mistress to me.

"Yet, so well did she keep the secret of her heir that not one of us knew who was to have Walhampton and the money.

"Now we know that it is to be young Master Charles we realise how cleverly she had planned.

"The house and estate are entailed to the little boy—that means no one can break it up until he makes his own decision when he is a man, and it also means that the place will be kept going, and most of us will be able to keep our jobs."

Eleven years ago Viscount St. Cyres died, and the blow was so great that his widow became a permanent invalid.

## TAXI STRIKE TO GO ON

EAST London taxi drivers who are on strike following the action of some of the proprietors in cutting down the meter percentage paid to drivers for Sunday work decided last night that the strike should continue until the owners agree to suspend the cut for two months.

A representative of the drivers said that if the proprietors would agree not to put the percentage cut into operation for two months the men would go back and in that period the position would be fully considered by the Transport and General Workers' Union.

### "LOVE AT FIRST SIGHT"

Advertisement for a housekeeper six weeks ago by Mr. Benjamin Kay, a Yorkshire farmer, had a sequel in this wedding at Selby. Mr. Kay, who at fifty-seven was regarded as a confirmed bachelor, is seen with his twenty-three-year-old bride, Miss Dorothy Tindall, a former nurse. They described their romance as "Love at first sight."

### NEVER WORKED—UP AT 4 TO SEE "DAD" OFF

The case of a young man who has never done a day's work in his life, yet rises at 4 a.m. to put his seventy-two-year-old father on the bus to go to work, was told at a conference of the Iron and Steel Trades Confederation at Newport on Saturday.

Another speaker said there were men working at a Rogerstone steel works who were over seventy-five and who went to work half an hour early so they could have a sit down before they started.

## FIREMAN FALLS FROM ENGINE FOOTPLATE

MISSED by his driver as the 6.19 express from Shenfield (Essex) pulled up at Stratford, London, E., last night, an L.N.E.R. fireman, E. Rawn, was found after a search lying severely injured on the line near Forest Gate, E., more than two miles back.

On arriving at Stratford Driver Adams was unable to say where the fireman had fallen from the footplate, and at once all signals were put at danger and the train service suspended while the search was made.

Rawn was taken to Queen Mary's Hospital and detained.

## DE VALERA SAVED WOMAN'S SIGHT

Mr. de Valera

BY A SPECIAL CORRESPONDENT

HOW Mr. de Valera, President of the Irish Free State, was instrumental in saving a London woman from blindness was told to me yesterday by a grateful husband.

The woman is Mrs. Adams, wife of the Rev. Joseph Adams, of Curzon-road, Muswell Hill, N.

"My wife has been suffering from an illness for over seven years," Mr. Adams said.

"Gradually her eyes were becoming worse and worse, and she had resigned herself to coming blindness, when I remembered that Mr. de Valera had had a serious operation on his eye in Zurich, and it was successful.

"I wrote him about it, and he replied personally in a long and very kindly letter.

"He recommended a London specialist first. I took his advice and my wife was operated on a few days ago at St. George's Hospital. One eye has been saved and my wife will not be blind."

## POLAND DEMANDS ABOLITION OF NAZI RULE IN THE 'FREE CITY' OF DANZIG

FROM OUR OWN CORRESPONDENT
WARSAW, Sunday.

A STRONGLY-WORDED note demanding respect for the Constitution and for Polish rights and interests in Danzig was sent by the Polish Government to the Danzig Senate to-day.

Poland demands the abolition of all Nazi enactments since July which violate the Constitution.

The Note follows a report received in Warsaw of a startling speech by Herr Foerster, Hitler's nominee in Danzig, at a conference of Nazi leaders in the Free City.

### Emergency Cabinet

Foerster is said to have declared that "within three months the League and Poland will be turned out from Danzig and the Free City included in Germany."

Alarmed at this threat, the Polish Government summoned an emergency conference at Warsaw and called in Dr. Pappee, Police Commissioner-General in Danzig, and M. Lipski, Polish Ambassador in Berlin, to discuss the situation.

As a result of this conference, Dr. Pappee took with him to-day to Danzig the Government's warning and demands.

Poland has now decided to follow a firmer policy against the Nazis, and, it is stated here, may ask the League High Commissioner to call in Polish police to intervene in Danzig against the Nazi terror.

## PALESTINE'S PUBLIC ENEMY No. 1 "CAPTURED BY BRITISH"

PALESTINE'S "Public Enemy No. 1"—Fawzki Kawkaji, chief of the Arab rebels—is reported to have been captured.

Kawkaji, said to have offered £500 reward for the capture of the British Commander-in-Chief, is believed to be among the prisoners taken after a battle with British troops in the valley of the Jordan, says Central News.

One British soldier was killed and two wounded in skirmishes with an armed Arab band during the week-end.

When the Arab Higher Committee called off the strike in Palestine, Kawkaji fled, and it was believed he had escaped into Transjordan.

Troops had been watching for his return in the Nablus area, where there are many Arab villages likely to shelter rebels.

## NORMA SHEARER'S RELAPSE

MISS Norma Shearer, the film star, has suffered a relapse, cables the Daily Mirror New York correspondent.

Friends announced yesterday that she will definitely retire from the screen, while Louis Mayer, chief of Metro-Goldwyn-Mayer, stated that plans for the actress "were being held in abeyance."

THE DAILY MIRROR, Tuesday, November 3, 1936.

Broadcasting - Page 19

# Daily Mirror

THE DAILY PICTURE NEWSPAPER WITH THE LARGEST NET SALE

GODFREY WINN'S
PARADE - - - - - P. 11
SERIAL - - - - - - - 21
DOROTHY DIX - - - 22
THE RUGGLES - - - 28

No. 10,273  Registered at the G.P.O. as a newspaper.  TUESDAY, NOVEMBER 3, 1936  One Penny

Amusements: Page 19

# FAMOUS K.C. DIES AS DINERS LAUGH AT HIS JOKES

BY A SPECIAL CORRESPONDENT

With 400 of the most distinguished patrons of sport, the arts and the theatre still laughing at one of his jokes, Sir Henry Curtis-Bennett, K.C., and fifty-seven-year-old 18st. "Falstaff of the Bar," collapsed and died at a London banquet last night.

HE was the second chairman of London Sessions to have dropped dead in less than a month. Sir Percival Clarke, the previous chairman, died on October 5 in his room in a London hotel.

Twenty-three years ago Sir Henry's father dropped dead at a meeting at the Mansion House within a month of his appointment as Chief Metropolitan Magistrate.

By another amazing coincidence Sir Henry's intimate friend, Mr. Frederick Freke Palmer, well-known solicitor, collapsed and died at a banquet in London in January, 1932, just as he had finished a speech full of humorous anecdotes, when he fell back into his chair.

Last night Sir Henry was replying to the toast of the "Guests" at the dinner of the National Greyhound Racing Society at the Dorchester.

A few moments before he rose to deliver his speech he turned to a friend and said: "I feel as nervous as a kitten to-night." "Oh, nonsense," was the answer, "the number of times you have spoken in public."

Sir Henry stood up. With tragic and unconscious prophecy, he began by saying that it might be the last speech he would make. On his appointment to the Bench he would have to learn to listen to other people.

For fifteen minutes he kept his audience rocking with merriment as he told story after witty story. Finally, he came to the tale of a journey which he had recently made from Scotland to England.

He said that the train seemed to be stopping far more frequently than usual, and at last, when it came to a Border town where it should not have halted, he put his head out of the window and asked a man in uniform why it had stopped.

"No, man replied, "Well, sir, we are getting a new engine, for this one does not seem to be able to get enough steam pressure. Somehow the train seems to be overladen to-night."

## Crash of Glass

As the guests were laughing at Sir Henry's story, obviously directed against himself, there was a crash of glasses.

Sir Henry was seen to stagger, put his hand to his side, and slowly topple over on to the floor, his bulk knocking chairs and cutlery out of the way and spilling the wine from the glasses which smashed to splinters as he slowly sank on to the carpet.

In a second his brother, Sir Noel Curtis-Bennett, was by his side, calling frantically for a doctor. Quickly two rushed to his side. One of them was Sir Henry Jackson. Screens were put around the top table.

A deep silence fell over the room, while the doctors brought water to Sir Henry's lips and fanned him with napkins.

Then an announcement was made that the dinner would be abandoned.

Guests filed slowly out.

Before Sir Henry Curtis-Bennett could be carried from the banqueting hall to an ambulance he had died.

Sir Henry had been a K.C. since 1919.

Murder trials in which he was briefed included those of Ronald True, Armstrong, Mrs. Thompson, Field and Gray, the Crumbles murderers, Patrick Mahon and Vaquier.

He acted as counsel for Miss Irene Savidge in the famous Savidge inquiry.

He was knighted in 1922, and had been at the Bar for thirty-four years.

This exclusive picture of Sir Henry Curtis-Bennett was taken at the dinner last night a moment before he fell to the floor and died.

As will be seen, Sir Henry was smiling broadly at a joke (told in adjoining column) about his weight. Guests round him, and even the waiters, were still laughing uproariously at the story when the great Judge and lawyer fell.

## £1,000,000 GEMS IN TO-DAY'S PAGEANT OF PARLIAMENT

BY A SPECIAL CORRESPONDENT

TIARAS in which one stone alone may be worth £1,000, priceless ermine and crimson velvet robes will make the House of Lords the scene of the most impressive pageant known in the modern world.

So great has been the rush to see the King make his first appearance in Parliament as Sovereign that more than 500 peeresses have been unable to obtain seats.

In the heavy gold carriage of state, drawn by eight horses, accompanied by a Sovereign's escort of Life Guards, the King will start from Buckingham Palace punctually at 11.20.

At 11.25 the procession will be in the Mall; 11.35, Horse Guards Parade; 11.40, Whitehall, and 11.45, House of Lords.

It will be the first Royal procession to Westminster for many years in which no woman has ridden.

The drive will be notable, too, as the first appearance of Lord Colebrooke in the recently revived office of Master of the Robes.

A woman secretary stood on guard by a telephone in Westminster last night while, with nerves on edge, Miss Florence Horsbrugh, M.P. for Dundee, was re-reading the speech she will make when she moves the address in reply to the King's Speech.

When a "Daily Mirror" representative asked if Miss Horsbrugh would come to the telephone to be congratulated on being the first woman to have the honour, the secretary was firm. "She has had so many congratulations, she needs protecting from them," declared the secretary.

"She's still nervous. She'll be nervous right up to the moment for making her speech."

Traffic Arrangements—see page 23

## DROPPED SPANNER SHOCK AT OPERA

BY A SPECIAL CORRESPONDENT

HERR Von Ribbentrop, the German Ambassador, and Frau Ribbentrop made their first public appearance in London society at the performance of "Der Rosenkavalier" by the Dresden State Opera Company at Covent Garden last night.

Nearly all the German colony in London were present.

The first excitement occurred when an electrician dropped a spanner in the middle of the first act.

The house was hushed for the singing of a newcomer to Covent Garden Marta Fuchs, when a terrific crash was heard back-stage. The singer jumped, then went on as though nothing had happened.

THE DAILY MIRROR, Wednesday, November 4, 1936.

# Daily Mirror

**Broadcasting - Page 19**

THE DAILY PICTURE NEWSPAPER WITH THE LARGEST NET SALE

GODFREY WINN'S PARADE .... P. 11
SERIAL ........ 21
DOROTHY DIX .... 22
THE RUGGLES .... 28

No. 10,274 Registered at the G.P.O as a newspaper. WEDNESDAY, NOVEMBER 4, 1936 One Penny

Amusements: Pages 18 and 19

# BANNED PLAY THAT PORTRAYS GOD TO GO ON SCREEN

BRITISH audiences are to be allowed to see God portrayed on the screen in the presentation of the negro play, "Green Pastures," which has been licensed by the British Film Censor, according to a statement by the London office of the producers, Warner Brothers, yesterday.

**The theatre production was banned six years ago because of the portrayal of God on the stage.**

An official of Warner Brothers said yesterday: "We have been officially informed by the film censor's office that they have passed the film, which—like the play—has a portrayal of God as a negro preacher.

"I understand that it has been passed without any conditions being imposed on the portrayal of God.

"The film was shown privately by us to many prominent Churchmen, and the Rev. Pat McCormick said he would like to show it in St. Martin-in-the-Fields.

"It was submitted to the film censor in June. His decision has only just been made known to us, and arrangements are being made to put the film on in the West End in a few weeks."

### "Fish Frys" in Heaven

"Green Pastures," of which the author, Marc Connelly, is now in London, is an episodic play about the Southern negro's ideas of heaven.

God is a pastor called "De Lawd" by the negroes, whose conception of the joys to be attained in heaven includes such delights as "fish frys." They translate their view of it into earthly comparisons.

In the American version of the play God is portrayed as a cigar-smoking individual sitting at a desk equipped with push-buttons which summon winged secretaries.

The part of God in the film is taken by a negro who was born on a Mississippi boat.

### Churchmen Disagree

Well-known Churchmen expressed opposing views on the portrayal of God on the screen when approached by the *Daily Mirror* last night.

"I object very strongly to the idea," Bishop Welldon said. "Any representation of God the Father on the stage or on the screen is profanity itself."

The Rev. Arthur Wellesley Orr, vicar of St. Paul's, Kingston Hill, however, said: "I see no objection provided the theme is reverently treated. Different races see Him in different ways, and no doubt the coloured races imagine Him as a negro."

### Took U.S. by Storm

"The Jews described heaven as full of gold and precious stones. That was their ideal—but some of us would prefer heaven to be a library full of books."

The film version of "Green Pastures" was received in America with widespread appreciation, cables our New York correspondent, and in August it took New York by storm.

Clergy were delighted with the film's sincerity, and it received the endorsement of the National Decency League, the Catholic organisation to prevent improper pictures.

In Ontario, Canada, the film was banned until protests by local clergy resulted in the ban's removal.

A striking scene of the negro conception of God taken from the film "Green Pastures." De Lawd (the negro name for God), played by a negro who was born on a Mississippi steamboat, is blessing a little child. On the right is a scene representing De Lawd with Noah.

## HEIRESS TO £10,000 STILL DOES HER OWN HOUSEWORK

**FROM OUR SPECIAL CORRESPONDENT**

DENHAM (Bucks), Tuesday.

I HAVE found to-night the mystery heiress who was left £10,000 by the seventy-year-old Scottish farmer father she had never seen.

She is Mrs. Eva Shand, a slim, brown-haired middle-aged woman, who lives quietly with her husband, Mr. Ernest William Shand, a retired compositor, and her beloved dog, Terry, at Lackaday, a creeper-covered bungalow on the Willowbank Estate, Denham.

**Not even her neighbours know that Mrs. Shand has inherited £10,000. She has not let it appear that she is a comparatively wealthy woman.**

She still does almost all her own housework. Her husband's chief pleasure still lies in the cultivation of their little garden.

The *Daily Mirror* published the news of the search for the heiress of Mr. Harry Reily, a retired farmer, who died about four months ago in Ayrshire.

Mr. Reily's wife had separated from him
(Continued on back page)

## BILL TO STOP EAST END RIOTS IN THE HOUSE NEXT WEEK

**BY OUR POLITICAL CORRESPONDENT**

THE Public Order Bill, banning political uniforms, will, I understand, probably be introduced in the Commons next week.

Sir John Simon has personally drafted the new measure, which will enable the Government to use Orders in Council in dealing with political disturbances and wearing of uniforms.

It is anticipated that the Bill will become law before Christmas.

In his speech last night in the Commons, the Prime Minister said that if ever there was a Bill which it was the duty of the whole House to attempt to shape, it was the Public Order Bill.

The Government believed that its proposals would go very far to discourage events recently seen in some parts of the country, and particularly in the East End of London.

Referring to trade, the Premier said that overseas trade had continued to expand.

Mr. R. D. Denman urged the Government in their Bill dealing with Ministerial salaries not to overlook the question of an official salary for the leader of the Opposition.

## ORDEAL 80 ft. FROM GROUND — ESCAPE ABLAZE BELOW

TWO men were fighting a fire in a burning building at York yesterday from an escape 80ft. above the ground when they discovered that the escape had caught fire.

The men, Police-Constables Stockdale and Drummond, were unable to turn off the water and had to descend carrying the powerful hose with them.

Flames were shooting from the window on to the ladder, and the men had to pass through them. They just had reached the bottom when the escape collapsed.

Stockdale's face was burned but Drummond escaped without injury.

The outbreak occurred in a warehouse in the centre of business property in Parliament-street.

### POLICE IN RIVERSIDE CHASE

After a thrilling chase by London police among Thames barges and riverside buildings a man made good his escape yesterday.

He made his way along the side of a warehouse—sometimes in the water, sometimes on the sides of barges—and disappeared after entering the warehouse.

've# Daily Mirror

THE DAILY PICTURE NEWSPAPER WITH THE LARGEST NET SALE

Broadcasting - Page 19

GODFREY WINN'S PARADE . . . . P. 11
SERIAL . . . . . . . . 21
DOROTHY DIX . . . . 22
THE RUGGLES . . . . 28

No. 10,275    THURSDAY, NOVEMBER 5, 1936    One Penny

Amusements : Pages 16 and 18

## FLAT ON CORONATION ROUTE COSTS £472 FOR WEEK

BY A SPECIAL CORRESPONDENT

Staggering prices are already being asked for furnished flats in London for Coronation week next May.

FOR seven days' occupation of a furnished service flat in the St. James's district—two bed and dressing rooms, one reception room and bathroom—I was asked yesterday to pay £472 10s.

This works out at an annual rental of nearly £25,000.

But so keen is the desire to see the Coronation, so enormous is the demand for luxury flats on the route, that it is believed someone will cheerfully pay this price.

Wealthy people in the British Isles and from the Dominions, the Colonies and from the United States are determined to be in the very centre of the Coronation festivities at any price.

The demand from America for Coronation week accommodation is one factor that has sent rocketing the price of furnished flats on and off the route.

For another furnished flat on the route in the St. James district, but containing only one bedroom, 300 guineas was asked for the week. And there is little fear, I was told, that it will not be let.

More surprising still perhaps are the prices now being demanded for luxury flats off the Coronation route in the West End.

At one great block of flats with no view of the Coronation procession, one hundred guineas for the week is being asked for one bedroom, one reception and one bathroom. True, it is beautifully furnished.

Furnished flats in fashionable squares behind Buckingham Palace, with no view of the Coronation, of course, can be had at prices from about twenty to fifty guineas for Coronation week, but many of these are on top floors—even the sixth and seventh—and some of them do not include service.

As I reflected on the prices—particularly on the £472 10s. a week flat—I wondered how many people could be fed for seven days on that money.

### M.P.'s Question in House

The British Medical Association some time ago gave a minimum diet for a family of five—Husband, wife and three children aged six-eight, ten-twelve and twelve-fourteen they declared could live on 22s. 6½d.

Taking these figures, I found that no fewer than 420 families could be fed for a week.

Major the Hon. J. J. Stourton (Cons., Salford S.) has given notice to ask the Prime Minister to-day, "What steps are being taken to guarantee them a fair share of reserved seats; if he can state what proportion of the processional route is either owned or controlled by the Government, and whether a large-scale erection of seats is contemplated for allotment and sale by the Government?"

The King, it was officially announced at Buckingham Palace yesterday, will hold his Coronation review of ex-Servicemen on Sunday, June 27.

The Daily Mirror also learns that the King is showing his continued interest in the ex-Servicemen by deciding to attend the British Legion Festival of Remembrance at the Albert Hall on Armistice night.

## EUTHANASIA BILL IN THE LORDS

EUTHANASIA (easy death) is to be debated by the House of Lords.

Lord Ponsonby yesterday introduced a Bill to provide in certain conditions for the administration of euthanasia to persons desiring it, and who are suffering from illnesses of a fatal and incurable character involving severe pain.

The Bill was read a first time.

£20,000 LEGS

Her legs are worth £20,000—at any rate, that's the amount they're insured for. She's Ann Leslie, in the Palace of Beauty at the Imperial Fruit Exhibition in Liverpool.

Miss Leslie is appearing in the new Marlene Dietrich film, "Knight Without Armour."

## £100,000 YACHT FOR MYSTERY FILM STAR

BY A SPECIAL CORRESPONDENT

A FAMOUS film star, I understand, will shortly take over the £100,000 yacht Flying Cloud—a vessel which rivals for luxury, power and elegance the Nahlin, in which the King took his holiday.

Flying Cloud, built for the Duke of Westminster in 1927, had £50,000 spent on her in 1924 by her second owner, Mr. Nelson Warden, the American millionaire, who purchased her for a honeymoon cruise when he married Miss Zoe Busler, a twenty-seven-year-old brunette.

Mr. Warden died, and his executors have disposed of the vessel to a London man professionally interested in yachting.

"The identity of the cinema star who will probably take over this magnificent yacht must be kept secret until arrangements are finally settled," I was told last night.

Mr. Warden installed Diesel engines capable of developing 15,000 horse-power, a wireless room, electrically-operated steering gear, and electrically-operated lifeboats which could be manned and launched in less than sixty seconds.

## DYING BRIDE'S LAST KISS—THEN TOLD HUSBAND 'DINNER IS READY'

FROM OUR OWN CORRESPONDENT
NEWARK, Wednesday.

"KISS me, Tom," were the words a bride of two weeks spoke to her husband after he had picked up her badly burned body in his arms. Then, with her last breath, she added: "Your dinner is in the oven."

The young woman was Mrs. Edna Kate Mitchell, twenty-three-year-old wife of Thomas Mitchell, a joiner, of Balderton, Newark. At an inquest to-night he told his tragic story to the deputy coroner, Mr. W. H. Franks.

He said that at noon yesterday he returned to his home and found his wife lying in the garden terribly burned. "Thank God you are here, Tom," she said.

He carried her into the house and put her on some rugs. She asked him to kiss her.

"I did so," added the husband "but her lips were terribly burned."

Mrs. Risdie, a neighbour, told how she saw Mrs. Mitchell in flames in the garden and with the aid of others put them out with some sacks.

The deputy coroner said that there was no evidence how the woman got on fire, but it was probable that she caught her clothing on the fire while preparing her husband's dinner. Accidental death was the verdict.

The couple were married two weeks ago at Beeston, Birmingham. Only two days ago the proofs of the wedding group pictures were received by them.

## WOMAN ACROBAT CRASHES ON STAGE

WHILE Dolinoff and the Three Raya Sisters, a Russian troupe, were performing a novelty acrobatic act at the Granada, Tooting, last night, one of the sisters, Mrs. Raya Dolinoff, crashed headlong to the stage from her husband's shoulders.

At once the curtain was lowered, and another act was substituted.

Mrs. Dolinoff was carried unconscious to her dressing room, and later was taken to St. James's Hospital, Balham, and detained suffering from severe concussion.

Mr. Dolinoff, the principal in the act, who was greatly distressed, said: "We have been performing the act for about a dozen years, and this is the first slip ever. I cannot account for it at all."

## FAMOUS K.C. TO FIGHT WIDOW'S CASE

LEARNING yesterday that Sir Stafford Cripps, K.C., is to take up her case without fee, Mrs. Annie Kirk, the Hull widow against whom the Court of Appeal ruled that a separation allowance made by a husband should cease on his death, expressed her thanks for the Daily Mirror's help for her cause.

"It is almost too good to be true," Mrs. Kirk told the Daily Mirror last night.

"My thanks for this are due to two quarters. First to my solicitors, Messrs. Pearlman and Rosen, who have been kindness itself to me, and secondly to the Daily Mirror, which has placed the facts of my case so accurately and kindly before its readers all over the country.

"If the women of England are behind me I hope I shall win this case. If I do I shall have to thank the sympathetic publicity given by the 'Daily Mirror' for it."

When the case goes to the House of Lords the ultimate decision will affect thousands of wives who found their allowances cut off at the death of their husbands from whom they were separated.

THE DAILY MIRROR, Monday, November 9, 1936.

# BEGIN THE WEEK

# Daily Mirror

Broadcasting - Page 18

THE DAILY PICTURE NEWSPAPER WITH THE LARGEST NET SALE

No. 10,278  Registered at the G.P.O. as a newspaper.  MONDAY, NOVEMBER 9, 1936  One Penny

## WELL
### SEE PAGE THREE

# PRAYING CHILDREN KILLED BY BOMB: MADRID IN FLAMES

## THE QUEEN MARY RACING THROUGH GALE ON FIRST RESCUE MISSION

THE Queen Mary was racing through heavy seas last night on her first rescue mission.

She turned from her course in answer to an S O S sent out by the German motorship Isis, when about 250 miles off Land's End.

It was not known how far from the Isis the Queen Mary was.

Earlier the Queen Mary reported that she was encountering heavy seas in a gale estimated at more than sixty miles an hour. She was making for Cherbourg, and was due at Southampton this afternoon.

### Hatches Stove In

The Isis, which reported that her hatches were stove in and that there was water in her holds, left Hamburg for New York last Tuesday. She is a vessel of 4,454 tons and belongs to the Hamburg-Amerika Line. She was built in 1923 at Hamburg.

Thirty steamers, mostly British, were held up at Deal last night by a gale sweeping the Channel.

A few got under way, but returned to their anchorage, finding conditions too severe in the Straits of Dover.

## 250,000 IN ANTI-JEW RALLY

Bukarest resembled a German town yesterday when storm troops wore their banned uniforms, complete with swastikas, and 250,000 people marched to an anti-Jewish rally organised by the National Christian Party, states Exchange.

No disturbance took place owing to the strict discipline enforced by the storm troopers of the party, the demonstrators satisfying themselves only with yelling "Death to the Jews," and chalking swastikas and anti-Semitic slogans on tramcars and the doors of offices and houses.

Wrecked by Shellfire...

Ruins of the church at Getafe, "the Croydon of Madrid," following bombardment by anti-Red artillery. On right are two bells fallen from the shattered belfry.

## NEWLY-WEDS' DUTY IS TO HAVE BABIES, SAYS VICAR

"I THINK it is the plain and bounden duty of every young married couple at the present time to have as many children as the health of the mother and their economic circumstances will allow."

This declaration by the Rev. R. H. Babington, vicar of St. Thomas's Church, West End, near Southampton, has caused much discussion among his parishioners.

The vicar, who is a young married man with three children, adds:

### "Prefer a Car"

"We must face the fact that children are refused often for selfish motives. A baby car is preferred to a baby boy or baby girl. The nursery is empty so that the garage may be full.

"Those who deliberately refuse parenthood, or restrict their family to one, except it be for the very gravest reasons, are not only doing wrong, but are storing up trouble and sorrow for the future."

REBEL 'planes swooping where General Franco's Army could not pierce, spread fire and death in the heart of Madrid yesterday.

So high are the casualties that late last night it was announced that doctors cannot estimate the dead and hundreds injured; fire stations were too busy to count the fires.

Eight women and children were killed at prayer when a **bomb fell on a church in which they were sheltering in Calle de Segovia,** in a working class district.

One of the first buildings to fall was a convent which had been converted into a home for refugees from nearby towns, hundreds of whom have rushed to the capital to escape rebel artillery fire.

One large bomb struck this building. The roof fell in and several women and children were killed.

Aided by a rain of shells from outside the city, the bombs razed many houses to the ground. Many more were still blazing late last night. Casualty wards in several districts were filled with the wounded.

After a day of desperate fighting the insurgents are still held at bay on the outskirts on the banks of the Manzanares river.

Every device of modern warfare—six-inch artillery, aeroplanes, tanks, flame throwers and the latest type of Whippet tanks—was used.

In the last stubborn stand, the defenders have resorted to medieval tactics, pouring boiling oil and water on the attacking forces from the upper stories of the houses.

### Two Britons Captured

General Miaja, on whom the loyal command fell when the Government fled to Valencia on Saturday, found an unexpected ally in a terrific rainstorm which flooded the city last night and made a rebel advance impossible.

Yesterday morning two members of the Scottish ambulance unit which left Glasgow in September were captured by the insurgents in no-mans-land.

Their names are given as Frederick McMahon, aged twenty-five, of Ravenhill-street, Belfast, and Joseph Boyd, aged twenty-nine, of Ulsterville-gardens, Belfast. They are both unmarried.

A Paris message says that M. Blum, the Premier, speaking on non-intervention in Spain yesterday, indicated that if Great Britain was prepared to raise the embargo on Spain, France would be willing to follow suit.

(Messages from B.U.P., Reuter and Exchange.)

### REVOLT IN CAPITAL: "PALACE CAPTURED"

Civil Guards in Madrid had revolted against the Government and occupied the Presidential Palace, according to a broadcast from Valladolid, says Central News.

The Presidential Palace was formerly the Royal Palace used by King Alfonso. It is 500 yards from the Casa del Campo, the former royal park, which the rebels claim to have occupied.

## MR. LANSBURY CALLS POLICE: 20 EJECTED AT MEETING

FOLLOWING interruptions, police were called to a Labour demonstration addressed by Mr. George Lansbury and Mr. Herbert Morrison at Bow Baths last night, and a number of men were ejected.

Mr. Lansbury, the chairman, had been speaking about three minutes when interrupters tried to drown his voice with cries of "Hail Mosley" and other remarks.

Mr. Lansbury declared that no attempt to break up the meeting would be permitted, and that police would be called in to preserve order.

While Mr. Edward Cruse, a member of the L.C.C., was talking there were further interruptions. Police who had been on duty outside the hall, were called in and started ejecting several young men.

About twenty had to leave. Each one gave the Fascist salute as he went out and this was returned by others in the audience.

Minor interruptions continued, some during Mr. Morrison's address.

Police officers remained in the hall and mounted officers were stationed outside.

THE DAILY MIRROR, Thursday, November 12, 1936.

# 22 WILL BE KILLED ON ROADS TO-DAY!

# Daily Mirror
Broadcasting - Page 18

ARE YOU SAFE? See Page 4

THE DAILY PICTURE NEWSPAPER WITH THE LARGEST NET SALE

No. 10,281 Registered at the G.P.O. as a newspaper. THURSDAY, NOVEMBER 12, 1936 One Penny

*Special Armistice Number*

# AT HIS MOTHER'S SIDE THE KING LEADS THE NATION

*On the Arm of Her Son*

The King helping Queen Mary down the steps as they left the Home Office, from which she had watched him lead the nation's homage as King, for the first time, in yesterday's Armistice Day Ceremony at the Cenotaph. Beside them is Sir John Simon, the Home Secretary, and following are the Duke and Duchess of York, the Duke of Kent, the Duchess of Gloucester. Other Armistice Day pictures on pages 5, 9, 15, 17 and 21.

THE DAILY MIRROR, Saturday, November 14, 1936.

## WE HAVE WARNED YOU!—SEE PAGE 10

# Daily Mirror

SATURDAY
NOV. 14 No. 10283
ONE PENNY

THE DAILY PICTURE NEWSPAPER WITH THE LARGEST NET SALE

Registered at the G.P.O. as a newspaper.

| QUIET CORNER - Page 14 | JANE - - - - - - 7 | RUGGLES - - - - 24 | GORDON FIFE - - - 20 | PIP & SQUEAK - - - 18 |
| DOCTOR'S DIARY - - 17 | SERIAL STORY - - - 21 | AMUSEMENTS - - - 17 | BROADCASTING - - - 16 | BELINDA - - - - - 22 |

# BALDWIN BETRAYS HIS CONVICTIONS FOR VOTES

# VICTORY—AT ANY PRICE!

### The Confession of the "Sealed Lips"...

"If I had gone to the country and said Germany was rearming and we must rearm, does anyone suppose that the country would have rallied to that cry? No. I cannot imagine anything that would have made the loss of the election more certain."
—Mr. Baldwin.

BALDWIN'S confession has shocked Britain and staggered the world.

In the forty-four astonishing words reproduced above he has written not only his epitaph, but has also forced a question which the whole Cabinet is in duty bound to answer.

What is the country to believe? Is everything that Mr. Baldwin and his twenty-one muddled Ministers have said to be cast into doubt by this calamitous revelation? These questions must be answered:—

1. WHY DID BALDWIN STAGE AN ELECTION ON FALSE PRETENCES?
2. WHY, THREE YEARS AFTER THE TRUTH OF GERMAN RE-ARMAMENT WAS KNOWN, IS THIS COUNTRY STILL UNPREPARED?
3. WHY WAS NOT CHURCHILL, THE OBVIOUS CHOICE, ENTRUSTED WITH THE VITAL TASK OF OUR DEFENCES?

Quietly and with deadly serenity, this most ghastly admission in the history of British politics has been announced.

The alarming story—incredible as it seems—of how this country's interests were risked for mere political gain has been revealed by Mr. Baldwin.

Never in the long and honourable record of our Parliament has a Prime Minister taken upon himself the ugly task of selling the destiny of England in order that his address might still continue to be 10, Downing-street.

Remember that this country was placed in a dangerous position. Remember that forces that menaced our very existence were at work. The Prime Minister knew in 1933 that Germany was arming with terrifying speed and ruthless determination.

Baldwin and his Cabinet, with an unsavoury eagerness to keep their jobs at all cost, smothered the truth—the truth that affects every man, woman and child

(Continued on page 2)

**WHY?** The Man! The Moment! Why not Defence Minister?

The Face That Did NOT Launch a Thousand 'Planes

THE DAILY MIRROR, Thursday, November 19, 1936.

# YOUTH OPENS ITS HEART—PAGE 12

# Daily Mirror

THE DAILY PICTURE NEWSPAPER WITH THE LARGEST NET SALE

THURSDAY
NOV. 19 No. 10287
ONE PENNY

Registered at the G.P.O. as a newspaper.

| QUIET CORNER - Page 16 | CASSANDRA - - - 14 | RUGGLES - - - - 22 | GORDON FIFE - - 24 | PIP & SQUEAK - - 20 |
| DOCTOR'S DIARY - - 10 | SERIAL STORY - - - 22 | AMUSEMENTS - - - 20 | BROADCASTING - - 18 | BELINDA - - - - 26 |

# "SOMETHING MUST BE DONE" —THE KING

The King, at his own request, made a special tour during his visit to South Wales distressed areas yesterday, to visit this site at Dowlais. Once it was a flourishing steelworks. Nine thousand men were employed; the village grew round the works to house their families. Look at it now—like a section of No Man's Land.

With bowed head the King walked through the scene of desolation where He men's hopes . . . and women's despair. Men who had worked there stood silent on the heaps of debris . . . watching him. At the end the King spoke to them. Ministers of the Crown beside him heard the words, "These works," he said, "brought all these people here. Something ought to be done to find them employment." Another picture on page 17. Story on page 3.

## BALDWIN UNREPENTANT—'PEACE AT ALMOST ANY PRICE'

"I have nothing to withdraw and nothing to retract. . . . If I were to describe my broad line of policy I would say it was peace at almost any price, but at the same time to be ready that no man might attack us. That means sacrifice."

MR. Baldwin made this comment on his recent statement in the House of Commons in a vigorous defence of his re-armament policy at Glasgow last night.

The Premier had earlier denied the suggestion that the information on which the Government rely on foreign air strength was incorrect. "Our information must be taken as more reliable than the deductions of any private person," he declared.

"We have recently been criticised," he said "on the grounds that we are entirely to blame for having failed to secure international disarmament. We have been blamed for embarking on a re-armament programme at all, and we have been blamed for not having started two years before we did.

"The Government of the day had no mandate. It is, I agree, a matter of speculation whether, in 1934, it would have been possible to have got a mandate for national re-armament.

"Putting himself back in 1934 I do not think there is a man in the country who would
(Continued on back page)

## ROYAL DUKE SEES NEUSEL WIN

THE Duke of Gloucester, paying a surprise visit, was a ringside spectator when Walter Neusel won on points against Ben Foord, British heavy-weight champion, at Harringay Arena, London, last night.

Neusel said afterwards: "One of the hardest fights of my life. I knew I had to make up a lot in the closing rounds, and I went all out."

"Well, it is all in the game," was Foord's comment. "Lots of people will say I deserved to draw."

Neusel is definitely to fight Max Baer at Harringay in February.

This announcement was made after last night's fight by Mr. Sydney Hulls, the promoter.
Report of fight, page 30; pictures, back page.

### MYSTERY OF CAR IN POND

Police early this morning were still investigating the mystery of a car which fell into a 50ft.-deep pond at Iron Acton, Gloucestershire, yesterday.

A diver may be needed to raise the car to find if anyone has been drowned.

### SPAIN—FRENCH ALARM

Late last night the French Ministers of War, Air and the Navy held a special conference in the Navy Ministry to consider the effect of the Italo-German announcement recognising General Franco's Government in Spain, says British United Press.

Afterwards it was learned that France has taken all precautionary measures in the Mediterranean, and it is suggested in official circles that Britain may take similar action.

Dictators Recognise Franco—Page 2.

THE DAILY MIRROR, Thursday, November 26, 1936.

**TRUE STORY: WHO IS MY MOTHER?** Page 12

# Daily Mirror

THURSDAY
NOV. 26  No. 10293
ONE PENNY

THE DAILY PICTURE NEWSPAPER WITH THE LARGEST NET SALE

Registered at the G.P.O. as a newspaper.

| QUIET CORNER - Page 16 | CASSANDRA - 14 | STARS' MESSAGE - 26 | AMUSEMENTS - 10 | BROADCASTING - 18 |
| BELINDA - 26 | RUGGLES - 29 | SERIAL STORY - 22 | GORDON FIFE - 22 | PIP & SQUEAK - 20 |

# STALIN CHALLENGES FASCISM AS 'PLOTTERS' ARE SHOT

## Europe Last Night:—

MOSCOW: Stalin declared to the world that Russia's new Constitution was a challenge to "Fascist barbarism"—an answer to the Berlin-Tokio anti-Red pact.

**Stickling, the German in Russia's latest sabotage trial, had his death sentence commuted to ten years' imprisonment. Six of the accused Russians were shot.**

**MADRID:** It was reported that shots were fired at a Russian ship crossing the Straits of Gibraltar by a Spanish insurgent vessel.

**LONDON:** Foreign Secretary (Mr. Anthony Eden) saw Signor Grandi immediately on his return from the Fascist Grand Council meeting in Rome. Italy's offer of a gentlemen's agreement in the Mediterranean—dependent on Britain recognising the conquest of Abyssinia—was renewed.

**PARIS:** Alarm at the alliance of Germany and Japan. The pact is seen as an opportunity for Germany and Japan to turn against Britain and demand colonial expansion.

Stalin's speech, which lasted three hours, was delivered at the opening of the All-Union Congress of the Soviets called to adopt the new Constitution.

Stalin called the Constitution "an indictment of Fascism, inspiring all civilised people fighting for democracy against Fascist barbarism."

The sole amendment which he suggested to the draft text was the organisation of a new Commissariat for military industries, which, he urged, should be the greatest military machine in the world.

Then he severely criticised those who wanted to deprive priests and former White Guards of suffrage.

## Berlin-Tokio Pact Terms

The new Constitution provides that the Union Council shall be popularly and directly elected.

Universal suffrage is also to be introduced, says Reuter.

The terms of the Berlin-Tokio pact provide
(1) Mutual exchange of information about Red activities;
(2) Mutual consultation on measures of defence against them;
(3) Appointment of a committee to supervise co-operation, and
(4) Invitation to other Powers to join in

Three "incidents" occurred in the Spanish war yesterday to add to the difficulties of the international situation.

In addition to the shots at a Russian ship,
*(Continued on back page)*

### THE KILL

Head of a silver fox crowning her hair, head of another nestling her shoulder, and "brush" and body for her fur—the Marchioness of Queensberry's striking mode, cynosure of all eyes at a Ritz Hotel cocktail party yesterday.

## 1937 PROSPERITY YEAR—NO NEED TO WORRY: MR. E. BROWN

THERE is no need to worry for two years. Employment is going up and up." Mr. Ernest Brown, Minister for Labour, said this at Bournemouth last night. He believes 1937 will be prosperity year. More insured people were at work at the end of last month, Mr. Brown said, than at any period since the dole began.

Inside two generations we had been granted such a mass of productive capacity so quickly that nine-tenths of our real problems were due to the fact that our capacity had not been big enough or speeds enough to cope with that production

### "GALLERYITES" AT DANCE

Women—and a few men—in day clothes watched the Red Cross Ball from the gallery of Grosvenor House last night. This was the first time that the public has been admitted to a social function of this kind.

# ARMED FARMERS READY TO INVADE GREATEST RANCH

**FROM OUR OWN CORRESPONDENT**
New York, Wednesday.

ARMED invasion threatens the world's largest cattle ranch near San Perlita, Texas, following the mysterious disappearance of two men, believed to have been murdered.

Two suspects have been questioned by Texas Rangers concerning the fate of the missing men, Luther Blanton, fifty-seven, and his son John, who went near the ranch on Friday to shoot ducks.

Hundreds of infuriated small ranchers living outside the one million acre ranch, often called the "Walled Kingdom of Kennedy," have threatened to tear down the fences and attack its guards.

The ranch has defied the Texas State's efforts to run a road through it.

## Rangers Intervene

To-day men from the small ranches gathered for an attack, but were restrained by Rangers, who promised they would enter the ranch to search for the men.

Mounted guards and cowboys with arms are patrolling the ranches' frontiers.

Dwellers outside allege that at least twenty people have entered and disappeared. Among them are two Mexicans. Rangers have been asked by the Mexican Consul at Brownsville to investigate their disappearance.

## "HOODWINKED" BY MR. BALDWIN

DECLARING that the people had been hoodwinked and deceived the Duke of Montrose, who recently left the Conservative Party to become a Liberal, criticised Mr. Baldwin in Glasgow yesterday.

He said that the natural impulse would be for the people to look elsewhere for a Prime Minister.

"It is Mr. Baldwin's duty to tell the whole truth to the country," he added. "It is not his business to say whether the people will not follow, that is for the people to say. It is for the people to say, when they have heard the truth, whether they will follow or not. If the Prime Minister does not trust the people, the people will not trust the Prime Minister."

## 'MIRACLE' THAT BANISHED BITTERNESS

"Bitterness of fifty-two years has been swept away in fifty-two days."

That was how Lord Molteson described the Anglo-Egyptian Treaty of Friendship when he spoke in the House of Lords last night.

He had remarked to Sir Miles Lampson, High Commissioner in Egypt, that the treaty has "changed the hearts of the people."

And Sir Miles had replied: "I am sure you are right. A miracle has happened."

## "PERSONAL" NOTE ON A COFFIN

SENT by a sorrowing fiancee, a casket of transparent paper, containing orchids and an envelope marked "Personal," lay on the coffin at an air crash victim's funeral at Rhos, near Colwyn Bay, yesterday—the day he was to have married.

The funeral was that of Mr. Charles Frederick O'Connell, twenty-six-year-old pilot, of Northern and Scottish Airways. Together with a woman passenger, Mrs. E. A. Miller, of Ramsey, Isle of Man, he was burned to death when his 'plane crashed while taking off at Blackpool last Friday.

He was to have married a Miss Henderson, of London.

Only men were present at the funeral, which was attended by representatives of Blackpool Airport and Northern and Scottish Airways.

THE DAILY MIRROR, Saturday, November 28, 1936.

# MARITZA'S MESSAGE OF THE STARS: Page 11

# Daily Mirror

SATURDAY NOV.28 No. 10295 ONE PENNY

THE DAILY PICTURE NEWSPAPER WITH THE LARGEST NET SALE

Registered at the G.P.O. as a newspaper.

| QUIET CORNER - Page 14 | CASSANDRA - 11 | STARS' MESSAGE - 11 | AMUSEMENTS - 9 | BROADCASTING - 16 |
| BELINDA - 22 | RUGGLES - 25 | SERIAL STORY - 21 | GORDON FIFE - 19 | PIP & SQUEAK - 18 |

# DOCTOR 'NO RIGHT IN HOMES OF WOMEN'

—SAYS WIDOW

"I am here to tell these medical gentlemen that a man with uncontrollable passion has no right to enter the homes of women."

THIS statement was made by a widow to the General Medical Council in London yesterday during cross-examination when she was giving evidence against a doctor.

She was Mrs. Lucy Matilda Jones, living at London-road, Morden, Surrey.

The Council directed that the name of Dr. James Ebenezer Boon, registered as of Bath-road, Bedford Park, London, W., be erased from the register.

The charge on which he was summoned to appear before the Council was that he had misconducted himself with Mrs. Jones while he stood in professional relationship with her.

Dr. Boon admitted an association with Mrs. Jones between February, 1924, and June, 1931, but denied that at any time he stood in professional relationship with her.

Mr. Laurence Vine, for Mrs. Jones, by whom the charge was brought, mentioned that eventually Mrs. Jones sued Dr. Boon for breach of promise at Kingston Assizes.

Dr. Boon had strongly denied asking Mrs. Jones to be his wife, but he was ordered to pay £300 damages and costs.

Mrs. Jones, in evidence, said she met Dr. Boon while her husband was a panel patient. Eventually the doctor attended them.

After her husband's death Dr. Boon saw her frequently. No other doctor attended her

### 4 Days After Marriage

Mr. George Pollock (for Dr. Boon) questioned Mrs. Jones about things she said in evidence at Kingston Assizes.

Mr. Pollock: Is it true you said there that if you had had a revolver you would shoot him, and is that your feeling still?

Mrs. Jones: No, but that is what I thought I should have done to stop him coming into my room.

Mr. Pollock: And after saying these things may I take it that you dislike Dr. Boon intensely?

Mrs. Jones made the reply quoted above.

Mr. Pollock: And in pursuance of your public duty four days after his marriage you

(Continued on back page)

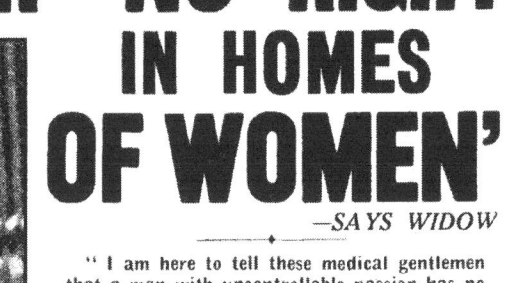

Mrs. Lucy M. Jones

Dr. J. E. Boon (with pipe) struck off the medical register.

## GLAMOUR OF TSARIST RUSSIA AT MIDNIGHT WEDDING RECEPTION

BY A SPECIAL CORRESPONDENT

THE glamour of Tsarist Russia was recaptured last night at a house in Hyde Park-square, London, W., when Colonel Jacob Maller, a former artillery officer in the Tsar's army, received 300 guests at a midnight wedding reception.

Earlier, Colonel Maller, a forty-seven-year-old widower, had married Mrs. Maud Margaret Barnett, an attractive blond of twenty-nine.

Among the guests were many of the former Russian nobility. They toasted the bride and bridegroom in vodka.

Two stalwart Cossacks danced the Russian dance of joy. Many of the guests wore Russian garb.

"If things in Russia had not changed," Colonel Maller told me, "my marriage would have been celebrated in a style similar to this."

### Sentenced to Death

Colonel Maller is the holder of the Cross of King George with double bar, its counterpart in British decorations being the Victoria Cross. He was sentenced to death during the revolution, and after perilous adventures escaped to England.

Colonel Maller's first wife died sixteen years ago. His son, an Oxford undergraduate, was killed in a motor accident at Oxford less than a year ago.

## MR. EDEN THINKS IT OUT

In chat with Baron de Cartier de Marchienne, Belgian Ambassador, in the Savoy Hotel yesterday. Then he told a luncheon gathering: "Belgium can count once more upon Britain's help if she is again the victim of an unprovoked aggression."— Story on page 2.

## "HOLIDAYS WITH PAY" BILL

THE Annual Holiday Bill, introduced by Mr. Rowson (Soc., Farnworth) and sponsored by eight colleagues, which provides for an annual holiday of not less than eight days, with pay for those who had been in the same employment for twelve months, was given a second reading in the House of Commons yesterday. Employers who fail to comply would be liable to a fine of £20.

The second reading was carried without a division.

## BRITAIN TO GET SHARE OF £10,000,000 ZAHAROFF WILL

THE British and French Governments will receive considerable sums in death duties from the fortune, estimated at £10,000,000, of Sir Basil Zaharoff, "mystery man of Europe," who died yesterday. (See page 4).

Two sisters, descendants of the Spanish Bourbons, will inherit the bulk of his fortune, says the British United Press.

They are the Countess d'Ostrorog and Mrs. Leopold Walford

### House of Silence

The chateau of Balincourt, Sir Basil's old home, became a house of silence when the news of his death was received.

"The stewards gave strict instructions that the gates were to be locked," said a member of the household.

"Instructions were given that the keys should be taken into the house and that no one should be admitted."

### U.S. REPORTS UNFOUNDED

## NO GUARDS FOR SOCIETY WOMAN

ON further inquiry yesterday the Daily Mirror learned that there is no truth in the reports appearing in American newspapers of threats against the life of Mrs. Simpson, a former U.S. society woman now living in London, or of special guards having been engaged for her protection.

We regret having given publicity in our later editions yesterday to these reports, for which there is no foundation.

THE DAILY MIRROR, Monday, November 30, 1936.

# I COULD PACK OUT YOUR CHURCH! Page 12

# Daily Mirror

MONDAY NOV. 30 No. 10296 ONE PENNY

THE DAILY PICTURE NEWSPAPER WITH THE LARGEST NET SALE

Registered at the G.P.O. as a newspaper.

| QUIET CORNER - Page 16 | CASSANDRA - - - 14 | STARS' MESSAGE - - 21 | AMUSEMENTS - - - 10 | BROADCASTING - - 18 |
| BELINDA - - - 26 | RUGGLES - - - 25 | SERIAL STORY - - 22 | GORDON FIFE - - 22 | PIP & SQUEAK - - 20 |

## EX-MILLIONAIRESS FIGHTS TO CLEAR DEAD MAN'S NAME

*"DAILY MIRROR" SPECIAL NEWS*

Once a millionairess and the owner of the most magnificent mansion in Surrey, a white-haired woman of seventy-two is planning a last fight to clear the name of her dead friend whose invention lost her £300,000.

MISS Dora Schintz, daughter of the Swiss "Nitrate King," once had nearly £500,000 of her own money as well as a life interest in £390,000.

Now she is living alone in an attic flat at Eastbourne on a small allowance of a relative, and on January 12 she will face her first public examination in bankruptcy at Kingston-on-Thames after an adjournment that has lasted five years.

It will be the first chance Miss Schintz has had of explaining how she came to lose her fortune in financing a company for Lionel Rapson, her former chauffeur.

Rapson got fame as the inventor of the low-pressure tyre, and once, with his sixteen-year-old son and two other drivers, drove a car 50,000 miles in forty-two days non-stop.

The company failed, and it was alleged in a Chancery action that Rapson had obtained "undue influence" over Miss Schintz—that he had lived in luxury on her money and been the means of ruining her.

"I have waited five years to prove how completely false those suggestions were," Miss Schintz told the "Daily Mirror."

"When those statements were made I was too ill to go to court to deny them. Rapson was there, but they never allowed him to speak

### Five Years Wait

"He died less than two years later without having had a chance to clear his name.

"There never would have been a chance for me to do it unless I had insisted on a public examination. I have had to wait five years to get that.

"Old as I am, I am determined to go on—to fight not only for Rapson, but for his widow and his only son."

Mrs. Rapson and her twenty-five-year-old son, Frederick, are also living at Eastbourne. Lionel Rapson did not leave a penny when he died—"That shows how honest he was," asserted Miss Schintz—and they have been helped by her ever since out of her small allowance.

Rapson's son acts as Miss Schintz's secre-

*(Continued on back page)*

### CAN IT BE? YES IT IS!

We are used to the vagaries of his hats, but in this case the individuality has spread to his coat.

Mr. Winston Churchill at the Duke of Westminster's shoot.

## 40-st. GIRL LIFTED FROM SHIP BY CRANE, THEN BARRED FROM LANDING

*"DAILY MIRROR" SPECIAL NEWS*

AFTER being lifted from a cross-Channel steamer by a crane, and wheeled along the quayside in a specially built truck at Dover yesterday, a German girl, weighing more than 40 stone, was refused permission to land, and had to return to Ostend by the next boat.

It is understood the papers of the girl, Miss Hilda Wilson, were not in order.

She had come from Ostend to England to appear in the freak sideshow of a London circus, and reached Dover at 3 p.m. By five o'clock, tired and miserable, she was on her way back to Belgium.

## JIM MOLLISON 'GOING STRONG' ON CAPE FLIGHT

JIM Mollison, with his co-pilot, M. Edouard Corniglion-Molinier, was "going strong" last night on his flight to the Cape.

Taking off from Croydon at 9.30 a.m. yesterday, he landed at Marseilles, and after refuelling continued his attempt to break the record.

Nine hours after leaving England he was sighted over Tunis, heading for Tripoli, says Reuter.

Some time after leaving Marseilles he was reported to have turned back for London and to have abandoned the attempt.

### Tank Overfilled

Apparently, however, his petrol tank had been overfilled. This was rectified.

Speaking to the *Daily Mirror* by 'phone from Marseilles, Mr. Mollison said his machine had behaved extremely well.

"We flew between ten and twelve thousand feet all the way. Weather conditions have been pretty foul, and reports here about the Mediterranean are not too good.

"But that doesn't matter," he said, "because we shall go above the clouds

"Sorry—I have to go. Listen, you can hear my engine. Sounds fine, doesn't she?"

## FOUR WOUNDED BY SHOT IN STREET

FOUR passers-by were taken to hospital—a man and two youths, with wounds in the legs, and a woman suffering from slight eye injuries—after a shot was fired in a Nottingham street.

A man will appear in court to-day in connection with the affair.

The injured are:—

Thomas Bridges, forty-six, railway carriage cleaner, of Tenfoot-street, Nottingham; George Bull, seventeen, of Ipswich-circus, Sneinton, Nottingham; Eric Bird, seventeen, of Stanley-terrace, Sneinton; and Sarah Ann Bridges, wife of Thomas Bridges.

Mrs. Bridges said she and her husband were walking along Sneinton-road when she heard a loud noise.

Her husband exclaimed: "I have got it," and staggered against her.

Though not hit, she was blinded by smoke for a moment. The two youths had been talking nearby.

Once Miss Dora Schintz owned this fleet of cars. Now she says: "I am managing to buy a car on hire purchase so that Fred can drive me round the country. But I suppose when the car is paid for my creditors will want that, too."

## WEDDING RING GIFTS FOR SPAIN

Wedding rings, engagement rings and bracelets were handed up to the platform at a meeting in the Albert Hall last night when a meeting was held in aid of the Spanish Medical Aid Committee. A collection realised £2,149.

The Marquesa de Belmonte and her daughter, members of a prominent Spanish Royalist family, arrived at Plymouth last night in the liner *Lafayette* from New York on a quest to discover if any of their relatives in Spain are still alive.

Italy warns the League on Spain: Page 3.

THE DAILY MIRROR, TUESDAY, December 1, 1936.

# GODFREY WINN'S QUESTION—TO YOU! Page 11

# Daily Mirror

TUESDAY
Dec. 1   No. 10297
ONE PENNY

THE DAILY PICTURE NEWSPAPER WITH THE LARGEST NET SALE

Registered at the G.P.O. as a newspaper.

| QUIET CORNER - Page 27 | CASSANDRA - - - 14 | STARS' MESSAGE - - 25 | AMUSEMENTS - - - 20 | BROADCASTING - - - 18 |
| BELINDA - - - - 26 | RUGGLES - - - - 29 | SERIAL STORY - - 22 | GORDON FIFE - - 22 | PIP & SQUEAK - - - 20 |

# FIRE WRECKS CRYSTAL PALACE: ROYAL DUKE WATCHES

WHEN THE END DREW NEAR: The central portion of the palace, its acres of glass a molten mass in the inferno below, its steelwork twisting under the intense heat.

**WITH FLAMES RISING TO A HEIGHT OF 500 FEET, STREAMS OF MOLTEN GLASS FORCING BACK FIREMEN AND SPARKS BEING HURLED THREE MILES, THE CRYSTAL PALACE, LONDON'S WORLD-FAMOUS £2,000,000 ALL-GLASS EXHIBITION BUILDING, WAS DESTROYED LAST NIGHT. ONLY ITS TWO 282-FOOT TOWERS WERE LEFT STANDING.**

MILLIONS watched the fire. It could be seen in Brighton, fifty miles away. An air liner pilot in mid-Channel, eighty miles away, sighted the glare. At midnight two-thirds of the building was in ruins. The fire was then under control.

Thousands raced from scores of surrounding towns and villages to see the spectacle. For three miles around roads were completely blocked by cars. Many fire engines found it impossible to get within half a mile.

In their news bulletin the B.B.C. advised crowds not to go too near because of the difficulties that faced the police.

Ninety engines were on the spot with 400 firemen. The entire London Fire Brigade was mobilised and every machine stood by.

The tremendous heat could be felt half a mile away. Firemen were unable to work near the flames for more than a minute. Several were injured and taken away.

The noise as the roof crashed could be heard five miles away.

Police cars raced through the thronged streets calling through their loudspeakers for

*(Continued on back page)*

The Duke of Kent chatting with Mr. Morris, chief of London Fire Brigade.

## DUKE OF KENT WEARS A FIREMAN'S HELMET

THE Duke of Kent, in evening dress, arrived by car shortly before midnight and chatted to fire fighters who took him up to the smouldering ruins.

At 2 a.m. he was still there—wearing gum boots and fireman's helmet.

A cascade of water from a fire hose fell over the Duke. He retreated, still smiling, to have a cup of coffee at a brigade motor canteen which had just arrived.

He stood at the counter surrounded by firemen.

After his coffee, which the Duke said was "very good," he went with the chief of the London Fire Brigade in a staff car for a tour round the glowing wreckage to see for himself the extent of the havoc.

Then he visited the fire brigade intelligence headquarters, which had been established in a waiting room at Crystal Palace Station.

There he saw firemen and gas engineers busy with maps, working out the positions of the various mains, and directing parties of workmen who had been roused from bed to go and cut off the gas.

THE DAILY MIRROR, Thursday, December 3, 1936.

**PAGE FOR EVERY HOUSEWIFE** — Page 27

# Daily Mirror

THE DAILY PICTURE NEWSPAPER WITH THE LARGEST NET SALE

THURSDAY
Dec. 3 No. 10299
ONE PENNY

Registered at the G.P.O. as a newspaper.

| QUIET CORNER - Page 16 | CASSANDRA - - - 14 | STARS' MESSAGE - - 21 | AMUSEMENTS - - - 20 | BROADCASTING - - 18 |
| BELINDA - - - - 26 | RUGGLES - - - - 29 | SERIAL AND FIFE - - 22 | DOROTHY DIX - - - 26 | PIP & SQUEAK - - 20 |

# THE KING WANTS TO MARRY MRS. SIMPSON: CABINET ADVISES 'NO'

**THE KING, THE "DAILY MIRROR" UNDERSTANDS, HAS TOLD THE CABINET OF HIS WISH TO MARRY MRS. SIMPSON, AMERICAN-BORN SOCIETY WOMAN NOW LIVING IN LONDON. THE CABINET HAS ADVISED AGAINST IT.**

LAST NIGHT THE KING AND THE PRIME MINISTER DISCUSSED THE MATTER AT BUCKINGHAM PALACE FOR ONE HOUR AND FORTY MINUTES. EARLIER IN THE DAY THE CABINET HAD SAT FOR TWO AND A HALF HOURS SEEKING A WAY OUT OF THEIR DIFFICULTY.

MR. BALDWIN LEFT THE HOUSE OF COMMONS HURRIEDLY IN THE MIDDLE OF A DEBATE TO DRIVE BY CAR TO THE PALACE.

On arrival there at ten minutes to six he was immediately received by the King. It was not until half-past seven, that, looking intensely serious and smoking his pipe, he drove away again.

This was the second audience Mr. Baldwin has had with the King within a week.

Twenty minutes after Mr. Baldwin had gone King Edward left Buckingham Palace by car alone.

Yesterday was a day of grave discussions in Whitehall and uncertainty in the City.

Prices of British Government securities fell sharply on the Stock Exchange. This, it was suggested, was caused by Cabinet difficulties (see columns 3 and 4).

## NOT EUROPE

Yesterday's "Manchester Guardian," in a leading article, stated:—

"There is reason to think that the hastily summoned Cabinet meeting of Friday was concerned not with the troubled state of Europe, but with a domestic problem that involves an important constitutional issue, since it bears on the relation of the King to his Ministers and his readiness to be guided, in all matters which may affect the welfare of the British Commonwealth, by the advice which the Prime Minister sees fit to offer.

"Of the validity of that principle, which serves as much for the assistance and support of the Monarchy as it does for the safety and ordered progress of the realm, there is no doubt; nor can one think that our present King, mindful as he is of the nationally beloved example of his father, King George V, would seek in any way to disturb the relations between Monarch and Ministers as they existed during the twenty-five years of the last reign."

The rate against the Coronation being postponed from the appointed day was increased by Lloyd's underwriters during the afternoon from twenty guineas per cent. to twenty-five guineas per cent. There was, however, very little business done at this rate owing to underwriters being absolutely full.

On leaving the Palace last night Mr. Baldwin did not go home, but drove back to the House of Commons, where he had dinner.

This is very unusual for Mr. Baldwin. Unless prevented by unforeseen and extremely urgent circumstances he always dines at home.

Just after nine o'clock he was driven to 10, Downing-street. When the car drove up at the door of No. 10 elaborate precautions were taken to ensure that the photographers did not get a clear view of Mr. Baldwin.

Mr. Baldwin's detective told the photographers to stand well back. Then one of Mr. Baldwin's private secretaries stepped out

(Continued on back page)

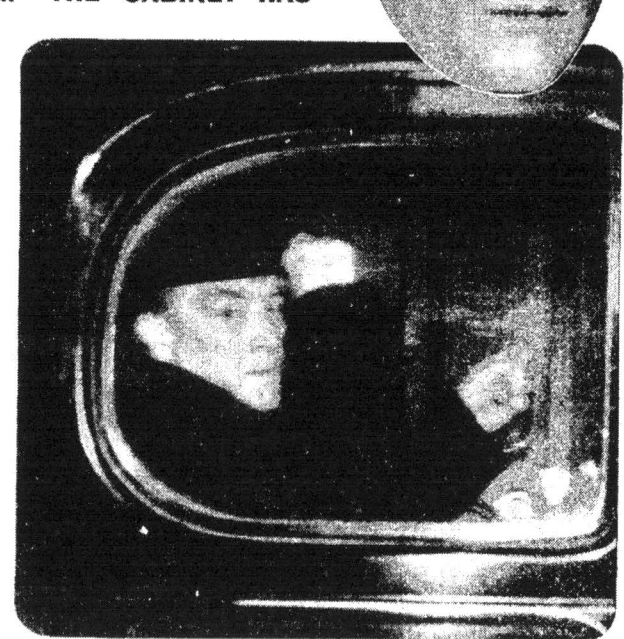

The Prime Minister arriving at Buckingham Palace to see the King.
—Daily Mirror exclusive photograph.

## SHARP DROP IN GOVERNMENT STOCKS

THE City has reflected the rumours in Whitehall of a serious political crisis.

A sharp slide was seen in prices for British Government securities on the Stock Exchange yesterday, and after the Exchange closed, War Loan stock fell another three-eighths to 105, making a fall on the day of 1 3-16 per cent.

Selling pressure developed suddenly during the afternoon without any tangible reason. There was certainly selling from the Continent. There were reports of impending important changes in the British Cabinet. Rumours also circulated of an adverse turn in the political situation affecting Spain.

There is no doubt that the fall was out of all proportion to the amount of selling experienced. Consols 2½ per cent. dropped 2¼ from the opening level. A similar drop was seen in Local Loans 3 per cent. stock, while War Loan 3½ per cent. stock fell 2⅜s. 5d.

The fall was the most severe for many months past. Reaction in this section spread to other sections of markets.

# Daily Mirror

THE DAILY PICTURE NEWSPAPER WITH THE LARGEST NET SALE

SATURDAY Dec. 5 No. 10301 ONE PENNY

## GOD SAVE THE KING!

# TELL US THE FACTS, MR. BALDWIN!

> "Suggestions have appeared that if the King decided to marry, his wife need not become Queen. These ideas are without any constitutional foundation.
>
> "There is no such thing as what is called a morganatic marriage known to our law. The Royal Marriages Act of 1772 has no application to the Sovereign himself....
>
> "This Act, therefore, has nothing to do with the present case. The King himself requires no consent from any other authority to make his marriage legal, but, as I have said, the lady whom he marries by the fact of her marriage to the King necessarily becomes Queen.
>
> "She herself therefore enjoys all the status, rights, and privileges which, both by positive law and by custom, attach to that position.... and her children would be in the direct line of succession to the throne.
>
> "The only possible way in which this result could be avoided would be by legislation dealing with a particular case. His Majesty's Government are not prepared to introduce such legislation.
>
> "Such a change could not be effective without the consent of all the Dominions. I am satisfied from inquiries I have made that this assent would not be forthcoming."
>
> —MR. BALDWIN IN PARLIAMENT YESTERDAY.

# THE NATION INSISTS ON KNOWING THE KING'S FULL DEMANDS AND CONDITIONS

## The Country Will Give You the Verdict

THE DAILY MIRROR, Wednesday, December 9, 1936.

# Daily Mirror

No. 10304    Registered at the G.P.O. as a newspaper.    ONE PENNY

*The four men who were in a vital conference with the King last night*

# THE KING AND BROTHERS HAVE FIVE - HOUR CONFERENCE WITH MR. BALDWIN AT FORT

**VITAL CONFERENCES BETWEEN THE KING, THE DUKE OF YORK, THE DUKE OF KENT, THE PREMIER, AND MR. WALTER MONCKTON, K.C., ATTORNEY-GENERAL TO THE DUCHY OF CORNWALL, LASTED FOR MORE THAN FIVE HOURS AT FORT BELVEDERE LAST NIGHT.**

### M.P.s ARE GROWING MORE CHEERFUL

After M.P.s had for days grown resigned to the view that the abdication of the King was imminent, there was a sudden change in outlook last night. Many were convinced that a happier issue was in sight.

MR. BALDWIN ARRIVED AT FIVE O'CLOCK, DINED WITH THE KING, HIS BROTHERS, MR. MONCKTON AND SIR ERIC MIEVILLE, PRIVATE SECRETARY TO THE DUKE OF YORK, AND DID NOT LEAVE UNTIL 10.5.

The Duke of Kent had been at the Fort throughout the day and the Duke of York arrived at 6.30; both left at 11 o'clock. Just before 1 a.m. the Duke of Kent returned to the Fort.

## Important Statement Expected To-day

An important statement is expected to be made in the House of Commons this afternoon by Mr. Baldwin.

**The Government were in close touch by telephone with the Dominions Premiers early to-day, the "Daily Mirror" understands. It is significant that a special session of the Australian Parliament is being held to-day.**

While the day's discussions were drawing to a close a specially chartered 'plane was landing in Marseilles after flying from London. The occupants of the 'plane, including a doctor and Mrs. Simpson's solicitor, later arrived at Cannes by car.

**Mr. Baldwin arrived at Downing-street from Fort Belvedere at eleven o'clock, accompanied by Captain Dugdale, Parliamentary Private Secretary.**

There had been little activity in Downing-street during the day until shortly after four o'clock, when Mr. Baldwin left No. 10 with Sir Eric Mieville and Mr. Walter Monckton. K.C., for Fort Belvedere.

**(Continued on back page)**

## LORD BROWNLOW'S 1 a.m. TALK

**BY A SPECIAL CORRESPONDENT**

The three men who left Croydon by an air liner on Government charter landed at Marseilles last night and motored ninety miles to Cannes, arriving at eleven o'clock.

THE MEN ARE:—

Dr. William Douglas Kirkwood, well known consultant, of Sloane-street, London, S.W.
Mr. Theodore Goddard, a partner in Theodore Goddard, and Co., solicitors, of Serjeants' Inn, London, who have acted for Mrs. Simpson.
Mr. Sidney Barron, solicitor's clerk.

All three were looking tired and exhausted when they arrived at the Mirimar Hotel, Cannes.

As their car drove up they jumped out and ran through the swing doors. Before anyone could speak to them they had entered a lift and gone to their rooms. They at once went to bed.

### MRS. SIMPSON
*A striking photograph of Mrs. Simpson, for which she posed yesterday, is on page 15.*

None of the hotel staff knew the men's identity.

All that the party carried as luggage were small attache cases.

At a quarter to one this morning a number of journalists went to the villa where Mrs. Simpson is staying and sent in a letter to Lord Brownlow asking him if he had any comment to make on Dr. Kirkwood's arrival in Cannes.

Speaking in the garden, Lord Brownlow said:

"I can tell you that Dr. Kirkwood has only come to Cannes as the personal doctor of Mr. Goddard. He will not come to the villa to-day. As a matter of fact, he is going to Monte Carlo.

### "A Personal Friend"

"Mr. Goddard assures me that Dr. Kirkwood is a personal friend of his, and is a practitioner in Sloane-street. He accompanied him as Mr. Goddard is in a poor state of health and is not accustomed to flying. Dr. Kirkwood's presence here has nothing to do with Mrs. Simpson."

Earlier Lord Brownlow had said: "Mr. Goddard is coming at Mrs. Simpson's suggestion to discuss details in regard to closing her London house. She has no intention of returning to London for a considerable time."

It is also believed that Mrs. Simpson will sign some important documents.

The air liner had taken off from Croydon in spite of reports of bad weather over France.

THE DAILY MIRROR, Thursday, December 10, 1936.

# Daily Mirror

No. 10305    Registered at the G.P.O as a newspaper    ONE PENNY

# THE KING DECIDES: ABDICATION PLANS

## DRAMATIC VISIT TO QUEEN MARY

**THE KING HAS DECIDED.**

**His abdication—unless he makes an eleventh hour change in his decision—is regarded by the Cabinet as imminent.**

**His Majesty's decision will be announced by Mr. Baldwin in the House of Commons this afternoon. Lord Halifax will make a similar statement in the House of Lords.**

**Last night the Labour and Liberal Opposition leaders were informed by the Government of the latest moves in the crisis, and advised that there is little hope of a happy solution.**

YESTERDAY AFTERNOON THE KING SLIPPED SECRETLY OUT OF FORT BELVEDERE—THE FIRST TIME HE HAD LEFT THE FORT FOR SIX DAYS—AND HE DROVE TO WINDSOR GREAT PARK, WHERE, IN ROYAL LODGE, HE HAD TEA WITH HIS MOTHER, QUEEN MARY.

This meeting was of the most moving character and had been arranged with the utmost privacy.

Elaborate precautions were taken to enable King Edward to leave the Fort unobserved.

### Over Rough-Track Roads

To avoid being seen, the King left by one of the rough track roads seldom used by cars and was able to make the two-mile journey without being seen.

His car had only to traverse 200 yards of public roadway before it crossed from his estate into the long private drive through Windsor Great Park to the Lodge.

No one working in the grounds was allowed to see the King leave the house. Workmen were told to remain hidden in a garage.

After spending half an hour with his mother the King returned as secretly to the Fort.

Queen Mary was accompanied by the Princess Royal and the Earl of Athlone. Later she dined with the Duke and Duchess of Kent.

In Mr. Baldwin's private room at the House of Commons last night a special Cabinet meeting was called and Ministers were frankly told of all developments.

The King had a further consultation with his brothers, the Duke of York and the Duke of Kent at Fort Belvedere during the day. The Duke of York did not return to London till 9 p.m. He looked pale and worn. In the event of abdication he will automatically succeed to the Crown.

Throughout the day dispatch riders with important messages from London had arrived at the Fort. The King's car drove out at 8.30 and shortly before eleven o'clock the royal shooting brake which has been used for the transportation of luggage left Fort Belvedere, and also a dispatch rider.

The Duke of Kent drove to Marlborough House shortly after 8 o'clock and at 10.15 a large car entered the gates with the Duke of York as its only passenger.

**M.P.s warned to be at the House to-day; Mrs. Simpson's drive.—Page 3.**

KING EDWARD VIII

### DIARY OF THE DAY'S EVENTS

Noon.—Mr. Walter Monckton, K.C., Attorney-General to the Duchy of Cornwall, and Sir E. Peacock back at No. 10.
1.15 p.m.—Cabinet meeting ended.
3.33 p.m.—Mr Baldwin made his statement in Commons
4.5 p.m.—Duke of York arrived at Fort Belvedere.
5.0 p.m.—Queen Mary meets the King at Royal Lodge, Windsor Great Park.
9.0 p.m.—Duke of York arrives back at 145, Piccadilly. The Prime Minister, Sir John Simon and Mr. Monckton at No. 10. Succession of messengers with brief cases.
9.15 p.m.—Mr. Malcolm MacDonald at No. 10.
10.0 p.m.—Sir John Simon and Mr. Monckton again at No. 10.
10.30 p.m.—Mr. Ramsay MacDonald at Colonial Office
11.20 p.m.—Mr. Monckton left No. 10 in the King's car.

THE DAILY MIRROR, Friday, December 11, 1936.

# Daily Mirror

No. 10306   Registered at the G.P.O. as a newspaper.   ONE PENNY

# KING EDWARD WILL BROADCAST TO-NIGHT

Edward VIII, immediately he signs the abdication papers to-night, will broadcast to the Empire "as a private person owing allegiance to the new King." The broadcast has tentatively been fixed for 10 p.m.

The British Empire yesterday received with utmost calm the announcement of the abdication. It welcomed with affection the accession of the Duke and Duchess of York.

The new King dined with his brother last night at Fort Belvedere.

The King's last message: Page 2; A toast "Across the Water": Page 3; Mr. Baldwin's revelations: Pages 4 and 5; Love ended a reign: Page 6; What the world thinks: Page 7.

### FLAG DROPS AS THE KING SIGNS

King Edward signed the Instrument of Abdication at 10 a.m. yesterday in his study on the ground floor of Fort Belvedere.

He signed in the presence of the Duke of York, the Duke of Kent and the Duke of Gloucester.

As the documents were signed, the flag of the Duchy of Cornwall, which has been flying over Fort Belvedere since his Majesty's arrival, was lowered. Later, it was run up again.

The Act of Abdication will be taken to the King to sign at Fort Belvedere to-night.

# Daily Mirror

No. 10307 — Registered at the G.P.O. as a newspaper. — ONE PENNY.

LATE·LON·ED

# EX-KING SAILED THIS MORNING IN YACHT

## The Son—and His Mother

### I CAN'T GO ON WITHOUT THE WOMAN I LOVE

### DISTRESS THAT IS FILLING MY HEART

## Escort of Two Destroyers

EX-KING Edward VIII broadcast to the world last night from the Augusta Tower of Windsor Castle. He was announced as his Royal Highness Prince Edward. He said:—

At long last I am able to say a few words of my own. I have never wanted to withhold anything. But until now it has not been constitutionally possible for me to speak.

A few hours ago I discharged my last duty as King and Emperor and now that I have been succeeded by my brother the Duke of York my first words must be to declare my allegiance to him. This I do with all my heart.

You all know the reasons which have impelled me to renounce the Throne, but I want you to understand that in making up my mind I did not forget the country, or the Empire which as Prince of Wales and later as King, I have for twenty-five years tried to serve; BUT YOU MUST BELIEVE ME WHEN I TELL YOU THAT I HAVE FOUND IT IMPOSSIBLE TO CARRY THE HEAVY BURDEN OF RESPONSIBILITY AND TO DISCHARGE MY DUTIES AS KING AS I WOULD WISH TO DO WITHOUT THE HELP AND SUPPORT OF THE WOMAN I LOVE. And I want you to know that the decision I have made has been mine, and mine alone.

This was a thing I had to judge entirely for myself. The other person most nearly concerned has tried up to the last to persuade me to take a different course. I have made this, the most serious decision of my life, only upon the single thought of what would in the end be best for all.

### One Matchless Blessing

This decision has been made less difficult to me by the sure knowledge that my brother, with his long training in the public affairs of this country and with the fine qualities he possesses, will be able to take my place forthwith without interruption or injury to the life and progress of the Empire.

And he has one matchless blessing, enjoyed by so many of you and not bestowed on me, a happy home with his wife and children.

During these hard days I have been comforted by her Majesty my mother and by my family. Ministers of the Crown, and in particular Mr. Baldwin, the Prime Minister, have always treated me with full consideration.

There has never been any constitutional difference between me and them and between me and Parliament. Bred in the constitutional traditions of my father, I should never have allowed any such issue to arise.

Ever since I was Prince of Wales and later on when I occupied the Throne, I have been treated with the greatest kindness by all classes of the people wherever I have lived or journeyed throughout the Empire.

For that I am very grateful. I now quit altogether public affairs and I lay down my burden. It may be some time before I return to my native land, but I shall always follow the fortunes of the British race and Empire with profound interest, and if at any time in the future I can be found of service to his Majesty in a private station, I shall not fail.

And now we all have a new King. I wish him and you, his people, happiness and prosperity with all my heart. God bless you all.

**GOD SAVE THE KING.**

A TOUCHING message to the nation and Empire, in which she refers to the "distress which fills a mother's heart," was issued by Queen Mary from Marlborough House last night. It read:—

To the people of this nation and Empire,—
I have been so deeply touched by the sympathy which has surrounded me at this time of anxiety that I must send a message of gratitude from the depth of my heart.

The sympathy and affection which sustained me in my great sorrow less than a year ago have not failed me now, and are once again my strength and stay.

I NEED NOT SPEAK TO YOU OF THE DISTRESS WHICH FILLS A MOTHER'S HEART WHEN I THINK THAT MY DEAR SON HAS DEEMED IT TO BE HIS DUTY TO LAY DOWN HIS CHARGE, AND THAT THE REIGN WHICH HAD BEGUN WITH SO MUCH HOPE AND PROMISE HAS SO SUDDENLY ENDED.

I know that you will realise what it has cost him to come to this decision; and that, remembering the years in which he tried so eagerly to serve and help his country and Empire, you will ever keep a grateful remembrance of him in your hearts.

I COMMEND TO YOU HIS BROTHER, SUMMONED SO UNEXPECTEDLY AND IN CIRCUMSTANCES SO PAINFUL TO TAKE HIS PLACE. I ASK YOU TO GIVE TO HIM THE SAME FULL MEASURE OF GENEROUS LOYALTY WHICH YOU GAVE TO MY BELOVED HUSBAND, AND WHICH YOU WOULD WILLINGLY HAVE CONTINUED TO GIVE TO HIS BROTHER.

With him I commend my dear daughter-in-law, who will be his Queen. May she receive the same unfailing affection and trust which you have given to me for six and twenty years. I know that you have already taken her fine qualities to your hearts.

IT IS MY EARNEST PRAYER THAT, IN SPITE OF, NAY THROUGH, THIS PRESENT TROUBLE THE LOYALTY AND UNITY OF OUR LAND AND EMPIRE MAY BY GOD'S BLESSING BE MAINTAINED AND STRENGTHENED. MAY HE BLESS AND KEEP AND GUIDE YOU ALWAYS. — MARY R.

---

Mr. Edward Windsor, ex-King Edward VIII, sailed from Portsmouth at 1.45 a.m. to-day on board the Admiralty yacht Enchantress with an escort of two destroyers, Wolfhound and Fury.

THIS followed a dramatic car dash to the coast after his radio farewell to the Empire.

The ex-King's car, with the blinds drawn, flashed in one of the gates of the dockyard.

He was accompanied by his equerry, Colonel the Hon. Piers Legh, his personal detective, and one member of his domestic staff.

He must have done the journey from Windsor in little more than an hour and a half. He at once boarded the Enchantress which had slipped alongside one of the jetties and was waiting with full steam up.

In the clear light of the starry night, with the hundreds of lights from vessels in the harbour, the Enchantress passed from the shores of England.

The last that could be seen of her was as she moved away, like a dream ship, showing her deck lights and with the port light gleaming blood red as a beacon in the darkness.

There had been tears in the voice of the ex-King as he spoke of "the woman I love" in his broadcast from Windsor Castle at 10 p.m.

*(Continued on back page)*

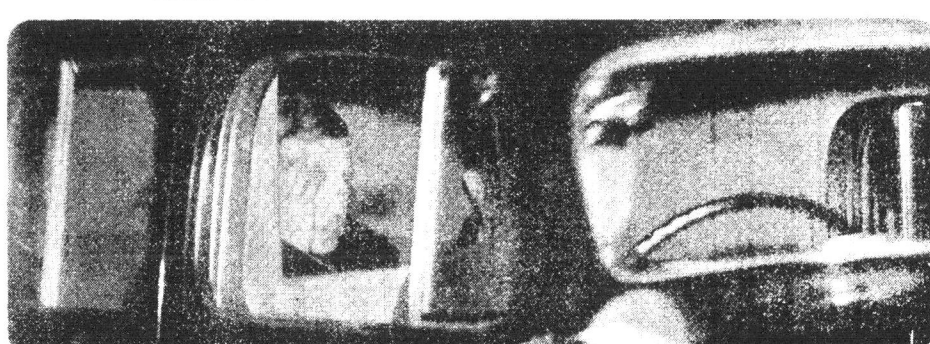

The former King Edward leaving Windsor Castle last night after his farewell broadcast, hand raised in salute to people who waved him good-bye.

THE DAILY MIRROR, Thursday, December 17, 1936.

# Daily Mirror

No. 10311    Registered at the G.P.O. as a newspaper.    ONE PENNY

# EIGHT MORE DIE IN THIRD DAY OF BRITAIN'S GREAT STORM

Eight more people died yesterday in the third day of the great gale that has swept Britain and is now—according to the weather forecast—almost at an end.

WIND gusts reported last night, however, reached 79 m.p.h. at Pembroke, 76 m.p.h. at Holyhead, and 71 at the Lizard.

Two men were drowned when a railway bridge collapsed into a flooded river near Cockermouth, Cumberland.

They were Mr. R. D. Gauld, of Manchester, the railway bridge engineer for the district, and a draughtsman named Riddart, of Barrow. Two others were rescued.

The bridge, which formerly carried passenger and mineral traffic by a cross route to Carlisle, is being demolished.

A gang of twenty men were cutting through the ironwork with acetylene burners. Suddenly the whole of the framework stretching halfway across the Derwent from the Brigham bank collapsed.

A Rhyl butcher, Mr. D. C. Williams, of Crescent-road, was returning to Rhyl accompanied by Mr. Leonard Barrett, of Vale Park, when their van skidded on a bridge, broke through the railings, and crashed into the river 25ft. below. Barret broke the windscreen and managed to get out, but Williams was trapped.

## The Ducks Escaped

A number of live ducks which Williams had bought at market floated to the surface in a crate half an hour after the accident. All were alive and were saved after floating some distance downstream.

The storm at sea brought further bereavement to relatives of one of the crew of the lost Fleetwood trawler Kodana when Mr. William Bird, mate of the trawler Cameo and brother of Skipper Perry Bird, a deck-hand in the Kodana, was washed overboard.

Two of the crew of the Leith drifter Margaret and Francis were drowned yesterday when their vessel was carried ashore on the Aberdeenshire coast.

Two workmen were killed yesterday in a collision between a cyclist and a pedestrian during the gale at Moresby, near Whitehaven, Cumberland. They were Wilson Rae, aged twenty-three, a collier, the cyclist, and Jacob Rudd, aged fifty. Rudd was a widower with a large family.

## BIGGEST FIRST NIGHT CROWD MOBS MARLENE

BY A SPECIAL CORRESPONDENT

NINETY minutes before Marlene Dietrich reached the Leicester-square Theatre last night for the premiere of her film, "The Garden of Allah," mounted police were called out to keep in check the biggest crowd that ever gathered for a London film first night.

When Marlene did arrive, the fans, wild with excitement, burst the police barricades. Some climbed on the roof and luggage grid of her car.

Police fought a way to the limousine in which Miss Dietrich was seen to be hiding between Douglas Fairbanks junior, and Miss Constance Collier.

### Shrank Behind Fur

She shrank behind the magnificent natural brown fox fur of her white satin cloak, obviously afraid that the crowd might tear open the door.

A few yards from the front of the theatre the car was unable to move.

Finally, a path was cleared, but as Miss Dietrich stepped out the police were again swept aside.

Douglas Fairbanks, his arm around her, rushed her up the red carpet into the theatre foyer. A mounted policeman whipped his horse across the pavement to keep the crowd from forcing their way through the glass doors.

A full review of the film will appear in Reginald Whitley's Film Notes to-morrow.

### 40,350 KILLED ON ROADS IN LAST SIX YEARS

Since January, 1931, approximately 40,350 people have been killed and 1,250,000 injured in road accidents, Captain Hudson, Parliamentary Secretary to the Ministry of Transport, told the Commons yesterday.

Steps would be taken to encourage highway authorities who had not already planted trees alongside roads under their control to make a special effort to do so in connection with the Coronation.

★ IN 6ft. OF GLAMOROUS FURS... ★

...that brought "Oh's!" of envy from the crowd of girl "fans" gathered round the doors—Marlene Dietrich arriving at the Leicester-square Theatre with Douglas Fairbanks, jun., for last night's premiere of "The Garden of Allah."

Top picture shows Claire Luce with marvellous white furs about her shoulders. Her escort, Lord Poulett, is a dishard of the evening cloak! His is lined with crimson.

## POLICE GUARD ON GERMAN EMBASSY

BY A SPECIAL CORRESPONDENT

SHOUTING "Hands off Spain, Hitler!" "Stop Hitler helping Franco!" 600 young people forced their way through theatre crowds in the heart of London's West End last night, protesting against German aid for rebel forces in Spain.

A hundred police were detailed to deal with the demonstration, organised by the Communist Party, the Independent Labour Party, and the Socialist League.

After police had moved on a crowd in Waterloo-place, near the Duke of York's Steps, other demonstrators reached Carlton House terrace, home of the German Embassy, which was guarded by a police cordon.

The leaders were not allowed to unfurl their flags, and the processions moved up Regent-street and Piccadilly-circus, pushing through theatre crowds and thrusting leaflets into private cars.

Traffic was held up while the demonstrators marched shouting round the Eros statue and afterwards back to Waterloo-place.

Finding this square entirely barred by police, the demonstrators marched to Holborn, where a meeting was held at a club.

# Daily Mirror

THE DAILY MIRROR, Thursday, December 24, 1936.

No. 10317    Registered at the G.P.O. as a newspaper.    ONE PENNY

LATE·LON·ED

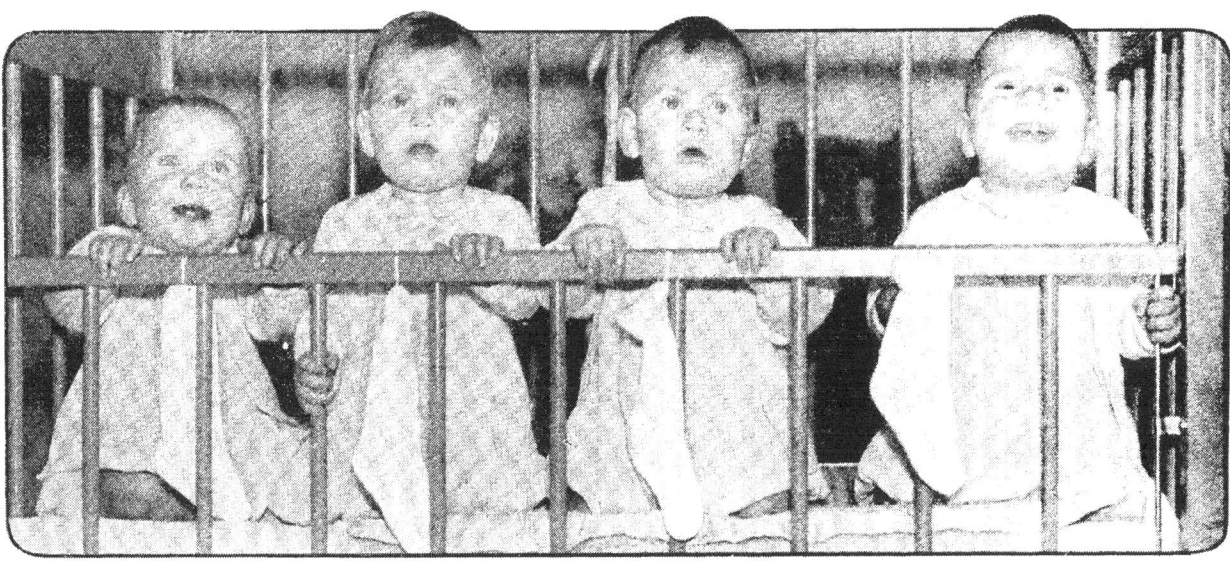

*A MERRY CHRISTMAS TO YOU ALL!*

★ *It's the old, old wish, and in this special picture the Miles Quads — Paul, Ernest, Michael and Ann — express it for us as they kneel behind the stockings that hang in their nursery at St. Neots, Huntingdonshire.*

*More pictures page 12.* ★

# THE KING GIVES BACK JOBS TO ALL AT SANDRINGHAM

### PAGES TO ENJOY— AND KEEP

SAVE the Christmas Party supplement in to-day's "Daily Mirror." It begins on page seven—twelve pages of good cheer that will help you to SPEND a merry Christmas.
SAVE THE SUPPLEMENT—PAGES 7 TO 18.

## FAMILY OF SIX HOMELESS IN COTTAGE BLAZE

A FAMILY of six were made homeless by a cottage fire at Ryme Intrinseca on the Dorset-Somerset border last night.

They are Mr. W. G. Young, his wife and two children, and Mrs. Young's sister and her mother, Mrs. Backholler.

Mrs. Backholler, who is bed-ridden, was rescued by her son-in-law.

Before the flames could be quelled the cottage had been almost destroyed.

While Fireman J. H. Smith, of Gravesend, was having a haircut last night he heard the clanging of the bell on the fire engine as it drove up the street.

Throwing aside the barber's sheet, he dashed into the road with his hair half cut, climbed on to the engine and went to the fire.

## BRITAIN TO HEAR THE POPE

The Pope's broadcast message from the Vatican will be relayed at 11.30 this morning in the B.B.C. National Programme, followed by an English version.

### "DAILY MIRROR" SPECIAL NEWS

THE King yesterday withdrew all notices given to workers on Sandringham estate by his brother, the Duke of Windsor.

He made the decision after conferences with heads of all departments of the estate.

More than sixty men in the forestry and farming departments and in the gardens were asked to accept six months notice by the ex-King when he visited Sandringham in October.

This action, it was stated, was necessary on the grounds of economy. The ex-King then decided that no man would be discharged until he had found other work.

In the case of farm workers this was not possible, however. I understand that the men had been told that they would have to leave in April.

Fourteen men on the gardening staff were given notice. Six of them have found other work.

The news of the withdrawal of notices was received with great joy in the villages round Sandringham.

"King George is a worthy successor to his father—the finest Squire who ever lived," declared workers as they toasted their new King's health last night.

The King, dressed in grey plus fours, cap and light overcoat, was one of the busiest workers on the Sandringham estate yesterday.

He became so absorbed in his tour of the estate that he was late for lunch.

The Queen and Queen Mary spent the whole morning giving the staff instructions for the Christmas festivities.

Princess Elizabeth and Princess Margaret Rose, with Lady Mary Cambridge as playmate, romped by the lake with spaniels from the kennels.

Sarah Churchill.

## FOG HOLD-UP

Measles has stopped the Princess Royal's annual Christmas party, greatest event of the year for children of Goldsborough village, Yorkshire.

The party, which the Princess has never failed to give since she went to Yorkshire, will be held on January 4, if the outbreak is over.

   ✦ · ✦ · ✦ · ✦

The Duke of Windsor is likely to visit Queen Marie of Rumania and her daughter, the Archduchess Anton of Hapsburg, during the Christmas holidays.

Thick fog enveloped parts of London and the Home Counties last night, causing serious congestion on the roads. Christmas holidaymakers bound for the coast were delayed by the fog.

Good news for 500,000 families—page four.

## SARAH CHURCHILL WEDS VIC OLIVER IN NEW YORK TO-DAY

FROM OUR OWN CORRESPONDENT

New York, Wednesday.

SOME time before they sail in the Aquitania for England at noon to-morrow, Sarah Churchill, the dancer daughter of Mr. Winston Churchill, and Vic Oliver, the actor-producer, will be married.

When and where the ceremony will take place is known only by Sarah and Vic.

For the past twenty-four hours the couple have been in hiding.

Eventually, when I discovered Sarah in her hotel, she was preparing for a dash to a secret destination.

### Bags Were Packed

Busily packing, Sarah told me: "Yes, we are getting married and shall sail for our honeymoon in the Aquitania to-morrow, but we absolutely refuse to reveal any details because we don't want a lot of fuss."

Vic Oliver said, "The wedding will take place near New York sometime to-day or to-morrow morning. As soon as it has taken place announcement will be made."

It is nearly four months since Miss Churchill left for the United States, and her intention to marry Mr. Oliver was rumoured.

A few days later her brother, Mr. Randolph Churchill, followed her to New York.

Miss Churchill is twenty-one. She appeared as a Cochran Young Lady in the revue "Follow the Sun," in which Vic Oliver was comedian.

Oliver's real name is Joe Plotz.

THE DAILY MIRROR, Monday, December 28, 1935.

# Daily Mirror
No. 10318    Registered at the G.P.O. as a newspaper.    ONE PENNY

# STREETS RED HOT IN BLAZE
## UNDER HEART OF BERLIN

FIRE raging in a tube railway 60ft. below the Potsdamerplatz, Piccadilly-circus of Berlin, last night, made city streets red hot and hid skyscrapers in a smoke screen.

Flames and clouds of acrid smoke, roaring through the ventilating shafts, spouted upwards, driving back squads of gas-masked firemen, enveloping holiday crowds.

All vehicles were forbidden to approach. The whole city's traffic was completely disorganised.

Fearing buildings might collapse all people in the square were ordered to leave.

All gas supplies over a wide area were cut off.

General Goering, Dr. Goebbels and General von Fritsch, Chief of Staff of the German Army, whose official residences are close by, rushed to the scene and supervised the rescue work.

### Where 19 Were Buried Alive

The half-mile section of railway affected is still under construction. Part of the tunnel collapsed in August, 1935, burying alive nineteen men.

First news of the fire was at five o'clock yesterday afternoon, when holidaymakers strolling along the Hermann Goering Strasse saw clouds of smoke pouring through chinks in the 14in. wooden beams which at present comprise the roadway while the tunnel is being built underneath.

The street was crowded with people visiting the nearby cafes and cinemas.

Nineteen fire brigades answered the alarm.

Through a loudspeaker the head of the fire brigade directed operations

Firemen were not able to descend into the burning tunnel, but tore up stretches of hot pavement and poured gallons of water in.

### Feeding Flames

Below baulks of timber and piles of boards and countless tar barrels and other building material added fuel to the flames.

But after five hours' work the fire was believed to be under control.

*(Messages from Reuter, British United Press and Exchange.)*

Flames and smoke belching from a station entrance to the Berlin underground at the height of the fire.

## FOUR MEN WOUNDED IN LONDON STREET SCENE

Four men were treated at the London Hospital yesterday for wounds stated to have been received in a scene in Collingwood-street, Bethnal Green, E.

Two of the injured men, Harry Cohen and John Jacobs, were operated on during the day and were detained. Their condition this morning was stated to be serious. The other two injured men were allowed to go home after treatment.

A man will appear at Old-street Police Court to-day in connection with the incident.

### RUSH FOR ICE CREAM ON CHRISTMAS SUNDAY

There was a brisk demand for ice-cream on the South Coast yesterday after the sunniest and mildest Christmas for seven years.

London provided a remarkable phenomenon. From Christmas Day until last night the thermometer on the roof of the Air Ministry varied by only two degrees—between 48 and 46.

Prince Edward, who now has a baby sister, out in his pram yesterday.

## DUKE OF WINDSOR TOASTS NEW BABY

WITHIN a few hours of her birth on Christmas Day, Britain's new baby Princess, daughter of the Duchess of Kent, was toasted in Vienna by the Duke of Windsor.

He was lunching with the British Minister, Sir Walford Selby, at the Legation, when he received news of the birth of his niece. At once he proposed the health of the new baby.

Last night the Duchess of Kent and her daughter were reported to be "going on very well." The doctors are so satisfied that, though a bulletin was expected on Saturday, none will be issued until to-day.

All day yesterday hundreds of messages of congratulation from all parts of the Empire continued to arrive at No. 3, Belgrave-square, the London home of the Duke and Duchess.

Many gifts of flowers for the Duchess had been sent specially from the country. Among them were flowers from the Sandringham estate, the gift of the Royal Family.

No decision has yet been taken about naming the new royal baby. It is suggested that among her names—and probably her first name—will be Mary, while another may be Alice, after her aunt, the Duchess of Gloucester, who was also born on Christmas Day.

## WOMAN LEAPS FROM WINDOW OF HOUSE TO ESCAPE FUSILLADE OF SHOTS— FRIEND AND CAPTAIN DIE TOGETHER

### FROM OUR OWN CORRESPONDENT
PEVENSEY BAY (Sussex), Sunday.

FLEEING before a fusillade of shots, a woman leapt from the window of a house here last night and ran to safety—leaving behind her two friends dying from wounds.

Captain Story, aged forty-three, had shot his housekeeper, forty-two-year-old Mrs. Holland, and then turned the revolver on himself.

Both Captain Story and Mrs. Holland came from the Brighton district. Five weeks ago Captain Story rented the house, Sea Change, a modern artistic white concrete house with a sunbathing roof.

At 6.45 last night he and Mrs. Holland were having dinner in the front room of Sea Change when a friend, Miss Hilda Drake, of Hampden Park, Eastbourne, knocked at the door.

She was let in by Mrs. Holland. Captain Story went upstairs. Mrs. Holland was about to follow when a revolver shot rang out.

With a cry Mrs. Holland tottered to the foot of the stairs, shot in the heart. Miss Drake went to her aid

More shots rang out.

### Race to 'Phone

Stricken with fear, Miss Drake jumped from the window into the main road and ran to a telephone box 200 yards away.

When police arrived Captain Story and Mrs. Holland were dead.

Captain Story had a bullet wound in his head. A revolver from which several shots had been fired lay near his hand.

Miss Drake was taken to her brother-in-law's house at Brodrick-road. She is suffering from shock.

Captain Story is believed to have been suffering from shell shock.

The house, Sea Change.

### £300 HAUL OF DRINKS

When a public-house in Liverpool-road, Islington, N., was opened last night it was found that thieves had cleared nearly all the stock of spirits—worth more than £300.

Made in the USA
Monee, IL
14 December 2020